Computer-Aided Design of User Interfaces IV

COMPUTER-AIDED DESIGN OF USER INTERFACES IV

Proceedings of the Fifth International Conference on
Computer-Aided Design of User Interfaces CADUI'2004
Sponsored by ACM and jointly organised with the Eight ACM
International Conference on Intelligent User Interfaces IUI'2004
13-16 January 2004, Funchal, Isle of Madeira

edited by

Robert J.K. Jacob
Tufts University,
Medford, MA, U.S.A.

Quentin Limbourg
Université catholique de Louvain,
Louvain-la-Neuve, Belgium

and

Jean Vanderdonckt
Université catholique de Louvain,
Louvain-la-Neuve, Belgium

KLUWER ACADEMIC PUBLISHERS
DORDRECHT / BOSTON / LONDON

A C.I.P. Catalogue record for this book is available from the Library of Congress.

ISBN 978-90-481-6807-1 (PB)
ISBN 9781-4020-3304-9 (e-book)

Published by Kluwer Academic Publishers,
P.O. Box 17, 3300 AA Dordrecht, The Netherlands.

Sold and distributed in North, Central and South America
by Kluwer Academic Publishers,
101 Philip Drive, Norwell, MA 02061, U.S.A.

In all other countries, sold and distributed
by Kluwer Academic Publishers,
P.O. Box 322, 3300 AH Dordrecht, The Netherlands.

Printed on acid-free paper

Printed in the Netherlands.

TABLE OF CONTENTS

Mixed-Reality Systems

Speech-Based Systems

Sponsors

Official IUI Web site: http://www.iuiconf.org
Official CADUI Web site: http://www.isys.ucl.ac.be/bchi/cadui

Gold Corporate Sponsors

Microsoft Research
http://research.microsoft.com/
Mitsubishi Electric Research Laboratories (MERL)
http://www.merl.com
Oliva Nova Model Execution Software
http://www.care-t.com

RedWhale software Corporation
http://www.redwhale.com

Other Corporate Sponsors

Conference Reviewing System (CRS)
http://www.conferencereview.com

HSBC
http://www.hsbc.nl

IBM Research
http://www.research.ibm.com/

Kluwer Academics Publishers
http://www.wkap.nl

Lucent Technologies
http://www.lucent.com/
The XIML Forum
http://www.ximl.org/

Conference sponsors

The City of Madeira and Madeira Tourist Authority
Board

Câmara Municipal de Funchal
http://www.cm-funchal.pt/

Scientific sponsors

American Association for Artificial Intelligence
http://www.aaai.org

Association for Computing Machinery
http://www.acm.org

ACM Special Interest Group on Computer-Human Inter-action
http://www.acm.org/sigart

ACM Special Interest Group on Computer-Human Inter-action
http://www.sigchi.org

ACM Belgian SIGCHI Chapter (BelCHI)
http://www.belchi.be

Association Francophone d'Interaction Homme-Machine
(AFIHM) http://www.afihm.org

Fonds National de la Recherche Scientifique
http://www.fnrs.be/

Institut d'Administration et de Gestion
http://www.iag.ucl.ac.be/

SIMILAR, The European research taskforce creating
human-machine interfaces SIMILAR to human-human
communication. http://www.similar.cc

Université catholique de Louvain
http://www.ucl.ac.be

University of Madeira
http://www.uma.pt

PROGRAM COMMITTEE MEMBERS

Ghassan Al-Qaimari, RMIT University, Australia
Elisabeth Andre, University of Augsburg, Germany
Simone Barbosa, Pontifical University Catholic de Rio de Janeiro, Brazil
Mathias Bauer, DFKI, Germany
Lawrence Bergman, IBM T.J. Watson Research Center, USA
Larry Birnbaum, Northwestern University, USA
Gaelle Calvary, IMAG Grenoble, France
Karin Coninx, Limburgs Universitair Centrum, Belgium
Mary Czerwinski, Microsoft Research, USA
Alain Derycke, University of Lille I, France
Prasun Dewan, University of North Carolina at Chapel Hill, USA
Jean-Daniel Fekete, INRIA Futurs/LRI, France
Steve Feiner, Columbia University, USA
Peter Forbrig, University Rostock, Germany
Elizabeth Furtado, University of Fortaleza, Brazil
Patrick Girard, University of Poitiers, France
Andreas Girgensohn, FX Palo Alto, USA
Mark Green, City University Hong Kong, Honk Kong
Peter Haddawy, Asian Institute of Technology, Thaïland
Kristian Hammond, Northwestern University, USA
Achim Hoffman, University of New South Wales, Australia
Anthony Jameson, DFKI and International University of Germany, Germany
Lewis Johnson, USC/Information Sciences Institute, USA
Peter Johnson, University of Bath, UK
Hermann Kaindl, Vienna University of Technology, Austria
Christophe Kolski, Université de Valenciennes, France
James Lester, North Carolina State University, USA
Henry Lieberman, MIT, USA
Maria-Dolores Lozano, University of Albacete, Spain
Claude Machgeels, Université Libre de Bruxelles, Belgium
Rob Miller, MIT, USA
Tom Moher, University Illinois at Chicago, USA
Faouzi Moussa, University of Tunisia, Tunisia
Kumiyo Nakakoji, University of Tokyo, Japan
William Newman, University College London Interaction Centre, UK
Erik Nilsson, SINTEF, Norway
Niels Ole Bernsen, Odense University, Denmark
Dan Olsen, Brigham Young University, USA
Philippe Palanque, University of Toulouse I, France
Cecile Paris, CSIRO, Australia

ACKNOWLEDGEMENTS

The editors would like to thank particularly Ion Voicu and Cristi Voicu, who significantly helped in the preparation and the editing of the final version of this book. They were supported by SIMILAR (www.similar.cc), the European research taskforce creating human-machine interfaces SIMILAR to human-human communication. The editors would like also to thank particularly the FNRS (Fonds National de la Recherche Scientifique) from Belgium (www.fnrs.be), who financially supported the conference and the editing of this book.

Chapter 1

THE INFLUENCE OF IMPROVED TASK MODELS ON DIALOGUES

Anke Dittmar and Peter Forbrig

Department of Computer Science, University of Rostock
Albert-Einstein-Straße 21 – D-18051 Rostock (Germany)
E-Mail: {ad,pforbrig}@informatik.uni-rostock.de
Tel.: +49-381-498 343{2,4} - Fax: +49-381-498 3426

Abstract   Model-based approaches support a flexible design process and the development of consistent device-dependent applications. However, their full strength
can only be achieved by expressive sub-models allowing to capture conceptual
knowledge as early as possible. In this paper we demonstrate how improvements to task models, which can be seen as the heart of model-based techniques, help to develop more appropriate models and prototypes of user interfaces (UIs).

Keywords: Abstract user interface models, Model-based design, Task modelling.

1.   INTRODUCTION

The development of user interfaces (UIs) is a co-operative, multidisciplinary process. In particular, the views of all stakeholders need to be
considered and agreements must be found. Model-based approaches accept
this nature of design processes as to be seen e.g. in many CADUI-papers.
Different declarative models and their relationships are used to represent important aspects of human-computer interaction on a conceptual level. For
example, task models describe the actions and the goals of users and their
domain knowledge. Abstract and concrete dialogue models are focused on
the description of UIs themselves. There can also exist models of users or of
specific environmental circumstances (e.g., specific tools and platforms). As
a consequence, model-based techniques support the development of design
spaces and prevent designers from following "first-solution strategies" too
often.

R. Jacob et al. (eds.), Computer-Aided Design of User Interfaces IV, 1–14.
© 2005 *Kluwer Academic Publishers. Printed in the Netherlands.*

In this paper, we concentrate on formal models about tasks, actions and task domains and their influence on abstract dialogue models and, to some extent, on abstract prototypes of UIs. Section 2 gives background information and points out some limitations of current approaches. Based on a formalization of domain knowledge (3.1) a hybrid notation for describing actions and states is suggested (3.2). This leads to more convenient task descriptions. An exploration of instantiating (3.3) and composing (3.4) actions evokes the reconsideration of temporal descriptions (3.5). Section 4 discusses the influence of the suggested improvements on developing abstract UI models. It is further argued that similar, but refined modelling techniques are applicable to task modelling as well as to dialogue modelling. Section 5 gives some conclusions. The ideas are illustrated by an example and tool support is discussed.

2.   FROM TASKS TO DIALOGUES - BACKGROUND

Most techniques which support a task-driven design process of UIs mainly exploit task structures (e.g., [2,10,15,20]). Fig. 1 depicts part of a task model from [10] in CTTE-notation [15]. Task hierarchies, task types and temporal relationships between sub-tasks are used to draw conclusions concerning the structure and the behaviour of corresponding UIs.

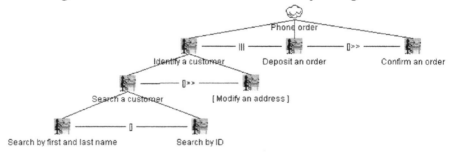

Figure 1. Part of a task model from [10].

A tool we developed to design dialogue models and to generate appropriate abstract prototypes of UIs is illustrated in Fig. 2. The designer can import a task model ((1) in Fig. 2) and assign several dialogue models to it which are based on *dialogue graphs* [5] ((2) in Fig. 2). A dialogue model consists of a set of nodes (views) and a set of transitions. Each view contains a set of elements which are created by mapping tasks to the view ((3) in Fig. 2). A transition is a directed relation between an element of a view and a view. It is distinguished between 5 types of views (single, multi, modal, complex and end view) and 2 types of transitions (sequential and concurrent). A dialogue model allows the generation of an abstract prototype in a WIMP style which can be animated (Fig. 3). Views are represented by windows, their elements by buttons and transitions by navigations between windows. In case of a sequential transition, the source view becomes invisible and the destination view will be visible and active if the associated button is pressed. Concurrent transitions allow for the source view to be visible. The temporal constraints of the underlying task model enable the buttons of abstract prototypes. Inconsistencies between the navigation structure of a dialogue model and the temporal relations between sub-tasks are reported.

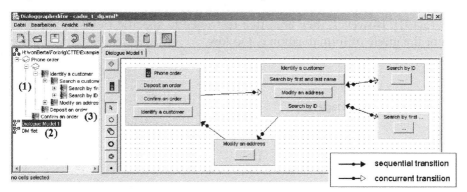

Figure 2. A dialogue graph assigned to Fig. 1.

Figure 3. An illustration of the generated abstract prototype of Fig. 2.

Our method is similar to [14] insofar as both approaches make the designer responsible for relating tasks to parts of the UI model and supply some form of model checking. So, we deliberately allowed the designer to decide which part of the conceptual task structure has to be reflected by the transition structure of a dialogue model. In the example, a user cannot execute `Search by ID` until he has "said" the interface (by navigation) that he intends to `Identify a customer` (Fig. 2,3). The sub-task `Search a customer` is not directly mapped. In contrast, a grouping of sub-tasks is not possible in [11]. In [16], a set of task sets (comparable to views in our approach) is generated by applying heuristics to the enabled task sets of a task model and by determining so called transition tasks. Approaches like [12,16] rather try to derive UI models (and abstract prototypes) from task models than to compare them.

Perhaps, many of us would accept Fig. 4b as part of a UI a system could offer its users to perform the task of Fig. 4a. However, there is no hint in the task model telling us that a mail has a sender, a receiver and a content. Although models and abstract prototypes as presented so far can already be used for discussions with stakeholders during early design phases, their limited expressiveness is obvious.

A main reason is the missing "introduction of domain and/or user models along with the task model to derive presentation and dialog models" as stated in [10]. Actually, there are approaches to relate task and domain knowledge in general (e.g., [7]) and for deriving models of UIs (e.g., [1,6,15,17]). However, they are often restricted to specific fields of application or the grade of formalisation is too low.

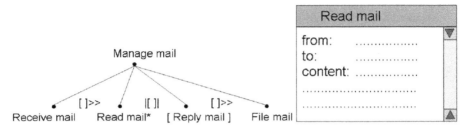

Figure 4. A task model of `Manage mail` (a) and a possible representation for sub-task `Read mail` (b).

Throughout the rest of the paper we will further explore this simplified mailing example to point out some modelling problems at the level of tasks. We will show how a stronger formalisation of task models and even minimal extensions like a new temporal operator can support a more appropriate mapping on abstract UIs. Let us start with the exploitation of formalised domain knowledge as proposed above.

3.   IMPROVEMENTS TO TASK MODELS

In [3] we suggest to tighten the link between actions and states within task models. A task is seen as a meta-action which includes a permanent development of models about actions, current states and goal states. For completing a task, humans have to perform a sequence of actions using objects of their environment (in the role of means and resources).

This results in creating or manipulating other objects (in the role of artefacts and side-effects). A deeper discussion can be found in [3]. Additionally, action and task models are defined as objects with a specific structure. We will use this idea in the following section.

3.1   A Formalisation of Domain Knowledge

Objects are specified by sets of attributes (name-value pairs). A pattern-instance relationship is defined between two objects O_P and O_I if there is a subset of attributes in O_P (a pattern schema) so that we can find for each attribute A in this subset an attribute A' with the same name in O_I. The value of A' has to be an instance of the value of A. Consequently, an object can be characterized intentionally by its attribute structure or extensionally by its actual set of instances. In addition, partial descriptions can be introduced to describe special subsets of instances of a (pattern) object. This can be expressed by partial equations.

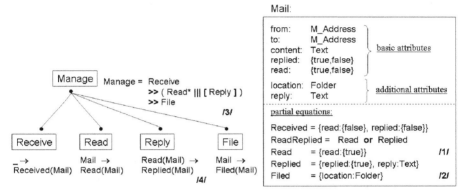

Figure 5. Action `Manage` enriched by preconditions and effects on artefact `Mail` (denoted by Pre→Eff) and the object description of `Mail`.

Object `Mail` (right part of Fig. 5) illustrates the proposed specification style. It represents a pattern for mail messages. There are partial descriptions specifying subsets of mail messages (instances) which are received, read, replied or filed by restricting ranges of attribute values (e.g., /1/) and introducing additional attributes (e.g., /2/). Furthermore, partial descriptions can be composed of others by using special operators. For example, `ReadReplied` describes all mail messages which are instances of `Read` or `Replied`. Hence, the operator `or` works on states.

The left part of Fig. 5 shows the enriched action model of Fig. 4a (outside an object O a partial description PD of O is denoted by $PD(O)$). For reasons of brevity, the artefact role is only considered in this paper. As mentioned earlier, actions are special objects. Their hierarchical decomposition is reflected in their sets of partial descriptions. The partial equation of a basic action contains predefined operations. For example, we support basic arithmetic and string operations, operations to read and write attribute values and to create and delete additional attributes. The partial equation of a non-basic action specifies the temporal relations between its sub-actions by using temporal operators. Tool support for creating and animating action models is illustrated in the appendix. However, some further points are worthy of mention regarding the example.

3.2   A Hybrid Notation for Action Models

Fig. 4a defines a behaviour which was not intended. Fig. 6 shows a STN with the desired one instead and an equivalent temporal equation. A temporal description in CTTE-notation is even more complex because the completion of iterative actions must be described explicitly. In addition, 'artificial' nodes must be introduced which destroy the conceptual hierarchical structure of the model. A hybrid notation as used in Fig. 5 unifies structural and procedural knowledge and can lead to more concise and, possibly, to more 'natural' descriptions than pure state or temporal notations.

The temporal equation /3/ guarantees that a mail message has been received before it can be read, replied, or filed. We do not need to specify this in the preconditions of the actions Read, Reply, and File. On the other hand, we can express knowledge about requested and resulting states of objects in preconditions and effects to shorten temporal descriptions. An example is the constraint that a mail message has to be an instance of the partial description Read (/4/) in order to reply to it. Of course, consistency checks of such hybrid models are useful, but their consideration is beyond the present paper.

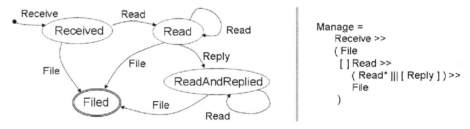

Figure 6. A STN with the desired behaviour and an equivalent temporal equation.

3.3   Two-fold Instantiation of Actions

Action models are patterns in a two-fold way. They describe a set of possible execution sequences of basic actions. In addition, if a pattern object occurs several times in the preconditions and the effects of an action tree it can be replaced consistently by the same instance. Necessary pattern names can be indexed (e.g., Mail[1], Mail[2],...) to distinguish between several instances currently used (Section 3.5). An instantiation for Fig. 5 can be found in the appendix.

3.4   Action Composition

As Paul entered his office on Friday morning the phone was ringing. "Hi Paul. Here's Stephen. Could you do me a favour and send your source code for checking the consistency of action models? Could you send some documentation as well? I have a problem that seems to be quite similar. I've sent you mail. Could you take a look at it? It's urgent!" Besides Stephen's mail Paul has got 7 other messages. And before he started to work on Stephen's mail he had to see what Ann has written...

An action model describes sequences of (unconsciously executed) operations under actual conditions of the domain [8]. Fortunately, humans cannot plan their whole activity by only one action. In other words, actions are situated and goal-directed. So, in the scenario above Paul obviously opened his mailbox to read and answer Stephen's mail immediately. Why did he react to Ann's mail in the next moment?

As mentioned before, we regard a task as a meta-action involving permanent adjustments to situations, goals, and actions. Paul had to combine, for example, his action models concerning the treatment of Stephen and Ann. Within a task-oriented approach we try to describe by the envisioned task model all those tasks which are supposed to be supported by the interactive system under design. In [9], the term (Target) Composite Task Model is used. The scenario reveals a phenomenon that often occurs when combining action models. The resulting structure is not necessarily a concurrent composition of the single actions. Instead, new actions are introduced to replace a set of sub-actions from different models. Such replacements can cause further restructurings, the creation of auxiliary sub-actions etc.

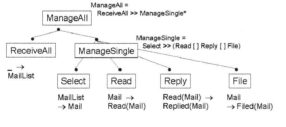

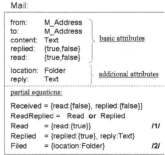

Figure 7. A composition of actions.   *Figure 8.* Paul has to reply to mail from Ann immediately...

Fig. 7 shows an action composition for managing many mail messages which is a more appropriate abstraction from the scenario as e.g. `Manage |||` `Manage |||` ... because Paul received several mail messages at once. In fact, every model has to handle different scenarios or lower-level abstractions.

Even so it has `Manage` (Fig. 4a). But, how can we describe, for example, that Paul has to reply immediately to all mail from Ann? Fig. 8 indicates two possible solutions. So far, only actions were informed about objects they use or manipulate.

We extend this uni-directional relation to a bi-directional one. In this case, an attribute `take_part:Manage` is added to the (artefact) object `Mail`. The partial description `FromAnnToPaul_Active(Mail)` determines a subset of sequences of basic actions of `Manage`. $A>>_TB$ means that `B` has to be started immediately after finishing `A`. Hence, if Paul has received mail from Ann his behavioural description is restricted in the intended way. `FromAnnToPaul_Passive(Mail)` specifies an order of states which mail from Ann to Paul has to go through.

Why can it be useful to 'source out' action knowledge to objects acted upon? We can argue in the same way as in Section 3.2 and even our simple example shows some advantages. If partial descriptions of actions restrict the kind of acting on single objects, it is often more convenient to attach these constraints to the objects themselves. Therefore, we could also weaken the preconditions in Fig. 7 because attribute `take_part` in Fig. 8 already says how to manage a single mail. In other words, `take_part` "saved" the knowledge about `Manage` from Fig. 5 into Fig. 7.

We are well aware that interactive systems have to support users in performing tasks in a variety of combinations under certain social, organizational and timing constraints. Before temporal operators are reconsidered in the next section, we would like to point out some effects of task composition. Roughly speaking, an action `A` with precondition `A` and effect `E` (denoted by `A{C→E}`) is described by a composed action `CA{CC→CE}` if `CC` guarantees `C` and `E` is achieved by `CE`. However, not only the effect is interesting but also an efficient execution. Let us take the action `ManageSingle*` of Fig. 7, which allows for an interleaved managing of mail.

It specifies sequences like ⟨`Select{m1→m1}`,`Read{m1→m1}`,`Select{m1→m2}`,`Read{m2→m2}`,`Select{m1→m2}`,`Reply{m2→m2}`,…⟩ where `ml` is an instance of `Mail-List`, `m1` and `m2` are instances of `Mail`. To observe the work on one particular mail message we hide all actions from execution sequences dealing with other mail and we get sequences like ⟨`Select{m1→m}`,`Read{m→m}`,`Select{m1→m}`,`Reply{m→m}`,`Select{m1→m}`,…⟩. It is easy to see that the following modification of `ManageAll` gives better results (preconditions and effects are omitted).

```
ManageSingle   = Select >> ManageSelected*
ManageSelected = Read [] Reply [] File
```

3.5 Reconsideration of Temporal Operators

The *|-operator. Temporal operators serve to describe some basic composition "patterns"' of actions or tasks. The set of operators offered by CTTE [15] is reproduced in Table 1.

Table 1. Temporal Operators of ConcurTaskTree notation.

[ ]	Choice	|>	Suspend & Resume
|-|	Order independency	>>	Enabling
|||	Concurrency	>>[ ]	Enabling with information exchange
|||[ ]	Concurrency with information exchange	*	Iteration
[>	Disabling	[...]	Optional

With the two-fold instantiation as introduced in Section 3.3, operators with information exchange are superfluous. By assigning preconditions and effects, and by following the instantiation rules, information exchange between sub-actions can even be described more precisely. However, it also becomes obvious that we need more than the *-operator for action repetition. In Fig. ?, one action instance of ManageSingle has to be completed entirely before a second one can be started. In reality, humans often perform similar actions concurrently. A new operator *| is introduced to describe finite sets of concurrent instances of actions. It is inspired by the replication operator ! as known from the π-calculus [12] ($!P \equiv P \mid !P$). Thus, ManageSingle*| allows an action instance like ⟨Select{m1→m1},Select {m1→m2},Read {m1→m1},Read{m2→m2},...⟩. Additionally, in order to explain the full semantics of action repetition, a closer look at the attached objects is necessary. It makes a difference whether we read mail again and again (Fig. 5) or whether we repeat ManageSingle from Fig. 7 on different mail messages. Fig. 9 illustrates two common instantiation patterns which generalize above examples. For simplicity, we abstract from partial descriptions of object O in preconditions and effects. BO can be instantiated by an arbitrary set of instances of O.

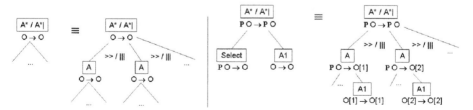

Figure 9. Two instantiation patterns for repetitive actions.

The >>ᴛ-operator. In [4], the distinction between task enabling and triggering is discussed. Triggers are proposed because they describe when actions finally occur. The $>>_T$-operator as introduced in the previous section could be useful for describing the immediate trigger type and, also, for describing environmental cues if $>>_T$ occurs in objects of the task domain.

4.   FROM TASKS TO DIALOGUE MODELS

While the focus of task models is more on the description of user needs abstract dialogue models focus on UIs (that is to say on the description of the artefact itself) [18]. As we have shown in Section 2, much of the requirements on dialogue models can (and should) be derived from task models. For example, the behaviour of a dialogue model has to obey the temporal constraints of its task model. Temporal descriptions of tasks can be mapped now more precisely on dialogue models, a conclusion we can draw directly from the previous section. So, the dialogue of Fig. 10 which allows for work on several mail messages concurrently would not be possible for the task ManageAll (Fig. 7) until ManageSingle * is replaced by ManageSingle *| in the temporal equation of ManageAll.

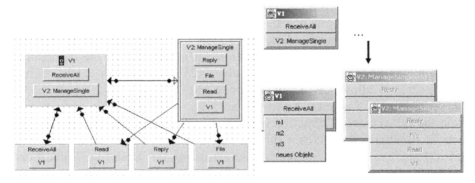

Figure 10. A dialogue graph for similar concurrent sub-actions (v2 is a multiple view) and two screenshots of the generated abstract UI-prototype.

However, we can go one step further. The formalization of domain knowledge also supports a more precise mapping on presentations. Furthermore, an abstract dialogue model (= behaviour + presentation) can be considered as a specific action model in a specific domain represented by Abstract Interaction Objects (AIOs) [19]. Although mail in Fig. 7 can refer to 'conventional' letters we are particularly interested in the subset of email messages and an appropriate software tool to manage them. A specialty of interactive systems is that their UIs represent both tools (functionality) and artefacts. Consequently, AIOs have to be assigned to actions and objects of the task model or to groups of them in order to specify a UI. For the description of AIOs, the same mechanisms as introduced in Section 3 can be used.

It is argued in [10] that different notations for task models and UI models are of advantage because these models are built by different people and are used independently. However, looking at object-oriented concepts and notations, for example, they are applied in very different context AIOs specify at an abstract level which parts of the underlying objects are visible, enabled, or active at which stage of execution. Abstract user actions are represented by function calls, navigation and data input. We can take a look at the example of Fig. 7 to roughly illustrate this idea. We should especially note the mapping of actions to view V1 (Fig. 10). For simplicity, an AIO associated to an object O is denoted by R_O. R_A is enabled/disabled if action A is enabled/disabled in the underlying action model.

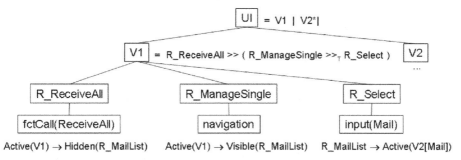

Figure 11. Part of an abstract user interface model.

Fig. 11 shows part of an appropriate abstract UI model. For example, the partial description Active(V1) in the precondition of fctCall(Receive All) defines that view V1 has to be active. By executing fctCall-(ReceiveAll), action ReceiveAll is completed. This enables the complex action ManageSingle in the action model and, thus, the associated AIO R_ManageSingle is enabled. If V1 and V2 are instantiated by windows, R_ReceiveAll and R_ManageSingle by buttons and R_MailList by a list of buttons, we get a presentation similar to the abstract prototype of Fig. 10. However, the UI description is only complete in connection with the underlying action model. Again, a hybrid notational approach was applied.

5. CONCLUSION

The pros and cons of using formal models to describe human work and, in particular, human-computer interaction are well known. On the one hand, formal models increase the guarantee that task knowledge and decisions made at a conceptual level are reflected in the final implementation of UIs. On the other hand, formal models are often rejected because they are "inappropriate for capturing the complexity of human experience and activity"

[4]. This is certainly true for at least two reasons. Often, formal models overemphasize a certain perspective on the subject of interest. Furthermore, some elements of the domain are not included in models but should be.

In this paper, an enriched, but more formalised description of tasks is proposed. However, the suggested hybrid notation of actions can ease modelling activities. It was shown that these improvements to task models (even a small modification like the introduction of a new temporal operator) allow a more precise mapping on abstract UI models. We provide prototypical tool support for some of our ideas, but there is still much to do. For example, domain knowledge is not fully exploited to derive abstract presentations.

REFERENCES

[1] Barclay, P.J., Griffiths, T., McKirdy, J., Paton, N.W., Cooper, R., and Kennedy, J., *The Teallach Tool: Using Models for Flexible User Interface Design*, in A. Puerta, J. Vanderdonckt (eds.), Proceedings of 3rd Int. Conf. on Computer-Aided Design of User Interfaces CADUI'99 (Louvain-la-Neuve, 21-23 October 1999), Kluwer Academics Pub., Dordrecht, 1999, pp. 139-157.

[2] Dittmar, A. and Forbrig, P., *Methodological and Tool Support for a Task-Oriented Development of Interactive Systems*, in A. Puerta, J. Vanderdonckt (eds.), Proceedings of 3rd Int. Conf. on Computer-Aided Design of User Interfaces CADUI'99 (Louvain-la-Neuve, 21-23 October 1999), Kluwer Academics Pub., Dordrecht, 1999, pp. 271-274.

[3] Dittmar, A., and Forbrig, P., *Higher-order task models*, in J. Jorge, N.J. Nunes, J. Falcão e Cunha (eds.), Proc. of 10th Int. Workshop on Design, Specification, and Verification of Interactive Systems DSV-IS'2003 (Funchal, June 2003), Lecture Notes in Computer Science, Vol. 2844, Springer-Verlag, Berlin, 2003, pp. 187-202.

[4] Dix, A., *Managing the Ecology of Interaction*, in C. Pribeanu, J. Vanderdonckt (eds.), Proc. of 1st Int. Workshop on Task Models and Diagrams for User Interface Design TAMODIA'2002 (Bucharest, 18-19 July 2002), Academy of Economic Studies of Bucharest, Economic Informatics Department, INFOREC Printing House, Bucarest, 2002, pp. 7-9.

[5] Elwert, T. and Schlungbaum, E., *Dialogue Graphs-A Formal and Visual Specification Technique for Dialogue Modelling*, in J.L. Siddiqi, C.R. Roast (eds.), Proceedings of the BCS-FACS Workshop on Formal Aspects of the Human Computer Interface FAHCI'96 (Sheffield, 10-12 September 1996), accessible at http://ewic.bcs.org/conferences/1996/formalaspects/papers/paper13.pdf

[6] Gamboa-Rodriguez, F. and Scapin, D., *Editing MAD* Task Descriptions for Specifying User Interfaces at both Semantic and Presentation Levels*, in Proc. of 4th Int. Conf. on Design, Specification, and Verification of Interactive Systems DSV-IS'97 (Granada, 4-6 June 1997), Springer-Verlag, Vienna, 1997, pp. 193-208.

[7] Johnson, P. and Wilson, S., *A Framework for Task-based Design*, in Proceedings of the 2nd Czech-British Symposium on Visual Aspects in Man-Machine Systems VAMMS'93 (Prague, 24-28 March 1993), Ellis Horwood, Chichester, 1993.

[8] Leontiev, A.N., *Activity, Consciousness, Personality*, Prentice Hall, Englewood Cliffs, 1978.

[9] Lim, K.Y. and Long, J., *The MUSE Method for Usability Engineering*, Cambridge University Press, Cambridge, 1994.

[10] Limbourg, Q., Vanderdonckt, J., and Souchon, N., *The Task-Dialog and Task-Presentation Mapping Problem: Some Preliminary Results*, in F. Paternò, Ph. Palanque (eds.), Proc. of 7th Int. Eurographics Workshop on Design, Specification, Verification of Interactive Systems DSV-IS'2000 (Limerick, 5-6 June 2000), Lecture Notes in Computer Science, Vol. 1946, Springer-Verlag, Berlin, 2000, pp. 227-246.

[11] Luyten, K., Clerckx, T., Coninx, K., Vanderdonckt, J., *Derivation of a Dialog Model from a Task Model by Activity Chain Extraction*, in J. Jorge, N.J. Nunes, J. Falcão e Cunha, J. (eds.), Proc. of 10th Int. Conf. on Design, Specification, and Verification of Interactive Systems DSV-IS'2003 (Madeira, 4-6 June 2003), Lecture Notes in Computer Science, Vol. 2844, Springer-Verlag, Berlin, 2003, pp. 203-217.

[12] Mori, G., Paternò, F., and Santoro, C., *CTTE: Support for Developing and Analysing Task Models for Interactive System Design*, IEEE Transactions on Software Engineering, Vol. 28, No. 8, August 2002, pp. 797-813. Accessible at http://giove.cnuce.cnr.it/ctte.html.

[13] Milner, R., *Communicating and Mobile Systems: the π-Calculus*, Cambridge University Press, Cambridge, 1999.

[14] Navarre, D., Palanque, P., Paternò, F., Santoro, C., and Bastide, R., *A Tool Suite for Integrating Task and System Models through Scenarios*, in C. Johnson (ed.), Proc. of 8th Int. Workshop on Design, Specification, and Verification of Interactive Systems DSV-IS'2001 (Glasgow, 13-15 June 2001), Lecture Notes in Computer Science, Vol 2220, Springer-Vrlag, Berlin, pp. 88-113.

[15] Paternò, F., *Model-Based Design and Evaluation of Interactive Applications*, Springer-Verlag, Berlin, 2000.

[16] Paternò, F., and Santoro, C., *One Model, Many Interfaces*, in Ch. Kolski, J. Vanderdonckt (eds.), Proc. of 4th International Conference on Computer-Aided Design of User Interfaces (Valenciennes, 15-17 May 2002), Kluwer Academics Publishers, Dordrecht, 2002, pp. 143-154.

[17] Puerta, A., Cheng, E., Ou, T., and Min, J., *MOBILE: User-Centered Interface Building*, in Proceedings of ACM Conf. on Human Aspects in computing Systems CHI'99 (Pittsburgh, 15-20 May 1999), ACM Press, New York, 1999, pp. 426-433.

[18] Traetteberg, H., *Model-based User Interface Design*, Ph.D. thesis, Mathematics and Electrical Engineering, Faculty of Information Technology, Norwegian University of Science and Technology, 2002.

[19] Vanderdonckt, J. and Bodart, F., *Encapsulating Knowledge for Intelligent Automatic Interaction Objects Selection*, in Proc. of the ACM Conf. on Human Factors in Computing Systems INTERCHI'93 (Amsterdam, 24-29 April 1993), ACM Press, New York, 1993, pp. 424-429.

[20] Vanderdonckt, J., Limbourg, Q., and Florins, M., *Deriving the Navigational Structure of a User Interface*, in M. Rauterberg, M. Menozzi, J. Wesson (eds.), Proc. of 9th IFIP TC 13 Int. Conf. on Human-Computer Interaction INTERACT'2003 (Zurich, 1-5 September 2003), IOS Press, Amsterdam, 2003, pp. 455-462.

APPENDIX: TOOL SUPPORT FOR TASK MODELLING

Task models can also be animated (but in a command-line style only). For reasons of clarity the output of the following scenario ⟨Receive, Read, Reply, Read, File⟩ has been shortened. Actions executable in the next step of the animation and the actual state of the instance mail1 are shown.

```
Parsing samples/mail/mail1.in...okay
Possible actions:
(1) [Manage, Receive]
Enter a number between 1 and 1 (0 to exit): 1
Environment:  [1]  Mail  -  replied=false  read=false  con-
tent="hallo paul..."
to="Paul" from="Ann"
Possible actions:
(1) [Manage, Read]
(2) [Manage, \_Read]              Enter...: 1
Environment: [1] Mail - read=true replied=false ...
%Possible actions:
(1) [Manage, Read]
(2) [Manage, \_Read]
(3) [Manage, Reply]              Enter...: 3
Environment:  [1]  Mail  -  replied=true  read=true  reply="hallo
Ann"
...
%Possible actions:
(1) [Manage, Read]
(2) [Manage, \_Read]              Enter...: 1
Environment: [1] Mail - read=true ...
%Possible actions:
(1) [Manage, Read]
(2) [Manage, \_Read]              Enter...: 2
Environment: [1] Mail - read=true ...
%Possible actions:
(1) [Manage, File]              Enter...: 1
Environment: [1] Mail - read=true replied=true content="hallo
paul..."
to="Paul" from="Ann" location="trash" reply="hallo Ann"
Action finished
```

Chapter 2

TASK-BASED WEB MODELLING: THE WEB OBJECT LIFE CYCLE MODELLING CONCEPT

Birgit Bomsdorf[1] and Gerd Szwillus[2]

[1]*FernUniversität Hagen, Praktische Informatik I,*
Universitätsstraße 1 – D-58097 Hagen (Germany)
E-Mail: birgit.bomsdorf@fernuni-hagen.de
URL: http://pi1.fernuni-hagen.de/mitarbeiter/bomsdorf.html
Tel: +49 2331 987-2962 – Fax: +49 2331 987-314
[2]*Universität Paderborn, Fakultät EIM, Institut für Informatik,*
Fürstenallee 11 – D-33102 Paderborn (Germany)
E-Mail: szwillus@upb.de
URL: http://www.uni-paderborn.de/cs/ag-szwillus
Tel: +49 5251 60-6624 – Fax: +49 5251 60-6620

Abstract   A web modelling approach is proposed, which uses a task model of the business as underlying basis and exploits it for adequate modelling of web sites including user interaction. We argue that a variant of classical task models, which emphasizes task objects and task views, is specially well-suited to support a model-based development of web sites. Its concepts and its practical use are discussed.

Keywords: Interactive web sites, Task based design, User-centred design, Web modelling.

1.   INTRODUCTION

In the early days of the WWW, web sites were created for fast and easy dissemination of information to web site visitors. Gradually, though, web sites have developed from this world of static HTML pages towards interactive sites. In addition to receiving general information, the visitor inputs data and is provided individually computed feedback from the web site. The visitor might order something, deliver or request information specific to the business, or request a specific service. In short, the dialogue going on is governed by the tasks of the user in relation to the business.

R. Jacob et al. (eds.), Computer-Aided Design of User Interfaces IV, 15–28.
© 2005 *Kluwer Academic Publishers. Printed in the Netherlands.*

If we look at current web modelling approaches, however, we see that they do not take the interactivity of web sites appropriately into account. Dialogue modelling – as done in HCI – is not a significant part of the process. Instead, the content-centred view on the domain objects is still the dominant issue of these approaches. We claim, however, that interaction design and feedback specification from the point of view of the users should be integral parts of a modelling technique for today's web sites. As the information presented and the user dialogues provided in the web are both dependent on events "occurring" in and with the business, while the users perform their tasks, we propose to include a task model of the business as underlying basis for a web modelling approach and exploit it for adequate modelling of interaction and for supporting the web site update process.

2.   MODEL-BASED APPROACHES

The model-based idea as such implies that the creation of some complicated artefact can be divided into the handling of several distinct levels dealing with separate aspects of the overall design. Following the motto "divide and conquer" the development is structured into separate design phases producing explicit, dedicated design documents – the models. Using explicit models results in typical benefits, such as verifiable and re-usable documents. Before dealing with our concrete web modelling approach, we first sketch and compare the existing HCI and web modelling approaches.

2.1   Model-based Approaches in HCI

In HCI there exist several model-based approaches for the development of user interfaces (e.g., [1,2,7,8,10,11,12,14,17]). Although a great number of variants of model-based approaches are discussed in HCI, there is a certain consensus about a collection of models and their importance for user interface (UI) development.

- Typically a model-based HCI approach starts with **task modelling**, describing the tasks from the user's point of view – the user's goals, activities, and basic actions are described. The model contains information about the **task objects** operated upon by the tasks, and includes information about the different types of users, referred to as **role model**.
- The task model is partitioned into different **views**, thus defining which tasks need to be dealt with together. This implies the visibility of means to trigger task execution and visibility of task objects to the appropriate user roles. These views can be seen as corresponding to dialogue elements showing subparts of the final user interface. This grouping is

guided by the necessity or usefulness for the user's ability to operate on a set of tasks at a time [3].

The behaviour of the user interface is described in two steps: first, the **navigation** between views is defined; second, the **processing** of user input events within single views is specified. Both parts together are referred to as the **dialogue** model of the user interface.

- The **navigation** model defines the visibility of the different views. It specifies which views are initially visible when a system is started, and which events in the user interface turn views visible or invisible. Hence, it defines the overall navigation structure of the user interface. As the views are derived from collections of tasks, the switch between different views is strongly dependent of the underlying task model structure.
- The **processing** model defines the details of user interaction within the single views. Typically, this is a state-based model, specifying the different states the user interface component can be in and the effects of events on the state. Effects can be state transitions, modifications of the output presented, application function calls, or arbitrary combinations of these.
- In a final step within model-based approaches the details of what views and their contents look like is defined in a **presentation** model.

Using this task-based model suite results in a user interface design which is strictly based upon the user task specification and concentrates on the functionality of the application as seen from the user's perspective.

2.2 Model-Based Development of Web Sites

Similar as in the field of HCI the model-based idea is applied to the development of web applications with the same general goals. Typically, a web site is modelled at the conceptual level to describe the information space, its structure and possible modifications independent from implementation issues. Model-based approaches, e.g., WebML [19], OOHDM [12], Strudel [14], RMM [8], and WSDOM [5], have their origin in the development of hypermedia systems and information systems, increasingly incorporating methods and techniques known from Software Engineering. SWCEditor is a recent approach concentrating on modelling web navigation [20]. Although there are significant differences between the approaches, there is consensus on the core of the activities to be performed and aspects to be modelled.

- Requirements are mostly captured by means of narrative **scenarios** and **use cases**, i.e. the objectives of the web site, the prospective user groups and their tasks are written down. The task specification is typically a high-level task enumeration, and no refined description of task internals.

- The **domain model** conceptually describes the objects of the business domain, their properties in terms of attributes, sub-object structures, and semantic relationships. In some approaches also the intended application functionality is specified. Techniques adopted for defining this model correspond to well-known structures from Software Engineering (such as the class model in UML) or database engineering (ER diagrams).

- Additionally, in some approaches **user-related domain models** are introduced (e.g., navigational class schema in OOHDM [18], audience object model in WSDM [5]), which are defined as views on the domain model, similar to external schemas as known from database development. Each user-related domain model represents a substructure of the complete model by identifying those parts which are relevant to a supposed type of user or role. Hence, these views describe properties, and semantic links to be shown to the users, while they are performing their role-specific tasks.

- The **navigation model** shows possible ways for the user to access the information space in terms of navigation elements, i.e. nodes and links. Hence, it defines the content and logical structure of the pages, as well as accessing criteria (such as filtering or indexing) and types of navigation (such as guided tours or object lists).

- The **presentation model** captures how content and navigation commands should be visualized to the user. Although this model varies in the degree of abstraction within different approaches, it is often called an **abstract interface design**. It shows the perceptual structure of single pages in terms of hierarchical grouping and intra-page links. It defines where additional files (images, audio, video) are to be inserted, and in which way links are to be presented (e.g., textually or graphically). The main meaning of abstraction in the context of this model concerns the independence from any particular language and from devices used to deliver the pages.

- The need for personalisation of web sites to individual users or user groups is generally increasing. It concerns user interface adaptation as well as the customisation of the underlying functionality, i.e. it is related to content, presentation, and navigation, thus affecting all the models described above. At the model stage personalization aspects are summarised by the term **personalisation model**, although they are often defined as special extensions of the existing models.

The main observation here is that there is no explicit model for user interaction and for the modification of content. It is not captured how the business functions work, i.e. which tasks are performed, and how they modify data, resulting in web site changes. Emphasis is on data modelling expressed in the domain model and on navigation within this information space.

2.3 Comparing HCI Models with Web Models

To strengthen the use and the role of task modelling within web modelling approaches, one could ask whether it would make sense to apply HCI modelling approaches directly to web modelling. The problem with this idea is that the objectives in both design fields were different from the very beginning:

- The primary goal of a user interface is to provide access to some application functionality, the **functional space**, to the user. It provides means to trigger functions and input data or parameter values to feed a given semantic functionality.
- The primary goal of a web site is to provide access to an **information space** to the unknown user. This space is described in terms of nodes carrying content connected by links allowing the user to navigate through the space, which is structured as a collection of web pages. Following a link means "going to another place", even if this may technically not be the case.

This is a shift in paradigm from modelling flow of action in user interfaces to modelling movement in information structures in the web. Let us look closer now into the single HCI models to find out more about the differences between the two fields.

As mentioned above, **task modelling** is used in both fields, although the degree of its use differs a lot. Both use task modelling for requirements gathering. Within the HCI approaches, however, task models are refined much further for describing the interaction model – they are richer in structure and content, e.g., defining conditions and sequencing of task execution. In consequence, task models are used as formal input to the subsequent constructive phases.

In web modelling, task models are used primarily as a means to explore requirements and are limited to high-level task descriptions (i.e. use cases or scenarios). They are used as starting point to describe either the global domain model or the user-related domain models (if supported). In WSDM [5], for example, task models are used to guide the design of the navigation, i.e. the content units and navigation tracks for different user groups, as well as the respective presentations. In OOHDM [18], task descriptions are analyzed to identify the data items, which are to be exchanged between the user and the web application. Hence, the task model is not exploited as a formal basis for the design of the site structure and interaction.

View modelling is used in both fields too, but with slightly different meanings. In the field of HCI, views are derived from the formal task model based on task grouping, leading to the definition of interaction elements for triggering tasks and information elements for displaying relevant task objects. Hence, the view definition originates essentially from task grouping. In web modelling, the term view is used for two different aspects: on one hand, user-related domain models are defined as views on the domain model, which are similar to the models of task objects in UI modelling. On the other hand, single nodes are considered as views on the underlying domain model. Defining such a view means to design the structure and content of a web page, typically derived from a data structure model of the web site. Hence, in web modelling the derivation of both kinds of views is strongly based on data modelling.

Navigation modelling means the transition between different views (logical "windows" or pages) in both fields. In a user interface, navigation corresponds to a transition between groups of tasks, hence UI navigation between views corresponds to movement within a function space.

Navigation in web modelling, however, means movement within an information space. The view model provides the necessary starting and end points for the movement, which may additionally transport data provided by the user for selection and filtering content from the underlying information base. Hence it is strongly data oriented. As interaction with the web site is mapped onto navigation too, there is no explicit orientation of the navigation model towards the functions provided by the web site to the visitor.

The **processing model** as introduced by the field of HCI is the most detailed part, specifying what is happening within single views.

In web modelling, there is no concept for specifying operations on a single view. As mentioned before, interaction is described and implemented by means of links. As links are used for different purposes, the definition of interaction is mixed with other modelling aspects. In existing web modelling approaches it is "visible" to the designer, e.g., in the form of extensions (new symbols, e.g., in [3]). From the viewpoint of the user, the effects of submitting information to the web site or invoking an application operation, for instance by clicking on a button, is mapped onto navigation. As described in [4] invoking operations is modelled as side effects of activating links. Hence, there is no explicit concept in web modelling for dealing with the user's action steps to execute a task – the user's movement possibilities are modelled along the information structures underlying the web site.

Altogether, a sequence of web interactions while performing a task is modelled as a sequence of pages the user has to navigate through. Hence, each dialogue state is represented by a single view (page) and a dialogue sequence is defined by means of links, without distinguishing between the navigation and processing dialogue. Furthermore, there is no explicit concept of defining groups of related task, i.e. views as introduced by HCI, which is important to match the mental model of the user and thus for supporting usability.

Based on the approaches as known from HCI and web modelling, we started to develop a web modelling approach with the objective to integrate benefits from HCI methods with the needs of web modelling. The overall goal is the strict user/task-orientation of the process throughout all development phases and the switch to data-centric issues only later in the process. Hence, the emphasis is on processes first and on information structures second, which is typically the other way round in web modelling approaches. Within our approach we are developing a system, referred to as Task-Object-Based Web Site Management system [2], [15], [16]. In the following, we will use WOLM (Web Object Life Cycle Model) as an abbreviation for this concept, as this model is the kernel model of our approach.

3.   TASK-OBJECT-BASED WEB SITES

Our approach is based strongly on an underlying task model, as is the case in HCI modelling. As mentioned above, a classical task model specifies primarily the task hierarchy, pre- and postconditions, and conditions for task execution. Most existing models take user roles and task objects into account too. Altogether, emphasis is on modelling of users' "action" while they are performing their tasks; modelling of "things", i.e. task objects, which are affected by those actions, comes second.

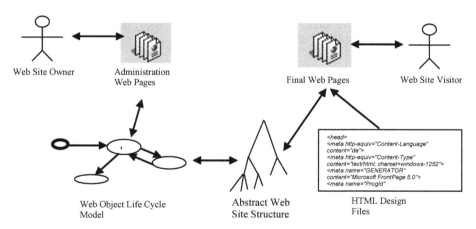

Figure 1. Overview of the concept

When applying the task model approach to web modelling, it is important to look at task modelling the other way round: The task objects modified during task execution are to be displayed in the web, and thus are of primary importance within the design process. Therefore, in our approach the core part is a **task object model**, referred to as **Web Object Life cycle Model**

(WOLM), describing the task objects which will ultimately be represented in the web as well as their modifications resulting from task execution. The second basic part of the approach is the **Abstract Website Structure (AWS)**, which structures the information described by the WOLM into web pages and parts of web pages. Fig. 1 gives an overview of the concept. In the following we discuss these two main parts and how they contribute to task-based modelling of web sites.

3.1   The Web Object Life Cycle Model

The WOLM contains **web objects** corresponding to the task objects of the business to be represented in the web site, as they have been identified during the task analysis phase. WOLM not only captures the objects' data structures as done in a domain model, but specifies the modifications they undergo during task execution as well. Technically, objects are described by means of a class specification, which specifies the properties of a given type of objects. The class specification contains attribute declarations, initialization information, and methods to be performed "on" the objects of the specified type. Object modifications are described as state transitions corresponding to the task description they are derived from. The different **web object states** represent "situations" or "configurations" a web object can be in. They are used to describe the changes a web object undergoes during its life time through execution of tasks. The following example shows a specification derived from the task model describing the user task "prolongate a book" while using a library system:

```
class Book
  { string signature;          task object specification

     ...
     prolongate() {…}             method

     ...                                              states
     field (prolongable,not_prolongable);
     prolongable -prolongate()->
        [numberProlongation < 3]: prolongable      transition
     prolongable -prolongate()->
        [numberProlongation >= 3]: not_prolongable
  ...}                              rule garding the transition
```

To define the dynamics, a WOLM class specification contains a definition of rules governing the transitions between states, specifying which state transitions are possible and what the respective target states are. Together with the state transition triggered by an event the effect of the transition on the object's attribute values is described. The performance of methods, i.e.

the execution of attribute modifications, may request input parameters from the user. The transition below, for example, specifies that within the login procedure the user has to fill in his "login" and "password":

```
not_logged_in -tryLogin(login, password)-> logged_in
```

The input request is an abstract model of the interaction process which will later on be mapped onto web site interaction elements.

WOLM specifies the modifications in the business from a strictly user centred point of view. It is a mirror of the task execution as performed in reality, described by the changes the task objects undergo. When specifying the state transition possibilities and their effects on objects, it is not defined where triggers for the state transitions originate. The model is explicitly concentrating on the effects and their interrelations between the objects. The model is independent from any web representation specification, hence the two design spaces "task model" and "web representation" are completely separated in this approach.

3.2   The Abstract Web Site Structure

The Abstract Web Site Structure (AWS) contains a hierarchy of elements structuring a web site, e.g., web pages, lists, graphics, text elements, links, and interaction elements such as buttons and text input fields. AWS is a pure structure model, as it defines **what** is shown on the web pages and does not specify **how** things look. While the WOLM defines the content to be displayed and the functions accessible, the AWS defines the distribution of the content onto web pages and the access to functions through the web pages, i.e. the AWS covers the specification of views, navigation and processing dialog. Before describing this let us consider the interrelations of both models.

AWS and WOLM are linked through references to single web objects or object lists, which are expressed in the AWS through specification of the web objects' properties. At runtime, the attribute values of linked WOLM objects are available as information source to the AWS, and therefore to the representation in the web. This concept is similar as in content management systems, which link abstract objects (typically database records) to web pages and derive the content of the pages from their contents.

Another important link between WOLM and AWS is the fact that different states of objects can lead to different AWS fragments representing an object. The AWS contains condition clauses defining which elements are shown and not. Hence, the state transition of an object related to an AWS fragment, can change its AWS representation by changing its state in the WOLM model. This mechanism allows the visualization of semantically important object state information to the web site visitor.

Furthermore, based on task grouping, the AWS is used to define views, which have a similar function as in HCI. A view in HCI specifies groups of related tasks to match the mental model of the user. A page in the AWS also groups related tasks; the modifications occurring within such a view are modelled within WOLM, while the corresponding changing representation is described within the AWS. The following AWS excerpt exemplifies a view on the task object "book" by means of which users of a library system can prolong an already borrowed book:

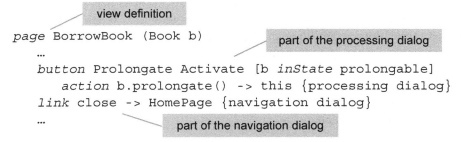

```
page BorrowBook (Book b)
    ...
    button Prolongate Activate [b inState prolongable]
        action b.prolongate() -> this {processing dialog}
    link close -> HomePage {navigation dialog}
    ...
```

The example also shows a part of the processing dialog: An abstract button `Prolongate` is defined. Activating it will invoke the function `prolongate` of the WOLM book object b. As denoted by the `this`- specification the same view, i.e. the same page, will be shown afterwards, of course in an updated version if necessary.

Basically, there exist two interaction elements in the web: text input fields and buttons. The user can click into text input fields and type text. If at some point this information is collected by the web site, e.g. by pressing the submit button of the corresponding form, the data is sent from the user's web browser to the server. This event triggering behaviour constitutes the second type of user interaction. When clicking on a button on a web page, as shown in the example above, the user triggers the execution of some application functionality.

The effect of a button click is twofold: first, reading user input from text input elements on the web page (if the button implements the "submit" functionality) and, second, displaying a new or redisplaying the same page (`this`). For the description of the navigation dialog we use a similar notation, e.g. `link close -> HomePage` specifies a link `close`, which will lead the user to the home page.

In the co-operation between AWS and WOLM, these two elementary functions are mapped onto two corresponding effects of a button press:

• First, the button can trigger a state transition of some WOLM object. In this case the values input by the web site visitor are transferred as parameters to this state transition. The state transition is then executed until the WOLM model has performed the corresponding modifications, including attribute modifications and inferred state transitions.

- Second, once the model is stable again, the same or some other page is displayed, using the "new" values of the WOLM model for this purpose.

Once an AWS is linked to a WOLM model, the remaining work to create the final web pages is to combine it with layout files containing templates for defining the visual representation.

3.3   Cooperation between the Components

WOLM and AWS cover very different design spaces within the web modelling approach. By means of the AWS the structure of information presentation, including the navigation structure between these elements is designed. Most important is the dependency of AWS parts of WOLM objects, defined by declarative constraints, and the variants in the representation, dependent on objects' states. Classical hyperlinks are modelled as well as the effect of interaction elements, and the two important components of a button element – the trigger of semantic changes and the display of some new page – are explicitly and separately specified. Hence, the two design spaces, modelling the functionality on one hand, and the displayed information structure and their properties on the other hand, are clearly separated, which allows to update, refine, and debug both parts independently of each other.

WOLM allows the designer to base the web site creation explicitly on a task model. The kernel model is a task object model specifying the web objects to be presented in the web, and defining their modification through task execution. The AWS contains both the view model as well as the model of the navigation and processing dialog. The views are defined by spreading the information to be displayed onto web pages and web page parts. The navigation is defined by specifying links from one node within the AWS to another one while the processing dialog is defined by abstract interaction elements whereby navigation within a view and between views is clearly separated.

Other than in HCI modelling, there is no dialogue model concentrated in a single component, which encapsulates the aspects "context" of a user interaction and its effect. These two aspects are separated in our approach, as the perceived context of an interaction is specified in the AWS, and the effect is specified in the WOLM kernel. This separation makes sense in the web modelling case, however, as designing these aspects needs developers with very different background and expertise.

In addition, exploiting the clear execution semantics of the WOLM allows the performance of a simulation of the model at a very early development stage. In addition, the "running" WOLM model can serve as underlying directing device for the live web site while the AWS deals with the resulting changes of the web presentation.

3.4   Status of the Work

To work successfully with a model-based approach such as WOLM, a tool environment is needed. We designed such an environment and identified the following suite of tools (Fig. 2):

- an **editor** to create and edit the WOLM,
- a **simulator** to execute the kernel model for to validate the dynamics of the specification,
- an **admin pages generator** to enable the web site owner to manipulate and define the contents of his web site via the simulator,
- an **AWS editor** to create and edit abstract web site structure documents, based upon an existing kernel WOLM model,
- an **AWS generator** to create an initial AWS automatically from the WOLM to allow fast and easy early-phase testing of the WOLM,
- a **layout Linker** tool to create and merge concrete HTML design files containing appropriate templates with the AWS, and
- a **runtime system** for WOLM, based upon the simulator, which incorporates the complete functionality for a living web site, including admin pages and a time stamp management for keeping the site up-to-date.

Most tools are currently under development and will soon be completed; emphasis up to now has been on the design and specification of the WOLM and AWS models, and their representation as XML files. A preliminary version of the runtime system has been developed and is working. In the context of language definition we currently look into applying the concept to realistically sized web projects.

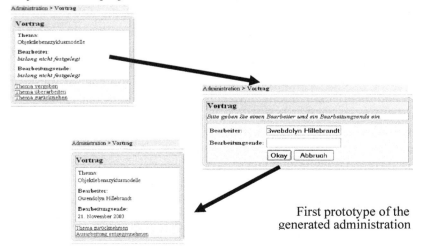

Figure 2. First prototype of the generated administration.

REFERENCES

[1] Bodart, F., Hennebert, A.-M., Leheureux, J.-M., Provot I., and Vanderdonckt, J., *A Model-based Approach to Presentation: A Continuum from Task Analysis to Prototype*, in F. Paternò (ed.), Proceedings of 1st Workshop on Design, Specification, and Verification of Interactive Systems DSV-IS'94 (Bocca di Magra, 8-10 June 1994), Eurographics Series, Berlin, pp. 25-39.

[2] Bomsdorf, B. and Szwillus, G., *From Task to Dialogue: Task-Based User Interface Design, A CHI'98 Workshop*, SIGCHI Bulletin, Vol. 30, No. 4, 1998, pp. 40-42.

[3] Bomsdorf, B. and Szwillus, G., *User-Centered Modeling of Interactive Web Sites*, accessible at http://www2003.org/cdrom/papers/poster/p327/p327-bomsdorf.htm

[4] Bomsdorf, B., *Task Modelling for Customisation of Web Applications*, in Proceedings of 10th International Conference on Human-Computer Interaction HCI International 2003 (Heraklion, 22-27 June 2003), Vol. 3, Lawrence Erlbaum Associates, Mahwah, 2003, pp. 33-37.

[5] Bongio, A., Ceri, S., Fraternali, P., and Maurino, A., *Modelling Data Entry and Operations in WebML*, in D. Suciu, G. Vossen (eds.), Proceedings of 3rd International Workshop on the Web and Databases WebDB'2000 (Dallas, 18-19 May 2000), Lecture Notes in Computer Science, Vol. 1997, Springer-Verlag, Berlin, 2000, pp. 201-214, accessible at http://www.research.att.com/conf/webdb2000/PAPERS/6b.pdf

[6] De Troyer, O., *Audience-driven Web Design*, in M. Rossi, K. Siau (eds.), Information modelling in the new millennium, IDEA Group Publishing, 2001, accessible at http://wsdm.vub.ac.be/Download/Papers/WISDOM/WSDMChapter.PDF

[7] Elwert, T., Forbrig, P., and Schlungbaum, E., *Meta Models for Task-oriented User Interface Development*, in C. Stary (ed.), Proceedings of the 1st Workshop on Cognitive Modelling and Interface Development (Vienna, December 1994), pp. 163-172.

[8] Hackos, J.T. and Redish, J.C. (eds.), *User and Task Analysis for Interface Design*, John Wiley & Sons, New York, 1997.

[9] Isakowitz, T., Kamis, A., and Koufaris M., *The Extended RMM Methodology for Web Publishing*, Working Paper IS-98-18, Centre for Information-Intensive Systems, New York University, New York, 1998, accessible at http://jmis.bentley.edu/rmm/papers/RMM-Extended.pdf

[10] Palanque, Ph. and Bastide, R., *Synergistic modelling of tasks, system and users using formal specification techniques*, Interacting With Computers, Vol. 9, No. 12, 1997, pp. 129-153.

[11] Paternò, F., Mancini, C., and Meniconi, S., *ConcurTaskTrees: A Diagrammatic Notation for Specifying Task Models*, in S. Howard, J. Hammond, G. Lindgaard (eds.), Proceedings of 6th IFIP TC 13 Conf. on Human-Computer Interaction Interact'97 (Sydney, 14-18 July 1997), Kluwer Academics, Dordrecht, 1997, pp. 362-369.

[12] Puerta, A., Cheng, E., Ou, T., and Min, J., *MOBILE: User-Centered Interface Building*, in Proceedings of ACM Conf. on Human Aspects in computing Systems CHI'99 (Pittsburgh, 15-20 May 1999), ACM Press, New York, 1999, pp. 426-433.

[13] Rossi, R., Schwabe, D., and Lyardet, F., *Web Application Models are More than Conceptual Models*, in P.P. Chen, D.W. Embley, J. Kouloumdjian, S.W. Liddle, J.F. Roddick (eds.), Advances in Conceptual Modeling, Proceedings of the ER'99 Workshops on Evolution and Change in Data Management, Reverse Engineering in Information Systems, and the World Wide Web and Conceptual Modeling (Paris, 15-18 November 1999), Lecture Notes in Computer Science, Vol. 1727, Springer-Verlag, Berlin, 1999, pp. 239-253.

[14] Stary, C., *Task- and Model-Based Development of Interactive Software*, in Proceedings of 15th IFIP World Computer Congress IFIP'98 (Vienna, 31 August-4 September 1998).

[15] Strudel Home Page, accessible at http://www.research.att.com/sw/tools/strudel

[16] Szwillus, G. and Bomsdorf, B., *Models for Task-Object-Based Web Site Management*, in P. Forbrig, Q. Limbourg, B. Urban, J. Vanderdonckt (eds.), Proceedings of 9th International Workshop on Design, Specification, and Verification of Interactive Systems DSV-IS'2002 (Rostock, 14-16 June 2002), Lecture Notes in Computer Science, Vol. 2545, Springer-Verlag, Berlin, 2002, pp. 267-281.

[17] Szwillus, G. and Bomsdorf, B., *Task-Object Models for the Development of Interactive Web Sites*, in Proceedings of 10th International Conference on Human-Computer Interaction HCI International 2003 (Heraklion, 22-27 June 2003), Vol. 1, Lawrence Erlbaum Associates, Mahwah, 2003, pp. 248-252.

[18] van der Veer, G., Lenting, B., and Bergevoet, B., *Groupware Task Analysis - Modelling Complexity*, Acta Psychologica, Vol. 91, 1996, pp. 297-322.

[19] Vilain, P. and Schwabe, D., *Improving the Web Application Design Process with UIDs*, in Proc. of 2nd International Workshop on Web Oriented Software Technology IW-WOST'2002 (Malaga, 10 June 2002), 2002, accessible at http://www.dsic.upv.es/~west2001/ iwwost02/papers/vilain.pdf

[20] WebML Home Page, accessible at http://webml.elet.polimi.it/webml.

[21] Winckler, M., Barboni, E., Farenc, C., and Palanque, P., *SWCEditor: A Model-based Tool for Interactive Modelling of Web Navigation*, in R. Jacob, Q. Limbourg, J. Vanderdonckt (eds.), Proceedings of 5th International Conference on Computer-Aided Design of User Interfaces CADUI'04 (Funchal, 13-16 January 2004), Kluwer Academics Pub., Dordrecht, 2004, pp. 55-66.

Chapter 3

MODEL-BASED DESIGN OF ONLINE HELP SYSTEMS

Milene Selbach Silveira[1], Simone D.J. Barbosa[1,2], and Clarisse Sieckenius de Souza[2]

[1] PUCRS, Faculdade de Informática (FACIN)
Av.Ipiranga, 668, Prédio 30 – Porto Alegre, RS 90619-900 (Brasil)
E-mail: milene@inf.pucrs.br
URL: http://www.inf.pucrs.br/~milene
Tel: +55 51 3203558 – Fax: +55 51 3203621
[2] PUC-Rio, Departamento de Informática,
R. Marquês de São Vicente, 225, 4º RDC, Gávea – Rio de Janeiro, RJ 22453-900, Brasil
E-mail: {simone,clarisse}@inf.puc-rio.br
URL: http://www.inf.puc-rio.br/{~simone,~clarisse}
Tel: + 55 21 3114-1500 ext. {4353,4344} – Fax: +55 21 3114-1530

Abstract   Online help systems are typically used as a last resource in interactive break-down situations. In this paper, we present a method for building online help based on design models according to a semiotic engineering approach. We show the benefits of having designers explicitly communicate their design vision to users, and we also point at the need to foster a new culture for online help. We show how this proposal opens a direct communication channel from designers to users, and we hope this will contribute to introducing this new culture.

Keywords: Design models, HCI design, Online help systems, Semiotic engineering.

1.   INTRODUCTION

How can we help designers build online help for a computer application? And how can we ensure that it will adequately tell users what to do with the application, what the application is for, why certain design decisions were made, and so on? Typical online help systems do not help their users much. The reasons for this inefficiency may lie in lack of time or planning or in excessive confidence in the intuitiveness of a fail-proof interface, or in a naïve

29

R. Jacob et al. (eds.), Computer-Aided Design of User Interfaces IV, 29–42.
© 2005 Kluwer Academic Publishers. Printed in the Netherlands.

acceptance of current standards [19]. Following Adler & Winograd's views [1] that attempting to build idiot-proof technology underestimates or hinders the users' intelligence and creativity to learn and transform software according to their needs, we believe the role of the online help system is to open new possibilities and give users resources to understand and go beyond the designer's original ideas, taking the most advantage of the technology. In this view, the construction of the online help system becomes a critical step in the design of human-computer interaction (HCI).

This work is based on Semiotic Engineering [7], which views the user interface as a message sent from designers to users, representing the designers' solution to what they believe is the users' problems. It is through this message that designers tell users what they have interpreted as being the users' needs and preferences, what the answer for these needs is and how they implemented their vision as an interactive system. In Semiotic Engineering, online help is an essential application component. This is where designers will explicitly "speak" to the users, revealing how the application was built, how it can be used and for what purposes.

This paper describes a model-based approach for online help system design, stemming from Semiotic Engineering and driven by two main pillars: communicability and the rhetorical layering technique used in the minimalist approach. In order to illustrate our approach, the design of a real application's help system is presented as a running example.

2.   A SEMIOTIC ENGINEERING VIEW OF ONLINE HELP

According to Semiotic Engineering, it is essential that users understand the designers' message so that they may better use and take advantage of the application. One way to make this message explicit is through a careful design of the application's online help system. The goal of our research [21] is to promote a novel perspective on online help design and usage. Users should be able to express more precisely their doubts and needs, and designers should be able to anticipate such doubts and needs, and to organize their response accordingly.

Our proposal for online help design draws from two related works: communicability evaluation [15] and the layering technique used in minimalist documentation [9]. Communicability evaluation is a qualitative HCI evaluation method which reveals potential breakdowns during interaction. These breakdowns are indicated by colloquial expressions which users can associate to their needs for help content. The minimalist approach to technical communication suggests that using small pieces of very relevant contextualized content is one of the best ways of providing information to users [5]. Its benefits are increased by the layering technique [9], through which related pieces of mutually accessible minimalist content are connected, and made available to users.

In our approach, users are offered a set of expressions from which they may choose one to indicate their doubts or trouble during interaction. In doing this, they obtain the contextualized help content associated to the chosen expression. For instance, if they can't see or interpret feedback for an action, users may ask "What happened?".

Some of the expressions used for accessing help were drawn from the communicability evaluation method, and others resulted from an analysis of existing help literature about users' most frequent doubts during interaction [4, 20]. A few of them are frequently found in commercial applications, such as "What's this?" and "How do I do this?". The current set of expressions we use for accessing help is:

What's this?	How do I do this?	What is this for?
Where is…?	Where was I?	What now?
What happened?	Why should I do this?	Why doesn't it?
Who can do this?	On whom does this depend?	Who does this affect?
Oops!	Is there another way to do this?	Help!

Both users and designers benefit from using these expressions: users have a greater chance of getting a relevant help response, and designers have an organisation principle directly driven by communicative breakdowns that they intend to circumvent or solve. Inspired by the layering technique [9], we allow users to access minimal pieces of help content about a certain user interface element or task first, and then access further help material, depending on their needs, and then on to as much further information as required.

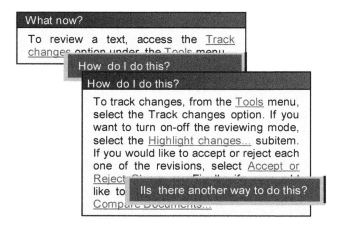

Figure 1. Help responses and their recurrence.

A simple example illustrating minimalist responses and the recurring use of expressions upon these is shown in Fig. 1. This is a fictitious example, based on some help content found in MS Word®, as a response to help requests about 'tracking changes'. Our proposal includes a standalone help module, where it is possible to find related information about the domain and the application as a whole, as well as usage scenarios, so designers may convey their global design vision in a consistent way. However, in this paper we will focus on the local (contextualised) help only.

3.   BUILDING ONLINE HELP SYSTEMS FROM HCI DESIGN MODELS

In this section we describe the extended HCI models involved in designing an online help system. We propose to use these models in a process comprising the steps illustrated in Figure 2.

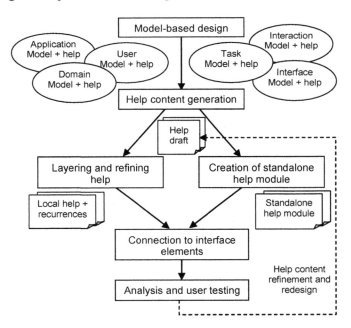

Figure 2. Steps used to build online help systems.

An implicit requirement of our proposal is that we capture design rationale, a task known not to be easy [10]. We should emphasize that the only relevant portions of design rationale for online help systems are those that directly affect the users' experience. In other words, all decisions that are related to software design, architecture and the like are unimportant for help purposes. The relevant information must be captured during the application design process. This is one of the reasons why we follow an extended model-based approach to HCI design. In general, model-based approaches in HCI promote the representation of interaction solutions in order for the designer to reflect on and make adequate design decisions. There is a variety of existing models: task models are the most widely used, but user, domain, presentation and dialogue models are also found in the HCI literature, among others [13,14,16,17,18,23,24,25]. We have carried out a series of studies about these models, in order to verify the possibility of reusing the existing information they provide in designing help and to identify the need for extensions. We have selected models for: domain, application, task, user, interaction and interface, and we have extended them to be able to represent information that is specific for help design.

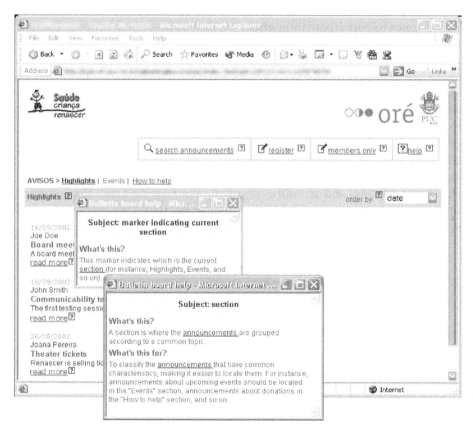

Figure 3. Help request and response.

In order to illustrate our approach, we will describe portions of an application we designed and developed for supporting the volunteer work in a nongovernmental organization [12]. The module we have chosen for illustration is the Bulletin Board, in which volunteers and employees of this organisation may post and verify announcements related to their work or to the organisation as a whole. These announcements may be classified according to different topics or divisions within the organisation, such as: Administration, Events, Meetings, and so on. Figure 3 illustrates a usage scenario in the actual application, in which a member of the organisation has looked for help about a section marker.

3.1   Model-based Design of Online Help

The information necessary for the construction of local help responses and for the standalone help module is derived from HCI models built during the design process. At this point we would like to emphasize the need for the help designer to participate throughout the design process in order to capture this information necessary for building the online help. His presence is essential to ensure the timely capture of help-specific information. As the models are created, the help designer should record the model components in a database which, towards the end of the process, contains all necessary information for generating the draft help content. This way, the help design process becomes more efficient and provides better results, for the information not only reflects the design product, but also includes the rationale underlying some relevant design decisions. If this information isn't captured throughout the design process, much of it would be scattered across numerous representations, and possibly forgotten. We now describe the information comprised in each model, highlighting (in boldface) the pieces of information that are essentially driven towards help system construction.

- *Domain model*: information related to the application domain, focused on its description, the **nature of work performed**, and the information elements (domain signs[1]) that belong to it.

- *Application model*: information related to the application being designed. The focus here lies in the application **description**, its **utility**, **advantages**, supported **activities**, **alternative courses of action**, and the application signs. Besides, it encompasses the roles users may play in this application, and for each role, the tasks related to it, and the necessary **basic knowledge**.

---

[1] A sign is a technical semiotic term that is usually taken to mean "something that stands for something else for someone". In this sense, every piece of data represented in a computer application is a sign to the designer, and every user interface element is a sign both to the designer and to the user(s).

- *Task model*: information related to the tasks users may perform. For each possible task, we represent its **description**, **utility**, **reason** why it should be performed (from the designer's point of view), its parent task (considering a hierarchical task decomposition), the operator[2] that connects it to the following task, which establishes in which way it should be executed, the tasks' preconditions, and the related domain and application signs.

- *User model*: information related to the targeted application users. For each user we represent his name, the roles he may play, and his profile, which indicates the way in which he would like to interact with the application.

- *Interaction model*: information about the possible forms of interaction in the application, that is, about how to effectively perform a certain task in the application. For the execution of each task there may be alternative courses of actions. For each alternative, there is the **reason** why it should be executed (from the designer's point of view), its precondition(s), the indication whether it is the **preferred alternative** (from the designer's point of view) and the actions necessary for its execution. For each action, there is the default value, as well as the way to **undo** it, besides the operator that connects it to the next action.

- *Interface model*: information about the interface elements of the application. For each element, we represent its type, the values it may assume, its default value, its location at the user interface, and the related domain and application signs.

As an example, consider a piece of the domain model, related to a couple of domain signs in our case study:

```
DOMAIN SIGN Marker indicating current section {
    DESCRIPTION (This marker indicates which is the current section (for instance,
    Highlights, Events, and so on.))
    PURPOSE (To quickly indicate the current section.)
}
DOMAIN SIGN  section {
    DESCRIPTION (A section is where the announcements are grouped according to
    a common topic.)
    PURPOSE (To classify the announcements that have common characteristics,
    making it easier to locate them. For instance, announcements about upcoming
    events are located in the "Events" section, about donations in the "How to help"
    section, and so on.)
}
```

and a piece of the task model:

---

[2]   The operators considered in this version are those proposed in [14].

```
TASK Provide the required information {
    TASK PARENT(Create an announcement)
    OPERATOR (sequence)
    SEQUENCE (1)
    ...
}
TASK Confirm the operation {
    TASK PARENT(Create an announcement)
    OPERATOR (sequence)
    SEQUENCE (2)
    ...
}
```

3.2   Help Content Generation using Templates

For each element–expression combination, a minimalist response is designed. In order to generate a draft of this response, we have created a help content template associated to each expression. This template is instantiated with information from the different HCI design models. For instance, for the "What's this?" expression, the content comes directly from the description of the related (domain or application) sign, which is represented in the corresponding (domain or application) model:

What's this?

Response: description(**Sign**)

A more elaborate generation may be illustrated by the "How do I do this?" expression, related to a task. In this case, we have the following:

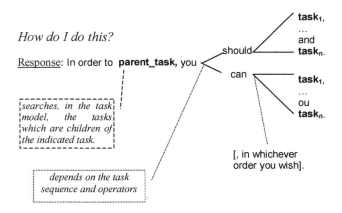

From the information contained in the models and these templates, a draft of the candidate help responses is generated for each pair expression–

element (where element may be a sign, task, alternative courses of actions, and actions). The help designer then selected which responses she would actually include in the application.

Let us consider the marker next to the name of the current section ("Highlights"). A sample response generated from the database is obtained as follows: This marker is a domain sign. The expressions related to (domain) signs are: "What's this?", "What is this for?", and "Where is...?". Taking as an example the expression "What's this?", and using the aforementioned template, the description element was retrieved from the domain sign component, resulting in the following draft answer:

> This marker indicates which is the current section (for instance, Highlights, Events, and so on).

With regard to the task model, the response for the expression "How do I do this?", related to the task "Create an announcement", would be:

> In order to create an announcement you should provide the required information and confirm the operation.

In case of procedural help content, animations may also be generated to show users how the interaction should occur, in a way similar to Cartoonist [22].

3.3   Layering and Refining Help and Creation of Stand-alone Help Module

Based on the interviews with users, domain analysis, and so on, the designer selects those elements which he believes users may have doubts or which he would especially like to explain or describe to users, and the expressions that will be used to access this help content.

As soon as these element–expression pairs are selected, the generated draft responses undergo a refinement process, in which technical communication specialists shape the text in order to better communicate the designer's message to users. Having done that, each help response is analysed by the designer to verify the possible recurrence points it may comprise. These points indicate the elements in the response to which further help expressions and content may be associated. This content may, in turn, contain additional recurrence points, and so on, deepening the help content about certain interrelated topics.

In our example, the draft text of the selected responses was refined and analysed with the purpose of finding possible recurrence points. For instance, in the response to the expression "What's this?"

> This marker indicates which is the current section (for instance, Highlights,

Events, and so on.)

The designer has verified a reference to another domain sign, in this case "section". She selected this word as a recurrence point within the response, and associated the expressions "What's this?" and "What is this for?" to it. The template for "What's this?" of a domain sign is: description(**Sign**); and the template for the expression "What is this for?" is: purpose(**Sign**). Thus, the response to "What's this?" is:

> A section is where the announcements are grouped according to a common topic.

And the response to "What is this for?":

> To classify the announcements that have common characteristics, making it easier to locate them. For instance, announcements about upcoming events are located in the "Events" section, about donations in the "How to help" section, and so on.

It is important to note that help responses are generated and refined beforehand and embedded in the application as static information, instead of being dynamically generated. This solution avoids execution delays in processing the possible expressions and responses for each element, and makes it possible to manually refine the generated draft responses, so that the manner of speech will seem natural and the communication will be more efficient.

Jointly with the layering and refinement of the help messages, the standalone help module may be created. In its most basic form, this module should contain help information about the domain and the application, as well as an explanation about how different kinds of help work (standalone and local). The domain and application portions of this module may be built and refined *pari passu* the construction and refinement of local help content. Afterwards, part of the local help content may also be included in the standalone module.

3.4   Connection to Interface Elements

Having refined the local help content, the expressions and their corresponding responses may be made available through the user interface, associated to the elements which, according to the help designer, may raise some kind of user doubt. This is achieved by adding a trigger or link to the corresponding help expressions and content. In our case study, the graphics designer created a symbol to function as a link to local help requests. The chosen symbol was an interrogation mark within a square, such as ?, placed next to the user interface element associated to the help expression

3.5   Analysis and User Testing

Having built the application prototype, the local help system and the standalone help module, the design team should carry out some preliminary testing in order to verify whether the expressions and the corresponding responses are consistent, as well as the general help information. Every connection to help should be tested, as well as every recurrent point within the responses.

Once the application is implemented it is ready for real user testing through communicability evaluation [15], to verify if the interface is conveying the designer's message and to investigate which problems might occur during interaction. In our case study, we set up a few sessions of communicability evaluation with six users with varying degrees of computer literacy. These users were selected specifically because they represented the majority of the targeted user population, as indicated by the analysis interviews.

In order to better observe interaction during testing and to be able to capture the problems that may occur in help usage, it is interesting that the help designer be present during observations, so that he may focus specifically on help issues. He may not only observe problems in accessing help expressions and in understanding their responses, but also find out user difficulties that hadn't been anticipated (and therefore had no associated help), or whose responses do not address the user's current problem. In our case study, this step made it possible to determine problems in the help content and in accessing help. These problems may be grouped into three classes: help content, "declining" help, and help culture.

Help Content. During testing, the help designer observed users having problems in situations unanticipated by her, which meant that the corresponding help was inadequate or altogether missing.

"Declining" Help. When a user, after many fruitless attempts to use the searching mechanism, made a local help request, she read the explanation, spontaneously said she understood it, but even so she decided to do something different from what was said in the help content, which made it impossible to carry out the task defined in the test scenario.

Help Culture. Most users did not access help, independently of their experience with the application or in using computers. There isn't a culture of asking for online help when you are in trouble. Few were those who asked for help and, when they did, some of them closed the help window before there was time for them to have read the help information. Only one user actually read the help text and followed what the explanation suggested.

4.   FINAL REMARKS

In this paper, we have shown why, in Semiotic Engineering, online help system is an essential part of an application. It is through help that the designer can directly communicate with the application users, revealing the reasons underlying his design and how users may make better use of it. In this approach, model-based design is of utmost importance, for it makes it possible to maintain the consistency between the design products built at each phase. This allows the designer to create and convey a cohesive message to users, in order to increase their chances of making sense of his message.

The users may also express their doubts more directly using one of the available local help expressions during interaction. The response will be a fragment of the designer's point of view and rationale when designing the application. Moreover, users may delve deeper into the help content from the recurrence points available at each help response, in an indefinitely long chain of associations driven by their local needs. This process is associated to some fundamental concepts in semiotic theory, namely semiosis and abduction.

In addition to all technical and theoretical efforts, we should also pay attention to introducing changes in the way users perceive help. As a rule, users access help only as a last resort [6]. They may have had frustrating experiences in the past, or not even understand what help is for. So, without fostering a culture for using help, the most carefully designed help won't improve the users' experience with software. Since this proposal opens a direct communication channel from designers to users, we believe it is a first step towards the introduction of this new culture.

By following a model-based approach, the cost of extending current design practices to design help according to our view is reduced. Using design models as a basis for context-sensitive help generation has been explored elsewhere [11]. The main differences in our work rely on the communication-oriented mechanism for accessing help content,, made available through communicability expressions. This mechanism empowers users, allowing them to choose between a set of expressions that express their immediate doubts in a more precise way, rather than relying on the designers' judgement of all the help content related to a certain user interface element.

In order to further increase the benefits of our work, our students at PUCRS and PUC-Rio are working on software tools for aiding the design of online help and integrating it to web and GUI applications.

REFERENCES

[1]   Adler, P. and Winograd, T., *Usability. Turning technologies into tools*, Oxford University Press, 1992.

[2]   Barbosa, C.M.A., de Souza, C.S., Nicolaci-da-Costa, A.M., and Prates, R.O., *Using the Underlying Discourse Unveiling Method to Understand Organizations of Social Volunteers*, in E. Furtado, J.C. Leite (eds.), Proceedings of Vth Symposium on Human Factors in Computing Systems IHC'2002 (Fortaleza, 7-10 October 2002), pp. ?.

[3]   Barbosa, S.D.J., de Souza, C.S., de Paula, M.G., and Silveira, M.S., *Modelo de Interação como Ponte entre o Modelo de Tarefas e a Especificação da Interface,* in E. Furtado, J.C. Leite (eds.), Proceedings of Vth Symposium on Human Factors in Computing Systems IHC'2002 (Fortaleza, 7-10 October 2002), pp. ?.

[4]   Baecker, R.M., Grudin, J., Buxton, W., and Greenberg, S., *Readings in Human-Computer Interaction: Toward the Year 2000*, Morgan Kaufmann Publishers, San Francisco, 1995.

[5]   Carroll, J.C. (ed.), *Minimalism Beyond the Nurnberg Funnel*, The MIT Press, Cambridge, 1998.

[6]   Ceaparu, I., Lazar, J., Bessiere, K., Robinson, J., and Shneiderman, B., *Determining Causes and Severity of End-User Frustration*, Technical Report, HCIL-2002-11, CS-TR-4371, UMIACS-TR-2002-51, University of Maryland, 2002, accessible at ftp://ftp.cs.umd.edu/pub/hcil/Reports-Abstracts-Bibliography/2002-11html/2002-11.pdf

[7]   de Souza, C.S., *The Semiotic Engineering of Human-Computer Interaction*. The MIT Press, Cambridge, 2004.

[8]   de Souza, C.S., Prates, R., and Carey, T., *Missing and Declining Affordances: Are These Appropriate Concepts?*, Journal of the Brazilian Computer Society, Vol. 7, No. 1, July 2000, pp.26-33.

[9]   Farkas, D.K., *Layering as a Safety Net for Minimalist Documentation*, In [5].

[10] Moran, T.P. and Carroll, J.M., *Design Rationale: Concepts, Techniques, and Use*, Lawrence Erlbaum and Associates, Mahwah, 1996.

[11] Moriyon, R., Szekely, P., and Neches, R., *Automatic Generation of Help from Interface Models*, in Proc. of ACM Conf. on Human Aspects in Computing Systems CHI'94 (Boston, 24-28 April 1994), ACM Press, New York, 1994, pp. 225-231.

[12] ORÉ Projeto, 2002, accessible at http://www.serg.inf.puc-rio.br/ore.

[13] Pangoli, S. and Paternó, F., *Automatic Generation of Task-Oriented Help*, in Proceedings of the 8th Annual ACM Symposium on User Interface and Software Technology UIST'95 (Pittsburgh, 15-17 November 1995), ACM Press, New York, 1995, pp. 181-187.

[14] Paternò, F., *Model-Based Design of Interactive Applications*, Springer-Verlag, Berlin, 1999.

[15] Prates, R.O., de Souza, C.S., and Barbosa, S.D.J., *A Method for Evaluating the Communicability of User Interfaces*, ACM Interactions, Vol. 7, No. 1, January-February 2000, pp. 31-38.

[16] Preece, J., Rogers, Y., Sharp, E., Benyon, D., Holland, S., and Carey, T., *Human-Computer Interaction*, Addison-Wesley, Reading, 1994.

[17] Puerta, A., *The Mecano Project: Comprehensive and Integrated Support for Model-Based Interface Development*, in J. Vanderdonckt (ed.), Proceedings of 2nd Int. Workshop on Computer-Aided Design of User Interfaces CADUI'96 (Namur, 5-7 June 1996), Presses Universitaires de Namur, Namur, 1996, pp. 19-36.

[18] Puerta, A., *A Model-Based Interface Development Environment*, IEEE Software, Vol. 14, No. 4, July/August 1997, pp.41-47.

[19] Purchase, H. and Worrill, J., *An empirical study of on-line help design: features and principals*, Int. J. Human-Computer Studies, Vol. 56, 2002, pp. 539-567.

[20] Sellen, A. and Nicol, A., *Building User-Centered On-line Help*, in B. Laurel (ed.), *The Art of Human-Computer Interface Design*, Addison-Wesley, Reading, 1990, pp. 143-153.

[21] Silveira, M.S., Barbosa, S.D.J., and de Souza, C.S., *Augmenting the Affordance of Online Help Content*, in A. Blandford, J. Vanderdonckt, P. Gray (eds.), People and Computers XV - Interaction without Frontiers, Proc. of the Joint AFIHM-BCS Conf. on Human-Computer Interaction IHM-HCI'2001 (Lille, 10-14 September 2001), Vol. I, Springer-Verlag, London, 2001, pp. 279-296.

[22] Sukaviriya, P. and Foley, J., *Coupling a UI Framework with Automatic Generation of Context-Sensitive Animated Help*, Proceedings of ACM Symposium on User Interface and Software Technology UIST'90 (Snowbird, 3-5 October 1990), ACM Press, New York, 1990, pp. 152-166.

[23] Tarby, J.-Cl, *The Automatic Management of Human-Computer Dialogue and Contextual Help*, in Proceedings of East-West International Conference on Computer-Human Interaction EWCHI'94 (St. Petersburg, 2-6 August 1994), Springer-Verlag, Berlin, 1994.

[24] Vanderdonckt, J. and Berquin, P., *Towards a Very Large Model-based Approach for User Interface Development*, in N.W. Paton, T. Griffiths (eds.), Proc. of 1st Int. Workshop on User Interfaces to Data Intensive Systems UIDIS'99 (Edinburgh, 5-6 September 1999), IEEE Computer Society Press, Los Alamitos, 1999, pp. 76-85.

[25] Vanderdonckt, J., Limbourg, Q., and Florins, M., *Deriving the Navigational Structure of a User Interface*, in M. Rauterberg, M. Menozzi, J. Wesson (eds.), Proceedings of 9th IFIP TC 13 International Conference on Human-Computer Interaction INTER-ACT'2003 (Zurich, 1-5 September 2003), IOS Press, Amsterdam, 2003, pp. 455-462.

Chapter 4

A DESIGN TOOLKIT FOR HYPERMEDIA APPLICATIONS BASED ON ARIADNE DEVELOPMENT METHOD

Susana Montero, Camino Fernández, Juan M. Dodero, Ignacio Aedo, and Paloma Díaz
Universidad Carlos III de Madrid, Departamento de Informática, Laboratorio DEI,
Avda. de la Universidad, 30 – E-28911 Leganés (Spain)
E-mail: {smontero@inf, camino@inf, dodero@inf, aedo@ia, pdp@inf}.uc3m.es
URL: http://www.dei.inf.uc3m.es/~smontero/
Tel: +34 91 624 9419 – Fax: +34 91 624 9129

Abstract   The development process of hypermedia applications implies very specific problems mainly related, first, to the use of navigational structures, interactive behaviours and multimedia compositions, and second, to the fact that are used by users with different levels of knowledge and skills, and also different security levels. This paper presents a design environment, AriadneTool, that allows a designer to model a hypermedia application, to validate such a design and to generate dynamically XML + SMIL implementation templates. This environment is based upon the Ariadne method which offers a set of integrated activities to model hypermedia applications in a systematic and iterative way. A practical example is shown to illustrate the use of the tool in the development of a hypermedia application.

Keywords: Development method, Design environment, Hypermedia applications, Hypermedia modelling.

1.   INTRODUCTION

The extremely high speed of demand on hypermedia systems, and in particular on web applications, have led to development processes where almost the only existing phase is coding, mainly using tools as NetObjects' Fusion or DreamWeaver with no method behind. But hypermedia development presents very specific problems [6,10,14] that can be summarised in: mecha-

43

R. Jacob et al. (eds.), Computer-Aided Design of User Interfaces IV, 43–54.
© 2005 *Kluwer Academic Publishers. Printed in the Netherlands.*

nisms to model sophisticated navigational structures, interactive behaviours and multimedia compositions which have to be usable and harmonic at the same time.

Traditional design methods lack intellectual mechanisms to analyse a design using abstractions and design entities related to the hypermedia domain (e.g., nodes, links, anchors and synchronisms). Some hypermedia methods provide designers with hypermedia specification tools including HDM [10], RMM [12] and OOHDM [14], but the key point of taking into account security issues is not addressed.

The proposal of this paper is the use of a graphical toolkit called AriadneTool, to support the development of hypermedia applications following a development method called Ariadne. The method applies an iterative process based on the evaluation of design solutions with potential users to determine their utility and usability. Compared to similar methods, Ariadne improves three significant aspects: it provides a mechanism to define time- and space-based constraints among contents; it offers a product to model the users structure based on roles and teams that can be used to support personalization and security; and it includes a security model to define the policy that will be applied during the hyperdocument operation.

2.   INTRODUCING ARIADNE AND ARIADNETOOL

Ariadne proposes a systematic approach to produce hypermedia applications. Compared to other hypermedia design methods such as HDM, OOHDM or RMM, Ariadne shares a number of similarities concerning the specification of the logical structure, navigation and interface layouts but it also improves or introduces mechanisms to deal in an integrated way with the six complementary views which have to be properly addressed by a development method [6], including navigation, presentation, control, security, processes and data. Several hypermedia methods and theirs CASE tools have been proposed including Autoweb [9], WebML [3] and OO-H [11]. However, these methods have the following weak points:

- Validation and integrity rules to test the correctness, completeness and integrity of the design.
- Contents modelling to organise and harmonise multimedia contents both in their temporal and spatial dimension.
- User modelling to model different types of application users and to apply personalisation as well as security constraints.
- Security modelling to model which contents should be delivered to which users, who can modify or personalise items and which constraints have to be applied.

- Evaluation stage to collect information about the potential usability of a system to improve features and functionality of application interface.

AriadneTool supports the Ariadne development method addressing these features as it is shown in the following sections. In particular, the main contributions of Ariadne are: the introduction of a specific mechanism to establish space and time-based relationships among contents, called alignments and synchronisations respectively; the inclusion of elements to define a users structure that can be used not only for security purposes (e.g., to define adaptive accesses); and, finally, the inclusion of a high-level security model which makes possible to specify a role-based security policy, simpler and easier to maintain than group-based policies [8], using the same design entities than those used to specify other hypermedia features such as the hypertext structure.

This method proposes a development process consisting of three phases: Conceptual Design, Detailed Design and Evaluation. Each of them generates a number of products covering the six views aforementioned Ariadne method is graphically described in Fig. 1. Arrows represent a sequence which is not unique but has been shown very helpful in different developments. Ariadne assumes an iterative process where the evaluation of prototypes is used to gather information to improve the design, whether conceptual or detailed. A detailed explanation of the method can be found in [4] and [6].

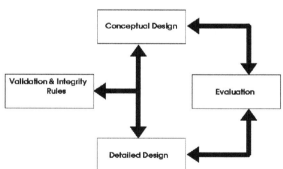

Figure 1. The Ariadne method.

AriadneTool is an environment devoted to the development of hypermedia applications based upon the above design process. The main components to support such mechanisms are (Fig. 2): (1) the `Front-End` that provides a perfect environment for elaborating the Ariadne Method products; (2) the `Validation and Verification Module` that holds the rules to validate and verify the completeness and correctness of the design, notifying any mistake or warning to the designer; (3) the `Dynamic Repository` that holds the components of the front-end in dynamic memory, so that access is faster; and (4) the `Central Repository` that holds the components in a persistent way. The development environment is implemented using SDK1.4, allowing us to obtain an independent operation platform. The Validation and Verification Module is represented by DTD documents in which the rules defining well-formed design products are specified. Elements designed in the different products of the method are stored in the Central Repository by JAXB1.1 which allows an automatic two-way mapping between Java objects stored in the Dynamic Repository and final XML documents. A module to translate synchronisation operations to SMIL specifications has also been included.

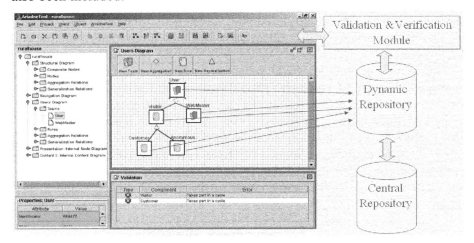

Figure 2. The Ariadne architecture.

3.   ARIADNE AND ARIADNETOOL WORKING TO-GETHER

In this section, a practical example is used to guide the application of the method with the use of the toolkit. The Ariadne Development Method establishes a systematic process composed by three phases: conceptual design, detailed design and evaluation. Each of these phases proposes a number of design products to specify and produce hypermedia and web applications. The conceptual design is focused on identifying abstract types of components, relationships and functions. The detailed design is concerned with specifying in a detailed way the system features, processes and behaviours the application should be generated with. Finally, the evaluation is concerned with using prototypes and specifications to assess the system usability. The method also provides a number of validation and integrity rules, both in the intra and inter phase level to check completeness, consistency and integrity among the various design products. These methodological foundations are the basis for AriadneTool. At this moment, the tool supports the design products of the conceptual design phase and the validation and integrity rules.

Figure 3. Example: Rural houses website.

The example shown in Fig. 3 illustrates a website about rural houses oriented towards providing information about houses, their equipments, booking and prices as well as places to visit or activities offered. The site will be accessed by different users that can be identified as, for instance, visitors who are anonymous users that browse the web-site, customers who are users that have booked some time a house so they can check their reservations and will be also notified of special offers, and the web-master who is the person in charge of administrating the site. Navigation tools should be offered to access all this information to all these users.

Taking this example site as an starting point, we will get through the phases of Ariadne method showing how to generate the products proposed by the method in the conceptual design phase: the structural diagram, the navigation diagram, the attributes and events catalogue, the internal diagram – including the spatial diagram and the timeline –, the users diagram, the categorisation catalogue and the validation and verification, which are the products included in AriadneTool.

3.1   Structural Diagram

In this diagram, the structural relationships that appear in the application domain are defined by means of composite nodes which are connected to their components (simple or composite) by means of two abstraction mechanisms: aggregation, that refer to a set of nodes as a whole, and generalisation, that represents an inclusion relation involving inheritance mechanisms. The structure of our example (Fig. 4) is defined as an aggregation of a *presentation* node, which is the entry point to the website (Fig. 3), and *main* composite which aggregates the *index* and the *information* nodes. The aim of this structure is to represent the fact that the website is made up of two frames. One frame holds the index node and the other one holds the information node. This last node generalises different kinds of information about what the website offers to visitors, such as how to get there or the features of the houses.

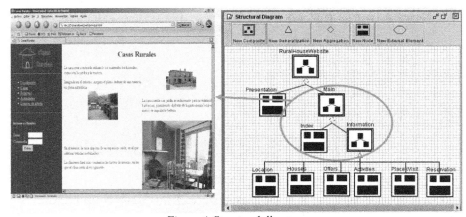

Figure 4. Structural diagram.

3.2   Navigation Diagram

The navigation diagram is where the navigation paths and tools the website offers to the users are specified. Navigation paths are settled among nodes using tagged links which can be uni- or bi-directional and n-ary [5]. For example in Fig. 5, from *presentation* node we browse both *index* and *houses* node. Since *information* is a generalisation composite, all its component (such as *houses*, *location*, and so on) will inherit the link *information* and, therefore, the *index* node has turned into a navigation tool, tagged with an NT. Moreover, we can define other navigation paths to external nodes of our application as, for instance, the payment link, used when paying our booking, to access the payment gateway, verify our visa number card and go back again to *reservation* node.

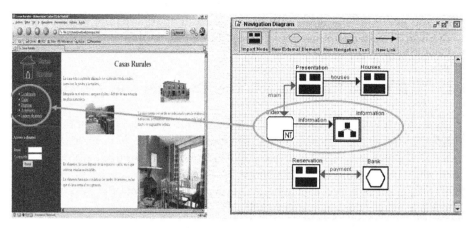

Figure 5. Navigation diagram.

3.3   Attributes and Events Catalogue

The attributes and the events catalogue are repositories where properties and behaviours are held so that they can be reused. The attributes catalogue collects properties which add semantic to modelling. For each attribute there is an entry including its name and its default value, so they can be associated to nodes, contents and links and the value can be overwritten. In the case of the events catalogue, they collect actions that take place when a condition is fulfilled. The same way, there is an entry for each event and they can be associated to nodes or contents.

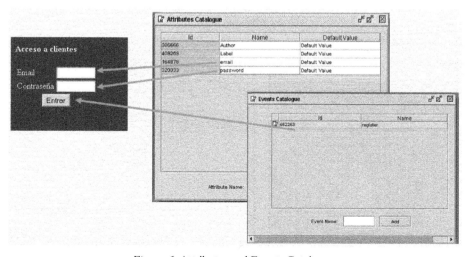

Figure 6. Attributes and Events Catalogue.

For example in Fig. 6, we could have two attributes associated to the email and password contents with the same name that holds the values typed by the user. These attributes could be used in an event that checks the values and send them to the server.

3.4   Internal Diagram - Spatial Diagram and Timeline

In order to provide more information about the nodes defined in the structural and navigation diagrams, an internal diagram is created for each node. This diagram consists of two subdiagrams; the spatial diagram and the timeline, where contents, anchors, attributes and events can be placed. The spatial diagram is a two dimensional space that represents the node visualisation area where contents are placed.

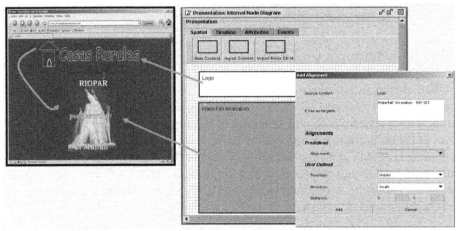

Figure 7. Spatial diagram.

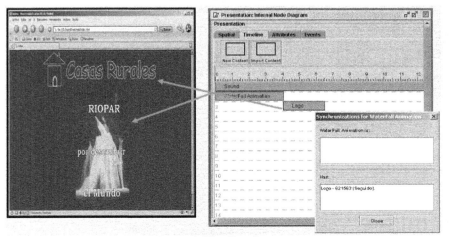

Figure 8. Timeline diagram.

In Fig. 7, our presentation node has two contents, the house logo and a waterfall animation. The waterfall animation content is coloured in blue because it acts as source anchor for information and index links. To create more harmonic presentations, space relationships can be set among contents. For example, the waterfall content will be always below the logo content. The other internal diagram is the timeline, which represents how the node evolves throughout a time interval. In Fig. 8, a sound is added which will be played during the time this node is being browsed. Moreover, to create more dynamic presentations, time relationships can be set among contents. In this case we have decided that the waterfall animation content is shown in the first place, and at the end of the animation the logo content appears.

3.5   Users Diagram

In the users diagram, the expected types of users of the application are identified inside roles and teams, with no individual users [2]. A role represents a job function or responsibility such as our visitors or the webmaster. Roles can be specified as hierarchical structures where roles are specialised into more specific roles by means of generalisation relationships. Fig. 9 shows how *visitor* role is specialised into *customers* and *anonymous* visitors. Roles can be grouped into teams that work together by means of aggregation relationships. For instance, all application users are grouped into *user* team. The users diagram makes possible to define user-dependent presentations as well as personalised hyperdocuments. For instance, only users that belong to the customer role will have access to offers node (Fig. 9).

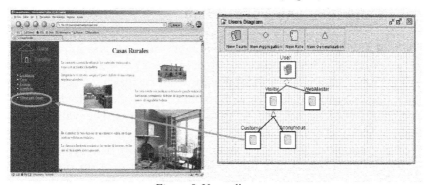

Figure 9. Users diagram.

3.6   Categorisation Catalogue and Access Table

The categorisation catalogue and the access table define who can do what in the system. The categorisation catalogue holds the security category assigned to each node or content defining the most permissive operation to be performed by a user. These categories are: browsing, personalising and editing following the security model described in [2] and [7]. In this case the category for all nodes and contents is browsing, that is all nodes can be read but not modified. The access table allows the definition of the security policies following a RBAC (Role Based Access Control) approach, assigning a manipulation category to each role for each node and content. For example (Fig. 10), the offer node can be only accessed by customers, so the rest of the users will have a no access category, except the webmaster role that needs to edit the page.

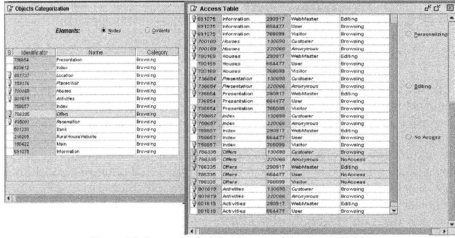

Figure 10. Categorisation Catalogue and the Access Table.

3.7   Validation and Verification

The tool also checks by means of a number of inter- and intra validation rules if each entity is fully and correctly described. For example, if visitor is specialised into a customer, at the same time that customer is specialised into a visitor, the inheritance mechanisms would always be applied. Therefore the designer would be notified of this misconception. The validation and verification module is in charge of checking the completeness and consistency of the modelling entities by means of ontologies. The elements stored in the dynamic repository are turned into an instance of an ontology that conceptualise a hypermedia application domain by means of an explicit number of elements, properties and axioms. After that, the instance is introduced into the Jess rule engine and several rules that check possible errors are run over the model and the results presented to the user. For example this rule checks that a team has to be made up of at least one role.

```
(defrule team-whithout-roles
```

```
(declare (salience -150))
(PropertyValue http://www.w3.org/1999/02/22-rdf-syntax-ns#type
  ?t http://ariadne/validator/laby#Team)
(not (PropertyValue http://ariadne/validator/laby#Valid
  ?t http://ariadne/validator/laby#Team))
=>
(assert (PropertyValue http://ariadne/validator/laby#Error
  ?t It/has/no/relation)))
```

4. CONCLUSION

AriadneTool is a design toolkit devoted to supporting the Ariadne development method. The main contributions of this method are, on the one hand, the multimedia modelling, offering mechanisms to organise and harmonise multimedia contents in different dimensions such as time and space, and, on the other hand, the user modelling that identifies the expected types of users of the application making it possible to define user-dependent presentations. Moreover, that modelling is used to define access policies in order to specify who can do what into the system.

With regard to the tool, the main contributions are, on the one hand, the validation and verification rules that help the designer to check completeness and consistency of its work, on the other hand, the automatic generation of documentation about the current design project, and, finally, since the conceptual modelling is serialised into XML format, using XML transformation language prototypes can be generated in HTML, SMIL or RDF.

AriadneTool has been evaluated by collecting feedback from the students in a course on Hypermedia Design. This feedback has been very positive, and a large majority believed that the tool supported well the method tasks and made much easier to use the Ariadne Method. The tool has also been used in a research project named ARCE, a web based system envisaged to cope with the lack of synchronism among assistance requests and responses in a multinational environment, whose main goal is to offer an efficient and reliable communication channel among the different agents involved in a disaster mitigation procedure [1].

Future work includes the support of the activities of the detailed design related to the specification of concrete elements from the abstract entities defined in the conceptual design. From this specification, prototypes will be generated in SMIL, XML and HTML. Moreover, a web design patterns repository will be integrated. Those web design patterns have already been formalised using ontologies for the designer to apply the pattern into the modelling phase using a task domain ontology. Finally, the ontology used in the validation and verification module is being used to generate semantic hypermedia applications that are made up of a domain ontology that describes the application domain in RDFS and its web resources using RDF.

ACKNOWLEDGMENTS

We'd like to thank Jose Ángel Cruz and Juan Francisco Arévalo for their cooperation in the development of AriadneTool. This toolkit is part of two projects funded by "Dirección General de Investigación del Ministerio de Ciencia y Tecnología" (TIC2000-0402) and "CAM" 07T/0024/2003.

REFERENCES

[1] Aedo, I., Díaz, P., Fernández, C., and Castro, J., *Supporting Efficient Multinational Disaster Response through a Web-Based System*, in K. Lenk, R. Traunmüller (eds.), Proc. of the 1st Int. Conf. on Electronic Government EGOV'2002 (Aix-en-Provence, 2-5 September 2002), LNCS, Vol. 2456, Springer-Verlag, Berlin, 2002, pp. 215-222.

[2] Aedo, I., Díaz, P., and Montero, S., *A Methodological Approach for Hypermedia Security Modelling*, Information and Software Tech., Vol. 45, No. 5, 2003, pp. 229-239.

[3] Ceri, S., Fraternali, P., and Bongio, A., *Web Modeling Language (WebML): a Modeling Language for Designing Web Sites*, in Proceedings of 9th International World Wide Web Conference WWW9 (Amsterdam, 15-19 May 2000), Computer Networks, Vol. 33, No. 1-6, 2000, pp. 137-157, accessible at http://www9.org/w9cdrom/177/177.html

[4] Díaz, P., Aedo, I., and Montero, S., Ariadne, A Development Method for Hypermedia, in H.C. Mayr, J. Lazanský, G. Quirchmayr, P. Vogel (eds.), Proceedings of 12th International Conference on Database and Expert Systems Applications DEXA'2001 (Munich, 3-5 September 2001), LNCS, Vol. 2113, Springer-Verlag, Berlin, 2001, pp. 764-774.

[5] Díaz, P., Aedo, I., and Panetsos, F., Labyrinth, *An Abstract Model for Hypermedia Applications. Description of its Static Components*, Information Systems, Vol. 22, No. 8, 1997, pp. 447-464.

[6] Díaz, P., Aedo, I., and Panetsos, F., *A Methodological Framework for the Conceptual Design of Hypermedia Systems*, in Proc. of the 5th Conf. on "Hypertexts and Hypermedia: Products, Tools and Methods" H2PTM'99 (Paris, Sept. 1999), 1999, pp. 213-228.

[7] Díaz, P., Aedo, I., and Panetsos, F., *Modelling Security Policies in Hypermedia and Web-Based Applications*, in S. Murugesan, Y. Deshpande (eds.), Proceedings of Conference on Software Engineering and Web Application Development Web Engineering'2001, LNCS, Vol. 2016, Springer-Verlag, Berlin, 2001, pp. 90-104.

[8] Ferraiolo, D.F., Barkley, J.F., and Kuhn, D.R., *A Role-based Access Control Model and Reference Implementation within a Corporate Intranet*, ACM Trans. on Information and Systems Security, Vol. 2, No. 1, 1999, pp. 34-64.

[9] Fraternali, P. and Paolini, P., *Model-Driven Development of Web Applications: The AutoWeb System*, ACM Transactions on Office Information Systems, Vol. 18, No. 4, 2000, pp. 323-282.

[10] Garzotto, F., Paolini, P., and Schwabe, D., *HDM-A Model-Based Approach to Hypertext Application Design*, ACM Trans. on Office Inf. Systems, Vol. 11, No. 1, 1993, pp. 1-26.

[11] Gómez, J., Cachero, C., and Pastor, O., *Conceptual Modelling of Device Independent Web Applications*, IEEE Multimedia, Vol. 8, No. 2, 2001, pp. 26-39.

[12] Isakowitz, T., Stohr, E.A., and Balasubramanian, P., *RMM: A Methodology for Structured Hypermedia Design*, Comm. of the ACM, Vol. 38, No. 8, 1995, pp. 34-44.

[13] Lowe, D. and Hall, W., *Hypermedia and the Web: An Engineering Approach*, John Wiley & Sons, New York, 1999.

[14] Schwabe, D. and Rossi, G., *Developing Hypermedia Applications Using OOHDM*, in Proc. of the Workshop on Hypermedia Development Processes, Methods and Models during the 9th ACM Conf. Hypertext'98 (Pittsburgh, 20-24 June 1998).

Chapter 5

SWCEDITOR: A MODEL-BASED TOOL FOR INTERACTIVE MODELLING OF WEB NAVIGATION

Marco Winckler, Eric Barboni, Christelle Farenc, and Philippe Palanque
Université Paul Sabatier, LIIHS -IRIT (Institut de Recherche en Informatique de Toulouse)
118, route de Narbonne – F-31062 Toulouse Cedex (France)
E-mail: {winckler, barboni, farenc, palanque}@irit.fr
URL: http://liihs.irit.fr/
Tel.: +33 (0)561 55 69 65 - Fax: +33 (0)561 55 62 58

Abstract   In spite of the apparent facility of building Web pages using current visual environments, the development on the Web application remains a complex task. As for other complex software one possible and promising way of dealing with this complexity is model-based approach. In this paper we present SWCEditor, a model-based tool (exploiting the StateWebCharts notation) aiming at supporting designers to build navigation models of Web applications. The State-WebCharts (SWC) notation is a formalism that provides abstract mechanisms to build navigation models of Web applications. This paper presents the SWCEditor, a tool supporting the creation, edition, visualisation and simulation of SWC models.

Keywords: Diagrammatic tools, Formal methods, Model-based approaches for the Web, Navigation modelling, Web application design.

1.   INTRODUCTION

Despite the apparent facility of building Web pages promoted by current visual environments, the development on the Web application remains complex and requires appropriate methods and tools. This inherent complexity is not only due to the huge number of pages that must be managed or the diversity of technologies employed (JavaScript, Java, Active-X, etc) but also to dynamic aspects such as on-the-fly page generation. In addition, Web applications require regular maintenance in order to update page content, to follow a particular business workflow, to include new features for supporting

R. Jacob et al. (eds.), Computer-Aided Design of User Interfaces IV, 55–66.
© 2005 *Kluwer Academic Publishers. Printed in the Netherlands.*

new task and/or users, and so on. Besides, Web development is often performed by several people (from different backgrounds) at a time and thus in a parallel manner. Another important feature of a Web project is the time to delivery or to update that can be as short as few hours. Designers can change almost immediately their design, so this makes Web development projects highly evolutionary in nature [12,14].

To deal with the complexity of Web development, modelling support is essential as it provides an abstract view of the application thus leaving details to later phases in the development process. By means of a formal description technique, models can help designers by decomposing complex applications in smaller and manageable parts, increasing communication into development team, reducing ambiguity, and providing support for verification prior to implementation.

Traditional methods and models successfully employed for the development of hypertext systems and traditional software have demonstrated that they are insufficient to deal with Web design due the intrinsic specificities of these systems [2,12]. Recently, some models have been proposed for supporting Web development such as WebML [1], OOHDM [15,16], and UML stereotypes [2]. Most of them propose solutions based on the concept of authoring-in-the-large introduced by the HDM approach [8], which means they provide abstract models describing the overall classes of information elements and navigation structures without much concern with implementation issues. An important limitation of the "authoring in-the-large" approach lies in the fact that it does not represent formally how users can interact with the Web application. Such representation is essential when it comes to the usability evaluation of these systems.

In [21], we have proposed a notation called StateWebCharts (SWC) to help Web designers to formally describe navigation of Web application. SWC is a notation extending StateCharts [7,9] which aims at providing dedicated constructs for modelling specific aspects of Web applications. It provides a visual notation easy-to-apply for Web designers and formal enough to allow automatic verification of the models, thus supporting the designer's activity throughout the design process. In this paper we present a tool, called SWCEditor that supports the edition, visualisation and simulation of SWC models. We describe hereafter how such a tool can support the design and the evaluation of the navigation of Web applications modelled using SWC notation. This paper is organised as follows: Section 2 discusses the role of models for describing navigation of Web applications. Section 3 presents briefly the StateWebCharts formalism. Section 4 presents the SWCEditor and a case study that highlights its functionalities and use. We then discuss the role of model-based approaches for Web navigation as well as future work in this field.

2.   MODELS FOR DESCRIBING NAVIGATION OF WEB APPLICATIONS

Research on navigation modelling has a long history in hypertext and hypermedia domain [6,20,23], which have strongly influenced the technology for the Web. State-based notations such as Petri nets [18] and StateCharts [3,11,13, 23] have been explored to model navigation for hypertext systems. However, such proposals are not able to represent some aspects of Web applications such as dynamic content generation, support to link-types (toward external states, for instance), client and server-side execution. However, some of them [3,18,23] do not make explicit the separation between interaction and navigation aspects in the models while this is a critical aspect for the usability of Web application.

More recent work devoted to Web applications, propose efficient solutions to describe navigation and architecture in a single representation, as it has been done by Connallen [2] using UML stereotypes, Fraternalli using WebML [1] and Schwabe using OOHDM [15]. These approaches mainly target data-intensive applications and even propose prototyping environments to increase productivity. The main inconvenience is that navigation is described at a very coarse grain (for instance navigation between classes of documents) and it is almost impossible to represent detailed navigation on instances of these classes or documents. The same problem appears in Kock [10]. Approaches such as Web UML stereotypes as in [2] and WebML [1] may reduce creativity at design time as they impose the underlying technology and as they do not provide efficient abstraction views of the application.

Many of these notations do not have appropriate tool support. Fraternali presents in [4] a survey of available tools and approaches to deal with the development of Web applications. Most of the tools presented in this survey are visual editors and environment for programming; that do not follow a model-based approach. Only a few, such as WebML and Web UML stereotypes feature tools supporting abstract modelling and partial code generation from models. However, as mentioned before, these two approaches present some limitations with respect to the representation of user interaction, which is essential in order to predict usability for instance. In addition, tools such as WebRatio and Rational Rose that support respectively WebML and UML Web Stereotypes do not provide tools for simulation and model analysis.

3.   THE STATEWEBCHART NOTATION (SWC)

StateWebCharts is a formalism based on StateCharts [7,10], which has been extensively used to model complex/reactive systems. StateCharts can be defined as a set of the states, transitions, events, conditions and variables and their inter-relations. There are numerous extensions to StateCharts to support different modelling needs and with different semantic. Hereafter we introduce the basics of SWC with respect to the extensions made over State-Charts, which give a view at glance of the domain addressed by SWC. More details about StateCharts and SWC can be found in [7,21], respectively.

In SWC, states are abstractions of containers for objects (graphic or executable objects). For Web applications such containers are usually (but not only) HTML pages. States in SWC are represented according to their function in the modelling. In a similar way, a SWC transition explicitly represents the agent activating it. Each individual Web page is considered a container for objects and each container is associated to a state. Links and interactive objects causing transition are represented by events. The semantic for a SWC state is: current states and their containers are visible for users while non-current are hidden. Fig. 1 presents all elements of the SWC notation.

Static states (Fig. 1a) are the most basic structures to represent information in SWC. A static state refers to a container with a static set of objects; once in a static state the same set of objects is always presented. However, the objects it contains are not necessarily static by themselves; they could have dynamic behaviour as we usually find, for example, in applets, JavaScript or animated images. Static is the default type.

Transient states (Fig. 1b) describe a non-deterministic behaviour in the state machine. Transient states are needed when a single transition cannot determine the next state for the state machine. Only completion or system events are accepted as outgoing transitions of transient states. Transient states only process instructions and they do not have a visual representation towards users. Frequently, they refer to server-side parts of Web applications, such as CGI or Java Servlets programs.

Dynamic states (Fig. 1c) represent content generated dynamically at runtime. They are usually the result of a transient state processing. The associated container of a dynamic state is empty. The semantics for this state is that in the modelling phase designers are not able to determine which content (transitions and objects) will be made available at run time. Designers can include static objects and transitions inside dynamic states; in such case transitions are represented, but the designer must keep in mind that missing transitions might appear at run time and change the navigation behaviour.

External states (Fig. 1d) represent information that is accessible through transitions but are not part of the current design. For example, consider two states A and B. While creating a transition from A to B, the content of B is not accessible and cannot be modified. Thus, B is considered external to the current design. Usually they represent connections to external sites. External states avoid representing transitions without a target state, however all activities (whatever it is entry, do, exit) in external states are null.

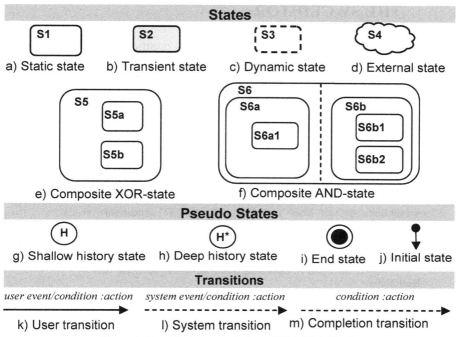

Figure 1. Graphical representation of StateWebCharts.

Events are classified in SWC notation according to the agent triggering them: user (e.g., a mouse click), system (e.g., a method invocation that affects the activity in a state) or completion (e.g., execution of the next activity in a row). A completion event is a fictional event that is associated to transitions without triggers, e.g. change the system state after a timestamp. Fictional completion events allow us to give the same representation for all transitions in SWC machines. This classification of event sources is propagated to the representation of transitions. Transitions whose event is triggered by a user are graphically drawn as continuous arrows (Fig. 1k) while transitions triggered by system or completion events are drawn as dashed arrows (Fig. 1l and 1m, respectively).

In order to represent behaviour such as those found in StateCharts, SWC provides the following pseudo-states (g) shallow history, (h) deep history, (i) end state and (j) initial state. These pseudo-states do not have any container associated to them. Pseudo-states and composite state in SWC are very close of the definition given by StateCharts (see [21] for details). Both states and transitions can have associated actions. When associated to transitions, actions represent what is executed by the system while traversing a transition. When associated to state, actions represent the activity performed by the state.

4.   THE SWCEDITOR

The SWCEditor is a prototype that supports creation, edition, visualisation, simulation and analysis of SWC models. It was built using Java and models are stored in a XML format. In the XML DTD, SWC elements are grouped in two main sections: a) state section, which contains the hierarchy of state and pseudo-states elements; and b) the transition section, which presents the list of all transitions in a model. Fig. 2 presents an extract of a SWC XML file.

```
<?xml version="1.0" encoding="UTF-8"?>
<!-- edited with SWCEditor -->
<swc>
    <CompositeState  id="root" label="root" file="null" initial="S1" concurrent="false">
        <BasicState  id="S1" label="main intro" type="BasicState" file="
                C:\swceditor\swceditor\demo\spider\spider_intro.html" >
        </BasicState>
        <BasicState  id="S2" label="schedule" type="BasicState"
                file="C:\swceditor\swceditor\demo\spider\spider_schedule.html">
        </BasicState>
        ...
    </CompositeState>
    <Transition id="t1" type="user" label="" source="S1" target="S2" trigger="mouseClick"
                guard="true" action="">
    </Transition>
    <Transition id="t2" type="user" label="" source="S1" target="S3" trigger="mouseClick"
                guard="true" action="">
    </Transition>
    ...
</swc>
```

Figure 2. XML file describing a SWC model.

4.1   Support for Creation, Edition and Visualization

One of the most basic requirements for model-based tools is to support the creation of new models and the updating of existing ones. Fig. 3 presents the edition of a basic state in a model. All attributes of a state are shown in a fill-in form; including actions and URL address for a container of objects. The URL field (see dialog "Edit Basic State" in Fig. 3) links an abstract representation of a state to a concrete Web page (a container of objects HTML, CSS, JavaScript, etc). As SWCEditor does not support code generation of Web pages, designers can use their preferred editor to implement the application. Once Web pages have been created, it is possible to associate each state to a corresponding Web page. This matching of states and Web pages is required for simulating the application in advanced phases of development. Even though the SWCEditor provides many facilities for creating new SWC models, it is also possible to imagine SWCEditor being used to visualize SWC specifications resulting from reengineering process of existing Web sites.

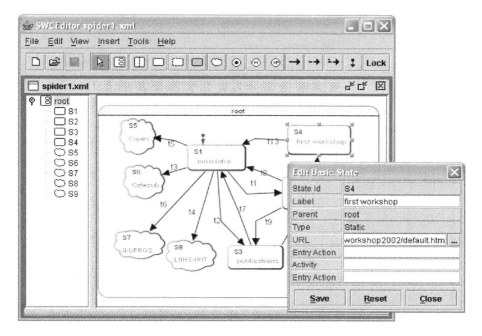

Figure 3. Editing function with SWCEditor.

4.2 Supporting for Simulation

During early evaluation phases of development designers have to check if abstract modelling will behave as expected. Simulations of models can be useful for that purpose. Fig. 4 presents how SWCEditor allows simulation of SWC models. First of all, let us to focus on the left part of the figure 4. There are two windows: the simulator window (at top-left) and the visualisation window (at bottom-left). The window simulator is composed of two panels showing: the set of active state (grey panel at left) and the set of enabled transitions at a time (white panel at right). The visualisation window is the main graphic editor of SWC models (the SWCEditor module).

In the current implementation, all interactions concerning simulation are performed over the simulator window. When an enabled transition is selected (by double-clicking) the system fires it immediately causing the changing of the system, which displays the next stable configuration. The interpretation of changes in the system is eased by an animation thus reducing the user's activity of comparing the current state with the previous one. The new active states become red in the visualization window, and the set of current active states and the set of current enabled transition are updated in the simulator window.

Simulator　　　　　　　　　　　　　　　　Browser

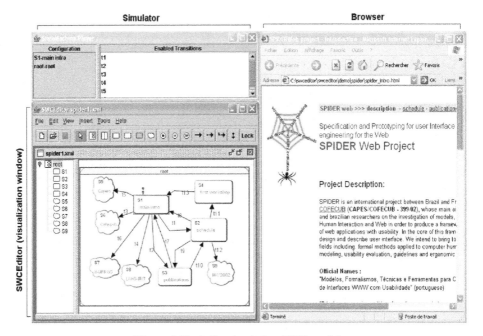

Figure 4. Tools for simulating SWC models.

If a container is associated to a state, it is possible to concurrently display the corresponding container (typically a Web page) in a browser during the simulation. The concurrent simulation of model and implementation is suitable during the prototyping activity. Thus, designers can follow the changes in the abstract specification at the SWCEditor as well as its concrete implementation at the Web browser. Fig. 4 shows in a browser window (at right part) the corresponding Web page for the current state in that simulation. The simulation can be used as a kind of automated walkthrough method for inspecting both navigation specifications and their corresponding Web applications. The task of testing the application for different displays is eased by repeating a simulation with different browsers.

Automated walkthrough is not the unique way for simulating models. In [22] it is described how navigation and task modelling could be synergistically exploited to improve the development process of Web applications as a means to evaluate Web applications at different phases of an iterative development process. That assessment technique consists in play scenarios over a model. By automatically simulating scenarios over navigation modelling it is possible to verify the system's conformance with the user requirements specified through task models.

4.3   Analysis of SWC Models

The main role of task analysis is to check if some properties hold on a model/application. As mentioned in Section 3, SWC is a formal notation which allows the description of low level interaction concerning navigation. Thus, SWC models provide information that can be employed by model checker tools to analyse some system properties concerning the usability. When employed in early phases of development, model checkers help to prevent usability problems in the implementation. We have identified 5 categories of analysis techniques suitable to be automated by model checkers and employed to analyse navigation models:

- *Static analysis:* checks directly a model without having to provide any additional information. For example: check if all states are accessible; if there is no duplicated states or links; if all transitions have a valid target, and so on.
- *Navigation path analysis:* given a start point and a destination for a navigation path it is possible to check: the availability of a path to the destination; the shortest path to destination; the occurrence of path constraints (for example, to get destination ones have to visit some arbitrary states first).
- *System properties analysis:* one can choose to check if the systems obey predefined rules such as if all states are accessible with a given number of links (more or less 5, for instance). Most of properties we are interested in to analyse concern the usability of the application. However, many others properties can be checked. Dhyani, Ng, and Bhowmick [19] have collected an impressive number of metrics that can be analysed over Web applications. They have classified Web metrics as: graph metrics, significance, similarity, search, usage and information theoretic. Many of Web metrics require a representation of the Web in a form of a direct graph or a description of the document and their relationships. This kind of information can be easily caught from SWC models.
- *Assessment of task and navigation models:* check if scenarios obtained from task modelling can be performed over a navigation modelling. This kind of analysis requires simulation of the system. The procedure to perform this assessment is described in [22].
- *Comparing alternative models:* if there is more than one navigation model for an application, it is possible to compare whether these models provide similar or equivalent navigation paths. By comparing alternative models, one can determine in which extension they are equivalent or not and if they support the same set of tasks.

Up to now, there is no analysis tool integrated to SWCEditor but this work is in progress. At present, we have selected a set of ergonomic rules that can be checked automatically or supported by semi-automatic tools. Our aim is to transform these ergonomic rules in a formal description that can be interpreted by model checker over SWC models.

5.   DISCUSSION AND FUTURE WORK

SWC models can be used in many different ways formalizing navigation for critical parts of the application or giving an abstract notation to support prototyping phases. However, most of advantages of having formalisms like SWC can only be fully exploited if appropriate software tools exist. The advantages of tool support for interactive design have been extensively discussed in the literature; they range from facilities for editing (such as provide automatic layout to avoid crossing lines in models) until advanced model analysis (i.e., prediction of system performance or automatic detection of conflicts in the system).

In the specific case of development of Web applications, designers can get many benefits from model-based approaches. Model-based tools can give abstract views of application and guide the implementation passing the interactive phase of prototyping (what is especially useful during the development of interactive systems such as Web applications) and supporting evaluation prior to implementation. Moreover, as discussed in [22] model-based tools can help designers to evaluate applications and supporting the rational redesign of Web applications.

Surprisingly, only a few tools such as WebRatio (available at http://www. webratio.com/), OOHDM-Web [15] and AutoWeb [5] support a model-based approach for Web applications. However, these tools are not based on a formal specification of the interface and they do not provide functions for simulating user interaction over the applications. Furthermore, due the lack of information about how users may interact with the application, these tools can hardly reap the benefits of advanced analysis of system properties.

We have presented in this paper our preliminary results of a prototype to deal with the creation until the analysis of navigation of Web application. The prototype presented here is based on a formal notation, called SWC. Our aim is to get more benefits from the fact SWC is formal and non-ambiguous to go further in the near future on the analysis of system properties. Even though the current implementation does not included all tools before mentioned to analyse system properties, SWCEditor provides, at least, the core functions enabling the development of such as tools. Our ongoing work consists in to develop and to integrate such as analysis tools to our prototype. We are also working on the development of more advanced visualisation features to make easier the interaction and edition of very large models.

ACKNOWLEDGEMENTS

This work has been partially supported by CNPq (Brazilian Council for Research and Development) and Capes/Cofecub (SpiderWeb project).

REFERENCES

[1] Ceri, S., Fraternali, P., and Bongio, A., *Web Modeling Language (WebML): a Modeling Language for Designing Web Sites*, in Proceedings of 9th International World Wide Web Conference WWW9 (Amsterdam, 15-19 May 2000), Computer Networks, Vol. 33, No. 1-6, 2000, pp. 137-157, accessible at http://www9.org/w9cdrom/177/177.html

[2] Connallen, J., *Building Web Applications with UML*, Addison-Wesley, Reading, 1999.

[3] Dimuro, G.P. and Costa, A.C.R., *Towards an Automata-Based Navigation Model for the Specification of Web Sites*, in Proc. of 5th Workshop on Formal Methods WFM'2002 (Gramado, 15-16 October 2002), accessible at http://gmc.ucpel.tche.br/ensinet/artigos/Dimuro-Costa.pdf

[4] Fraternali, P., *Tools and Approaches for Developing Data-intensive Web Applications: a Survey*, ACM Computing Surveys, Vol. 31, No. 3, 1999, pp. 227-263.

[5] Fraternali, P. and Paolini, P., *Model-Driven Development of Web Applications: The AutoWeb System*, ACM Transactions on Office Information Systems, Vol. 18, No. 4, 2000, pp. 323-282.

[6] Halasz, F. and Schwartz, M., *The Dexter Hypertext Reference Model*, Communications of the ACM, Vol. 37, No. 2, 1994, pp. 30-39.

[7] Harel, D., *StateCharts: A Visual Formalism for Computer System*, Science of Computer Programming, Vol. 8, No. 3, 1987, pp. 231-271.

[8] Garzotto, F. and Paolini, P., and Schwabe, D., HDM-A Model for the Design of Hypertext Applications, in Proceedings of the 3rd Annual ACM Conference on Hypertext Hypertext'91 (San Antonio, 15-18 December 1991), ACM Press, New York, 1991, pp. 313-328.

[9] Horrocks, I., *Constructing the User Interface with Statecharts*, Addison-Wesley, Reading, 1999.

[10] Koch, N. and Kraus, A., *The Expressive Power of UML-based Web Engineering*, in D. Schwabe, O. Pastor, G. Rossi, L. Olsina (eds.), Proc. of 2nd Int. Workshop on Web-oriented Software Technology IWWOST'2002 (Malaga, 10 June 2002), accessible at http://www.dsic.upv.es/~west2001/iwwost02/papers/koch.pdf

[11] Leung, K., Hui, L., Yiu, S., and Tang, R., *Modelling Web Navigation by StateCharts*, in Proc. of 24th Int. Conf. S.A., IEEE Computer Society Press, 2000.

[12] Murugesan, S. and Deshpande, Y., *Web Engineering: Managing Diversity and Complexity of Web Applications Development*, Lecture Notes in Computer Science, Vol. 2016, Springer-Verlag, Berlin, 2001.

[13] Oliveira, M.C.F. de, Turine, M.A.S., and Masiero, P.C., *A Statechart-Based Model for Modeling Hypermedia Applications*, ACM Transactions on Office Information Systems, Vol. 19, No. 1, April 2001, pp. 28-52.

[14] Sano, D., *Designing Large-Scale Web Sites: A Visual Design Methodology*, John Wiley & Sons, New York, 1996.

[15] Schwabe, D., Pontes, R.A., and Moura, I., *OOHDM-Web: An Environment for Implementation of Hypermedia Applications in the WWW*, SigWEB Newsletter, Vol. 8, No. 2, June 1999, pp. 18-34.

[16] Schwabe, D., Rossi, G., and Barbosa, S.D.J., *Systematic Hypermedia Application Design with OOHDM*, in Proc. of the 7th ACM Conference on Hypertext Hypertext'96 (Washington, 16-20 March 1996), ACM Press, New York, 1996, pp. 116-128.

[17] Silva, P. P. da, and Paton, N.W., *UMLi: The Unified Modelling Language for Interactive Applications*, in Proc. of 3rd Int. Conf. on the Unified Modeling Language UML'2000 (York, 2-6 October 2000), Lecture Notes in Computer Science, Vol. 1939, Springer-Verlag, Berlin, 2000, pp. 117-132.

[18] Stotts, P.D. and Furuta, R., *Petri-Net-Based Hypertext: Document Structure with Browsing Semantics*, ACM Trans. on Information Systems, Vol. 7, No. 1, January 1989, pp. 3-29.

[19] Dhyani, D., Ng, W.K., and Bhowmick, S.S., *A Survey of Web Metrics*, ACM Computing Surveys, Vol. 34, No. 4, 2002, pp. 469-503.

[20] Turine, M.A.S., Oliveira, M.C.F., and Masieiro, P.C., *A Navigation-Oriented Hypertext Model Based on Statecharts*, in Proceeding of 8th ACM Conf. on Hypertext Hypertext'97 (Southampton, 6-11 April 1997), ACM Press, New York, 1997, pp. 102-111.

[21] Winckler, M. and Palanque, P., *StateWebCharts: a Formal Description Technique Dedicated to Navigation Modelling of Web Applications*, in J. Jorge, N.J. Nunes, J. Falcão e Cunha (eds.), Proc. of 10th Int. Workshop on Design, Specification, and Verification of Interactive Systems DSV-IS'2003 (Funchal, June 2003), Lecture Notes in Computer Science, Vol. 2844, Springer-Verlag, Berlin, 2003, pp. ?.

[22] Winckler, M., Palanque, P., Farenc, Ch., and Pimenta, M., *Task-Based Assessment of Web Navigation Design*, in C. Pribeanu, J. Vanderdonckt (eds.), Proceedings of 1st Int. Workshop on Task models and Diagrams for User Interface Design TAMODIA'2002 (Bucharest, 18-19 July 2002), Academy of Economic Studies of Bucharest, Economic Informatics Department, INFOREC Printing House, Bucharest, 2002, pp. 161-168.

[23] Zheng, Y. and Pong, M.C., *Using Statecharts to Model Hypertext*, in Proceedings of the European Conference on Hypertext Technology (Milan, 30 November-4 December 1992), ACM Press, New York, 1992, pp. 242-250.

Chapter 6

BEHAVIOUR MODELLER
The Systematic Generation of Statechart from Functional Relations and Scenarios for Prototyping User Interfaces

Akihiko Urushihara[1], Satoshi Kanai[1], Takeshi Kishinami[1], and Toyoaki Tomura[2]

[1] *Det. of Systems & Information Engineering, Graduate School of Engg., Hokkaido University,*
nishi 8 cho-me kita 13 jyo, kita-ku, Sapporo 0608628, JAPAN
E-mail: {kanai, kishinami}@coin.eng.hokudai.ac.jp, aurushi@minf.coin.eng.hokudai.ac.jp
URL: http://minf.coin.eng.hokudai.ac.jp/
Tel.: +81 11-706-6448 – Fax: +81 11-706-6448
[2] *Asahikawa National Collage of Technology,*
6-1 2-chome 2-jyo syunkoudai Asahikawa City JAPAN
E-mail: tomura@asahikawa-nct.ac.jp
Tel.: +81 166-55-8027 – Fax: +81 166-55-8027

Abstract Designing user interface (UI) behaviour can be regarded as a mapping from product functions and a set of UI control scenarios to state-transition-based UI specification. However, in current UI prototyping tools, UI designers must directly describe the UI specification from scratch, and the specification is not explicitly related to the product functions. In this paper, we present a "Behaviour Modeller" to systematically support this mapping process. In the modeller, required functional relations of the product are modelled as a functional relation diagram (FRD), while UI control scenarios are modelled as sequence diagrams (SDs). The UI element Statechart (SC) templates are also introduced to enable efficient generation of the specification. The modeller automatically generates an SC as the complete state-transition-based UI specification from an FRD, SDs and templates. The designer can easily modify a complex SC only by inserting or removing functions in the FRD and by changing the scenario in SDs. The effectiveness of the method and tool was confirmed by application to UI design for consumer products.

Keywords: Embedded system, Prototyping, Scenario, Statechart, State vector, User interface.

R. Jacob et al. (eds.), Computer-Aided Design of User Interfaces IV, 67–80.

1.   INTRODUCTION

1.1   Background and Purpose

Rapid development of embedded systems for consumer products such as cellular phones is strongly needed in the electronic appliance manufacturers. User Interface (UI) control software accounts for a large part of recent embedded software used in these systems, and usability assessment using UI prototype in the early design stage of the UI development process becomes more important. Thus, efficiency of development of UI control software is a key to shorten the overall. However, the current bottleneck is design of the UI behaviour specifications.

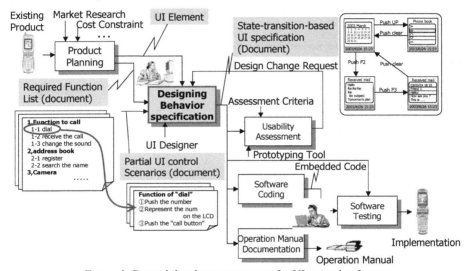

Figure 1. General development process for UI control software.

Fig. 1 shows the general development process of UI control software that has been investigated by us from several Japanese electronics manufacturers. As shown in the figure, designing the UI specification can be regarded as a mapping process from the product function list, partial UI control scenarios and UI elements to the complete state-transition-based UI specifications. The function list is an enumeration of the product functions. The UI control scenario shows how a user sequentially interacts with the UI to use a particular function, and UI elements are input and output UI objects such as buttons and display fields on the product.

However, from our investigation, the function list and the state-transition-based UI specifications are mostly expressed only as written documents, and the mapping is done manually. It is difficult to re-use specifications in subsequent processes such as usability assessment, software coding/testing, and manual documentation. Therefore, the computer-aided tool that can digitally transform the required function list into the state-transition-based UI specifications is needed. The purpose of this study was to establish a method for automatic generation of SC specifications expressing UI behaviour from a function list of the product, scenarios of each function, and UI elements of the product. The following approach was taken to reach this goal.

1. A functional relation diagram (FRD) is introduced to digitally describe the functional relations of the product, and a systematic and automatic method for generating the SC for function selection from the FRD dependent on the UI elements is proposed.
2. A method for automatically generating the SC for function execution from scenarios expressed by sequence diagrams (SDs) by evaluating the state vectors dependent on the UI elements is proposed.
3. The behaviour modeller to digitally support the methods of 1) and 2) is implemented and its effectiveness was confirmed by the results of a case study on UI design for consumer products.

Our approach is outlined in Section 2. The method for generating the SC for function selection from the FRD is described in detail in Section 3, and the method for generating the SC for function execution from scenarios for each function is described in detail in Section 4. Implementation of the tool and results of a case study are described in Section 5.

1.2   Related Work

Several methods for representing UI behaviour by state-transition-based specifications have been proposed. An Interactive Object Graph (IOG) [2] is an extended Statechart to which the data objects and data flows between states and data objects are attached. The IOG is effective in describing interaction objects in the UI. Jacob *et al.* [7] proposed a UI specification where event-based discrete interactions and continuous interactions such as data flow or constraint-like components are combined for Non-WIMP UI specification. However, the above two methods did not sufficiently address how to describe the functional specification and the process from the functions to a behavior specification. Therefore, it is difficult for the UI designer to modify behavior specifications corresponding to changes of the functions. Of course, these methods could extend the functionality of the SC, and can be considered as complements to our SC-based approach.

On the other hand, XIML [11] was proposed as an XML-based common representation for interaction data. It is readable to both humans and computers, and is consistently reusable from design to evaluation of the UI. But it does not have a graphical representation, and capturing the UI behaviour intuitively by designers is hard.

Based on these considerations, we use the SC for the UI specifications.

The reasons are that 1) the concept and notation of the SC are standardized by the UML and are widely accepted, 2) the SC has not only a graphical representation, but also a standard XML document format (XMI), and 3) it enables top-down step-by-step definition using state hierarchy by designers.

Several commercial CASE tools have become available recently. CASE tools based on UML [13,14] can be used to help UI designers to schematically specify the behaviour of the UI control software using sequence diagrams, collaboration diagrams, and Statecharts (SCs). Moreover, UI prototyping tools [9,12] can also be used to model state-transition-based UI specifications using a "mode tree" or a set of finite state machines.

These tools can store UI specifications in digital form, but they still have the following problems. Firstly, UI designers must directly generate complex state-transition-based UI specifications from scratch, and they cannot handle the specifications in relation to product functions. This is not good for the process of designing UIs for consumer products, in which required functions often change even during the design process. Secondly, scenarios are widely used by UI designers as a specification method since they are easier for designers to use than state-transition-based specifications. However, these tools do not have functions to model the scenarios and convert them to state-transition-based UI specifications. Thirdly, the format of state-transition-based UI specifications is not open and their re-use is limited.

Recently, a methodology for developing UI specifications has also been proposed. Horrocks [5] proposed a general guideline for constructing UI specifications with SC using practical examples. But the supporting tools for it were not discussed. Puerta [10] proposed sophisticated model-based UI development methodology and tools. In his approach, the models of user-task, dialog, and presentation are interrelated to provide a formal UI specification. But they did not discuss the model of product functions and of state-transition-based UI behaviour specification.

On the other hand, there have been a number of studies on the generation of UI specifications from scenarios. Whittle *et al.* [17] reported a method for generating an SC from multiple scenarios expressed by sequence diagrams. In their method, however, the functions of the product are not explicitly modelled, and the SC-based UI specification cannot be managed in relation to product functions. Elkoutbi *et al.* [3] also proposed a method similar to that of Whittle et al. for generating a UI specification from scenarios. They also proposed another method [4] for generating a Petri-Nets-based UI specification from sequence diagrams and Use Case diagrams. In both approaches, the generation of an SC-based UI specification from scenarios could be automated. However, in both methods, the relation of product functions were not captured and modelled, and the modification of the SC-based UI specification could not be done efficiently.

2. FUNCTIONAL OUTLINE OF THE BEHAVIOUR MODELLER

Fig. 2 shows an outline of our behaviour modeller. The basic concepts of modelling UI behaviour in the modeller are based on the following assumptions:

1. The behaviour consists both of the behaviours of the input and output UI elements themselves and the behaviour of the UI controller.
2. Each behaviour can be specified by the SC.
3. The SC structure for the UI controller mainly consists of the SC for controlling function selection (ex. "Mode Selection") and the SC for performing the function according to the scenario in the selected function
4. The behaviours of three kinds of SC for input/output UI elements and UI controller are logically interconnected by action-event chains. The user sends an event to and receives actions from the UI controller via the SCs of input/output UI elements.

Based on these concepts, the modelling process in the behaviour modeller consists of three sub-processes:

1) Generation of the SC for function selection from the FRD corresponding to the function list and from the UI element SC template.
2) Generation of the SC for function execution from the SDs expressing the scenarios for each function and from the UI element SC template.
3) Completion of the SC for the UI controller by integration of the SC for function selection with the SCs for function execution.

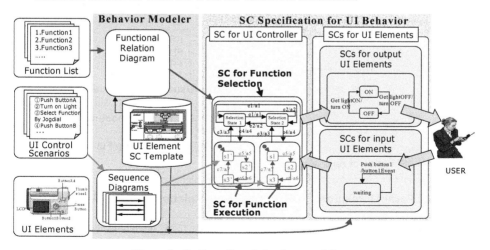

Figure 2. Outline of our behaviour modeller.

3.   GENERATION OF THE STATECHART FOR FUNCTION SELECTION FROM A FUNCTIONAL RELATION DIAGRAM

The process for generation of the SC for function selection involves two steps: 1) combination of the product function list and UI elements using an FRD, and 2) automatic generation of the SC for function selection from the FRD using UI element SC templates. The details of these steps are described in the following sections (3.1-3.3).

3.1   Functional Relation Diagram (FRD)

A functional relation diagram (FRD) is a tree expressing relations and hierarchy among product functions. Fig. 3 shows an example of an FRD. Among the nodes at different levels of the tree, the *hierarchical relation* between a function and its sub-functions is defined. Among the nodes at the same level of the tree, either an *exclusive relation* or *parallel relation* is defined. An *exclusive relation* means that one function is selected from the functions at that level and executed, while a *parallel relation* means that all of the functions at that level are executed concurrently.

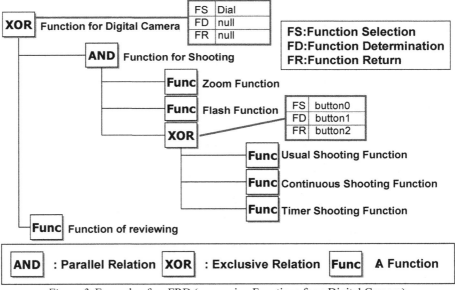

Figure 3. Example of an FRD (expressing Functions for a Digital Camera).

Moreover, as shown in the Fig. 3, at the branch of the exclusive relation, "function control attributes" are attached to the FRD. The attributes, which show the logical relation between UI elements and function control, include the attributes of 1) *Function Selection* (the UI elements that are used to se-lect one function from a set of sub-functions in the function selection mode), 2) *Function Determination* (the UI elements that are used to enter the se-lected function from the function selection mode), and 3) *Function Return* (the UI elements that are used to escape from the selected function to the function selection mode). These function control attributes enable generation of the SC for function selection from an FRD.

Function Chaining Graph [16] and Activity Chaining Diagram [1] whose notations were similar to our FRD have been already proposed for task mod-elling. However, these diagrams aimed to describe and/or relations among input/output information processed by a certain UI function, not to describe and/or relations among product functions. IDEF-3 [6] also has extended no-tation similar to above diagrams.

3.2   Statechart Templates for UI Elements

The *SC template* for a UI element consists of two pre-defined SC struc-tures: one for a particular type of input UI element and one for the function selection behaviour in the UI controller corresponding to that element type. A typical template includes a simple push button, slide switch, cross key, thumb wheel and Jog-dial. An example of an SC template for Dial is shown in Fig. 4.

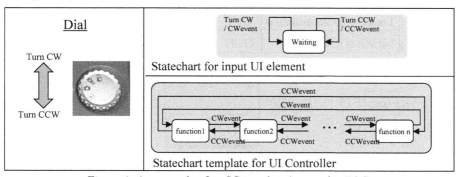

Figure 4. An example of an SC template (expressing Dial).

Only by specifying a particular type of UI element in the function control attributes of the FRD can an SC of the input UI element and its function se-lection part in the SC of the UI controller be generated automatically. Even if it is necessary to change the design of an input UI element, the GUI de-signer only has to change the attribute to the new type of UI element, and new structures of the SCs automatically replace the old one based on the templates. The concept of this SC template eliminates the necessity of de-scribing and re-building the complex structure of the SC behaviour for the UI specification from scratch.

3.3   Automatic Generation of the SC for function selection

By using the FRD and SC templates for UI elements described in sections 3.1 and 3.2, it is possible to automatically and systematically generate the SC for function selection for function control. The generation process consists of the following three steps, and is as shown in Fig. 5.

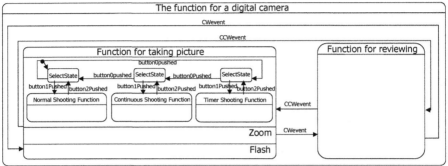

Figure 5. Generation of the SC for function selection for UI controller.

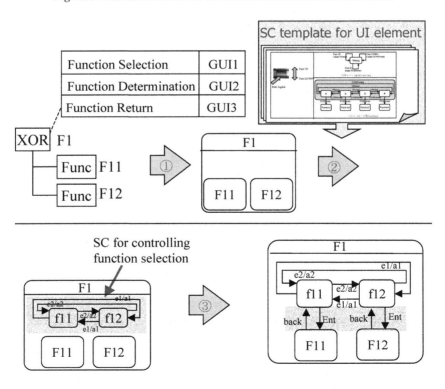

Figure 6.   The SC for function selection for a digital camera.

1) A set of states is generated on the basis of function relations described in the FRD. The functions in exclusive relations (e.g., F11 and F22) are mapped to sequential sub-states in the parent state of SC, and their parent function (e.g., F1) is mapped to the parent state. On the other hand, the functions in a parallel relation are mapped to concurrent sub-states in the parent state.

2) The state transitions for function selection in the case where one of the sub-states is selected are inserted inside their parent state. The structure of the state transition (e.g., f11, f12) is determined on the basis of the UI element specified in the *Function Selection* attribute and is generated from the SC templates for the UI element.

3) The states of the function selection part (f11, f12) are respectively connected to the sub-states (F11, F12) by two bi-directional transitions. The transition outgoing to the sub-state is labelled with the event name that the UI element specified in the *Function Determination* attribute has. The transition incoming from the sub-state is also labelled with the event name that UI element specified in the *Function Return* attribute has.

As an example of this process, Fig. 6 shows the SC for function selection generated from the FRD shown in Fig. 3.

4. GENERATION OF THE STATECHART FOR FUNCTION EXECUTION FROM THE UI CONTROL SCENARIOS

To complete the SC of UI behaviour for the UI controller, we have to model the SC for function execution for each function and insert it into the SC for function selection. Modelling the SC for function execution is based on combining UI control scenarios and consists of four steps as shown in Fig. 7: 1) modelling Sequence Diagrams (SDs) for UI control scenarios, 2) identifying unique states from an SD by evaluating the state vector, 3) identifying the transitions between states by classifying messages and tracing a lifeline of the UI controller in an SD, and 4) combining SCs for function execution of different scenarios to form one SC.

4.1 Sequence Diagram (SD)

In this paper, a UI control scenario is described as a Sequence Diagram (SD). An SD is defined in UML [15] as a method for describing standard behavioural specification for object-oriented software. Examples of an SD are shown in Figure 8. The SD specifies object interactions arranged in time sequence. It shows the sequence of messages exchanged among objects. In this paper, three objects are defined in the SD: "User", "UI Elements", and "UI controller". A vertical thin line in the SD represents the *lifeline* of the object and represents the life of the object during the interaction, a horizontal arrow represents a *message* between two objects, a tall thin rectangle shows an *activation* that represents the duration of the object's action in time.

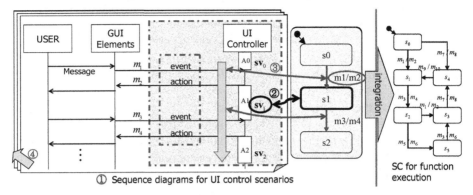

Figure 7. The outline of generating the SC for function execution.

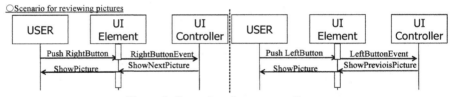

Figure 8. Examples of a sequence diagram.

In our study, multiple UI control scenarios were assumed to exist in one function. Thus, multiple SDs may be defined for a function, and the SC for function execution for a function must be generated from combining these SDs. The method to combine the SDs to form one SC is explained in the following sections.

4.2　State Identification from a Scenario using the State Vector

It is difficult for a UI designer to manually identify the same states in many SDs. We therefore use state vectors (STVs) of the UI controller for this purpose. A STV is a vector of values of the state variables [14]. The domain of a state variable is a set of states in the SC of one output UI element. The UI controller has a unique state if it shares an identical STV. Here, the different SVs are defined as $sv_1, sv_2, ..., sv_m, ..., sv_M$, and a set of these STVs is defined as $SV = \{sv_1, sv_2, ..., sv_m, ..., sv_M\}$, where M is the number of states of the UI controller, and a STV is defined as $\mathbf{sv}_m = \left(v_{m1}, v_{m2}, ..., v_{mp}, ..., v_{mP} \right)$, where v_{mp} indicates a p-th state variable value and is one of the states in the SC of the p-th output UI element, and P is the number of output UI elements. Change in this STV is triggered by an incoming event to the UI controller from an input UI element. In response to this event, the controller generates an outgoing action to an output UI element, resulting in a change in the states of some output UI elements. Therefore, one activation on the UI controller object corresponds to a STV, namely, a state of the UI controller. We can therefore define the one-to-one relation between a STV and a state of the UI controller. As a result of this operation, all of the unique states of the UI controller in one SD can be identified.

4.3 Transition Identification and Integration of the Statechart

For the set of states described in Section 4.2, transitions can be identified from the SD to form a part of the SC. The SC for function execution is generated by combining the SDs. The method is similar to that of Whittle [14] and involves following steps as shown in Fig. 7.

1. Do 1.1 to 1.3 from the top of the lifeline of the UI controller object in an SD.
    1.1. Select a pair of an incoming event to the UI controller (m_1) and an outgoing action from it (m_2) if the pair exists in the same gap between two successive activations (A_0 and A_1) on the UI controller lifeline.
    1.2. Using the state vector, identify the states $s_{CURRENT}$ and s_{NEXT} for these two activations (A0, A1).
    1.3. Connect the transition from the current state $s_{CURRENT}$ to the next one s_{NEXT} and attach the event/action pair (m_1/m_2) on this transition.
2. Take forward the current state to the next one and repeat the step 1 until the next state (activation) disappears.
3. Set the current SD to the next one, and repeat 2 until the next SD disappears.

As a result, combining all of the SDs expressing UI control scenarios for one function generates an SC specification for function execution in the UI controller. Then, by embedding these SCs for function execution inside the state for that function already defined in the SC for function selection, final UI specification expressed by the complex SC of the UI controller can be completed.

5.   BEHAVIOUR MODELLER AND A CASE STUDY

5.1   Implementation of the Behaviour Modeller

The proposed methods for SC modelling in previous sections were implemented in a Java-based tool. A snapshot of the tool is shown in Fig. 9. So far, the function of generating the SC for function selection from FRD has been completed in the tool. JGo [17] was used for handling the SC schematically in our tool.

5.2   A Case Study for the UI of a Digital Camera

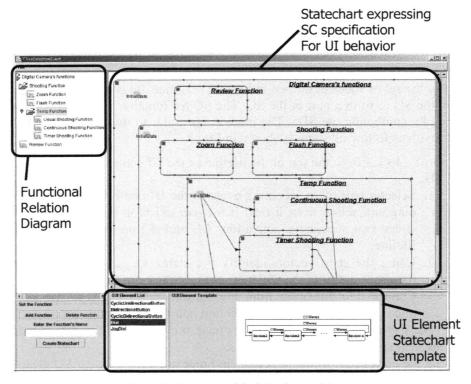

Figure 9.   Prototype of the behavior modeler.

To confirm the effectiveness of the proposed methods and the tool, we carried out a case study on modeling of the SC of the UI for a currently available digital camera (CANON Powershot A20). Fig. 3 shows the FRD for the major functions of the camera. Three buttons (flash button, zoom button and dial) on the camera were assigned to the function control attributes. Based on this FRD, the SC for function selection was automatically generated as shown in Fig. 6. Examples of SDs expressing the UI control scenarios for "Normal Shooting Function" are shown in Fig. 8, and the complete SC that contains the SC for function execution generated from these SDs is shown in Fig. 10. By manually tracing all transitions of the SC in Fig. 10, it was found that the state-transition behaviour of this SC specification matches the real behaviour of the camera.

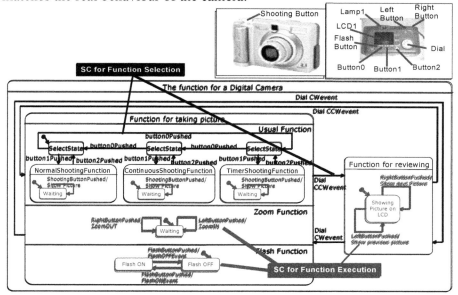

Figure 10. Complete SC for controlling the UI in a digital camera (Cannon Powershot).

6. CONCLUSION

The conclusions of this study are summarised as follows.

1. A method to automatically and systematically generate the SC for function selection of UI behaviour that contains function selection control logic from a functional relation diagram and SC templates of the input UI elements is proposed.
2. By identifying the unique states using state vectors, a method to automatically combine multiple Sequence Diagrams for UI control scenarios to form a SC for function execution is proposed.
3. A Java-based Behaviour Modeller was implemented and the effectiveness of the methods and tool was confirmed by applying them to modelling an SC of the UI for real consumer products.

The most interesting feature of our approach is the systematic and automatic generation of the SC for function selection from FRD and SC templates. The UI designer can easily change the SC only by directly inserting or removing functions at the FRD level and by replacing the input/output UI elements. As future work, we plan to move in two directions. One direction is to connect our modeller to a 3D Mechanical CAD system in order to easily evaluate the usability of a UI in a 3D virtual prototype, and the other direction is to generate a test case from the SC specification.

REFERENCES

[1] Bodart, F., Hennebert, A.-M., Leheureux, J.-M., Provot, I., Vanderdonckt, J., and Zucchinetti, G., *Key Activities for a Development Methodology of Interactive Applications*, in D. Benyon, P. Palanque (eds.), Critical Issues in User Interface Systems Engineering, Springer-Verlag, Vienna, 1995, pp. 109-134.

[2] Carr, D.A., *Specification of Interface Interaction Objects*, in Proc. of the ACM Conference on Human Factors in Computing Systems CHI'94 (Boston, 24-28 April 1994), ACM Press, New York, 1994, pp. 372-378.

[3] Elkoutbi, M., Khriss, I., and Keller, R.K., *Generating User Interface Prototypes from Scenarios*, in Proc. 4th IEEE International Symposium on Requirements Engineering RE'99 (Limerick, 7-11 June 1999), IEEE Computer Society, 1999, pp. 150-158.

[4] Elkoutbi, M. and Keller, R.K., *User Interface Prototyping based on UML Scenarios and High-level Petri Nets*, in M. Nielsen, D. Simpson (eds.), Proc. of 21st Int. Conference on Application and Theory of Petri Nets ICATPN'2000 (Aarhus, June 2000), Lecture Notes in Computer Science, Vol. 1825, Springer-Verlag, Berlin, 2000, pp. 166-186.

[5] Horrocks, I., *Constructing the User Interface with Statechart*, Addison-Wesley, Reading, January 1999.

[6] *Information Integration for Concurrent Engineering IDEF3 Process Description Capture Method Report*, 1995, accessible at http://www.idef.com/.

[7] Jacob, R.J.K, Deligiannidis, L., and Morrison, S., *A Software Model and Specification Language for Non-WIMP User Interfaces*, ACM Transactions on Computer-Human Interaction, Vol. 6, No. 1, March 1999, pp. 1-46.

[8] JGo Ver.5 Northwood Software, accessible at http://www.nwoods.com/go/jgo.htm.

[9] Protobuilder, accessible at http://www.gaio.com/.

[10] Puerta, A.R., *A Model-Based Interface Development Environment*, IEEE Software, Vol. 14, No. 4, July/August 1997, pp. 40-47.

[11] Puerta, A.R. and Eisenstein, J., *XIML: A Common Representation for Interaction Data*, in Proc. of the 7th International ACM Conference on Intelligent User Interfaces IUI'2002 (San Francisco, 13-16 January 2002), ACM Press, New York, 2002, pp. 214-215.

[12] Rapid Plus, accessible at http://www.e-sim.com/.

[13] Rational Rose, accessible at http://www.rational.com/products/rose/index.jsp.

[14] State Mate Mugnum, accessible at http://www.ilogix.com/.

[15] Unified Modeling Language Ver.1.5, accessible at http://www.omg.org/uml/.

[16] Vanderdonckt, J., Tarby, J.Cl., and Derycke, A., *Using Data Flow Diagrams for Supporting Task Models*, in P. Markopoulos, P. Johnson (eds.), Sup. Proc. of 5th Int. Eurographics Workshop on Design, Specification, Verification of Interactive Systems DSV-IS'98 (Abingdon, 3-5 June 1998), Eurographics Association, Aire-la-Ville, 1998, pp. 1-16.

[17] Whittle, J. and Schumann, J., *Generating Statechart Designs from Scenarios*, in Proc. of 22nd International Conference on Software Engineering ICSE'2000 (Limerick, 4-11 June 2000), ACM Press, New York, 2000, pp. 314-323.

Chapter 7

MAUI: AN INTERFACE DESIGN TOOL BASED ON MATRIX ALGEBRA

Jeremy Gow and Harold Thimbleby
University College London, UCL Interaction Centre (UCLIC),
Remax House, 31-32 Alfred Place – London WC1E 7DP (United Kingdom)
E-mail: {j.gow, h.thimbleby}@ucl.ac.uk
Tel.: +44 (0)207 679 {5232, 5204} – Fax: +44 (0)207 679 5295

Abstract   We describe MAUI, a user interface design tool that is based on a matrix algebra model of interaction. MAUI can be used to build and analyse designs for
interactive systems, such as handheld devices. This paper describes MAUI, its
advantages and underlying mathematical approach. MAUI is implemented in
Java and XML, which allows flexible integration with other parts of the design
life cycle, such as prototyping, implementation and documentation.

Keywords: Finite state machines, Matrix algebra, User interface design, XML.

1.   INTRODUCTION

Regardless of how attractive they are, many interactive systems remain
complex and hard to use, and many result in frustration and accidents. They
are often built informally, and it is not obvious what their problems are nor
how to avoid them. The research field of Human-Computer Interaction
(HCI) aims to improve the user experience, but it suffers from a lack of analytic tools that both support clear formal reasoning and support design and
evaluation at a practical scale. The theoretical approaches that have the formal power to specify interactive systems are technical and beyond the reach
of real designers; and the practical development tools that create real interactive systems are so informal that systems are inevitably developed in *ad hoc*
ways.

This paper introduces MAUI, a matrix algebra based User Interface (UI)
development and analysis tool that provides a simple, general and rigorous

81

R. Jacob et al. (eds.), Computer-Aided Design of User Interfaces IV, 81–94.
© 2005 *Kluwer Academic Publishers. Printed in the Netherlands.*

approach to design. It is sufficiently powerful to handle many complex interactive devices and because of its simplicity raises clear and well-defined design and research questions.

MAUI allows the designer to model an interactive device as a finite state machine (FSM), a technique that has successfully been used in HCI [14]. From this representation, an *event algebra* is generated, essentially a decomposition of the FSM's transition matrix into matrices representing individual user actions [16]. We represent the FSM in linear algebra to permit equational reasoning about UI events. Properties of the interface can be formally stated as theorems of this event algebra, and checked efficiently via matrix calculations – though a user of MAUI need not know or care about the internal implementation technique. MAUI stands for **Matrix Analysis of UIs**.

Regardless of how attractive they are, many interactive systems remain complex and hard to use, and many result in frustration and accidents. They are often built informally, and it is not obvious what their problems are nor how to avoid them. The research field of HCI aims to improve the user experience, but it suffers from a lack of analytic tools that both support clear formal reasoning and support design and evaluation at a practical scale. The theoretical approaches that have the formal power to specify interactive systems are technical and beyond the reach of real designers; and the practical development tools that create real interactive systems are so informal that systems are inevitably developed in *ad hoc* ways.

This paper introduces MAUI, a matrix algebra based UI development and analysis tool that provides a simple, general and rigorous approach to design. It is sufficiently powerful to handle many complex interactive devices and because of its simplicity raises clear and well-defined design and research questions.

MAUI allows the designer to model an interactive device as a finite state machine (FSM), a technique that has successfully been used in HCI [14]. From this representation, an *event algebra* is generated, essentially a decomposition of the FSM's transition matrix into matrices representing individual user actions [16]. We represent the FSM in linear algebra to permit equational reasoning about UI events. Properties of the interface can be formally stated as theorems of this event algebra, and checked efficiently via matrix calculations — though a user of MAUI need not know or care about the internal implementation technique. MAUI stands for **Matrix Analysis of UIs**. There are three key ideas behind the system:

1. **Specification.** Algebraic properties can correspond to usability issues. This is explored in Sections 5 and 6. MAUI maintains an algebraic specification which can be checked against the evolving design.
2. **Simplicity**. The simplicity of the formalism means that the system can verify and generate relevant properties automatically. Hence the designer

does not need to get involved in proof, and can gain insights into the interface design from properties and inconsistencies pointed out by MAUI.

3. **Integration.** MAUI allows integration with other design tools and processes via XML. For example, fast prototyping with SVG (Scalable Vector Graphics) [5], an XML open standard version of Flash.

Fig. 1 shows a UI simulation in SVG. The interface design was specified in MAUI, and automatically combined with an SVG image to make an interactive graphical simulation.

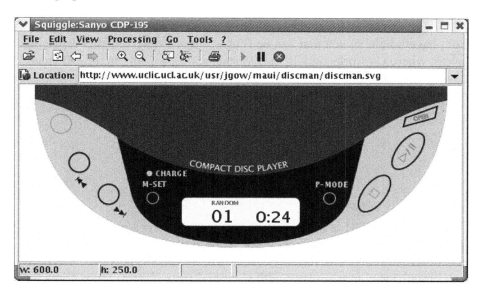

Figure 1. An SVG simulation of the Sanyo CDP-195 portable CD player. The graphics are hand-coded, but the simulation code is automatically generated from the interface design in MAUI. Viewed using the Squiggle SVG browser.

2. FSM MODELS

Formal techniques have found a wide variety of applications in UI design — e.g., for a collection of recent work, see [12]. Finite state machines are a basic formalism with a long history in this area, starting with Parnas [13] and Newman [11] in the 1960s, and reaching a height of interest in User Interface Management Systems (UIMS) work [18]. See [3] for a textbook introduction with applications of FSMs in HCI.

Finite State Machines (FSMs) are a simple and well understood formalism used throughout computer science. An FSM consists of a finite set of states connected by labelled transitions. In this paper we assume that the states are those of the UI, and that labelled transitions correspond to those

events that change the interface's state. Events usually consist of user actions, but may include other influences on the system. Examples of events
are the user pressing a button, selecting a menu item or doing nothing for
two seconds. We denote events with a box notation: Event

Fig. 2 shows an extremely simple example: an FSM model of a light
switch. It has the states On and Off, and a Switch event that flips between
them. This model is *deterministic*, in that every event has at most one effect
in any state. A non-deterministic version might define Switch in the Off state
so that it may turn the light on or blow the bulb. The model in Fig. 2 is also
unguarded, in that every event is possible in every state. A guarded version
might have a light switch that can be flicked Up or Down (together replacing
Switch), where Up works only in the On state and Down only in the Off state.

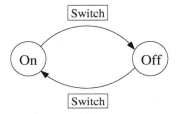

Figure 2. A simple FSM model of a light switch.

Formally, an FSM is a tuple $\langle S, \Sigma, s_0, \delta \rangle$, where S is a set of states, Σ an
alphabet (of events, in this case), $s_0 \in S$ the initial state, $\delta \subseteq S \times \Sigma \times S$ the
transition relation. The definition is standard. In MAUI, however, the FSM
model is enhanced in two ways: with *signs* and *state classes*. Signs allow the
designer to distinguish between the interface's state and those features observable by the user. An interface has a collection of signs, and each state
displays some subset of them. Examples of signs are highlighting a menu
item, displaying the time, or playing some music. Each sign may be associated with several states. Formally, we add to the FSM tuple a set of signs Ψ
and a function $\omega\colon S \rightarrow \mathbf{P}(\psi)$, which yields the subset of observable signs in
each state.

State classes are used to reduce the effort in describing interface models,
and for MAUI to classify theorems. Event transitions and signs only have to
be defined once for a state class, and are inherited by all the states that are
members of the class. A state may be a member of several state classes. Two
classes are allowed to assign different transitions to the same state and event
– the model will simply be non-deterministic. State classes are presentational
and do not change the semantics. As a modelling technique, FSMs have the
advantage of being a standard, simple formalism, and therefore more accessible to the technically-minded interface designer. They are also easy to
simulate, which is is good for prototyping.

FSMs can be used *in theory* to model any finite, discrete concurrent or sequential system, and so are widely applicable to UI design. For example, a related state diagram formalism is used in [9] to model virtual environments.

However, FSMs also have a well known disadvantage in that they scale badly. Because each state is represented explicitly, the size of an FSM increases dramatically with the complexity of the modelled system – a combinatorial explosion. This is a potential problem, as the model may become too large for the designer to comprehend or for a computer to store and analyse. Fortunately, there are a number of ways in which the combinatorial explosion can be mitigated:

- **Abstraction**. Details of the design can be excluded from the model. Useful formal analyses can be still carried out on abstract models.
- **Modularisation**. Large interface designs can often be broken down into a number of distinct, independent models.
- **Higher-Level Formalisms**. Models can be built in equivalent higher-level formalisms and compiled down to FSMs for analysis. The designer need never see the underlying FSM; this is the approach of Esterel [1], LTSA [10] and other languages.
- **Implementation techniques**. There are numerous compact implementation techniques appropriate for FSMs, including BDDs [4] and symbolic techniques.
- **Pragmatism**. MAUI works with an event algebra that captures UI properties; if there is an unmanageable combinatorial explosion then this *might* suggest that the user model is also extremely complex. Thus we claim that if MAUI cannot handle the specification of the device, the designer should have a good idea of *why* the FSM is so complex, how the users will cope with it, and whether this is acceptable.

3. EVENT ALGEBRAS

Analysis in MAUI uses a formalism consisting of states and events, represented by vectors and matrices respectively. For example, the states On and Off from Fig. 2 are represented as vectors:

$$s_{off} = (1\ 0) \qquad s_{on} = (0\ 1)$$

Events are represented as matrices that transform these state vectors according to the FSM model. For example:

$$\boxed{Switch} = \begin{pmatrix} 0 & 1 \\ 1 & 0 \end{pmatrix}$$

Checking that these definitions conform to Fig. 2 is a matter of elementary matrix multiplication:

$$s_{off} \boxed{\text{Switch}} = s_{on} \qquad s_{on} \boxed{\text{Switch}} = s_{off}$$

This can be read purely algebraically as a description of the light switch, without reference to the underlying vectors and matrices. However, the real advantage is that these matrices form an *event algebra* in which we can make assertions about user actions *independently of any particular state* [16]. For our toy example, we can state the following property:

$$\boxed{\text{Switch}}\, \boxed{\text{Switch}} = \begin{pmatrix} 1 & 0 \\ 0 & 1 \end{pmatrix} = I$$

where I is the identity ("do nothing") matrix. This tells us that pressing $\boxed{\text{Switch}}$ twice has the same final effect as doing nothing! This is an inherent property of $\boxed{\text{Switch}}$, no matter what state the system is in. The strength of this approach is that similarly concise statements can be made about far more complex interfaces with many states. We look at some more interesting examples below.

Given a MAUI interface model $\langle S, \Sigma, s_0, \delta, \psi, \omega \rangle$, we formally define its event algebra with a bijection $\eta: \{1 \ldots |S|\} \leftrightarrow S$ mapping states to element indices; η generates a representation function $\Re$ that maps states and events to the vectors and matrices that denote them. For state $s \in S$ define the *state vector* $\mathbf{s} = \Re\, [\![s]\!]$ by

$$\mathbf{s}_i = \begin{cases} 1 & if\, \eta(i) = s \\ 0 & otherwise \end{cases}$$

For event $\boxed{\text{E}} \in \Sigma$ define the *event matrix* $E = \Re\, [\![\boxed{\text{E}}]\!]$ by

$$E_{ij} = \begin{cases} 1 & if\, \delta(\eta(i), \sigma, \eta(j)) \\ 0 & otherwise \end{cases}$$

The algebra of these vectors and matrices, equipped with multiplication and an initial state vector $\Re\, [\![s_0]\!]$, provides another model of the UI, based on the original FSM. For brevity in this paper, we write the event $\boxed{\text{E}}$ to denote the matrix $E = \Re\, [\![\boxed{\text{E}}]\!]$; in general capital letters $A, B, \ldots$ denote matrices that may or may not be events or products of events.

4.   USING MAUI

MAUI's own interface (Fig. 3) is a conventional GUI design, with windows representing different aspects of a system's functionality: *Design, Simulation, Statistics* and *Analysis* (described in Section 5). There are also menus for basic functions such as opening and saving files.

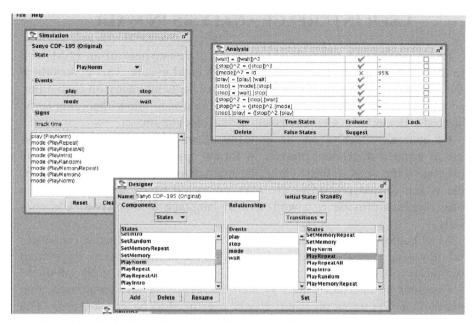

Figure 3. MAUI being used to analyse the design of the Sanyo CDP-195 from Fig. 1.

The Design window displays the current interface design and allows the user to edit it. The window is split into a *Components* panel and a *Relationships* panel. The Components panel can be set to display a list of either states, state classes, events or signs. Selecting a component from this list results in the *Relationships* panel displaying a list of related components. The type of related components displayed can be set by the user. For example, selecting a state from the Components panel causes its state transitions to be displayed in the Relationships panel. The user can also choose to view the classes the state belongs to, or the signs associated with it. The Components lists may have items added, deleted or renamed, and the Relationships panel may be used to edit transitions, class membership, etc.

The Simulation window shows an interactive simulator, ideal for basic tests. The Simulation window does not aspire to be photorealistic, which is currently handled externally by SVG and other mechanisms. The Statistics window shows statistics that are useful for comparing the complexity of different designs. For example, minimum, maximum and average path length between two states [14]. Another example is the overshoot recovery cost. A common user error is an overshoot caused by doing an event, say $\boxed{\text{E}}$, once too often. MAUI can calculate the overshoot recovery cost as the minimum number of events that correct an overshoot: it determines a product of events R such that $\boxed{\text{E}}\,\boxed{\text{E}}\,R = \boxed{\text{E}}$. The Analysis window allows the user to explore the interface design's event algebra, as discussed in Section 3. The following section describes how this works in MAUI, and its utility in UI design.

5. USER INTERFACE ANALYSIS IN MAUI

Event algebras in themselves are simply a restatement of an FSM with the transition function 'broken up' into individual events. This makes them well-suited for making statements about how events interact with each other, and hence for usability analysis. Crucially, matrices allow theorems to be checked efficiently by elementary numerical calculation.

Of course, reflecting on the usability of an interface design is an extremely context-dependent process. A formal approach does not relieve the designer of the need to think about the implications of their design, and decide which formal properties are relevant to the user's experience. What event algebras provide is a well-defined language to talk about UIs concisely.

MAUI allows the designer to specify a set of event algebra properties that they wish their design to conform to. As the design evolves, the system provides feedback on which parts of the specification are currently satisfied.

Consider an interface button $\boxed{A}$ such that $\boxed{A}\,\boxed{A} = \boxed{A}$, an idempotence that tells us that if $\boxed{A}$ needs pressing, it only ever need to be pressed once. The button would avoid the possibility of an overshoot error (pressing once too often). This would be suitable for the specification of a $\boxed{\text{Play}}$ or $\boxed{\text{Stop}}$ button.

Another example is undo. Allowing the user to undo their actions is a common usability requirement. We can express the requirement that user actions $\boxed{B} \ldots \boxed{C}$ act as an undo for action $\boxed{A}$ by: $\boxed{A}\,\boxed{B} \ldots \boxed{C} = I$. The designer may want each event to be easily undone, and so have a short undo sequence (ideally one action) for each event $\boxed{A}$. Some events are inherently irreversible, and so have no $\boxed{B} \ldots \boxed{C}$ that yields the identity. This can be determined by straightforward calculation (to show the matrix is singular); the designer can specify in MAUI that an event must be reversible, or tat is must be irreversible. Further, some events although in principle invertible, are merely irreversible for the user, as there is no sequence of events whose corresponding matrix product is the inverse of the event.

Another kind of usability issue the designer may be interested in is permissiveness [15]: allowing many different sequences of actions to achieve any given task, ones that commute or distribute, etc:

$$\boxed{A}\,\boxed{B} = \boxed{B}\,\boxed{A},\ \boxed{A}\,\boxed{B}\,\boxed{C} = \boxed{A}\,\boxed{B}\,\boxed{A}\,\boxed{C},\ \boxed{A}\,\boxed{B} = \boxed{C}\,\boxed{D}\,\boxed{E}$$

A related usability concept is that efficient shortcuts should be available for expert users: $\boxed{A}\,\boxed{B} \ldots \boxed{C}\,\boxed{D} = M$ – where, in turn, M can be factored as a product of user events, but its total cost (to the user) is less. So far we have shown how universal statements about interface models can be made in MAUI. In some cases a property will only be of interest for a certain subset of states. This can be done by restricting properties to particular state classes. For example, we can claim for a class, 'For C: $\boxed{A} = \boxed{B}$' if for all $s_{\eta(i)} \in C$, the

i^{th} row *of* $\boxed{A}$ and $\boxed{B}$ are equal. Another use for state classes is dealing with predictable effects of actions. We can state that event $\boxed{A}$ always puts an interface into one of the states in class C if we can show that for every non-zero j^{th} column of $\boxed{A}$ the state $s_{\eta(j)}$ is not in C.

The designer manages the specification through MAUI's Analysis window. This presents a list of the currently specified properties, with options to add, delete and edit them. MAUI distinguishes between three basic types of property: equality of two event/state expressions; the reversibility of an individual event; and predictability of an event. These are displayed in the property list as '$A = B$', 'E is reversible' and 'A results in C'. Choosing to create or edit a property brings up an editing panel that allows these properties to be composed from the existing events, states and state classes in a straightforward way. Predefined events and states, like the identity and so on, are also provided. More complicated properties can be built up in the editing panel by either negating properties or restricting properties to a particular state class.

The Analysis window monitors how the current interface design conforms to the designer's specification. Unsatisfied properties are highlighted, and annotated with a percentage of *how* true they are. For an equality theorem the percentage of states for which it holds is used, by calculating the percentage of equal matrix rows. Other measures could be used. The designer can also request detailed information about why a property is not true in the form of counter-example states, and can 'lock' any true property, so that MAUI forbids changes to the UI that make it false.

One feature that makes MAUI stand out as a design tool is its ability to suggest to the designer properties of the interface model. At the designer's request the system can automatically generate true theorems not already in the specification, as well as 'near-theorems' – non-theorems of the equality type that are true for a high percentage (e.g., > 95%) of states. The value of near-theorems is that they may represent properties which the designer could choose to make universal, for a more clear and consistent design. The automatic suggestion mechanism currently works by enumerating all identities up to a certain complexity, with some redundant theorems being pruned because they can be derived from simpler theorems. In order to manage the amount of suggestions generated by MAUI, the designer can vary both the theorem complexity level and the percentage threshold for near-theorems.

Ivory and Hearst [8] point out the current lack of automated support for critiquing UIs, that is "methods that not only point out difficulties but propose improvements." Following their terminology, MAUI's ability to suggest properties that are *or should* be true is a simple form of support for critiquing analytical models. No other technique in their survey provides this kind of support.

6. EXAMPLES

The MAUI suggestion mechanism was used to analyse the design of a portable CD player, the Sanyo CDP-195. The 29 state model captured the behaviour of four events: [Play], [Stop], [P-Mode] and [Wait] (for 6 seconds). The [P-mode] button selects one of seven play modes (Normal, Random, Intros,…). The suggestion mechanism generated the following 97% near-theorem: $[\text{P-Mode}]^7 = I$. Reflecting on why this is almost universally true, we found that the [P-Mode] button cycled through the seven play modes and returned to the original state, irrespective of whether the player was at rest, playing or paused – *except for in one state*. In this state, the display gave the CD information, but $[\text{P-Mode}]^7$ took the user to an equivalent state with no display except '– –'. Merging these two states would have no effect on the functionality of the interface, but would make $[\text{P-Mode}]^7 = I$ true and, we suggest, the device more understandable to the user. MAUI's suggestion for a design property thus leads to a simpler and more consistent interface design.

As a second example, the Nokia 5510 mobile phone menu system [16] can be specified by 5 event matrices, over 188 states. We can automatically (and quickly) find theorems including: $[\text{Up}][\text{Cancel}] = [\text{Cancel}]$, $[\text{Down}][\text{Cancel}] = [\text{Cancel}]$, $[\text{Cancel}]^4 = [\text{Cancel}]^5$, $[\text{Up}][\text{Down}] = I$.

7. DESIGN INTEGRATION VIA XML

MAUI can store UI designs in an XML format. This is ideal for integrating the formal analysis done in MAUI with other stages of the design cycle: prototyping, documentation, implementation, alternative analysis tools etc. For proof-of-concept, so far we have written XSLT stylesheets to convert designs to:

1. **Graphviz.** Visualisations of interface state graphs were produced by converting XML designs into AT&T's Graphviz format [6].
2. **HTML+Javascript.** HTML simulations are a simple, portable way to share designs with other people over the web.
3. **SVG+Javascript.** Hand-coded SVG [5] was added to the MAUI-generated XML and automatically transformed into SVG+Javascript, for a more sophisticated graphical simulation. We intend to adapt an existing SVG editor to integrate a graphical design editor with MAUI, to avoid the need to write the SVG graphical elements by hand, as at present.
4. **Mathematica.** In the hands of an expert user, *Mathematica* could do larger and far more complex analyses than are done in MAUI, although it is far less accessible than our system, both in terms of ease of use and price (MAUI is free).

Reusing the design data in each stage means there is no need to reimplement the design several times, with the possibility of errors occurring at each stage. Fig. 4 shows fragments of XML describing the Sanyo CDP-195 mentioned in Section 5. The XML was generated by MAUI, except for the hand-coded `form` element which contains the graphical design. It was automatically transformed to the graphical simulation shown in Fig. 1.

```
<fui>
 <name>Sanyo CDP-195</name>
 <event id="play"/>
 <event id="mode"/>
 ...
 <form width="600" height="250">
 ...
   <signs>
    <text id="track" ... x="260" y="195">01</text>
    <text id="time" ... x="320" y="195">0:24</text>
    ...
   </signs>
 </form>
 <function>
  <initial ref="StandBy"/>
  <state id="StandBy">
   <change event="play" to="PlayNorm" />
  </state>
  <stateclass id="PlayState">
   <change event="stop" to="NoAction" />
  </stateclass>
  <state id="PlayNorm" class="PlayState">
   <change event="play" to="PauseNorm" />
   <change event="mode" to="PlayRepeat" />
   <sign ref="track"/> <sign ref="time"/>
  </state>
  ...
 </function>
</fui>
```

Figure 4. XML description of the Sanyo CDP-195 portable CD player generated by MAUI, except for the content of the `form` element, which is hand-coded SVG.

8.   FURTHER WORK

In developing MAUI our highest priority is to apply it to more real-world case studies. We have argued for the generality of MAUI's design methodology, and given some examples. However, further work with a wider range of examples is needed to establish the scope of the method, both in terms of types of system and types of usability analysis. MAUI is a research tool, but a separate question is how accessible we could make our formal methodology to designers or HCI researchers. The real question here is 'which ones?'

MAUI's approach to formal analysis is an attempt to be simple enough for more technically-minded designers to grasp and to still be useful. Any further development will need to consider more about the abilities and requirements of designers and/or HCI researchers. Sometimes a user will follow a detour to achieve some straightforward goal, as in $AB \dots CD = AD$, etc. An interesting future development might be to make some of MAUI's analyses available to end users, not just designers. "Would you like to know a better way to do what you have just done?" In Hyperdoc [14], the end user could ask the system to find event sequences that set signs to particular values. There are many techniques for compressing matrices. In MAUI, an interesting possibility to explore would be to compress matrices and hence help a designer determine tighter class definitions and nearly (or completely) redundant transitions, as well as transitions that if changed might reduce the model. MAUI's statistics could be extended in many ways, such as incorporating expectations based on Markov models [17]. MAUI could constrain design changes to maintain statistics, as it currently does for theorems.

9.   CONCLUSION

We have described MAUI, a design tool in which formal models of UIs can be built and analysed. Integration with other design processes, especially graphical prototyping, is achieved using XML. Design specifications are expressed and easily verified using event algebras, with the novel feature that the system can suggest to the designer properties that are true or nearly true.

Our approach can be related to a great deal of previous work on modelling UIs with finite state machines and related formalisms. For instance, VEG [2] is a recent example based on BNF grammars. MAUI's algebraic style of specification, based on the global properties of events, is a key difference with such methods. Also, more sophisticated interface models are typically employed in order to ease the specification process. This is a less important difference, as such techniques could be adopted by MAUI.

Many systems, like LTSA [10] or the Play-Engine [7], aim for comprehensiveness, and thus tend to lose sight of clarity in usability and effective use by typical mathematically naïve designers. Usability itself is a very complex field, and we feel that the interaction between usability research and various schemes for combining rapid prototyping and modelling are not best helped by the usual goals of universality. We imagine that as a body of design and usability related theorems is developed (e.g., that many pairs of actions, such as ⎡Up⎤ and ⎡Down⎤, should be inverses), these will be embedded into MAUI, thus making it a convenient tool for designers and researchers not only to build, simulate and generate prototype interactive systems, but to check a wide range of their properties.

ACKNOWLEDGEMENTS

Harold Thimbleby is a Royal Society Wolfson Research Merit Award Holder. Jeremy Gow is funded on the award. We are grateful to Paul Cairns for constructive comments.

REFERENCES

[1]   Berry, G., *The foundations of Esterel*, in G. Plotkin, C. Stirling, M. Tofte (eds.), Proof, Language and Interaction: Essays in Honour of Robin Milner, The MIT Press, Cambridge, 1998.

[2]   Berstel, J., Reghizzi, S.C., Roussel, G., and Pietro, P.S., *A Scalable Formal Method for Design and Automatic Checking of User Interfaces*, in Proc. of the 23rd International Conference on Software Engineering ICSE'01 (Toronto, 12-19 May 2001), IEEE Computer Society Press, Los Alamitos, 2001, pp. 453-462.

[3]   Dix, A., Finlay, J., Abowd, G., and Beale, R., *Human Computer Interaction*, Prentice Hall, Englewood Cliffs, 1998.

[4]   Drechsler, R., *Binary Decision Diagrams: Theory and Implementation*, Kluwer Academics Publishers, Dordrecht, 1998.

[5]   Ferraiolo, J., Jackson, D., and Jun, F., *Scalable Vector Graphics (SVG) 1.1 Specification*, Recommendation, W3C, 2003, accessible at http://www.w3.org/TR/SVG11.

[6]   Gansner, E. and North, S., *An Open Graph Visualization System and its Applications to Software Engineering*, Software Practice & Experience, Vol. 30, No. 11, 2000, pp. 1203-1233.

[7]   Harell, D. and Marelly, R., *Come, Let's Play: Scenario-Based Programming Using LSCs and the Play-Engine*, Springer Verlag, Berlin, 2003.

[8]   Ivory, M.Y. and Hearst, M.A., *The State of the Art in Automating Usability Evaluation of User Interfaces*, ACM Computing Surveys, Vol. 33, No. 4, 2001, pp. 470-516.

[9]   Jacob, R.J.K, Deligiannidis, L., and Morrison, S., *A Software Model and Specification Language for Non-WIMP User Interfaces*, ACM Transactions on Computer-Human Interaction, Vol. 6, No. 1, March 1999, pp. 1-46.

[10] Magee, J., *Behavioral Analysis of Software Architectures Using LTSA*, in Proc. of 21st International Conference on Software Engineering ICSE'99 (Los Angeles, 16-22 May 1999), ACM Press, New York, 1999, pp. 634-637.

[11] Newman, W.M., *A System for Interactive Graphical Programming*, in Proceedings of the AFIPS 1968 Spring Joint Computer Conference (Atlantic City, 30 April - 2 May 1968), Vol. 32, American Federation of Information Processing Societies, Thomson Book Company, Washington, 1968, pp. 47-54.

[12] Palanque, P. and Paternò, F., *Formal Methods in Human-Computer Interaction*, Springer-Verlag, Berlin, 1997.

[13] Parnas, D.L., *On the Use of Transition Diagrams in the Design of a User Interface For an Interactive Computer System*, in Proc. of the 24th ACM National Conference (26-28 August 1969), ACM Press, New York, 1969, pp. 379-385.

[14] Thimbleby, H., *Combining Systems and Manuals*, in J.L. Alty, D. Diaper, S.P. Guest

(eds.), People and Computers VIII, Proceedings of the BCS-HCI Conference on Human-Computer Interaction HCI'93 (Loughborough, 7-10 September 1993), Cambridge University Press, Cambridge, 1993, pp. 479-488.

[15] Thimbleby, H., *Permissive User Interfaces*, International Journal of Human Computer Studies, Vol. 54, No. 3, 2001, pp. 333-350.

[16] Thimbleby, H., *User Interface Design with Matrix Algebra*, ACM Transactions on Computer-Human Interaction, Vol. 11, No. 2, 2004, pp. 181-236.

[17] Thimbleby, H., Cairns, P., and Jones, M., Usability Analysis with Markov Models, ACM Transactions on Computer-Human Interaction, Vol. 8, No. 2, 2001, pp. 99-132.

[18] Wasserman, A.I., *Extending State Transition Diagrams for the Specification of Human Computer Interaction*, IEEE Transactions on Software Engineering, SE-11, No. 8, 1985, pp. 699-713.

Chapter 8

GOLIATH: AN EXTENSIBLE MODEL-BASED ENVIRONMENT TO DEVELOP USER INTERFACES

David Julien[1], Mikal Ziane[1,2], and Zahia Guessoum[1]

[1]*Laboratoire d'Informatique de Paris 6, Thème OASIS,*
8, rue du Capitaine Scott, F-75015 Paris (France)
E-mail: {david.julien,mikal.ziane,zahia.guessoum}@lip6.fr
Tel.: +33- 1 44 27 {5480, 8746, 8743} - Fax: +33- 1 44 27 70 00
[2]*Université René Descartes,*
12, rue de l'école de médecine, F-75005 Paris (France)

Abstract   Despite the success of visual interface builders, user interfaces are still too difficult to develop. Model-based approaches are promising but have a high threshold of use. In this paper, we describe GOLIATH, an easy-to-use Model Based User Interface Development Environment (MB-UIDE) with an extensible architecture. The models of GOLIATH are simple enough to be used by developers who currently use visual interface builders. However, these models are rich enough to better support the links between the interface and the functional core of the application than current MB-UIDEs.

Keywords: Model-based interface design, Multi-agent system.

1.   INTRODUCTION

Despite the success of visual interface builders, user interfaces are still too difficult to develop. Even if interface elements can be assembled graphically in visual builders, "*the behaviour of user interfaces is generally implemented by complex, hand crafted software systems*" [1]. In particular, it is difficult to ensure that what is displayed by the interface corresponds to the state of the application. Moreover, "*changing an existing interface to reflect changing requirements and to take account of user feedback is a laborious and often somewhat ad hoc process*" [1]. Model-Based User Interface Development Environments (MB-UIDEs) [6,9,11,12,13,14] automatically or

95

R. Jacob et al. (eds.), Computer-Aided Design of User Interfaces IV, 95–106.

semi-automatically generate interfaces according to a declarative specification which consists of several models describing different aspects of the interface. Unfortunately, they have not yet caught on. Among the reasons to explain this lack of success, [7] mentions the unpredictability of the resulting interfaces and the threshold of use of these environments.

In this paper, we describe GOLIATH, an easy-to-use MB-UIDE with an extensible architecture. The models of GOLIATH are simple enough to be used by developers who currently use visual interface builders. However, these models are rich enough to better support the links between the interface and the functional core of the application than current MB-UIDEs. This paper is organised as follows. Section 1 introduces MB-UIDEs and their main models. Sections 2, 3 and 4 present the application, presentation and dialogue models of GOLIATH. Section 5 describes its multi-agent architecture. An address book example is used across the paper and its interface is presented in section 6. Section 7 discusses potential drawbacks of GOLIATH's approach.

2.   MB-UIDES

MB-UIDEs specify interfaces using models which typically include the application model, the presentation model and the dialogue model. Fig. 1 shows a typical mapping of these models to the ARCH architectural model of interactive systems [?].

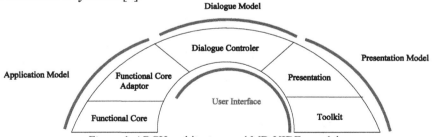

Figure 1. ARCH architecture and MB-UIDEs models.

The Application Model. It describes the application's data and functionality. Corba's IDL is a standard way to describe an API independently from its programming language, and was used to describe MASTERMIND's application models [13]. Teallach [6] relies on the ODMG object model which is consistent with their particular focus on database applications. Since Corba's IDL gives very little information about the semantics of the application, Mastermind extended it with pre-conditions and reports. This makes it easier to avoid proposing invalid choices to the final user, and to refresh the presentation when some data have changed. GOLIATH's application model, even though it is much simpler than Corba's IDL, significantly improves on these extensions for further automatisation.

The Presentation Model. It has two roles. First, it describes the presentation elements of the targeted toolkits. Second, it allows defining new elements by composition. The salient aspects of GOLIATH's presentation model are its independence from toolkits (even though each presentation model specification is bound to a specific toolkit), and its ability to ease the automation of the aforementioned behavioural aspects.

The Dialogue Model. It describes the links between the functional core and the presentation. It mainly defines what is displayed in the presentation, the functions to call (when and with what arguments) and the consequences of user actions. Most MB-UIDEs define the dialogue through a task model. However, Paternò [8] highlights that *"designers find often them difficult to apply, [...]. The reason for this problem is that it is not easy when analysing an existing application or envisioning a new one to know immediately the structure and the elements of the task model"*. Since GOLIATH targets developers accustomed to visual interface builders, it introduces a simple and concrete dialogue model. This model is defined in terms of abstract containers which are more concrete than abstract tasks.

From models to running interfaces. Despite significant effort, transforming a set of models into a running interface is still a problem for MB-UIDEs [10]. These transformations require often deep knowledge. So it is not easy to have all the needed knowledge from the outset. In order to facilitate the representation and integration of this knowledge, we propose to use a multi-agent system [5].

3.   THE APPLICATION MODEL

GOLIATH's application model is a language much simpler than Corba's IDL which is used by Mastermind, and essentially relies on the definition of data types and function signatures. Moreover, GOLIATH's application model supports the definition of pre-conditions and dependency declarations. Preconditions and dependency declarations make it easier to avoid proposing invalid choices to the final user and to automate refreshing the presentation. A term of this language is a data term, a pre-condition or a dependency declaration. A data term is a variable of some type, a constant of some type, or an application-data term. An application-data term is the output of a function call without side-effects, or part of this output if the function has several OUT parameters. The parameters of a function call are data terms of the appropriate types.

3.1   Function Signatures and Notifications

Functions with side-effects (that is mostly which modify application data) are denoted with a '+' before their identifier. Notifications, denoted by a '*', allow identifying application-data modifications which do not depend on side-effects function calls (for instance a modification of a mail box, after the reception of new e-mail, does not rely on any function call). They are more precise than MASTERMIND's report mechanism: parameters allow precisely identifying which data has changed.

Example of function signatures and notifications from the AddressBook application model:
getContact (IN AddressBook anAddressBook,
    IN ContactKey aContactKey, OUT Contact aContact)
contactExists (IN AddressBook anAddressBook,
    IN ContactKey aContactKey, OUT Boolean exists)
isDateValid (IN Date data, OUT Boolean valid)
+updateContact (INOUT AddressBook anAddressBook,
    IN ContactKey aContactKey, IN String firstName, ..., IN Date birthDate)
+removeContact (INOUT AddressBook anAddressBook,
    IN ContactKey aContactKey)
*newMail(OUT Integer mailId)

3.2   Pre-Conditions

Contrarily to MASTERMIND's pre-conditions which are informal, GOLIATH's pre-conditions can be automatically evaluated. Their syntax is the following: <precondition> ::= <function-call> (("if" | "ifNot") <data-term>)+

Example: a call to *updateContact* of the form updateContact(AB, CK, _, ..., BD) is valid if CK is a ContactKey of an existing contact in the AddressBook AB, and if BD is a valid Date.
updateContact (AB, CK, -, ..., BD)
    if exists from contactExists (AB, CK)
    if exists from isDateValid (BD)

3.3   Dependency Declarations

The presentation of displayed data-term has to be updated when its value changes. GOLIATH can deduce at run-time that this value has changed thanks to two mechanisms: inference from a call to a side-effect function, and notification by the application. When the application is not able to notify some changes, it is still possible to declare that a data term is potentially out-of-date. This allows GOLIATH to remind the developer to take appropriate measures if necessary. These inferences rely on dependency declarations of the following form: <dependency> ::= <function-call> "impacts" <data-term> | <notification> "impacts" <data-term> | "unknown" "impacts" <data-term>

Example: *removeContact* modifies the result of *contactExists*.
removeContact(AB,CK) impacts exists from contactExists(AB,CK)

4.   THE PRESENTATION MODEL

Like every presentation model, GOLIATH's allows to describe and compose new presentation elements. Toolkit presentation models describe the basic presentation elements, from which designers can compose new presentation elements.

GOLIATH's presentation elements. Each presentation element has an interface part. It defines actions fired, data handled and existing slots in a presentation element. A slot defines a customizable place in a presentation element. It allows to define containers (like windows) or to delegate some internal rendering to an external presentation element (for instance a presentation element which displays a list of items may delegate the rendering of each item to a specialised presentation element). Furthermore, each composite element defines a list of sub-elements, a set of mapping between its interface and the sub-elements interface, and a set of behaviours to define dynamic modifications. These aspects are not described in this article.

Actions and data handled. In order to support the automatic updating of the presentation, meanings are associated to each action of presentation elements.

Example: newContactSelected (EXPLICIT DATA_MODIFICATION
An action to select a contact in a list is explicit (the user has to click on the item) and modifies the selected data.

A data handled by a presentation element is mainly described by an identifier, a type, a list of associated actions and a description of its content. Associated actions allow identifying which action will be fired in case of modification of the presentation data. Thanks to this information, pre-conditions and dependency declarations depending on a presentation data can be automatically re-evaluated when a DATA_MODIFICATION action linked to the presentation data is received.

Example: The *ContactEditor* presentation element allows to edit data describing an addressbook contact. Here is what concerns the *birthDate* presentation data:

```
birthDateModified ( DATA_MODIFICATION)...
birthData:Date {
    actions = { birthDateModified )
    content = independent-content (
        day: Integer (...)
        month: Integer (...)
        year: Integer (...))
```

The meanings of the birthDateModified action, which is linked to *birthDate*, include DATA_MODIFICATION. Hence, GOLIATH can deduce when any data-term including this *birthDate* has to be re-evaluated.

5.   THE DIALOGUE MODEL

Since GOLIATH targets developers accustomed to visual interface builders, it introduces a simple and concrete dialogue model. This model is defined in terms of abstract containers. Each of them represents an independent part of the interface linked to a composite presentation element, and describes what operations the final user can trigger and what data will be displayed in it.

Operations. It is mainly composed of a call to a function with side-effects and a set of conditions to control its triggering. A condition typically corresponds to an action defined in the composite presentation element associated to the abstract container which holds the operation. When one of the conditions is validated, the function is called. If the function call is not authorized (because its pre-conditions are not verified), all of the conditions are forbidden (by disabling the presentation elements which trigger the actions).

Example:
```
operation UpdateContact (
    triggers = ( update ),
    function-call= updateContact(myAddressBook, contactKey, contact.firstName, ...,
    contact.birthDate)
...)
```
The UpdateContact operation describes how to update a contact in an addressbook when the "update" action is fired. "myAddressBook" and "contactKey" are local variables of the abstract container, while "contact" references data handled by its presentation element.

Views. A view binds a data term with a data variable of the composite presentation element associated to the abstract container which holds the view. The data term is automatically re-evaluated and the presentation updated when a relevant modification is detected.

Example:
view DisplayContact (
   data-term = contact from getContact(myAddressBook, contactKey),
   pdata = (contact) ...)
This view displays a contact returned by the *getContact* function. "myAddressBook", "contactKey" and "contact" are defined above.

6.   AN EXTENSIBLE ENVIRONMENT

In order to foster extensibility and flexibility, GOLIATH's models are interpreted by a multi-agent system [5]. Unlike the PAC approach [4], which decomposes the interface in many agents, GOLIATH limits the number of agents by associating one agent to each component of the ARCH architecture. Each agent is composed of an extensible set of services which allows running an interface from the models. Agents communicate by sending messages to each others (Fig. 2A). These messages are requests for services. To respond to the request, agents activate the requested services. Broadcasted messages are allowed when information has to be sent to all agents.

The Functional Core Agent and the Toolkit Agent are wrapper agents. They encapsulate the functional core and the toolkit. Consequently, they provide a standard interface (through an Agent Communication Language) to communicate with the functional core and the toolkit, independently of their implementation language.

The Presentation Agent interacts with the Toolkit Agent to generate automatically the physical presentation according to presentation models. The Application Agent allows providing higher level functions from the functional core.

The Dialogue Agent manages the relationships between the presentation and the application. New services may be introduced in this architecture. Our goal is to foster the introduction of interface-designers' knowledge to further relieve them of tedious tasks. For instance, a service has been introduced into the dialogue agent to manage the consistency of the presentation regarding the application state (Fig. 2B).

The five Goliath's agents

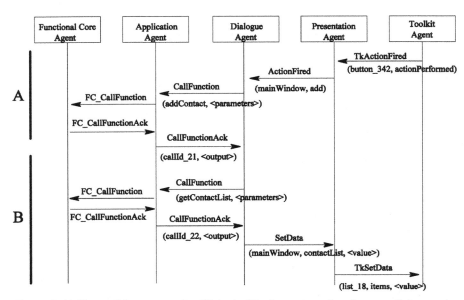

Figure 2. A) The toolkit agent sends a TkActionFired message when the user clicks on a button. This message is received by the presentation agent which determines the concerned presentation element and the action name. The dialogue agent waits for ActionFired message to determine if an operation is triggered. In that case, it sends a CallFunction message to the application agent and waits for its acknowledge.
B)When an addContact call-acknowledge message is detected, our consistency service evaluates the consequences of this function call. The different models provide information whose analyses allows to identify that the current displayed contact list is incoherent with current application contact list. Therefore, the consistency service recovers an up-to-date contact list from the application and updates the presentation.

7.   A CONCRETE EXAMPLE

The GOLIATH environment is operational. The Application, Dialogue and Presentation Agents are implemented in the (CAML) language [3]. The implementation language for the Functional Core Agents and the Toolkit Agents depends on the implementation language of the underlying applications and toolkit libraries. In the current version of GOLIATH, Functional Core Agents encapsulating Java and CAML functional cores, and Toolkit Agent encapsulating Java/Swing, have been tested successfully. GOLIATH has been used for designing a user interface for an address book application (Fig. 3).

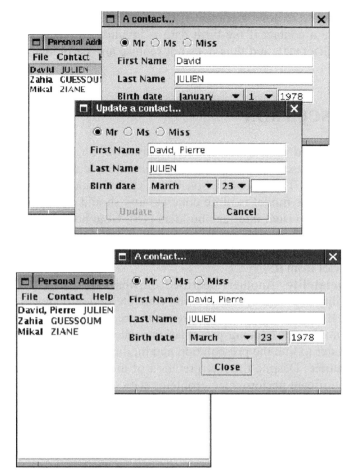

Figure 3. On the upper picture, the address book user interface before the update. The "Update" button has been automatically disabled because the new date edited is invalid (preconditions of "updateContact" function is thus unverified). On the lower picture, the same interface just after a contact update. The various windows have been updated automatically.

The AddressBook interface consists of four abstract containers: the main container, the consult container, the update container and the add container. The main container has a view on the contact list of the address book, and the consult/update containers hold a view on a selected contact in the aforementioned list. The update (resp. add) container holds an operation which triggers *updateContact* (resp. *addContact*) function. From these abstract containers described by the user-interface developer, GOLIATH generates a running interface and automatically updates the main interface after each add/update/remove action, as well as other interfaces displaying updated or removed contacts. Moreover, some buttons and menu items are enabled or disabled according to operations they trigger. For instance, the final user can not consult/update/remove a contact if there is no selected contact, and can not add/update a contact if the birth date is invalid. This behaviour is fully managed by GOLIATH, and thus does not require any particular design decision.

8.   DISCUSSION

High threshold of use. According to Myers et al., MB-UIDEs have a high threshold of use [7] because programmers must learn new languages to define the models. This is one reason why GOLIATH does not rely on a task model. Its dialogue model is more concrete and should be attractive to programmers used to visual interface builders [15]. Note however that dialogue models are abstract enough not to be bound to any specific toolkit. Moreover, it is quite possible to add a task model to GOLIATH and then derive a dialogue model from it.

Unpredictability. Another identified drawback of MB-UIDEs is their unpredictability [7]. Again, thanks to its concrete dialogue model, we claim that GOLIATH's resulting interfaces are quite predictable. The focus of GOLIATH was not on introducing presentation-related heuristics, but rather on making it easier to link the presentation and the functional core.

Performance. Despite the interpretation of models, we have not yet noticed any significant performance problems with GOLIATH. To validate it on large and sophisticated interfaces, we are currently designing, with GOLIATH, a visual tool to edit GOLIATH's models. If a performance problem appears, it will certainly not be due to the multi-agent system: the number of agents is quite limited. If interpretation is not efficient enough, code generation should be considered.

9.   CONCLUSION

GOLIATH is a MB-UIDE targeted at developers used to visual interface builders. Thanks to its concrete dialogue model, it alleviates two important drawbacks of current MB-UIDEs: the unpredictability of the resulting interfaces, and the threshold of use of these environments. Moreover, thanks to its more precise models and an additional service, GOLIATH makes it easier to avoid proposing invalid choices to the final user and to refresh the presentation when some data have changed

REFERENCES

[1] Barclay, P.J., Griffiths, T., McKirdy, J., Paton, N.W., Cooper, R., and Kennedy, J., *The Teallach Tool: Using Models for Flexible User Interface Design*, in A. Puerta, J. Vanderdonckt (eds.), Proceedings of 3rd Int. Conf. on Computer-Aided Design of User Interfaces CADUI'99 (Louvain-la-Neuve, 21-23 October 1999), Kluwer Academics Pub., Dordrecht, 1999, pp. 139-157.

[2] Bass, L. Little, R., Pellegrino, R., Reed, S., Seacord, R., Sheppard, S., and Szczur, M.R., *The UIMS Tool Developers' Workshop: A Metamodel for the Runtime Architecture of an Interactive System*, SIGCHI Bulletin, Vol. 24, No. 1, 1992, pp. 32-37.

[3] CAML, *The CAML Language*, INRIA, Rocquencourt, 6 October 2001, accessible at http://caml.inria.fr

[4] Coutaz, J., *PAC: An Object-Oriented Model for Dialog Design*, in H.-J. Bullinger, B. Shackel (eds.), Proceedings of 2nd IFIP Conference on Human-Computer Interaction Interact'87 (Stuttgart, 1-4 September 1987), North Holland, Amsterdam, 1987, pp. 431-436.

[5] Ferber, J., *Multi-Agent System: An Introduction to Distributed Artificial Intelligence*, Addison-Wesley, Reading, 1999.

[6] Griffiths, T., Barclay, P., Paton, N.W., McKirdy, J., Kennedy, J., Gray, P.D., Cooper, R., Goble, C., and Pinheiro da Silva, P., *Teallach: a Model-based User Interface Development Environment for Object Data-bases*, Interacting with Computers, Vol. 14, No. 1, pp. 31-68.

[7] Myers, B.A., Hudson, S.E., and Pausch, R., *Past, Present, and Future of User Interface Software Tools*, ACM Transactions on Computer-Human Interaction, Vol. 7, No. 1, 2000, pp. 3-28.

[8] Paternò, F., *Model-Based Design and Evaluation of Interactive Applications*, Springer-Verlag, Berlin, 1999.

[9] Pinheiro da Silva, P., *User Interface Declarative Models and Development Environments: A Survey*, in P. Palanque, F. Paternò (eds.), Proceedings of 7th International Workshop on Design, Specification, and Verification of Interactive Systems DSV-IS'2000 (Limerick, 5-7 June 2000), Lecture Notes in Computer Science, Vol. 1946, Springer-Verlag, Berlin, 2000, pp. 207-226.

[10] Pinheiro da Silva, P., Griffiths, T., Paton, N.W., *Generating User Interface Code in a Model-Based User Interface Development Environment*, in V. Gesù, S. Levialdi, L. Tarantino (eds.), Proceedings of ACM Int. Conference on Advanced Visual Interfaces AVI'2000 (Palermo, 23-26 May 2000), ACM Press, New York, 2000, pp. 155-160.

[11] Puerta, A.R., *A Model-Based Interface Development Environment*, IEEE Software, Vol. 14, No. 4, 1997, pp. 40-47.

[12] Puerta, A., Cheng, E., Ou, T., and Min, J., *MOBILE: User-Centered Interface Building*, in Proceedings of ACM Conf. on Human Aspects in computing Systems CHI'99 (Pittsburgh, 15-20 May 1999), ACM Press, New York, 1999, pp. 426-433.

[13] Szekely, P.A., Sukaviriya, P.N., Castells, P., Muthukumarasamy, J., and Salcher, E., *Declarative Interface Models for User Interface Construction Tools: the MASTERMIND Approach*, in K. Unger, L. Bass (eds.), Proceedings of IFIP Working Conference on Engineering for Human-Computer Interaction EHCI'95 (Grand Targhee Resort, 14-18 August 1995), North Holland, Amsterdam, 1995, pp. 120-150.

[14] Vanderdonckt, J. and Berquin, P., *Towards a Very Large Model-based Approach for User Interface Development*, in N.W. Paton, T. Griffiths (eds.), Proc. of 1st Int. Work-

shop on User Interfaces to Data Intensive Systems UIDIS'99 (Edimburgh, 5-6 September 1999), IEEE Computer Society Press, Los Alamitos, 1999, pp. 76-85.

[15] Vanderdonckt, J., Limbourg, Q., and Florins, M., *Deriving the Navigational Structure of a User Interface*, in M. Rauterberg, M. Menozzi, J. Wesson (eds.), Proc. of 9th IFIP TC 13 Int. Conf. on Human-Computer Interaction INTERACT'2003 (Zurich, 1-5 September 2003), IOS Press, Amsterdam, 2003, pp. 455-462.

Chapter 9

TRANSFORMATIONAL DEVELOPMENT OF USER INTERFACES WITH GRAPH TRANS-FORMATIONS

Quentin Limbourg and Jean Vanderdonckt
IAG – School of Management, Université catholique de Louvain,
Place des Doyens 1 – B-1348 Louvain-la-Neuve (Belgium)
{limbourg,vanderdonckt}@isys.ucl.ac.be
URL : http://www.isys.ucl.ac.be/bchi/members/{qli.jva}
Tel : +32 10/47 {83 84, 85 25} – Fax : +32 10/47 83 24

Abstract   In software engineering transformational development aims at developing
software systems by transforming a coarse-grained specification to final code
(or to a detailed specification) through a sequence of small transformation
steps. Transformational development is known to bring benefits such as: cor-
rectness-preserving of the development cycle, explicit mappings between development steps, reusability and reversibility of transformations. No piece of
literature provides a systematic formal system applying transformational development to user interface engineering. To fill this gap, a methodology, called
TOMATO, is described in three facets: 1) A development cycle is defined to
outline possible transformations. 2) A language for supporting the methodology is presented relying on graph transformations, a mathematical system for
expressing specifications and transformation rules. 3) A tool implementation,
using a visual syntax, is illustrated.

Keywords: Forward engineering, Graph grammar, Graph theory, Mapping problem, Program transformation, Reverse engineering, Transformational approach.

1.   INTRODUCTION

A state of the art [18] in the field of engineering methods of user interface shows that no method provides an integrated view of the abstractions
needed to build a user interface along with an explicit mechanism to manipulate these abstractions throughout a development cycle. More specifically,
there is no general logical mechanism to incorporate and manipulate design
knowledge in user interface creation tools [2,13] nor any system for relating

107

R. Jacob et al. (eds.), Computer-Aided Design of User Interfaces IV, 107–120.

abstractions needed for this purpose. This problem has been referred to as the *mapping problem* by Puerta and Eisenstein in [16].

This paper addresses the lack of a disciplined and explicit mechanism for supporting user interface development in a transformational approach from early requirements to the final code. We draw the bases of such a mechanism along with the explicit definition of an algorithmic method able to perform automatically (or semi-automatically) the transformation of specification models.

A *UI specification model* consists in a series of representations (called *component models*) pertaining to various facets of the UI such as: user's task, domain objects, UI presentation and dialog, user's characteristics, computing platform, physical environment of interaction, etc [14,18]. A consistent effort has been done in the literature to integrate these specification models in an explicitly articulated and coherent manner. TOMATO methodology (standing for "formal meThOdology for MApping user interface specificaTiOn models) is composed of a development cycle and a language (Tomato-L). It is aimed at supporting transformational development of UIs. Within Tomato any UI artefact is internally represented by a set of models that are analyzable, editable, and processable by software means [14]. Each model is stored in a model repository in a UI specification language based on graph theory. This UI internal representation is then subject to production rules that progressively transform abstract concepts into concrete concepts so as to finally create a full description of a final UI [20]. Once this description is obtained, a rendering tool can be used to produce the running code. Such renderers have already been developed and discussed (www.uiml.org).This paper is focused on the transformation development that leads to the final description.

In the context of model-based development environments [18], at least four works can be cited: Mobi-D [13,14,15,16], Teallach [6], TIDE (www. uiml.org) and TERESA [12]. All these works represent significant attempts to incorporate design knowledge for a user interface design tool. The above tools are advanced in the sense that they support the explicit mappings between the different models, the different views, and steps of the method. In Tomato methodology, these mappings are not hand coded and built-in in the software. Rather, they are graphically expressed in the environment, which allows to exploit these mappings in a flexible way. With respect to the application of graph transformations to user interface development, two contributions can be mentioned: Freund *et al.* [5] and Sucrow [19]. Both approaches make an interesting use of graph transformations but have a too narrow conceptual coverage to address a fully defined UI development cycle.

The purpose of this paper is not to prove that a complete and consistent set of rules can be achieved to store a comprehensive part of design knowledge. Rather, it is intended to show how we can apply transformations from the abstract to the concrete domain in a seamless manner. The remainder of this paper is structured as follows: first, the transformation development life cycle supported by the Tomato methodology will be described. Then, the underlying language and its supporting tools are discussed. An example is presented to introduce the method. Finally, a related work section shows that this type of work remains unprecedented. The conclusion summarizes the main benefits of the approach, while contrasting with potential shortcomings.

2. TRANSFORMATIONAL DEVELOPMENT WITH TOMATO

2.1 Context and Aim

An example is herby exposed in order to better introduce TOMATO methodology. A simple scenario is proposed: a doctor at the hospital has to record information on her patient medical history. For this purpose, she has to input identity information, medical history i.e., general pathologies, heart pathologies, and other problems.

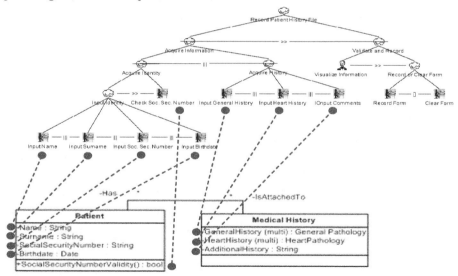

Figure 1. A Conceptual Model (Domain + Task).

Using TOMATO methodology, a developer may initiate the development by a conceptual schema expressing either domain concepts or a task specification or both. Fig. 1 shows a domain and task specification along with the mappings between both models. In this example, input tasks are mapped onto the attribute or the attribute set they are concerned with. Tasks involving a system function are mapped onto domain operations. Having this specification, the designer can pick up a derivation heuristic in a database and generate a detailed specification of the desired UI. The heuristics exploited in this example are listed in Fig. 2. These heuristics are expressed in natural language for the good comprehension of the example. The resulting specification is illustrated by Fig. 3.

Now the developer is told that her system is not suited for patients admitted through the emergency service. In this case a handheld platform has to be used. In consequence, the developer selects an appropriate derivation to transform the specification of the UI of Fig. 3 into a specification suited for a small display device. The resulting specification is illustrated by Fig. 4.

R0: generate a "main" window;
R1: for each multi-valued class attribute, generate a group box whose name is the name of the attribute;
R2: for each multi-valued class attribute whose domain is enumerated and is associated with a group box, generate a checkbox whose label is the label of the enumerated value;
R3: for each class attribute of type string and not multi-valued, generate a label and an input field whose, respectively, caption and name is the name of the attribute. The label and the input field being topologically bound together;
R4: for each attribute of type long string, generate a multiple line edit box;
R5 for each operation class, generate a button whose label is the name of the operation;
R6 (A and B) : each object belonging to a same window are placed following an order depending on the task they allow to accomplish.

Figure 2. Heuristic sample of the working example.

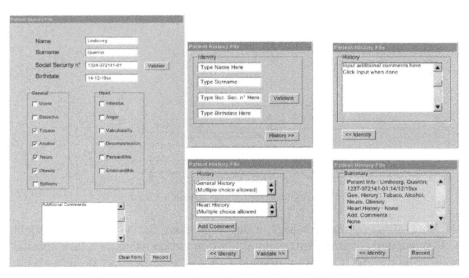

Figure 3. (Left) & 4 (Right) Recording Patient History File.

The initial specification has been split up into four smaller interaction spaces. Navigation between these interaction spaces has been automatically generated. Some widgets have been replaced by a degraded equivalent (e.g., a group of text boxes has been replaced by a multiple selection list box [22,23]). Because patient information is scattered between several interaction spaces so that the task of checking the information before recording the file can not be done appropriately, a summary interaction space in generated. This example shows a possible application of Tomato methodology. Next section exposes this methodology in a systematic way.

2.2   Development Cycle: TOMATO Cycle

Tomato cycle complies with transformational development theories. Transformational development can be viewed as a development process that takes as input a high level specification and produces as output a more concrete specification (i.e., implementation oriented) or an executable program. The transformation process itself takes the form of a sequence of small transformation steps. Each step preserves some desirable properties (e.g., correctness or consistency [9]).

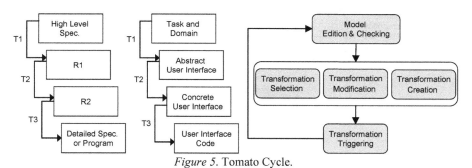

Figure 5. Tomato Cycle.

Fig. 5 illustrates the sequence of abstractions and designer's tasks to transform a high level specification into a refined specification through the following steps [3]: task and domain, abstract user interface, concrete user interface, and user interface code.

With such a transformational development, the role of the developer is very different from traditional approaches. In traditional approaches, the developer receives a specification, tries to fully understand it and implements what he has understood in a specific development environment. With transformational approaches [10], the developer receives a specification, tries to fully understand it, edits it, selects/modifies/creates an appropriate transformation and applies it to the initial specification in order to finally obtain a refined specification. Properties of the resulting model can then be checked against a set of rules expressing coherence or usability properties.

Regarding the role of the developer, three types of transformations can be identified [10]: manual transformations require intervention of the developer at each stage for choosing the appropriate transformation, semi-automatic transformation and fully automatic transformation. TOMATO cycle adopts a manual approach i.e., the developer builds the sequence of transformation himself. This is explained by the fact that transformations are heuristics. There is no single way to transform a task model into a presentation, or a presentation adapted to a large display to a presentation adapted to a small display, etc.

2.3   THE TOMATO-L

TOMATO-L is a language that enables the expression of concepts needed to build a user interface. TOMATO-L structure is defined in Fig. 6.

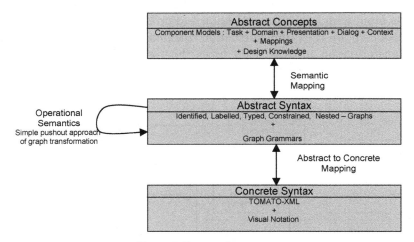

Figure 6. TOMATO Language.

2.3.1   Abstract Concepts

The *abstract concepts* we consider to formalise with graph structures consist in abstractions needed to build a UI in a model-driven approach [11]. It is impossible to list here all language elements. Nonetheless, these abstractions can be categorised into three main classes.

1. **Component models** partition concepts needed to construct a UI. Component models allow building several views on a UI. These views help to answer questions like: what tasks does my UI support? What objects does it manipulate? How does it look like? How does it behave? Component models have been listed in [14]. They consist in: (1) a *task model* represents a decomposition of user tasks in interaction with a system in order to reach a specific goal, (2) a *domain model* represents the concepts ma-

nipulated by the user while interacting with the system, (3) a *presentation model* consists in a specification of a hierarchy of graphical elements composing a UI along with their respective topological constraints, (4) a *dialog model* represents the dynamic aspects of a presentation model. Dialog modelling can concern different levels of granularity. We focus here on navigational aspects i.e., window transitions. 5) a *context model*. The context model essentially serves to describe in which conditions a specific UI specification is valid or not. It is beyond the scope of this paper to discuss extensively the context model. Schematically, our context model is composed of [3,12] (a) a user model describing the main characteristics of some user's users ? stereotypes (b) a platform model containing the description of hard- and soft- resources exploited to render a UI (c) an environment model describing environmental factors affecting the way users interact (noise or light level, stress conditions,…).

2. **Mappings** are relationships between component models [15,16]. These relationships are very interesting as they realize the integration of component models into one whole specification instead of having a collection of unrelated abstractions (this partly provides seamlessness to our method). Concretely, expressing mappings allows us to answer questions like: what objects do I need to accomplish this task? (task-domain mapping) What graphical objects support this task or represent this object? (<task, domain>-presentation mapping).

3. **Design Knowledge** is the knowledge that is put into practice while building a UI [13]. In our perspective, applying design knowledge means manipulating component models and mappings. Design knowledge allows answering questions like: what widgets are more appropriate to represent such domain object? How should I lay out objects into a container? Which navigation is preferred by a user stereotype? What kind of transition should I have between two windows? [24]. More detailed examples are provided in Section 2.4.

2.3.2   Abstract Syntax and Operational Semantics

The *abstract syntax* is defined as the hidden structure of a language, its mathematical background [9]. Our abstract syntax takes the form of a directed graph. A graph g is defined as a quadruple (V, E, source, target) such that (1) V is a finite set of vertices (2) E is a finite set of edges (3) source: E $\rightarrow$ V is an injective function assigning a source to each edge of E (4) target: E $\rightarrow$ V is an injective function assigning a target to each edge of E. To enable the expression of a specification model within a graph structure we *enrich* the initial definition of graph with several interesting features. Most important features are: (1) labelling: enables each edge or node to be labelled

(2) typing: enables edges and nodes to be classified into types (3) constraining: enables to attach to nodes and edges constraints of various types (e.g., cardinality constraint) (4) nesting: enables to nest a graph into another graph.

After expressing models, the abstract syntax of TOMATO-L expresses design knowledge via *graph grammars*. Graph grammars are set of rules, called *productions*. Productions aim, in this context, at transforming the graph representing UI artefacts. In order to transform graphs (i.e., UI artefact transformation), a grammar is applied to an initial graph, called *host graph* leading to a *resultant graph*. A resultant graph is said *final* if there is no more applicable production to this graph. It is said *intermediate* in the opposite case. The application of a production is called a *graph transformation step* [7], for short *a derivation*.

The *operational semantics* of a language describes the way an automaton (called interpreting automaton) transforms an input into an output [9]. The behaviour of the automaton for graph transformation depends on the chosen transformation technique. The technique used in this work is known as *Single PushOut approach* (SPO). It is illustrated in Fig. 7.

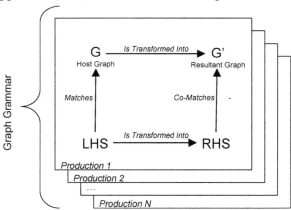

Figure 7. Production and Grammar in the Single Pushout Approach of Graph Transformation.

When a Left Hand Side (LHS) matches into a host graph G, it is replaced by a Right Hand Side (RHS). G is resultantly transformed into G'. All elements of G not covered by the match are considered as unchanged.

In order to achieve a better level of expression of productions, the mechanism of LHS match is complemented with 1) Positive Application Conditions (PAC), expressed as textual Boolean expressions on variables of the LHS and 2) Negative Application Conditions (NAC). A NAC is an additional condition to a production that contains a graph with which the host graph *must not* match with. In addition, several technical problems may arise while applying a grammar to a host graph e.g., conflicts between rules, occurrence of dangling edges or dependencies between rules leading to an indeterminable resultant graph. We deal with this problem by adopting a conservative and cautious approach by (1) identifying production conflicts a priori when possible, (2) erasing all dangling edges in resultant graphs, (3) constraining the application of productions to a specific order (programmed graph rewriting).

2.3.3   Concrete Syntax

The *concrete syntax* of a language is its external appearance. Tomato-L has two concrete syntaxes: (1) a graphical syntax which consists in the notation used in this paper. Its elements are just boxes, arrows and labels. The advantage with this notation is that it is visual. The disadvantage is that it can not, as is, be manipulated by an automaton (2) a textual syntax (called TOMATO-XML) of XML files is also provided.

Existing UI Description Languages (UIDLs) like XIML (http://www. ximl.org), UIML (http://www.uiml.org), and XHTML are limited to the expression of a concrete syntax. TOMATO concrete syntax is governed by an XML schema. It is logically derived from its abstract syntax as its structure is twofold: a set of nodes describing the elements populating the model at hand, a set of relationship describing the relationships between these different elements. An excerpt of an instance file in shown in Fig. 8.

2.4   TOOL IMPLEMENTATION

The principles exposed above could be put into practice in various programming environment enabling an easy expression and manipulation of graph structures (e.g., Prolog). An environment called AGG (Attributed Graph Grammars tool) is used for this experiment. AGG can be considered as a genuine programming environment based on graph transformations [7]. It provides:

1)   A programming language enabling the specification of graph grammars.

2)   A customisable interpreter enabling graph transformations. AGG was chosen because it allows the graphical expression of directed, typed and attributed graphs (for expressing specifications and rules). It has a powerful library containing notably algorithms for graph transformation [7], critical pair analysis, consistency checking, positive and negative application condition enforcement. AGG user interface is described in Fig. 8. Frame 1 is the grammar explorer. In Fig. 8, frames 2, 3 and 4 enable to specify sub-graphs composing a production: a negative application (frame 2), a left hand side (frame 3) and a right hand side (frame 4). The host graph on which a production will be applied is represented in Frame 5.

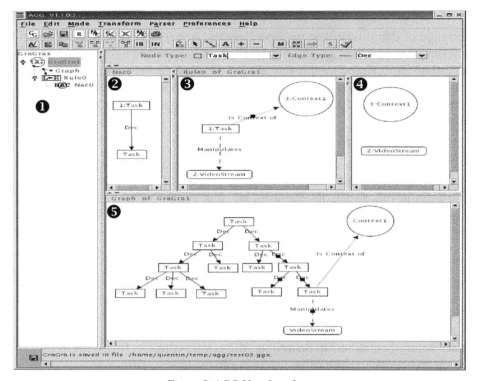

Figure 8. AGG User Interface.

Fig. 9 illustrates a rule used to perform the example exposed in section 2.1 (R1 in Fig. 2). It asserts that for every possible multi-valued attribute, a group box is generated. The group box's name is the name of its corresponding attribute. A negative application condition (left) avoids an infinite iteration of this rule. In order to ensure a possible manipulation of the output produced by AGG, an export function towards TOMATO textual syntax has been realised. An import function is currently under development.

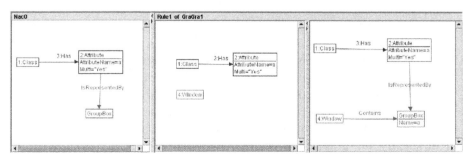

Figure 9. Composition of a rule: a NAC (left), a LHS (center), a RHS (right).

Experiments showed that AGG is a proper environment for defining and applying rules. Unfortunately, it shows poor in terms of usability for specifying large UI models. Indeed, it may appear somewhat abstract to the designer to describe a UI appearance with a set of nodes and relationships. An external tool for visually ("WYSIWYG" style) manipulating abstract and concrete UI models is under development in our lab. At this time, the tool allows specifying graphically a UI in terms of concrete widgets. A property sheet allows the detailed specification of the widget properties. The tool exports the specification of the created UI in a syntax that is compliant with Tomato concrete syntax. An import function, and consequently a rendering function, of Tomato concrete syntax are currently being developed. The main features of our tool experimentation can be summed up as follows.

1) A 'design editor' allows the creation and the consolidation of models exploited in the development process. A specific environment enables the design of UI appearance by direct manipulation of widgets.
2) A 'design derivator' enables the transformation of a model into another model.
3) A 'rule editor' enables the definition of new transformation rules.
4) A 'rule validator' enables the designer to identify conflicts within a set of rules. The critical pair analysis technique is used for this purpose.
5) A 'design analyser' enables the verification of desirable properties of the manipulated artefacts such as basic consistency rules, type checking or even usability properties (i.e., IFIP properties like reachability, browsability).

3. CONCLUSION

In this paper, a formal development methodology (Called TOMATO-M) enabling the construction of user interfaces through a set of transformations has been presented.

This methodology relies on: 1) the representation of manipulated abstractions with directed, labelled, attributed, and typed graphs. 2) the progressive transformation of higher level specification models to lower level specification code via the application of graph transformations 3) the expression of design knowledge with an explicit and developers accessible language.

The traditional role of the developer is challenged with TOMATO as it consists in 1) the expression of specification models under the form of graphs 2) the access, definition, extension, restriction, testing, verification and, ultimately, the application of appropriate transformations corresponding to design heuristics. The advantages of such a method can be summed up as follows:

- A *logical expression of design knowledge*: rather than having concepts of components models used in the process being hard coded and built-in within the design tools. All design rules, heuristics, algorithms can be expressed through productions that can be logically and mathematically defined.

- A *flexible production process*: productions can be gathered in graph grammars to be executed on graphs representing the starting models (e.g., task, domain, and user) to obtain the final models (e.g., presentation and dialog). This process is flexible in the sense that it can be controlled (forward, backward, and both) by the tool engine, thus providing developers with a great degree of freedom.

- A *reusable and combinable way of using design knowledge*: any form of design knowledge, once expressed in the Tomato language, can be reused at any time, can be refined when experience is growing, can be stopped when needed, and can be combined with other rules to obtain a more or less sophisticated production process. Using the same graph grammar also reinforces the consistency of produced results.

- A *visual and mathematical expression*: while the developer can graphically express productions in AGG tool, each production is stored as a graph transformation rule, a mathematically sound concept.

- A *coverage for many particular methods*: each method or tool typically promotes its particular process. As productions can be arranged in bidirectional ways and can start from any model, we believe that multiple entry points and top-down or bottom-up approaches can be supported. For example, linking and deriving rules from Teallach [6] can be expressed in TOMATO. Similarly, multiple UIs for multiple contexts of use could be obtained through different graph grammars.

On the other hand, preliminary results obtained with the TOMATO method revealed that some abstraction effort is required by the person who is responsible to incorporate the design knowledge. But once the designed knowledge is introduced into the tool it can be experimented with a limited experience of the language [21].

ACKNOWLEDGEMENTS

This work has been supported by the Cameleon research project (http://giove.cnuce.cnr.it/ cameleon.html) under the umbrella of the European Fifth Framework Programme (FP5-2000-IST2), which we gratefully acknowledge. This work gave birth to the USIXML language (User Interface eXtensible Markup Language – www.usixml.org) that is used across the members of the Cameleon project. The authors would like to thank Cameleon partners who contributed to V1.2 of USIXML: Lionel Balme, Gaëlle Calvary, Cristina Chesta, Alexandre Demeure, Joëlle Coutaz, Jean-Thierry Lechein, Fabio Paternò, Stéphane Raymond, Carmen Santoro, and Youri Vanden Berghe. This paper is related to USIXML V1.4, an extension of USIXML V1.2 with dialog model, more inter-model mappings, a context model made up of user, platform, and environment, and the concrete user interface level.

REFERENCES

[1] Baresi, L. and Heckel R., *Tutorial Notes on Foundations and Applications of Graph Transformation, an Introduction From a Software Engineering Perspective*, in Proceedings of 1st Int. Conference on Graph Transformation, ICGT'02 (Barcelona, 7-12 September 2002), Springer-Verlag, Berlin, 2002, pp. 402-429, accessible at http://link.springer.de/link/service/series/0558/bibs/2505/25050402.htm

[2] Brown J., *Exploring Human-Computer Interaction and Software Engineering Methodologies for the Creation of Interactive Software*, SIGCHI Bulletin, Vol. 29, No. 1, January 1997, pp. 32-35.

[3] Calvary, G., Coutaz, J., Thevenin, D., Limbourg, Q., Bouillon, L., and Vanderdonckt, J., *A Unifying Reference Framework for Multi-Target User Interfaces*, Interacting with Computers, Vol. 15, No. 3, June 2003, pp. 289-308.

[4] Engels, G. and Schürr, A., *Encapsulated Hierarchical Graphs, Graph Types and Meta Types,* in Proceedings of Joint Compugraph/Semagraph Workshop on Graph Rewriting and Computation, Electronic Notes in Theoretical Computer Science SEGRAGRA'95 (Volterra, 28 August-1 September 1995), Vol. 2, July 1995.

[5] Freund, R., Haberstroh, B., and Stary, C., *Applying Graph Grammars for Task-Oriented User Interface Development*, in Proceedings of International Conference on Computing and Information ICCI'1992 (Toronto, Ontario, 28-30 May 1992), IEEE Computer Society Press, Los Alamitos, 1992, pp.389-392.

[6] Griffiths, T., Barclay, P., Paton, N.W., McKirdy, J., Kennedy, J., Gray, P.D., Cooper, R., Goble, C., and Pinheiro da Silva, P., *Teallach: A Model-Based User Interface Development Environment for Object Databases*, Interacting with Computers, Vol. 14, No. 1, 1 December 2001, pp. 31-68.

[7] Ehrig, H., Engels, G., Kreowski, H-J., and Rozenberg, G., *Handbook of Graph Grammars and Computing by Graph Transformation*, Applications, Languages and Tools, Vol. 2, World Scientific, Singapore, 1999.

[8] Mens, T., *Conditional Graph Rewriting as a Domain-Independent Formalism for Software Evolution,* in Proc. of International Conf. Applications of Graph Transformations with Industrial Relevance AGTIVE'1999 (Kerkrade, 1-3 September 1999), Lecture Notes in Computer Science, Vol. 1779, Springer-Verlag, Berlin, 2000, pp. 127-143.

[9] Meyer, B., *Introduction to the Theory of Programming Languages*, Prentice Hall, New York, 1990.

[10] Partsch, H., and Steinbruggen, R., *Program Transformation Systems*, ACM Computing Surveys, Vol. 15, No. 3, September 1983, pp. 199-236.

[11] Paternò, F., *Model-Based Design and Evaluation of Interactive Applications*, Springer-Verlag, Berlin, 2000.

[12] Paternò, F., and Santoro, C., *One Model, Many Interfaces*, in Proceedings of 4th International Conference on Computer-Aided Design of User Interfaces CADUI'2002 (Valenciennes, 15-17 May 2002), Kluwer Academics Publishers, Dordrecht, 2002, pp. 143-154

[13] Puerta, A.R., and Maulsby, D., *Management of Interface Design Knowledge with MOBI-D*, in Proc. of 2nd ACM International Conference on Intelligent User Interfaces IUI'97 (Orlando, 6-9 January 1997), ACM Press, New York, 1997, pp. 249-252.

[14] Puerta, A.R., *A Model-Based Interface Development Environment*, IEEE Software, Vol. 14, No. 4, July-August 1997, pp. 41-47

[15] Puerta, A.R. and Eisenstein, J., *Interactively Mapping Task Models to Interfaces in MOBI-D*, in Proceedings of 5th International Eurographics Workshop on Design, Specification and Verification of Interactive Systems DSV-IS'98 (Abingdon, 3-5 June 1998), Springer-Verlag, Vienna, 1998, pp. 261-273.

[16] Puerta, A. and Eisenstein, J., *Towards a General Computational Framework for Model-Based Interface Development Systems Model-Based Interfaces*, in Proc. of ACM International Conference on Intelligent User Interfaces IUI'99 (Los Angeles, 5-8 January 1999), ACM Press, New York, 1999, pp. 171-178.

[17] Rozenberg, G., *Handbook of Graph Grammars and Computing by Graph Transformation*, Foundations, Vol. 1, World Scientific, Singapore, 1999.

[18] Szekely, P., *Retrospective and Challenges for Model-Based Interface Development*, in Proc. of 2nd International Workshop on Computer-Aided Design of User Interfaces CADUI'96 (Namur, 5-7 June 1996), Presses Universitaires de Namur, Namur, 1996, pp.1-27.

[19] Sucrow, B., *On Integrating Software-Ergonomic Aspects in the Specification Process of Graphical User Interfaces*, Transactions of the SDPS Journal of Integrated Design & Process Science, Vol. 2, No. 2, June 1998, pp. 32-42.

[20] Vanderdonckt, J. and Bodart, F., *Encapsulating Knowledge for Intelligent Automatic Interaction Objects Selection*, in Proc. of the ACM Conf. on Human Factors in Computing Systems INTERCHI'93 (Amsterdam, 24-29 avril 1993), ACM Press, New York, 1993, pp. 424-429.

[21] Vanderdonckt, J., *Assisting Designers in Developing Interactive Business Oriented Applications*, in H.-J. Bullinger & J. Ziegler (eds.), Proceedings of 8th International Conference on Human-Computer Interaction of HCI International'99 (Munich, 22-26 August 1999), Ergonomics and User Interfaces, Vol. 1, Lawrence Erlbaum Associated Pub., Mahwah, 1999, pp. 1043-1047.

[22] Vanderdonckt, J., *Advice-Giving Systems for Selecting Interaction Objects*, in N.W. Paton & T. Griffiths (eds.), Proceedings of 1st Int. Workshop on User Interfaces to Data Intensive Systems UIDIS'99 (Edinburgh, 5-6 September 1999), IEEE Computer Society Press, Los Alamitos, 1999, pp. 152-157.

[23] Vanderdonckt, J. and Berquin, P., *Towards a Very Large Model-based Approach for User Interface Development*, in N.W. Paton & T. Griffiths (eds.), Proc. of 1st International Workshop on User Interfaces to Data Intensive Systems UIDIS'99 (Edimburgh, 5-6 September 1999), , IEEE Computer Society Press, Los Alamitos, 1999, pp. 76-85.

[24] Vanderdonckt, J., Limbourg, Q., and Florins, M., *Deriving the Navigational Structure of a User Interface*, in M. Rauterberg, M. Menozzi, J. Wesson (eds.), Proc. of 9th IFIP TC 13 Int. Conf. on Human-Computer Interaction INTERACT'2003 (Zurich, 1-5 September 2003), IOS Press, Amsterdam, 2003, pp. 455-462.

Chapter 10

A DISTRIBUTED USAGE MONITORING SYSTEM

Philip Gray[1], Iain McLeod[1], Steve Draper[2], Murray Crease[3], and Richard Thomas[4]

[1]*Computing Science Department, University of Glasgow,*
17 Lilybank Gardens – Glasgow G12 8QQ (Scotland)
E-mail: {pdg,mcleodia}@dcs.gla.ac.uk
URL: http://www.dcs.gla.ac.uk/~pdg –
http://www.dcs.gla.ac.uk/contacts/searchresults.cfm?rowid=362
Tel: +44 141 330 {4933, 4256} – Fax: +44 141 330 4913
[2]*Psychology Department, University of Glasgow,*
58 Hillhead Street – Glasgow G12 8QB (Scotland)
E-mail: s.draper@psy.gla.ac.uk
URL: http://www.psy.gla.ac.uk/~steve/
Tel: +44 141 330 4961 – Fax: +44 141 330 5086
[3]*NRC-IIT e-Business, 46 Dineen Drive, Fredericton – New Brunswick E3B 9W4 (Canada)*
E-mail: murray.crease@nrc-cnrc.gc.ca
URL: http://iit-iti.nrc-cnrc.gc.ca/personnel/crease_murray_e.html
Tel: +1 506 444 0496 – Fax: +1 506 444 6114
[4]*Computer Science & Software Engineering, The University of Western Australia,*
35 Stirling Highway – Crawley 6009 (Australia)
E-mail: rct@csse.uwa.edu.au
URL: http://www.cs.uwa.edu.au/~richard
Tel: +61 8 9380 2733 – Fax: + 61 8 9380 1089

Abstract   We are developing a distributed computer system that supports usability and interaction studies, by handling the collection, storage and analysis of usage data, such as that generated by user-computer interaction and associated sensing devices (e.g., cameras). Data sources may be distributed as may be the data repositories and data consumers (other computer processes and human investigators). The system supports dynamic configuration of the entire process, including changes in the goals of the investigation itself. In this paper we describe the system's key features, including a generic and evolvable data transport and processing network, a set of tools for capturing and cleaning usage data, a tool for instrumenting software for data capture, and a system for managing the entire process. We also report on several trials of the system, identifying successes, failures, lessons learned and areas for future development.

Keywords: Usability testing tools, Usage monitoring.

121

R. Jacob et al. (eds.), Computer-Aided Design of User Interfaces IV, 121–132.
© 2005 *Kluwer Academic Publishers. Printed in the Netherlands.*

1.   INTRODUCTION

Usage data is central to investigative activities in a number of domains, including usability testing and educational research. In these studies data is taken primarily from events generated by user manipulation of keyboards, mice and other computer input devices, along with other observational data, such as screen dumps and images or video streams from cameras. Although there are a number of software tools that support the capture, storage and analysis of such data, it remains difficult to manage such usage data, especially when the data is being collected from a number of machines, perhaps distributed over a large area and the analysis is being carried out by a number of researchers remotely from the data collection.

The Grumps Project at the University of Glasgow has been developing a set of software tools to address the opportunities and challenges of distributed usage monitoring, especially in the case of exploratory studies that do not have clearly defined and unchanging initial hypotheses and assumptions. We call studies of this type *REDDIs: Rapidly Evolving Data Driven Investigations* [9]. Rather than focusing on a static set of fixed data sources such as log files, it focuses on explorations by an investigator where the question evolves as much as the answer, as in data mining. The findings are as likely to be an unanticipated pattern in the data as a specific answer to a defined question. Calling them 'investigations' rather than 'experiments' highlights the fact that they may or may not have a prior hypothesis, let alone manipulate the circumstances being studied. These investigations depend upon data, and the possibility of collecting it easily (as opposed to using other methods, such as surveying human users); they are as much about what it is possible to learn from these sources as about answering prior questions. To call them "data driven" is to further emphasise their orientation to a particular technical opportunity. On the other hand, and in contrast to their log file precursors and to data mining, the possibility is now emerging of changing or post-processing the data collected rapidly, in response to new interests, guesses, and hypotheses of the investigator; hence they are potentially "rapidly evolving", and so also not simply passive, post hoc, archaeological analyses of what comes to hand.

This paper describes the Grumps software framework designed to support REDDIs and the current tools that reside in that framework, for software instrumentation, event capture, event transport, processing and storage, and data preparation and analysis. Section 2 describes the key features of our approach to supporting usage monitoring. Section 3 surveys the framework and tools. Section 4 discusses the results of some early evaluations of our prototypes, while Section 5 looks at some related work. The paper concludes with a consideration of future directions for our work.

2.   THE GRUMPS APPROACH

In the Grumps Project we have begun to develop a model of usage-based studies. At a high level of abstraction, such studies can be represented by the diagram in Fig. 1.

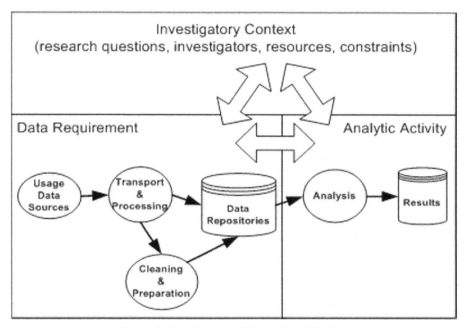

Figure 1. Key Aspects of Usage-Based Studies.

The three key constituent aspects of a usage-based study are:
- **Investigatory context.** This includes the investigation goals or research questions, the investigators, the resources (subjects, machines, time, money) and constraints that motivate and drive the rest of the investigation effort.
- **Data requirement.** This describes the sources of raw usage data and other related data, the process of preparing it for study and the mechanisms for communicating it and storing it as necessary.
- **Analytic activity.** The activity that relates data to investigation goals, by finding relevant patterns, correlations, etc.

The relationship of these three aspects – the ways in which they influence or determine aspects of one another – depends on the type of investigation. Thus, in the case of formal, hypothesis-driven experiments, the investigation goals determine a fixed formulation of the analytic activity (the experimental plan) and the data requirement is derived from that. In the case of most data mining, the analysis and investigatory contexts cause changes in one another, but typically there is no change to the data collection. However, in the case of REDDIs, it is possible to start with any aspect of the investigation and derive the other aspects as needed. Furthermore, in the course of the investigation, the aspects may change; for example, a usage monitoring opportunity may arise that stimulates research questions, leading to analysis that generates new questions which in turn require new data to be gathered, perhaps of a new form.

The Grumps software framework, designed to support both experiments and REDDIs, is a dynamically configurable system that implements the data requirement aspect. The key features of our system are:

- **Generic.** The system is not restricted to any predetermined set of data sources. It can handle any source of usage data, direct (e.g., keystroke logs) and indirect (camera output), even including the results of think-aloud protocol collection, as long as that data can be described in our simple usage data model (Section 3.1.1) .
- **Fundamentally distributed.** Subject to security access, the sources of data can located anywhere, and the data processors and consumers can be anywhere (Section 3.1.2).
- **Component-based.** A Grumps Usage Data System consists of a set of dynamically deployable components including data sources (event generators), data sinks (file archives or databases), routing components and data processors (filters, abstractors, aggregators). The components can be modified through run-time change of parameters as well as by dynamic replacement (Section 3.1.2).
- **Heterarchic.** It is possible to use (some) Grumps tools usefully in a stand-alone mode, but also integrated piece-wise fashion, starting from any point in the usage data handling process.

3.   THE GRUMPS SOFTWARE FRAMEWORK

3.1   Support for Data Capture and Transport

3.1.1   Modelling Usage Data

Grumps usage data can be created by a number of different devices or processes. Raw usage data, which is the output from data capture devices, therefore, has a simple and flexible structure, to accommodate the variety of data being collected and the need to modify it easily into other forms. Raw usage data is organized into distinct sequences of usage events, called sessions. A session is a collection of usage events organized around an application-significant grouping of usage events. For example, it might be all the events collected from a user-computer interaction from login to logout of a single user. A session is currently defined as follows:

```
Raw usage session = <session_id, start_time, end_time,
    user_id, machine_id, exit_reason>
```

Events belonging to a usage session are currently defined as follows:

```
Usage action event = <action_id, session_id, time-
    stamp, type, body>
```

Session and action ids are unique identifiers for the data items. Timestamps provide a way of ordering the events. The body holds variant fields determined by the nature of the collection device and its configuration. These current definitions and indeed our modelling of usage data in general is still the subject of ongoing work (Sections 4 and 6).

Examples of a typical instance of a session and a usage action event within that session are given in Table 1. This data comes from a relational database storing the results of one of our ongoing field trials. This study is further discussed in Section 4.1.

Table 1. Session and event within a session, as logged in a repository.

SessionID	StartTime	EndTime	UserID	MachineID	UARExitReason
5253	1045142859063	1045144730173	87858268	bo715-11-02	User Logged Out

ActionID	Session	Time	Body	Type
1251079	5253	1045143002268	`<p>adagide.exe</p>` `<wl>58</wl>` `<wt>62</wt> <wr>806</wr>` `<wb>568</wb> <ws>nor</ws>`	9

Note that the event record stores an XML representation of keystroke data generated by an operating system monitor process. Event type is sometimes inferrable from the body, but not in the general case (e.g., the body might be a pixmap generated by a camera). In addition, explicitly including the event type helps tools that behave differently based on the event type.

3.1.2   Data Transport and Processing

Usage data is handled by a network of data processing components. See Fig. 2. These components are known as GRUMPS Units (or GUs) and connected in a graph, called a GRUMPSNet [2]. Each GU receives data in the form of events, optionally transforms these events (for example compresses them or combines events from multiple sources), and passes them to other GUs in the network. This decouples each step in the data pipeline, facilitating dynamic reconfiguration of the GrumpsNet in response to changes in investigatory context, data requirements or analytic activity.

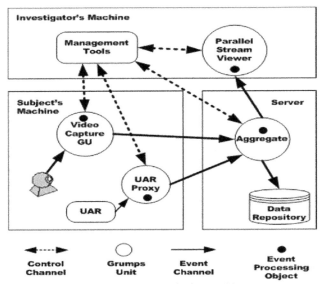

Figure 2. An example GrumpsNet.

Fig. 2 illustrates a hypothetical GrumpsNet that can be used to support many usability studies combining data captured about user activity (via the UAR component, Section 3.1.2) and images of the user captured via a webcam. The data from these two sources is then combined by connecting them to the aggregator GU. The aggregator generates "super sessions" that associates sessions from the two separate streams of captured data, thus creating an association between the streams. The aggregator's output is sent to a parallel stream viewer GU that displays the output to an investigator in real-time. Note that the output of the aggregator is also sent to one or more data repositories. For clarity, this is not shown, but it could be done through an XML-to-SQL transformation GU.

Dynamic configuration and reconfiguration of a GRUMPSNet is done through Control Events. A Control Event contains code which can be sent to a GU and executed remotely. Values can also be returned via reply events. In this way, components of the network can be connected to or disconnected from each other, or even replaced altogether by components with different functionality. A GU can also be interrogated via standard control events to bind, unbind, edit and discover properties at runtime. These properties contain information about the current state of the GU – by registering remote listeners on the properties, other parts of the network can keep track of the state of a GU and even veto changes. For example, our data collection network in Fig. 2 could be reconfigured to add a GU between the two sources and the aggregator that controls the sources, switching off video collection during a period with no user activity.

3.1.3   Data Production

We have produced several different data capture devices that can be connected to a GrumpsNet. These include:

- **User Action Recorder.** This is a tool, written in C++, that registers with operating system hooks in Microsoft Windows and captures keystrokes, window focus and mouse events. To provide user privacy, it can be configured to provide various levels of obfuscation of user data (e.g., replacing specific characters by a single generic alphanumeric character).
- **Specially instrumented Java applications.** We have developed a system, iGuess [8], that allows the customizable instrumentation of an executable Java application (no source code is needed), inserting a Grumps Unit into the instrumented application.
- **Independent applications.** We have constructed a Grumps Unit tailored for the capture of images from a webcam.

In general data sources constructed via any of these three methods can provide three levels of increasing power, depending on their conformance with the Grumps data and control models. At the lowest level, any component that can produce data (e.g., write data to a file) is a potential Grumps data source. Clearly, in this case the data format may limit the utility of the usage data, since it does not conform to the Grumps schema and thus may be inappropriate for some uses. Sources that produce data conforming to the Grumps schema, on the other hand, can be processed using our set of data cleaning, preparation and analysis tools (Section 3.2). Finally, data sources that offer a control interface can be dynamically configured at run-time as well, providing the maximum level of Grumps functionality.

3.2   Support for Data Preparation and Analysis

Once collected data must be cleaned, transformed to make it amenable for analysis and subjected to additional processing to extract information (e.g., statistical analysis). In the Grumps framework these operations can be performed:

- By Grumps components in the network, e.g., prior to storage in a repository, filtering, abstraction, aggregation, etc.
- As relational operations on database tables.
- Via processing using other general and special purpose utilities.

As part of field trials (Section 4.1) we have constructed a number of useful general purpose data preparation routines, packaged as T-SQL stored procedures. We have also built a viewer for parallel data streams, useful for visualising heterogeneous sequential data.

4.   EARLY USES OF THE FRAMEWORK

4.1   Evaluation and Field Trials

We have tested components of the Grumps framework in several settings, including:
1. Two data capture episodes involving a first year undergraduate university programming laboratory; a third has now been running for 6 weeks.
2. A study of the effects of interruption on user behaviour.
3. A study of the "Think Aloud Screen" at Simula Labs in Norway [6].

These studies have been quite different, enabling us to examine issues arising from the range of usage-based studies, including:
- **Data capture constraints.** The programming study had strong security and engineering constraints. The data had to be anonymised at source and had to run with minimal disruption to network and users.
- **Scale.** The two programming lab studies were carried out over several months, the second collecting over four million actions from 141 students. The study at Simula involved about 50 users over several sessions. The interruption study, on the other hand, is collecting data in 1 week sets from a total of four users.
- **Collaboration.** The programming lab study involved several concurrent investigations involving different researchers located in the UK and Australia. The Norwegian study and the Interruption study have single investigations.
- **Investigation Type.** The studies have ranged from highly exploratory studies to well-defined experiments. Thomas *et al.* [9] presents a brief account of the use of the Grumps system in of the programming laboratory studies, identifying issues of data capture, transport, cleaning, preparation and analysis.

4.2   Lessons Learned

While we anticipated that the support of REDDIs would demand a high degree of flexibility across every aspect of data collection, storage and processing, we have found flexibility to be important for other reasons, too.

GrumpsNet, due to its component based nature, affords many different connection methods. For example, "GrumpsNet Lite", a version of Grumps-Net uses local caching of events in files in transport rather than direct streaming of events across the network. This proved to be useful in the programming lab studies, reducing network traffic during peak times. Its simplicity also appealed to the network administrative staff who were understandably concerned to run a system with a high degree of robustness and reliability and a minimum impact on other processes.

In order to support different data sources, low-cost exploration of different questions and the sharing of data between investigations, we have found it important to keep the original raw data in a form that has minimal fixed attributes. XML has proved useful as a representation for the variant part of the data, since it is easy to transform into other formats via XSL, e.g. SQL for storage, SMIL for visualisation, HTML for printing.

We have found that there are important and costly demands and constraints on individual studies that have emphasized the importance of configurability. For example, some studies require heavyweight anonymisation and data access controls that prevent subjects from viewing usage data temporarily stored on their machines. For other investigations, such features are only an impediment to efficient research activity and are not needed. A framework like Grumps should make it possible to customise such facilities with minimum impact on the rest of the usage monitoring system.

Raw usage is fundamentally temporal and thus sequential. This has implications for the way the data is modelled and handled. In many cases it is important to have direct sequence information, independent of timestamp, both for efficiency in performing sequencing operations (e.g., over millions of events) and for checking that no events have been lost (e.g., dropped video frames due to an unreliable network connection). Synchronisation of events from independent data sources remains an area for further work.

Complicated investigations can involve a large number of concurrent data sources, a complicated transport network, considerable data cleaning and data preparation for analysis. This results in many intermediate files and database tables, not to mention a range of subsequent complex analyses, again requiring intermediate results to be stored. All of this complexity can place severe management demands on investigators. Particularly in the programming lab studies we have become aware of the importance of higher-level investigation management support and the need for reusable representations and packaged processing routines. Handling intermediate processing has become a key bottleneck in the process and is now a major focus of our attention for future development.

5.   RELATED WORK

There are many existing systems that support usage-based studies, including commercial products and research systems. These range from built-in logging facilities, like those in the BlueJ programming environment [7] through web testing systems such as WebQuilt [5] to full-featured human behaviour experimentation environments like those from Noldus (www. noldus.com). Such systems, where loggable events are determined by what is exposed by the system or related medium (e.g., http requests), can be efficient, but its value depends on the match to monitoring needs. Thus, a system that records interactions only at the command level can miss important information (e.g., whether the command is invoked via menu, accelerator or toolbar), while logging at too low a level of abstraction can generate too much data. The Grumps system makes it possible to tailor the level of abstraction to the requirements of the problem. This was used successfully in our programming lab studies when, for the second study, specialised command logging was added to the programming environment [9].

The KALDI system [1] provides integration of data capture, transport and analysis. However, it has opted to capture usage data via one approach, viz., specialising the Java windowing classes. This restricts the genericity of the system compared to Grumps.

Hilbert and Redmiles' internet-based usage data capture system [4] provides powerful distributed transport of events and is designed to deal with the problems of scale arising from large-scale usage studies. However, their code instrumentation approach requires modification of source code.

The Grumps data transport system is similar to DataGrid [3] which uses a dataflow graph to represent the processing of data for experimental purposes. In DataGrid, processing is specified in a language that can be used to construct and configure the data processing. We have not yet done this in Grumps, although it should be feasible given the dynamic configurability of the GrumpsNet infrastructure (Section 6 below).

6.   CONCLUSIONS AND FUTURE WORK

The Grumps Usage Monitoring System offers a generic approach to the support of both experiment and exploratory studies of human-computer interaction. It is scalable, dynamically configurable and able to support the evolution of a study as findings generate new research and evaluation questions.

Although we have built and developed a working prototype and learned from its deployment in real trials of different kinds, there remains much to be done to achieve our aims. A key requirement, that we are tackling at the moment, is description languages for all three aspects of an investigation. In particular we need to be able to describe all potential data that can flow through a GrumpsNet plus the capture, transport and processing of the data performed by the network. Specifications in this language can be generated by tools like iGuess and used to create a GrumpsNet and to control its operation at runtime; the specifications can also be used to describe tracked changes in the system. These descriptions might also be reused between studies, forming investigatory patterns.

The current set of Grumps data preparation tools have not been fully integrated into GrumpsNet. In particular, we have not addressed the question of tool support for constructing *sequences* of these operations using higher level descriptions so that we can replace one implementation (e.g., a database macro) with another (e.g., a special purpose grumps component). This will be a key requirement for the GrumpsNet modelling language. Also, iGuess, our code instrumentation system, is limited to Java at present. However, the same approach is applicable to any bytecode-based language, e.g., C#. We intend to extend iGuess to handle this and possibly other languages, as opportunities allow.

ACKNOWLEDGEMENTS

This work was funded by EPSRC Grant GR/N38114. We wish to thank Malcolm Atkinson, Margaret Brown, Quintin Cutts, Huw Evans, Gregor Kennedy, Rebecca Mancy and Karen Renaud, who have all contributed to the work described in this paper.

REFERENCES

[1] Al-Qaimari, G. and McRostie, D., *KALDI: A Computer-Aided Usability Engineering Tool for Supporting Testing and Analysis of User Performance,* in Blandford, A., Vanderdonckt, J., Gray, Ph. (Eds.), *Interactions sans frontières – Interactions without frontiers,* Proceedings of the Joint AFIHM-BCS Conf. on Human-Computer Interaction IHM-HCI'2001 (Lille, 10-14 September 2001), Vol. I, Springer-Verlag, London, 2001, pp. 153-169.

[2] Evans, H., Atkinson, M., Brown, M., Cargill, J., Crease, M., Draper, S., Gray, P.D., and Thomas, R.C., *The Pervasiveness of Evolution in GRUMPS Software,* Software: Practice and Experience, Vol. 33, No. 2, February 2003, pp. 99-120.

[3] Foster, I., Vöckler, J., Wilde, M. and Zhao, Y., *The Virtual Data Grid: A New Model and Architecture for Data-Intensive Collaboration,* in Proceedings of 1st Biennial Conference on Innovative Data Systems Research CIDR'2003 (Asilomar, 5-8 January 2003), accessible at http://citeseer.nj.nec.com/554758.html

[4] Hilbert, D.M. and Redmiles D.F., *Extracting Usability Information from User Interface Events,* ACM Computing Surveys, Vol. 32, No. 4, December 2000, pp. 384-421.

[5] Hong, J.I., Heer, J., Waterson, S., and Landay, J.A., *WebQuilt: A Proxy-based Approach to Remote Web Usability Testing,* ACM Transactions on Office Information Systems, Vol. 19, No. 3, July 2001, pp. 263-285, accessible at http://citeseer.nj.nec.com/454004.html.

[6] Karahasanovic, A., Anda, B., Arisholm, E., Hove, S.E., Jørgensen, M., and Sjøberg, D., *A Think-Aloud Support Tool for Collecting Feedback in Large-Scale Software Engineering Experiments*, Simula Research Laboratory Technical Report 2003-7, 2003, accessible at http://www.simula.no/publication_one.php?publication_id=603.

[7] Kölling, M., Quig, B., Patterson, A., and Rosenberg, J., *The BlueJ System and its Pedagogy*, The Journal of Computer Science Education, Special Issue on Learning and Teaching Object Technology, Vol. 13, No. 4, December 2003, pp. 249-268.

[8] Mcleod, I.A., *IGUESS: Instrumentation of Bytecode in the Production of Grumps Event Sources*, B.Sc. thesis, University of Glasgow, Glasgow, 2003.

[9] Thomas, R.C., Kennedy, G.E., Mancy, R., Crease, M., Draper, S., Evans, H., and Gray, P.D., *Generic Usage Monitoring of Programming Students*, in Proc. of Australian Society for Computers in Learning in Tertiary Education ASCILITE'2003 (Adelaide, 7-10 December 2003), The University of Adelaide, Adelaide, 2003.

Chapter 11

DIALOGUE-BASED DESIGN OF WEB USABILITY QUESTIONNAIRES USING ONTOLOGIES

Elena García Barriocanal, Miguel A. Sicilia Urbán, León González, and José R. Hilera
Computer Science Department, Polytechnic School, University of Alcalá,
Ctra. Barcelona, km. 33.6; 28871, Alcalá de Henares, Madrid (Spain)
{elena.garciab, msicilia, leon.gonzalez, jose.hilera}@uah.es
Tel:+34 91 885 66 63 - Fax: +91 885 66 46

Abstract   Questionnaires are nowadays widely used usability evaluation instruments, and several generic usability questionnaires are available. But these generic artefacts are not always appropriate to evaluate a given setting, and constructing a questionnaire from scratch is a complex task requiring both expertise and resources, so that discount-usability approaches to questionnaire-based evaluation can make a good option in many cases. In this work, a novel knowledge-based approach to design Web usability questionnaires is described. The questionnaire model comprises different ontologies including concepts regarding questions and questionnaires, the different measures that can be obtained and the tasks that have to be carried out by users in order to evaluate a specific kind of Web application. As a proof of concept for the model, a prototype questionnaire design application is also described. The application demonstrates how facts can be gathered through a guided dialogue with the user, and how the system can use this information to tailor the resulting questionnaire to the concrete situation.

Keywords: Computer-aided questionnaire design, Ontologies, Usability evaluation, Usability questionnaire.

1. INTRODUCTION

Usability can be defined as the capability of the software product to be understood, learned, used and attractive to the user, when used under specified conditions [15]. Developing usable Web applications entails significant costs, since usability must be considered in all the phases of the development

R. Jacob et al. (eds.), Computer-Aided Design of User Interfaces IV, 133–146.
© 2005 *Kluwer Academic Publishers. Printed in the Netherlands.*

life cycle [18], including evaluations at different process stages. Evaluations can be carried out using different methods, like testing, inspection or inquiry, which in turn comprise different techniques, like user testing [8], heuristic methods [21] and questionnaires [23], respectively. In this work, we focus on the use of questionnaires as a usability evaluation technique. Questionnaires can be used not only to collect factual information about users, but to obtain their likes, dislikes, needs, and understandings of the system by asking them about some concrete interface aspects. Questionnaires are widely used instruments in usability evaluation for many reasons, e.g. they are reusable, they can be used remotely, and they are a convenient vehicle for massive administration and so on. But the correct construction and configuration of a questionnaire may increase evaluation costs in terms of time and resources, because previous experience is needed in order to develop an appropriate questionnaire with a minimum figure of validity and reliability. If the questionnaire is not well-designed, biased results will be obtained, because it would not collect data about what testers really want to measure. Nonetheless, as pointed out by Brooke [4], the use of "quick and dirty" questionnaires – i.e. with no demonstrated validity and reliability –, is justified to allow low-cost assessments of usability in the evaluation of industrial systems. Several existing predefined questionnaires with good scores in validity and reliability measures can be used for that purpose, e.g., QUIS [14] or WAMMI [16], but they are not always directly applicable. Depending on the application domain, these questionnaires may not cover all the desirable aspects that must be evaluated, as occurs in educational Web applications, where a very specific set of parameters must be taken into account to obtain useful measures [6]. This fact points out to the necessity of constructing some kind of questionnaire-tailoring tools that could be used as "discount-usability" artefacts [22]. As a matter of fact, some tools that allow the construction of generic questionnaires are available, but very few ones are concerned with the specifics of usability evaluation. An exception is Perlman's user interface questionnaire page (http://www.acm.org/perlman/question. html), a Web-based tool that reads questionnaires and options from files and form data, administers a questionnaire, and e-mails data to the administrator. However, this system has limited applicability, since it's based on a generic, predefined questionnaire, and it does not provide guidance for the evaluators in the definition of the tasks that participants would have to perform to carry out the evaluation.

In this paper, we approach a computer-aided design process of usability questionnaires using a logic-based knowledge representation, in an attempt to overcome the just described limitations. Concretely, we use ontologies to represent both the concepts and the concrete information surrounding the design of a usability questionnaire. The integration and use of ontologies provides design flexibility, enables the sharing of conceptual and factual structures, and constitutes a sound basis for reasoning [19]. The design process is intended for novice users or projects lacking resources, so that it can be considered a "discount usability" approach [22], as previously mentioned. Ontologies have already been applied in Web application development, as in [1], where learning systems are designed taking into account a multi-layer authoring task conceptualization, or IIPS [17], an intelligent system which is aimed at building and maintaining data-intensive Web sites using both interface and domain ontologies. In the usability area some ontological modelling representation techniques exist, like OSM [2] which provides a structured but informal representation of the ontology of a system, forming a basis for usability assessment. But the issue of questionnaire design have not been addressed yet in any of these efforts.

The rest of the paper is structured as follows. In the second section the core components of the model and the relationships between them are described, motivated in the context of usability evaluation. In the third section, a case study illustrating some of the benefits of this ontological approach is provided. Finally, conclusions and future research directions are provided in the fourth section.

2.   A QUESTIONNAIRE MODEL FOR USABILITY EVALUATION

As the complete questionnaire ontology comprises a large amount of concepts, – ranging from usability evaluation generic knowledge to specific evaluable elements and tasks –, here we limit ourselves to describe the essential elements that are directly connected to the objective of the paper. Concretely, we will first sketch the overall structure of the model and then a more detailed account of some key concepts and relationships will be provided.

2.1   Overall Structure of the Ontology

As it has been described in the previous section, the design of a Web usability questionnaire can be made easier if a model that support the whole process is available. This model should represent all the essential concepts (also called terms or entities) that play a significant role in the evaluation, and it should also be rich and precise enough to enable certain subsequent automated 'intelligent' techniques aimed at aiding in the design of a questionnaire suitable for the application at hand. The elements that must be covered include the following: (a) questionnaire structure, including sections, (b) usability attributes considered, (c) functionalities provided by the Web application, and (d) the tasks that would be carried out by participants. In Fig. 1, a UML [24] diagram showing the main model entities is provided. The model described in this paper is just a view of a more comprehensive one which comprises other terms in the domain of questionnaires in usability evaluation. Some of these concepts are described in [12] (e.g., usability techniques and methods, participants' profile, etc.), and they enable the representation of all the surrounding knowledge needed to develop applications that facilitates an "enhanced" usability evaluation using attitude questionnaires [13].

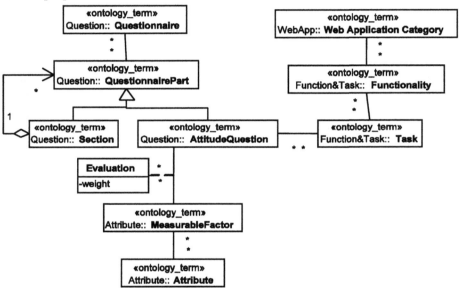

Figure 1. Core classes of the usability questionnaire model.

As we are aimed to design close-ended attitude questionnaires, we represent here exclusively the knowledge about the questions that enable the collection of user opinions according to his/her personal experience. Since it is possible that participants had never used the application before, a collection of typical tasks is provided so that they can create for themselves an opinion about the system. Each task is intended to evaluate a specific functionality of the application, and in addition, we have considered that usually each kind of Web application contains a minimum well-defined set of typical functionalities. Another important part of model describes the attributes that can be evaluated using the questionnaire. According to [20], a usability attribute can be defined as a system feature that contributes to make the system more easy-to-use. Attitude questionnaires measure user satisfaction about the application, and they can also indirectly measure the perception of the users about other usability attributes. In consequence, we have called "measurable factors" to the concrete system features that are used to estimate the intended usability attributes. These factors may have a different impact on different usability attributes, but exclusively satisfaction [15] can be directly obtained from the overall questionnaire result. A question may contribute to more than one measurable factor, and a given factor may be measured through more than one question, possibly having different weights.

2.2   Key Ontology Concepts

The elements of the model are structured in four interrelated ontologies: a "Web applications" ontology, a "functionalities and tasks" ontology, a "usability attributes" ontology and a "questionnaires" ontology, showed as UML namespaces in Fig. 1. The principles of the METHONTOLOGY approach [9] have been applied for ontology engineering, but following a literature-based process as described in [25]. In the rest of this section, a number of concepts and relations embodied in the ontology are described using description logics syntax [3]. For the sake of brevity, only elements relevant to understand the subsequent case study are provided.

2.2.1   Web Application Ontology

The Web application ontology describes the most common kinds of applications available through the Web, along with their structure. Web applications (*WA*) can be classified according to their business or information handling model. Concretely, we have adopted the taxonomy described in [5]. According to this, it can be stated the following: $WA \sqsubseteq \exists hasType.WAType$, so that $e - Commerce \sqsubseteq WAType$, among others. Assertions $WA(app1); e - Commerce(e - shop); hasType(app1, e - shop)$ can be used to denote that the Web application app1 is an e-shop. Depending on its type, a Web application usually comprises different characteristic parts ($WA \sqsubseteq \forall includes.WAPart$), and these parts are also typed, e.g., an e-shop usually contains a registration page, a search page, a shopping cart, etc, i.e: $WAPart \sqsubseteq \exists URL.(String) \sqcap \exists hasPartType.WAPartType$.

2.2.2   Functionality and Task Ontology

This ontology models both the typical functionalities (*TypFunct*) of the Web application (and/or its application parts) and the tasks that will be provided to the user as part of the evaluation. Some functionalities may be modelled as prerequisites for others transitively. Tasks may require input/output parameters, (*TInParam*) and (*TOutParam*), respectively:

WAPartType ⊑ ∃ *usuallyHas.TypFunct*
TypFunct ⊑ ∀ *hasPrerreq.TypFunct* ⊓ ∃ *isTypEvaluatedBy.Task*
Task ⊑ ∀ *requires.TInParam* ⊔ ∀*requires.TOutParam*

2.2.3   Attribute Ontology

This ontology describes usability attributes and the different factors that can be measured using a questionnaire. There is no agreed upon definition of usability [27]. Our model allows some degree of flexibility through the use of analogy and influence relations among attributes in the same or different "attribute list". Two attributes of different lists are analogous if they define the same concept using different terminology. For example, learnability as defined in Nielsen's list [20] is essentially the same that "time to learn" as defined in Shneiderman's one [26]. In addition, some attributes may influence positively others. For example, Dix defines a categorization of usability attributes at different abstraction levels [7], where flexibility is positively influenced by customisability, among others:

Att ≡ ∃ *definedIn.AttList* ⊓ (∀ *isAnalogous.Att* ⊔ ∀ *inflPos.Att*)
AttList ≡ ∀ *contains.Att* ⊓ ∃ *contains.Att*
definedIn ≡ *contains⁻ (symmetric relation)*

Several attributes can be measured (directly o indirectly) using a questionnaire. For example, WAMMI measures five factors –measurable factors in our model–, including learnability. This factor constitutes in turn an element that must be taken into account to evaluate other usability attributes, like efficiency. Some of the model terminology needed to reflect this knowledge is the following:

Att ⊑ ∀ *isMeasuredBy.MeasurableFactor*
MeasurableFactor ⊑ ∀ *measuresOpinionAbout. Attribute*
measureOpinionAbout ≡ *isMeasuredBy⁻*

2.2.4   Questionnaire Ontology

Here we deal with attitude questionnaires with close-ended questions which may contain different sections. The model represents this fact using a composite structural design pattern [10]. A questionnaire is made up of several questionnaire parts. Each part is a question or a section, and sections may contain other questionnaire parts:

Questionnaire ≡ ∀ *isMadeUpOf.QnnPart* ∩ ¬*Section*
Question ⊆ *QnnPart; Section* ⊆ *QnnPart*
Section ⊆ ∃ *contains.QnnPart*

Finally, each question is intended to contribute to one or more measurable factors possibly with different weights:

Weight ⊆ ∃ *weights.MeasurableFactor* ∩ ∃ *value.(real)*
Question ⊆ ∀ *hasWeight.Weight*

The rest of the terms of these four ontologies are integrated as sketched Fig. 1 above.

3. AN ONTOLOGY-BASED APPROACH FOR QUESTIONNAIRE DESIGN: A CASE STUDY

The model described above can be used to implement usability evaluation computer aided tools. Here we describe a prototype tool that guides the questionnaire design process through a dialogue with the user. The information needed in the different steps of the design process does not require any depth knowledge about usability evaluation, so that this approach can be considered a useful tool for novice information architects and Web designers. The tool has been developed as a Web wizard that leads the designer through the questionnaire design. During wizard execution the specific features of the concrete application that must be evaluated are asserted as instances and relations in the ontology. The application is modelled according to the characteristic defined in the predefined Web application types described above.

The first step in the dialogue collects basic application data like name, a brief description and URI, creating an instance of *WA* concept: *WA (app1); URL(app1,"http://...").* In the second steps the designer specifies the application type by navigating the *Web application ontology* (Fig. 2). Concretely, the system enables navigation from the more general categories of Web applications to more specific ones –pressing *Refine* button– until no more subclasses or instances of selected terms are found (a process similar to that described in [25]). For example, in left part of Fig. 2, subclasses of *WAType* are shown, and in the right part of the same figure, the commerce application category is expanded, in this case retrieving the following instances of the ontology: *CommerceSite(e – shop); CommerceSite(e – mall); CommerceSite(virtual – market Place); CommerceSite(e – auction).* When the designer finishes the selection of the application type, the corresponding type is asserted, for example: *hasType(app1, e – shop)*.

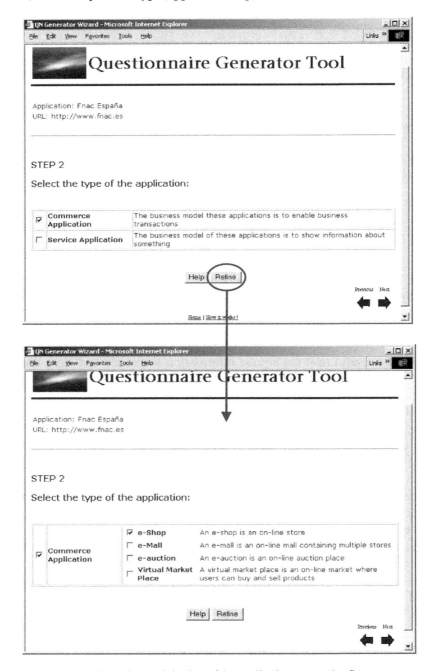

Figure 2. Second step: Selection of the application type and refinement.

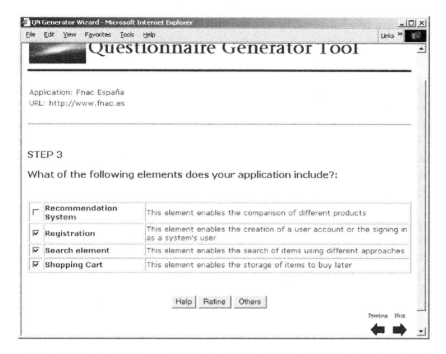

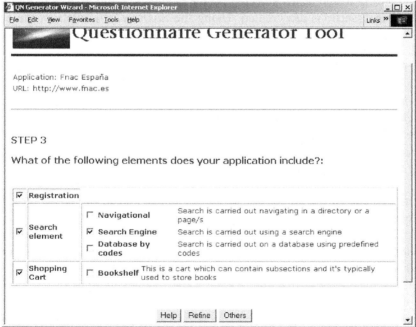

Figure 3. Third step: Selection of the elements that must be evaluated.

This navigational search through the ontology provides two main advantages: On the one hand, designers are able to use different abstraction levels to classify their application – the more specific type, the more concise become in the following steps. An on the other hand, designers are able to catalog the system using several terms at the same time, so that the approach provides a large flexibility to be used within a wide scope of applications.

Once the application type is specified, the wizard shows the parts that the selected kind of application usually includes to support its typical functionalities. Following the example, Fig. 3 shows the parts that an e-shop normally includes: recommendation system, shopping cart and searching and registration facilities.

The tool retrieves these elements using semantic relationships, e.g.:

WAType $\subseteq$ *∀usuallyIncludes. WAPartType*
WAPartType(RecommendationSystem); WAPartType(RegPage)
WAPartType(SearchPage); WAPartType(CartPage)
usuallyIncludes(e – shop, RecommendationSystem)
usuallyIncludes(e – shop, CartPage)
usuallyIncludes(e – shop, RegPage)
usuallyIncludes(e – shop, SearchPage)

According to the terms selected by the designer in the interface, the corresponding assertions are created. Using the *hasPartType* relation, the specific parts of the application can be linked to typical application parts (depending on the application type). For example, if the designer specifies that app1 contains a registration page and a shopping cart page, we have:

WAPart(app1RegPage); WAPart(app1CartPage)
includes(app1, app1RegPage); includes(app1, app1CartP age)
hasPartT ype(app1RegPage,RegPage)
hasPartType(app1CartPage,CartPage)
URL(app1CartPage "http : //..."); URL(app1RegPage, "http : //...")

On the basis of the previously selected elements, tasks are retrieved using the relationships among the concepts of the *functionality and task ontology*. In the next step of the construction process, designer is asked for specific parameters required by the tasks, in order to contextualize them. To do so functionalities are obtained by traversing *usuallyHasfunctionality* from the selected instances of *WAPartType*. As the wizard shows the *typical* functionalities of the selected parts, the concrete functionalities that the application implements have to be asserted:

WAPart $\subseteq$ *∃hasFunct.Funct*

$Funct \sqsubseteq \exists isLike.TypFunct \sqcap \exists isEvaluatedBy.ConcTask$
$ConcTask \sqsubseteq \forall needs.ConcTaskInParam \sqcap \forall needs.ConcTaskOutParam$
$ConcTaskInParam \sqsubseteq \exists type.TaskInParam$
$ConcTaskOutP aram \sqsubseteq \exists type.TaskOutParam$

According to the selected functionalities the designer is asked for the parameters required to complete each task (e.g., element to add in the shopping cart, element and search criteria, etc.). Using this information task instances are created. The use of the *functionality and task ontology* also enables some other features like the establishment of pre-required between tasks. For example, the task use to evaluate a shopping cart part requires the sign in and/or the registration task. Subsequently the designer is asked to select the usability attributes. To do so, he is able to select a complete list or some of its attributes using a refinement process similar to the one illustrated in Fig. 2. A default list of attributes can be selected if desired. Finally, questions are retrieved in accordance with the selected attributes and functionalities, coming up with a complete questionnaire as illustrated in Fig. 4.

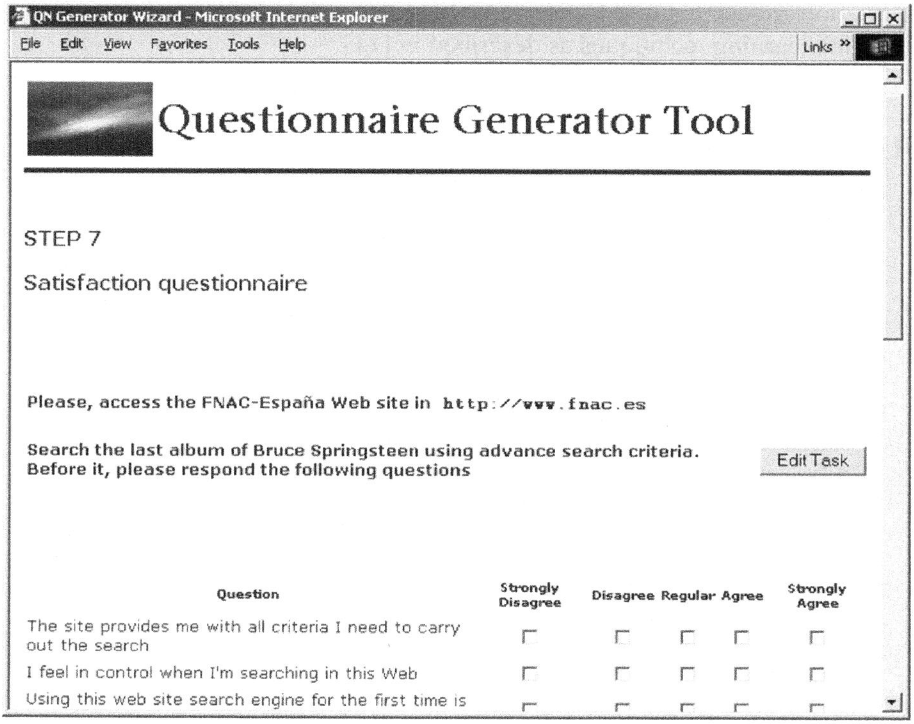

Figure 4. Example of generated questionnaire.

Once the design is completed, an editable Web form is automatically created that allows the administration of the questionnaire, and stores collected data in a relational database form consistent with the ontological model [12].

4.   CONCLUSION

A new approach to design usability attitude questionnaires has been described, intended to be used as a "discount usability" tool. The approach is based on a knowledge representation comprising four ontologies: *Questionnaire ontology, attribute ontology, functionality and task ontology* and Web *application ontology*. The use of a well-defined ontological model allows for different applications like the one presented in this paper: a dialogue-based construction of questionnaires.

It can be especially useful to novice information architects and designers since the tool is able to suggest both the functionalities and the task that should be evaluated, depending on the type of the Web application. Ontology-based approaches to questionnaires also enable a common, shared information model for questionnaire results, that could be later exploited by machine learning techniques as described in [11].

REFERENCES

[1] Aroyo, L. and Dicheva, D., *Authoring Framework for Concept-Based Web Information Systems,* in Proceedings of the Workshop on Concepts and Ontologies in Web-based Educational System, during International Conference on Computers in Education ICCE'2002 (Auckland, 3-6 December 2002), CS-Report 02-15, Technical University of Eindhoven, Eindhoven, 2002, pp. 41–48.

[2] Blandford, A. and Green, T.R.G., *OSM: An Ontology-Based Approach to Usability Evaluation*, in Proc. of Workshop on Representation in Interactive Software Development, Queen Mary & Westfield College, July 1997.

[3] Borgida, A., *On the Relative Expressiveness of Description Logics and Predicate Logics*, Artificial Intelligence, Vol. 82, No. 1-2, 1996, pp. 353-367.

[4] Brooke, J., *SUS: A 'Quick and Dirty' Usability Scale*, in P.W. Jordan, I.L. McClelland, B. Thomas, and B.A. Weerdmeester (eds.), Usability Evaluation in Industry, Taylor and Francis, London, 1996.

[5] Ceri, S., Fraternali, P., and Matera, M., *Conceptual Modelling of Data-Intensive Web Applications,* IEEE Internet Computing, Vol. 6, No. 4, 2002, pp. 20-30.

[6] Díaz, P., Sicilia M.A. and Aedo, I., *Evaluation of Hypermedia Educational Systems: Criteria ad Imperfect Measures*, Proc. of International Conference on Computers in Education ICCE'2002 (Auckland, 3-6 December 2002), IEEE Computer Society, Los Alamitos, 2002, pp. 621-626.

[7] Dix, A., Abowd, G., Beale, R., and Finlay, J., *Human-Computer Interaction*, Prentice Hall, New York, 1998.

[8] Dumas, J.S. and Redish, J.C., *A Practical Guide to Usability Testing*, Intellec, Bristol, 1999.

[9] Fernández, M., Gómez-Pérez, A., Pazos, J., and Pazos, A., *Building a Chemical Ontology Using METHONTOLOGY and the Ontology Design Environment*, IEEE Intelligent Systems, Vol. 14, No. 1, 1999, pp. 37-46.

[10] Gamma, E., Helm, R., Johnson, R., and Vlissides, J., *Structural patterns*, in Design Patterns, Addison Wesley, Boston, 1995, pp. 163-175.

[11] García, E., Sicilia, M.A., Hilera, J.R., and Gutiérrez, J.A., *Extracting Knowledge from Usability Evaluation Databases*, in Proceedings of the 8th IFIP TC. 13 International Conf. on Human Computer Interaction INTERACT'01 (Tokyo, 9-13 July 2001), IOS Press, Amsterdam, 2001, pp. 713-715.

[12] García, E., Sicilia, M.A., Hilera, J.R., and Gutiérrez, J.A., *Computer-Aided Usability Evaluation*, A questionnaire case study, Advances in Human Computer Interaction, Typorama, 2001, pp. 85–91.

[13] García, E., Sicilia, M.A., González, L., and Hilera, J.R., *Machine Learning Techniques in Usability-Evaluation Questionnaire Systems*, in Proceedings of 2nd International Conference Learning ICDL'02 (Cambridge, 12-15 June 2002), IEEE Computer Society Press, Los Alamitos, 2002.

[14] Harper, B., Slaughter, L., and Norman, K., *Questionnaire Administration via the WWW: A Validation and Reliability Study for a User Satisfaction Questionnaire*, in Proc. of the WebNet World Conference (Toronto, 31-5 October 1997), accessible at http://www.lap. umd.edu/webnet/paper.html

[15] ISO/IEC/JTC 1/SC 7. ISO/IEC FDIS 9126-1, Software Engineering - Product quality - Part 1: Quality model, Technical Committee of International Organization for Standardization, 2000.

[16] Kirakowski, J., Claridge, N., and Whitehead, R., *Human Centered Measures of Success in Web Site Design*, in Proc. of the 4th Conference on Human Factors and the Web HFWeb'1998 (New Jersey, 5 June 1998), 1998.

[17] Lei, Y., Motta, E., and Domingue, J., *An Ontology-Driven Approach to Web Site Generation and Maintenance*, in Proc. of 13th International Conference on Knowledge Engineering and Knowledge Management EKAW'02 (Sigüenza, 1-4 October 2002), 2002, pp. 219–234.

[18] Mayhew, D., *The Usability Engineering Lifecycle*, Morgan Kaufmann, San Francisco, 1999.

[19] Menzies, T., *Cost Benefits of Ontologies*, ACM SIGART Intelligence, 1999, accessible at http://menzies.us/pdf/99sigart.pdf

[20] Nielsen, J., *Usability Engineering*, Morgan Kaufmann, San Francisco, 1994.

[21] Nielsen, J. and Mack, R., *Usability Inspection Methods*, John Wiley and Sons, New York, 1994.

[22] Nielsen, J., *Guerrila HCI: Using Discount Usability Engineering to Penetrate the Intimidation Barrier*, in R.G. Bias and D.J. Mayhew (eds.), Cost-Justifying Usability, Academic Press Professional, Boston, 1994, pp 245–272.

[23] Oppenheim, A.N., *Questionnaire Design, Interviewing and Attitude Measurement*, Pinter Pub Ltd, 1992.

[24] Rumbaugh, J., Jacobson, I., and Booch, G., *The Unified Modelling Language Reference Manual*, Addison Wesley, Boston, 1998.

[25] Sicilia, M., García, E., Díaz, P., and Aedo, I., *A Literature-Based Approach to Annotation and Browsing of Web Resources*, Information Research, Vol. 8, No. 2, 2003, accessible at http://informationr.net/ir/8-2/paper149.html

[26] Shneiderman, B., *Designing the User Interface*, Addison-Wesley, New York, 1998.

[27] van Welie, M., van der Veer, G., and Eliëns, A., *Breaking down usability*, in A.M. Sasse, Ch. Johnson (eds.). Proceedings of 7th IFIP TC.13 International Conference on Human-Computer Interaction INTERACT'99 (Edinburgh, 30 August-3 September 1999), IOS Press, Amsterdam, 1999, pp. 613–620.

Chapter 12

CREATING CONTEXTUALISED USABILITY GUIDES FOR WEB SITES DESIGN AND EVALUATION

Céline Mariage and Jean Vanderdonckt
Institut d'Administration et de Gestion, Université catholique de Louvain
Belgian Lab. of Computer-Human Interaction (BCHI)
Place des Doyens, 1 – B-1348 Louvain-la-Neuve (Belgium)
E-mail:{mariage,vanderdonckt}@isys.ucl.ac.be
URL: http://www.isys.ucl.ac.be/bchi/members/{cma, jva}
Tel.: +32-10-47 {8391, 8525} – Fax: +32-10-478324

Abstract   This work addresses the problem of creating usability guides for web sites design and evaluation. We present a web-distributed tool, called MetroWeb, to
help web designers create and/or access to contextualised usability knowledge
during the whole design process, in order to develop user-centred applications.
The developer creates her own usability knowledge bases, which can be composed of other usability bases diffused by the tool, and uses this knowledge
when designing and/or evaluating her web site. The usability knowledge forms
a semantic network, in which various searching paths linked to user-centred
design and evaluation are represented.

Keywords: User-centred design and evaluation, Tools for working with guidelines, Web
usability guides.

1.   INTRODUCTION AND MOTIVATIONS

Usability knowledge exists in many forms today, both and explicitly
within people, guides, and tools: guidelines, patterns, design rules, conventions, and standards. Although this knowledge is supposed to be used continuously throughout the development life cycle, there is often a gap between
the constitution of this knowledge and its true usage during design and
evaluation. This gap is also often reflected in the existence of separate, independent processes and tools intended to support design and evaluation at the

147

R. Jacob et al. (eds.), Computer-Aided Design of User Interfaces IV, 147–158.
© 2005 *Kluwer Academic Publishers. Printed in the Netherlands.*

same time. For instance, software exist that capitalise usability knowledge to be used by developers, but once evaluators use the knowledge capitalised by one of these tools in order to assess the usability of the developed user interface (UI), the tool stops and another tool starts, thus preventing members of the development team to link usability problems with related knowledge and to accumulate this knowledge as the organisation experience is growing. In addition, each tool typically remains focused on one aspect at a time: an online style guide only provides guidelines, but no testing of them, some UI evaluators can perform testing, but with little or no access to the usability knowledge.

There is almost no task-based tool to support the constitution of a style guide among stakeholders so as to share it with developers afterwards during the development life cycle. Moreover, the process of progressively introducing guidelines in a standard remains mostly manual, without any tool support.

To address the above shortcomings, a generic tool is presented that permits to create a *contextualised usability guide*, which represents a set of guidelines linked to significant usability knowledge, like an interface object on which the guideline can be applied, or an evaluation method that is able to assess the guideline. The usability knowledge can be expanded at any time, disseminated at any time and explicitly used during design and evaluation in a continuous way, shared by everyone implied in the web site development.

Although the tool presented can manage usability knowledge about any potential type of interface and a large spectrum of evaluation methods, we focus it on UIs for the web with heuristic or expert-based evaluation [1]. The tool is web-distributed to manage usability knowledge in a flexible and autonomous manner that can be run on multiple computing platforms.

Our main objectives are (1) to provide a tool responding to design questions with guidelines and resources exploitation, (2) to permit to automate searching paths related to user-centred design and evaluation process, (3) to support the usability guide creation task.

The paper is organised as follows: Section 2 reports on the most significant pieces of work related to the main goal. Section 3 presents the semantic network defining the fundamental usability concepts required to be manipulated in a usability knowledge base, in regard to searching paths linked to usability evaluation. Section 4 explains how to create a usability style guide with the tool. Section 5 presents how to use the guide in web site development. Section 6 reports on the design and development of the tool. Section 7 summarises the main points of the paper and presents some future work.

2.   RELATED WORK

In the 'Tools for Working with Guidelines' (TFWWG) approach [11], tools were developed for accessing and retrieving guidelines organised either as a database or hypertext [4], in order to diffuse and promote usability knowledge to use during UI design.

First, usability guides were diffused on paper, but rapidly appeared guides on hypertext support. Hyperlinks joined guidelines to resources (e.g. references or ergonomic criteria).

After that, hypermedia permitted to usability guides to link usability knowledge to illustrative examples, presented in various format like screen shots or video sequences.

These first supports did not permit efficacy information research. For that reason appeared tools managing usability knowledge bases and permitting efficacy research information and structure usability knowledge. Some of these tools are: i) SIERRA [9,12], which manages a usability knowledge database used with a hypermedia system; ii) Sherlock [4], which manages usability guidelines by a client-server system, evaluating automatically some guidelines or offering advice about how to solve detected design problems; iii) GUIDE [5], which permits to manage a guidelines base, linking guidelines used to a particular application and storing these experiences in cases in order to be reused by case-based reasoning; iv) the TELE-environment [3], which consists of a multimedia learning environment for the web, managing interactive examples and cases linked to usability guidelines, in order to help developers understand and apply guidelines during the web design.

Unfortunately, these tools manage only one base at a time and for that reason remain too rigid in a development cycle. Moreover, there do not support continuous evaluation usage, except Sherlock [4] that is supporting some steps of the evaluation process. User-centred design is not really supported by these tools, because the guidelines contextualisation is poor. Various design questions are not covered by the tools, e.g. "which are the guidelines appropriated to this context of use, in this particular development phase and linked to some ergonomic criteria".

We present in this paper the MetroWeb tool that enables the management of multiple guidelines bases with a more precise contextualisation of the guidelines. This contextualisation is guided by a semantic network managing possible searching paths needed in web usability design and evaluation. Moreover, many users are able to share the tool (evaluator, designer, developer, etc.).

3.   THE METROWEB SEMANTIC NETWORK

This section presents the semantic network we want to support with the MetroWeb tool, in order to respond to design questions. In fact, it's frequent that, during the user-centred design cycle of the web site, the designer needs to assess to particular guidelines, e.g. guidelines dedicated to the elaboration of forms. Guidelines can also be appropriated to such a development phase, like the specifications. The designer can be interested in which evaluation methods she can use to assess a set of guidelines. When she decides to choice such interaction object to put in a web page, she can need to access to the guidelines linked to this object. If she wants to assess ergonomic criteria in her site, like consistency e.g., she needs to know which guidelines are linked to these criteria. In parallel, to which criteria are linked such guidelines is important to know. In a particular context of use, like the use of the web site by people with disabilities, particular guidelines (e.g., accessibility guidelines), have to be respected. Moreover, the designer needs to access to illustrative examples of the guidelines, references or related guidelines. The complete information related to guidelines is summarised in Fig. 1. The semantic network we define is aimed to respond to these questions.

The core concept of the MetroWeb network is the *guideline*. A guideline consists of a design and/or evaluation principle to be observed to get and/or guarantee a usable user interface [2]. Guidelines can be found in many different formats with contents varying both in quality and level of detail, ranging from ill-structured common sense statements to formalized rules ready for automatic guidelines checking [6]. A guideline can be characterised, or contextualised, by other concepts like ergonomic criteria, linguistic level or model.

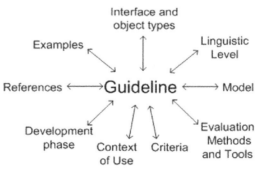

Figure 1. Fundamental Concepts of MetroWeb.

The organisation of fundamental concepts around the guideline enables browsing the knowledge base from multiple entry points toward any target information in a reversible way: for instance, from task model to guidelines and vice versa. An entity-relationship schema exists that structures considered usability concepts into 40 entities and 34 relationships.

Ergonomic criteria are criteria that lead to an elaborated, efficient, sophisticated, user friendly UI [2]. Nielsen's linguistic model [7] separates human-computer interaction into seven layers ranging from the highest level (the closest of the human world) to the lowest level (the closest to the computer world). In a guideline evaluation process, other interface information has to be specified: interface and object types, context of use, development phase. Indeed, evaluator needs more information about the guideline than the guideline itself. For example, she needs to know to which types of user, task and environment the guideline applies. This information forms the context of use [5]. The evaluation methods and tools must also be specified, in order to illustrate to the evaluator how to resolve the usability problems encountered. Positive and negative examples and bibliographic references reinforce also the evaluation when present. If the evaluator needs to assess a particular interactive object of a particular interface, she can consult all the guidelines linked to that particular point. If an evaluator wants to evaluate a specified guidelines base in the evaluated interface, she can consult the evaluation methods and tools permitting guidelines base assessment. Navigation can be made by whatever input point and by direct manipulation. These concepts are structured in a semantic network. This network allows different types of reasoning because it contains several facets [8]:

- **Definitional**: any entity of interest is described by its own definition in the guidelines base, i.e. by the attributes. Moreover, relationships link entities, e.g., the entity Web-Site is a subtype of the super type UI-type and is the super type of Intranet, Extranet and Internet. Decomposition relation can also link objects to sub-objects, e.g. a Concrete Interaction Object (CIO) [10] can be composed by other CIOs. In this way, usability knowledge is attached to the highest level of application possible.

- **Assertional:** assertions can be added between guidelines, e.g., the guideline stating that, in a web site, each image should have an alternative text is no more valuable when another image with the same alternative text stays next to the image.

- **Implicational**: implications can be incorporated between contents. For example, if you consider a guideline, then you also need to check if it respects other guideline(s) implied by this one, e.g., a guideline stipulating that web site look must be consistent in the entire application applies to all the objects of the interface. To evaluate this, the consistency has to be assessed in each web page of the web site. For that reason, each guideline part of the consistency criteria must be assessed in each page of the web site to evaluate. If the evaluation concerns several web sites, we must verify each application page. The consistency evaluation is called inter-application, and no more intra-application.

- **Executable:** in our network, associations between evaluation tools and guidelines are specified so that any usability knowledge content that can be automated is delegated to a tool to be executed.
- **Pedagogic:** the usability knowledge managed by MetroWeb, e.g. evaluation methods and tools, can generate tutorial, guided tours, pro's and contra's argumentation of the design cases, and teaching of design through examples. This pedagogic facet is shared by other TFWWGs [3,11].

These 5 facets permit to support different searching paths linked to user-centred design.

4.   CREATING USABILITY GUIDES WITH METROWEB

Once the fundamental aspects are known, there is a need to identify interactive tasks that manipulate this knowledge in a user-centred way. Our tool permits to create usability guides to be used during the web site development. In this section we develop the different tasks to hold to get a usability guide with the tool. We present also the evaluation tasks involving the use of the usability guides. First the creation itself of usability guides is decomposed into several tasks (Fig. 2): collecting, organisation and incorporation of the guidelines into a method.

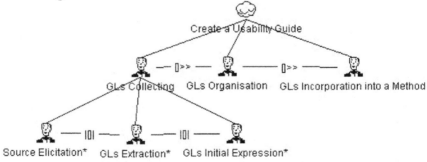

Figure 2. Tasks of Usability Guide Creation.

The collection of the guidelines depends on the user's needs. Does the user want to use existing usability guides or create her own? She can also use existing sources to create her guide, contextualised to the organisation needs (types of web sites analysed, development phases to cover, evaluation objectives like code verification of home pages or semantic analysis, etc.). Our tool permits the management of multiple guidelines bases, whatever the source. The guidelines collection can be divided in source elicitation, guidelines extraction and initial expression.

The organisation of the guidelines is the main goal of the tool. The guideline itself is structured on a hierarchy. Each guidelines base created can manage sections and subsections, as deep as needed. Fig. 3 shows the implemented interface: the left part contents hierarchy in one base, and the right part shows the guidelines belonging to one subsection. The guidelines details appear when the user selects a guideline.

Contextualisation of the guidelines is permitted by the semantic network supported by the tool. All the themes presented in Fig. 1 can contextualise the guidelines and form a contextualised usability guide. For example, an organisation that wants to develop usability guides about Intranet will collect specific guidelines linked to this topic.

The incorporation of the guidelines into a method is largely supported by our tool. In fact, it supports heuristic inspection that assesses UIs in comparison with a list of principles or guidelines. A heuristic inspector can use MetroWeb to access to the guidelines she wants to verify in the interface. Links to usability knowledge reinforce the applicability of the guidelines. Even if heuristic inspection is supported by the tool, other methods can be linked to guidelines, in order to guide the evaluation process, whatever the method used.

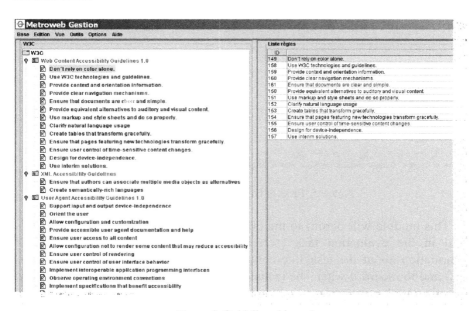

Figure 3. Guidelines hierarchy.

5.   USING USABILITY GUIDES IN WEB SITES DESIGN AND EVALUATION

Once a base is created, it can be used for various evaluation and teaching purposes (e.g., browsing them, searching specific guidelines freely or design question searching, or by teaching, see Fig. 4). A guidelines checklist can gather guidelines previously input by identifying sections relevant for evaluation (e.g., include, exclude, copy, import from various guideline bases).

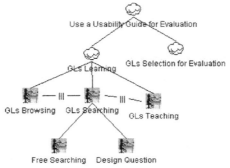

Figure 4. Tasks of Guidelines Learning.

The evaluation reporting task will be totally supported by our tool (Fig. 5), by a specific evaluation module, actually under development.

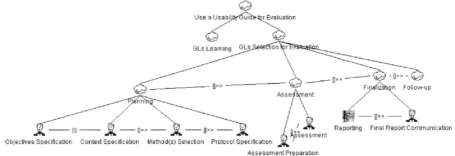

Figure 5. Tasks of Guidelines Use for Evaluation.

This module will permit to the evaluator to choice the information to record in the evaluation task (screen shots, guidelines, scenarios, meta-information about the task like contact information of the evaluator, date, etc.) and to record it when she evaluates her site. The tool supports partially the other evaluation tasks (except the follow-up) by providing information helping the evaluator judgments (e.g., information about which methods to use in such evaluation context).

6. THE METROWEB TOOL

The tool is intended to support usability guides creation. The created guides are contextualised in order to provide complete information about how to apply the guidelines in a web development cycle. Fig. 6 shows the implemented tool. The tool is developed in Java Swing, on top of Borland Interbase databases, which is open source and can work on multiple platforms. Different views are provided to the user, corresponding to her task.

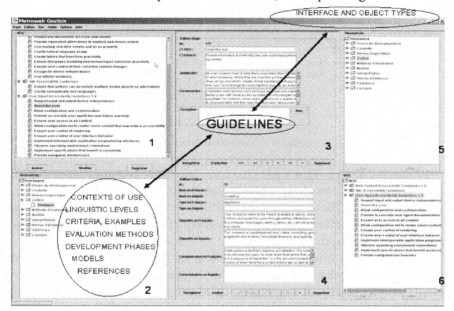

Figure 6. The MetroWeb Tool: complete view.

The complete view (Fig. 6) presents in one screen the guidelines and resources hierarchy, details and links. A guideline is no longer presented isolated from its context of application and related concepts. All the concepts related to the guidelines (Fig. 1), except the interface and objects types, are actually implemented. The left part shows the guidelines hierarchy in bases and sections (1 & 2). The central part contains details of guidelines and resources linked to guidelines (3 & 4).

The right part contains types of links (and linkage attributes) between guidelines and resources (5 & 6). Knowledge manipulation is direct because user can move from a specific view to another, directly by moving slide bars. By moving up or down the horizontal slide bar, the complete view (Fig. 6) becomes detailed view of guidelines or resources (Fig. 7), contextualised by it hierarchy and links.

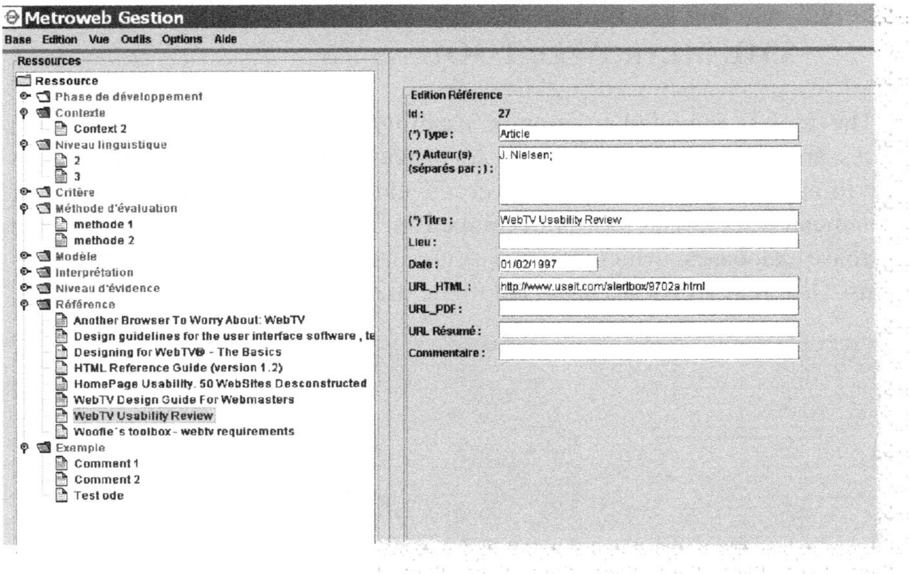

Figure 7. MetroWeb detailed view.

By moving left or right slide bar, complete view becomes more detailed guidelines or resources views, called normal views (Fig. 8), keeping either it hierarchy or links. These navigation facilities between coordinated views are corresponding to different design and evaluation questions that can be raised frequently in development teams.

At **design time**, it is possible to quickly identify usability knowledge required to address questions like: "for this interactive task, what are the previous UI implementations (examples) that have been recorded with usability qualities?" (this enables people in an organisation to build an organisation memory of their usability practise over time), "what guidelines do I need to consider to design a form in a web page?", "what are the most important design options impacting usability to be decided at design time?".

At **evaluation time**, it is possible to find answer to questions like: "what are the guidelines that need to be considered to check this UI against this style guide or standard?", "what should I do to make my web page compliant with W3C Web Accessibility Initiative (WAI) guidelines?", "what level of support can I count on to automate this task?", "Can I use the same guidelines both at design and evaluation time?", "how to store evaluation results so as to reuse them later on?".

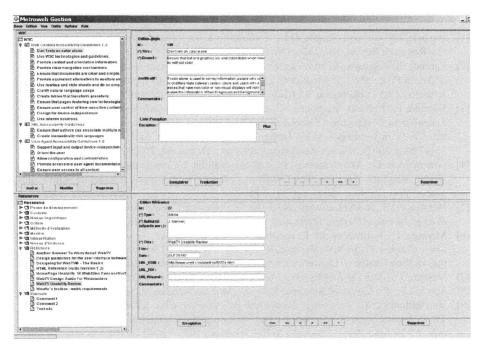

Figure 8. MetroWeb normal view.

7. CONCLUSION

The tool presented in this paper permits to support user-centred design and evaluation of web sites, by the creation of multi-bases usability guides, and the use of them during the whole development cycle. The tool, with respect to existing work, is original for the following characteristics: continuity (usability knowledge gathered in the phase of style guide constitution is reused consistently), integration (design and evaluation can be supported simultaneously), multi-bases (multiple knowledge bases can be used at the same time, for instance to evaluate guidelines belonging to different sources), collaboration (since the tool is web-based itself, implemented in Java/Swing, it can be installed and used locally or remotely), level of support (several phases concerning usability in the development life cycle are covered). Our future work concerns the implementation of the evaluation module, aimed to support the usability problems reporting, tightly coupled with a system that supports the designer and the evaluator in automating the evaluation of guidelines contained in METROWEB [13,14].

REFERENCES

[1] Bastien, J.M.Ch. and Scapin, D.L., *Evaluating a User Interface with Ergonomic Criteria*, Research Report, No. 2326, INRIA, August 1994.

[2] Farenc, C., Palanque, P. and Vanderdonckt, J., *User Interface Evaluation: is it Ever Usable?*, in Proc. of 6th International Conference on Human-Computer Interaction HCI International'95 (Yokohama, 9-14 July 1995), Elsevier, Amsterdam, 1995, pp. 329-334.

[3] Furtado, E., Furtado, V., Sousa, K., and Belchior, A., *An Online Multimedia System for Learning to Design User Interfaces*, in Ch. Kolski, J. Vanderdonckt (eds.), Proc. of 3rd Int. Conf. on Computer-Aided Design of User Interfaces CADUI'2002 (Valenciennes, 15-17 May 2002), Kluwer Academic Publishers, Dordrecht, 2002, pp. 229-242.

[4] Grammenos, D., Akoumianakis, D., and Stephanidis, C., *Integrated Support for Working With Guidelines: The Sherlock Guidelines Management System*, Interacting with Computers, Vol. 12, No. 3, 2000, pp. 281-311.

[5] Henninger, S., *A Methodology and Tools for Applying Context-Specific Usability Guidelines to Interface Design*, Interacting with Computers, Vol. 12, No. 3, 2000, pp. 225-243.

[6] Mariage, C., Vanderdonckt, J., and Pribeanu, C., *State of the Art of Web Usability Guidelines*, Chapter 41, in R.W. Proctor, K.-Ph.L. Vu (eds.), « The Handbook of Human Factors in Web Design », Lawrence Erlbaum Associates, Mahwah, 2004.

[7] Nielsen, J., *Usability Engineering*, Academic Press, Boston, 1993.

[8] Sowa, J.F., *Principles of Semantic Network*, Morgan Kaufmann, San Mateo, 1991.

[9] Vanderdonckt, J., *Accessing Guidelines Information with SIERRA*, in Proc. of IFIP TC.13 International Conference on Human-Computer Interaction Interact'95 (Lillehammer, 27-29 June 1995), Chapman & Hall, London, 1995, pp. 311-316.

[10] Vanderdonckt, J. and Bodart, F., *Encapsulating Knowledge for Intelligent Automatic Interaction Objects Selection*, in Proc. of the ACM Conf. on Human Factors in Computing Systems INTERCHI'93 (Amsterdam, 24-29 April 1993), ACM Press, New York, 1993, pp. 424-429.

[11] Vanderdonckt, J., *Development Milestones towards a Tool for Working with Guidelines*, Interacting with Computers, Vol. 12, No. 2, December 1999, pp. 81-118.

[12] Vanderdonckt, J., *Visual Design Methods in Interactive Applications*, Chapter 7, in M. Albers, B. Mazur (eds.), « Content and Complexity: Information Design in Technical Communication », Lawrence Erlbaum Associates, Mahwah, 2003, pp. 187-203.

[13] Vanderdonckt, J. and Beirekdar, A., *The Impact of Internationalization on Guidelines Contents and Usage*, in Proceedings of 2nd International Conference on Universal Access in Human-Computer Interaction UAHCI'2003 (Creete, 22-27 June 2003), Vol. 4, C. Stephanidis (ed.), Lawrence Erlbaum Associates, Mahwah, 2003, pp. 1544-1548.

[14] Vanderdonckt, J., Beirekdar, A., Noirhomme-Fraiture, M., *Automated Evaluation of Web Usability and Accessibility by Guideline Review*, in Proceedings of 4th International Conference on Web Engineering ICWE'04 (Munich, 28-30 July 2004), N. Koch, P. Fraternali, M. Wirsing (eds.), Lecture Notes in Computer Science, Springer-Verlag, Berlin, 2004.

Chapter 13

USABILITY TESTING OF INTERACTION COMPONENTS
Taking the Message Exchange as a Measure of Usability

Willem-Paul Brinkman[1], Reinder Haakma[2], and Don. G. Bouwhuis[3]

[1]*Brunel University, Uxbridge – Middlesex UB8 3PH (United Kingdom)*
E-mail: willem.brinkman@brunel.ac.uk – URL: http://www.brunel.ac.uk/~csstwpb/
Tel.: +44 1895 274000
[2]*Philips Research Laboratories Eindhoven, Prof. Holstlaan 4 – 5656 AA Eindhoven*
(The Netherlands)
E-mail: reinder.haakma@philips.com
[3]*Technische Universiteit Eindhoven, P.O. box 513 – 5600 MB Eindhoven (The Netherlands)*
E-mail: d.g.bouwhuis@tue.nl

Abstract   Component-based Software Engineering (CBSE) is concerned with the development of systems from reusable parts (components), and the development and maintenance of these parts. This study addresses the issue of usability testing in a CBSE environment, and specifically automatically measuring the usability of different components in a single system. The proposed usability measure is derived from the message exchange between components recorded in a log file. The measure was validated in an experimental evaluation. Four different prototypes of a mobile telephone were subjected to usability tests, in which 40 subjects participated. Results show that the usability of the individual components can be measured, and that they can be priorities on their potential for improvement.

Keywords: Component-based software engineering, Log file analysis, Sequential data analysis, Usability evaluation, Usability testing.

1.   INTRODUCTION

Although Component-Base Software Engineering (CBSE) is becoming more popular, so far, no empirical usability testing methods have been developed that correspond well with this engineering approach. CBSE is a sub-discipline of software engineering, which is primarily concerned with the

159

following three functions: development of software from pre-produced parts; the ability to re-use those parts in other applications; and easy maintenance and customisation of those parts to produce new functions and features [3]. Instead of building an application from scratch, the CBSE approach focuses on building artefacts from already made components (e.g., pop-up menus, radio buttons, and list boxes). The idea behind the engineering concept is that components can easily be re-used in other systems since they are autonomous units, free of the context in which they are deployed. The promise of CBSE is reduced development cost and time since ready-made and self-made components can be used and re-used.

The development organisation for CBSE differs from the 'traditional' engineering organisation that focused on writing new software and not on composing an application from existing software. Therefore, an empirical usability testing method in which the usability of an individual component can be measured after they are deployed in an application is of course welcome. The usability of components has not yet been measured individually. Several authors [2],[5][11] have proposed analysing the user interaction with a component to determine the usability of individual component. To reduce the amount of work and to overcome the low reliability of existing usability evaluation methods [4], employing automatic procedures has been suggested [2] to determine the performance-oriented aspects of usability on the basis of usage logs.

2.   ARCHITECTURE OF INTERACTIVE SYSTEMS

The following three sections introduce the concepts: interaction component, router, and layer. With these concepts it is possible to identify interactive system architectures on which the testing method can be applied, such as for example the CNUCE agent model [9]. The general architecture described here is based on the ideas of the Layered Protocol Theory [11], which decomposes the user-system interaction into different layers that can be designed and analysed separately.

2.1   Interaction Components

Interaction components define the elementary units of interactive systems, on which behaviour-based evaluation is possible. An interaction component is a unit within an application that directly or indirectly receives signals from the user. These signals enable the user to change the physical state of the interaction component. Furthermore, the user must be able to perceive or to infer the state of the interaction component. Therefore, an interaction component should provide feedback. Without the possibility of perceiving the state, users cannot separate the component from the whole system and are not able to control it. Without the ability to control the feedback, users' behaviour is aimless.

2.2 Routers

Another element in the general architecture is the Router. Routers are binding elements that direct the communication flow between interaction components, and do not have to have an own state. This component's only function may be merging the messages of two lower-level interaction components into a message for the high-level interaction component or vice versa.

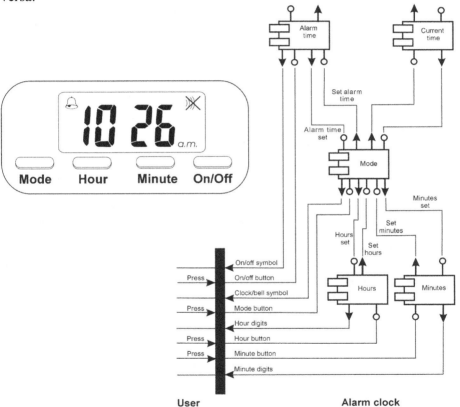

Figure 1. Front and component structure of an alarm clock.

2.3 Layers

The points where input and output of different interaction components are connected demarcate the border between layers. An interaction component operates on a higher-level layer than another interaction component, when the higher-level interaction component receives its user's messages from the other interaction component. With the definition of interaction components, routers, and layers it is possible to describe the architecture of a regular alarm clock to illustrate these concepts. With this alarm clock, users can set the alarm time by setting the clock in the right mode, changing the hours and minutes digits, and finally activating the alarm. Figure 1 shows the interaction components involved. The Hour and Minute interaction components are located on the lowest-level layer, where they manage the state of the hour and minute digits. The Mode interaction component is placed on the middle-level layer. The component is responsible for the mode of the alarm clock, and consequently whether the current or the alarm time is visible or set. To indicate that the alarm time is displayed, a small icon of a bell is shown in the top-left corner of the display. The Alarm Time and Current Time interaction components, which keep the corresponding times, make up the top-level layer in the architecture. The Alarm Time interaction component shows a small icon in the top-right corner of the display to indicate whether the alarm is activated or not.

3.   THE TESTING METHOD

3.1   Test Procedure

The test procedure of the testing method roughly corresponds to the normal procedure of a usability test. Subjects are observed while they perform a task with the system. The task is finished once subjects attain a specific goal that would require them to alter the state of the interaction component under investigation. In advance, subjects are instructed to act as quickly as possible to accomplish the given goal. As subjects perform the task, messages sent to the various interaction components are recorded in a log file. Once they reach the goal, the recording stops.

3.2   Component-Specific Usability Measure

The number of messages received by a component is a powerful measure to study the difference in usability between two versions of a component [1]. This raw measure forms the basis for a usability measure that can be applied on different components in a single system. Instead of a direct comparison, the proposed method compares the performance of an (fictional) ideal user with that of real users. The method looks at the performance of a component as if higher-level components operated optimally. This way the inefficiency of higher-level component is compensated for. In this context, inefficiency means that a component requests more lower-level messages than optimal required. The method assumes that lower-level components only sent messages upwards intended by users (no effectiveness problem) and messages sent by an ideal user are also sent by real users.

Valuable information for evaluators is which interaction components should be changed to create the largest usability improvement of the whole system, i.e. impact assessment and effort allocation [6]. The impact an interaction component has on the overall performance can be estimated by assigning an effort value to each message received. These effort values are based on the effort value of the lowest-level messages that are linked to higher-level messages. At the lowest-level layer, weight factors of an arbitrary unit are assigned to the messages, which present the user effort value to send a single message. This can be a number for each keystroke or for the time users need to make an elementary message. The users' effort, to make these elementary actions, is regarded as similar throughout task execution. In the next section, an example is worked out to explain the performance evaluation in detail.

3.2.1   Example

Imagine a drawing application. A circle and polygon are drawn. Now, the task is to change the circle's colour into red and remove its black outline. If users perform the task optimally, they first select the circle by clicking on it, and then they open the Right Mouse Button Menu (RMBM) and choose the option Properties. The application comes up with a property window, where the users select the red box in the Fill tab sheet (Fig. 2). They also check the "No Line" check box on the "Outline" tab sheet. Finally, the users click on the "Ok" button of the property window and the circle changes accordingly. Figure 3 presents the message exchange between the relevant interaction components of the drawing application when the task is conducted in this optimal way.

In this example, (imaginary) recordings are also made of the behaviour of a (imaginary) real user who has three problems: first, with selecting an object; second, with setting the right tab sheet; and third, with distinguishing a circle from a polygon. The real user selects objects with a selection window instead of clicking on the objects themselves. Furthermore, the real user takes the polygon for a circle, and consequently makes two selections. After the circle is selected, the real user searches for the right tab sheet, starting with General, then Detail and ending with the right tab sheet. Fig. 4 shows the message exchange between the same interaction components as before, but now for the real user.

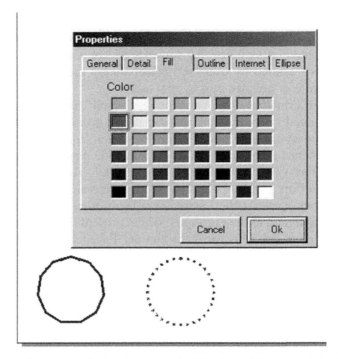

Figure 2. Property window for setting the fill colour of the selected circle.

3.2.2   Analysis of the Example

In this example, a value 1 is assigned to all Click messages (Fig. 3 and 4). After effort values are assigned to the lowest-level messages, the effort values are calculated for the messages sent upwards. The effort value of a message sent upwards is, in principle, the sum of the effort values of the messages received between this and the previous message sent upwards. Fig. 3 gives the effort values for the messages sent upwards in the case of the ideal user. Take for example the Call message sent upwards by the RMBM at event 4. Two Click messages, each having an effort value 1, were received before this message was sent (see event 3); therefore, an effort value of 2 is assigned to this message. The calculation starts at the lowest-level layer and works its way upwards. This means that first the effort value for the Selection and RMBM interaction components is calculated, followed by the effort value for the messages sent upwards by the Properties and finally by the Visual Drawing Objects (VDO) interaction component.

If messages are sent upwards through actual task execution (the real user), the inefficiency of lower-levels is removed from the effort value. The effort values of the messages that are also sent upwards in optimal task performance receive a similar effort value as if these messages are sent upwards in optimal task performance. If another type of message or a message with another effect is sent upwards compared to that in optimal task performance, it will receive the sum of the effort values of messages received. However, if this message is of the same type as messages sent upwards in optimal task performance, it may not exceed the maximum optimal effort value of messages of this type. For example, the Select messages, sent upwards by the Selector in Fig. 4 at event 2 and 4, have an effort value of 1 because the ideal user made a Select message that has the same effect with only an effort value of 1.

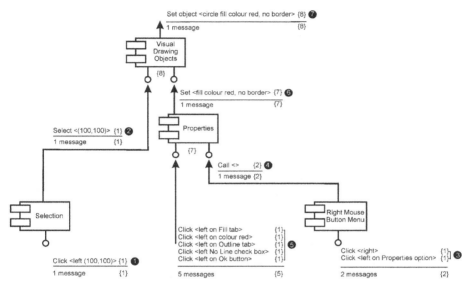

Figure 3. Message exchange between the components of the drawing application in the case of optimal task execution (ideal user). Effort values are given within brackets. The numbers in the black circles give the event sequence of the task execution.

The total effort for the control of an interaction component is the sum of the effort values of the messages received (third and fourth column of Table 1), which, in the case of real users, is later on corrected for the inefficiencies of a higher-level. Without correction, the total effort still may include inefficient high-level demands, which should not be charged to the interaction component. Therefore, the analysis only looks at the number of messages sent upwards that are required to fulfil the optimal request of higher-level layers. This corrected value is called the user effort and is also given in Table 1. It is calculated by first taking the total effort in the case of the real user (fourth column) and dividing it by the number of messages the real user sent upwards (second column); and second, by multiplying the result by the number of messages the ideal user sent upwards (first column). This correction assumes that the same number of messages have to be received to send a message upwards again, which is the case when the state of the interaction component is reset after a message is sent upwards.

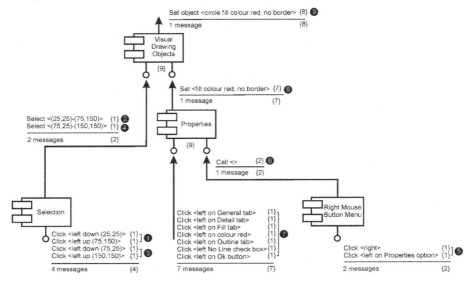

Figure 4. Message exchange between the components of the drawing application in the case of observed task execution (real user). Effort values are given within brackets. The numbers in the black circles give the event sequence of the task execution.

Table 1. The extra user effort and the parameters to calculated it.

	Sent upwards		Total effort			
	Optimal	Observed	Optimal	Observed	User effort	Extra
Properties	1	1	7	9	9	2
VBO	1	1	8	9	9	1
Selection	1	2	1	4	2	1
RMBM	1	1	2	2	2	0

The extra user effort is a measure of the effort difference when a real user or an ideal user controls an interaction component. The extra user effort is the result of the subtraction of the total effort made by the ideal user from the user effort made by the real user. Table 1 shows the extra user effort per interaction component. The Selection interaction component is charged with 1 extra keystroke. Although the real user made an inefficient selection two times, only the average extra user effort per selection is taken into account because the repetition is attributed to inefficiency of higher-level layers. The RMBM interaction component, with its optimal performance, is subsequently charged with no extra user effort. The Properties interaction component is charged with two extra keystrokes; the two keystrokes for searching the right tab sheet. The VDO interaction component is charged with only one extra keystroke; the one keystroke, an ideal user would need to select the polygon. Finally, ordering the interaction components by their extra user effort creates the priority list of the most effective improvements; putting the Properties component on top of the list.

4.   EXPERIMENTAL VALIDATION

An experiment was conducted to study the method and to validate the proposed component-specific usability measure. The experiment compared prototypes with variations in their usability. The use of predefined usability variations had to emphasise the validity of the usability measures. All usability variations addressed the complexity of dialogue structures that can be understood in terms of Cognitive Complexity Theory (CCT) [7]. This theory holds that the cognitive complexity increases when users have to learn more rules.

4.1   Prototypes

A mobile telephone was chosen for the experiment because of its relatively complex user interface architecture. Two interaction components of a mobile telephone were manipulated. They were responsible for the way subjects could activate functions in the telephone (Function Selector), and send text messages (Send Text Message). For each of these two interaction components two versions were designed. In one version of the Function Selector (FS), the menu was relatively broad but shallow, i.e. all eight options available within one stratum. In the other version, the menu was relatively narrow but deep, i.e. a binary tree of three strata. Users tend to be faster and make fewer errors in finding a target in broad menus than in deep menus [10].

In terms of CCT, the deep menu structure requires subjects to learn more rules to make the correct choices when going through the deep menu structure. In the more usable version (simple version) of the Send Text Message (STM) component, the component guided subjects through the required steps. The less usable version (complex version) left the sequence of steps up to the subjects. All these options were presented as icons that forced the subjects to learn the icon-option mapping rules in the complex version. Furthermore, they also had to learn in which order to choose the options. Combining these versions led to four different mobile telephone prototypes.

The experimental environment was programmed in Delphi 5, and included PC simulations of all mobile telephone prototypes and a recording mechanism to capture the message exchange between the interaction components [1].

4.2   Procedure and Subjects

All 40 participating subjects were students of Technische Universiteit Eindhoven. None of them used a mobile telephone on a daily or weekly basis. The kinds of tasks they had to perform with the mobile telephone were calling to someone's voice-mail system; adding a person's name and number to the phone's address list; and sending a text message. The application automatically assigned the subjects in a random order to a prototype. At the end of the experiment, subjects were asked to evaluate the mobile telephone and the two components with a questionnaire on the computer. The computer gave the questions in a random order. The questions addressed both the ease-of-use and satisfaction of the overall mobile phone, and the FS and STM components separately [1]. After the experiment, the subjects received NLG 22.50 (roughly €10) for their participation.

4.3   Results

The extra user effort was calculated for the two interaction components per prototype over all types of tasks (Table 2). For each prototype a multivariate analysis of variance was conducted on the extra user effort. The analyses took the components as an independent within-subject variable. The results revealed a significant difference in prototype 2, which was equipped with the narrow/deep version of the FS component and the simple version of the STM component. As expected, designers confronted with this prototype should focus their attention on the FS component rather than on the STM component. With prototype 3, designers should focus on the STM component, although the analysis failed to reach a significant level.

The ability to say something about the accuracy of the extra user effort measurement is limited. For the versions of the STM interaction component, a difference of 29 keystrokes was found in the extra user effort, whereas a difference of 64 keystrokes was found in the overall number of extra keystrokes. A relative similar deviation was found for the difference between the versions of the FS component, 55 versus 105 keystrokes. An explanation for the difference between extra keystrokes and extra user effort is that the extra keystrokes measure also includes the additional effect usability problems had on other components with usability problems.

After the multivariate analyses, the validity of extra user effort measure was examined by correlating it with other measures obtained in the experiment. Table 3 shows the partial correlations between these measures and the extra user effort to control the FS and the STM components. All correlations were controlled for the versions of the other interaction component. Only significant partial correlations, in the expected direction, were found; except for the correlations between the mobile telephone satisfaction and extra user effort for STM component. The results validate the extra user effort measure as a component-specific usability measure.

Table 2. Results of multivariate analyses of variance on the extra user effort for the four prototypes with the components as independent within-subject variable.

Prototype	Versions components	Extra effort FS	STM	df Hyp.	Err.	F	p
	Simple						
1	Broad/shallow	0	2.2	1	9	1.34	0.277
2	Narrow/deep	47.7	13.6	1	9	34.91	<0.001
	Complex						
3	Broad/shallow	0	33.6	1	9	4.85	0.055
4	Narrow/deep	61.6	39.5	1	9	1.78	0.215

Table 3. Partial correlation between extra user effort regarding the two components and other usability measures.

Measure	Function Selector	Send Text Message
Objective		
Extra keystrokes	0.64**	0.44**
Task duration	0.63**	0.39**
Perceived		
Overall ease-of-use	-0.43**	-0.26*
Overall satisfaction	-0.25*	-0.22
Component-specific ease-of-use	-0.55**	-0.34**
Component-specific satisfaction	-0.41**	-0.37**

$*p. < .05. **p. < .01.$

5. CONCLUSION

The benefit of the proposed empirical testing method is the ability to evaluate the usability of an individual component in a single system. Something, overall measures (e.g., task duration, number of keystrokes) cannot do. Other sequential data analysis methods (for a survey see [5]) take only lower-level events for their analysis. They pre-processed this data to create data that relates to more high-level concepts. However, these compound messages leave more room for discussion about the system interpretation of the lower-level messages as they lack a direct relation with higher-level system components. Extending the log file with recording of the system's status makes it possible to construct the system interpretation of the lower-level into higher-level message (e.g., [8]). However, directly logging the higher-level messages when users interact with the system avoid the task of creating a tool to pre-process the data later on.

The proposed analysis also has its limitations. It assumes that the usability of a component will not influence other components. However, factors like the user (e.g., memory load or inconsistency [1]), the environment and even the system architecture can create relations between the components that can disturb the analysis. For instance, the system architecture can be a factor if an unclear input method for entering a character on a mobile phone can cause users to create unwanted characters that will be sent to higher-level String components. These unintended messages to higher-level component should not be charged to the usability of String components. Therefore, future evaluators should convince themselves that lower-level components have no ineffectiveness problem. The so-called Standardised Reception Coefficient [1] can help them to inspect the components for ineffectiveness.

REFERENCES

[1]   Brinkman, W.P., *Is Usability Compositional?*, Ph.D. thesis, Technische Universiteit Eindhoven, Einhoven, 2003.
[2]   Brinkman, W.P., Haakma, R., and Bouwhuis, D.G., *Usability Evaluation of Component-Based User Interfaces*, in Proceedings of IFIP 8th TC.13 International Conference on Human-Computer Interaction INTERACT'01 (Tokyo, 9-13 July 2001), IOS Press, Amsterdam, 2001, pp. 767-768.
[3]   Haakma, R., *Layered Feedback in User-System Interaction*. Ph.D. thesis, Technische Universiteit Eindhoven, The Netherlands, 1998.
[4]   Heineman, G.T. and Councill, W.T., *Component-Based Software Engineering: Putting the Pieces Together*, Addison-Wesley, London, 2001.
[5]   Hertzum, M. and Jacobsen, N.E., *The Evaluator Effect: A Chilling Fact About Usability Evaluation Methods,* International Journal of Human-Computer Interaction, Vol. 13, No. 4, 2001, pp. 421-443.
[6]   Hilbert, D.M. and Redmiles, D.F., *Extracting Usability Information From User Interface Events*, ACM Computing Surveys, Vol. 32, No. 4, 2000, pp. 384-421.
[7]   Hilbert, D.M. and Redmiles, D.F., *Large-Scale Collection of Usage Data to Inform Design*, in Proceedings of 8th IFIP TC.13 International Conference on Human-Computer Interaction INTERACT'01 (Tokyo, 9-13 July 2001), IOS Press, Amsterdam, 2001, pp. 569-576.
[8]   Kieras, D. and Polson, P.G., *An Approach to the Formal Analysis of User Complexity*, International Journal Man-Machine Studies, Vol. 22, No 4, 1985, pp. 365-394.
[9]   Lecerof, A. and Paternò, F., *Automatic Support for Usability Evaluation*, IEEE Transactions on Software Engineering, Vol. 24, No. 10, 1998, pp. 863-888.
[10] Paternò, F., *Model-Based Design and Evaluation of Interactive Applications*, Springer, London, 2000.
[11] Snowberry, K., Parkinson, S.R., and Sisson, N., *Computer Display Menu*, Ergonomics, Vol. 26, 1983, pp. 699-712.
[12] Taylor, M.M., *Layered Protocols for Computer-Human Dialogue, I: Principles*, International Journal Man-Machine Studies, Vol. 28, No. 1, 1988, pp. 175-218.

Chapter 14

INFIGURA, AN INTEGRATED DESIGN TOOL
Exploiting Semantics and Patterns for Web Development

Thomas Tiedtke, Thomas Krach, and Christian Märtin
Augsburg University of Applied Sciences, Department of Computer Science
Baumgartnerstrasse 16 – D-86161 Augsburg (Germany)
E-mail: { tiedtke, krach, maertin}@informatik.fh-augsburg.de

Abstract   This paper presents a tool for the computer-supported design of website interaction structures and interfaces. The *InFigura* tool incorporates user experience patterns and prototyping. It enables interdisciplinary cooperation. This allows easier and faster development of high-quality websites.

Keywords: Interface and Interaction Design, Patterns, Prototyping, Usability, Web
Development.

1.   INTRODUCTION

The construction of highly usable websites requires the integration of advanced user interface and interaction design methods into web design approaches. However, such unified approaches and appropriate integrated tool
support are still quite rare.

Most current proposals for improving website design either model web
applications like traditional software systems [3], or focus on visual design
aspects alone [27]. Both approaches neglect the interdisciplinary facets of
web development. Better solutions could be achieved by combining sound
conceptual models with state-of-the-art software development technology,
and communicative visual design, where all system aspects are modelled
from a user's perspective [7].

The *InFigura* tool presented in this paper is built around such a user-
centered approach for web development. Its main purpose is to assist information architects in developing the structures and semantic elements of web-

171

R. Jacob et al. (eds.), Computer-Aided Design of User Interfaces IV, 171–184.
© 2005 *Kluwer Academic Publishers. Printed in the Netherlands.*

sites. It also supports interdisciplinary cooperation that is vital for the production of high quality websites and other multimedia products.

Usability engineering is an essential activity of interactive system design. It is needed to create interactive software and media that enable positive user experiences. *InFigura* supports usability engineering by integrating patterns and usability guidelines. The tool also allows fast and easy user testing with automatically generated prototypes [17].

The presented tool combines the advantages of automated processes – made possible by a centralized and consistent database – with the flexibility and creativity of interactive design methods. The tool emphasizes the importance of user experience for web design that has a great effect on conversion rates and customer loyalty [20] and thus has direct impact on the economic success of a web project [7]. Conceptually *InFigura* is not restricted to websites. It could also be used to design user interfaces for interactive devices like mobile PDAs or set-top boxes. In a first step the *InFigura* prototype has been developed as a website development tool, in order to concentrate on a well known field. The adaptation to other user interface types is planned in a later step.

In Section 2 we describe current approaches and tools used for developing web sites and work to which *InFigura*'s approach is related. The architecture and basic concepts of the *InFigura* tool are presented in Section 3, its workflow process, including prototyping, in Section 4. A short discussion in Section 5 and future prospects in Section 6 conclude this paper.

2.   RELATED WORK

Two different lines of *interface design* meet at web development: classic GUI design for software systems, applying style guides and usability rules, and the approach used by visual designers with their wish to create "flippy and cool" designs [29]. So far, no unified interaction design methods have been established.

Today most information architects still use standard software environments for developing websites. There are few *tools* offering integrated support for interaction and interface design and the modelling of websites. One approach for designing web site structures and web pages is described in [12], a sketch-based system with different zoom views on the website. Real support of the website's semantics, however, is missing, as well as prototyping. In [8], a schema-based tool with an explorer-like interface is described. But information architects rather need tools with intuitive handling, like the drawing applications they are used to.

Professional web design tools like DreamWeaver [13] or FrontPage [14] as well as IDEs like Eclipse [9] enable web designers or software developers to edit the *code* of user interfaces in a WYSIWYG manner. They lack the integration of the information and interaction architecture (semantics). With these tools a user, e.g., creates a *syntactic* link element, but not a *semantic* navigation element.

The *experience a user gains, by using a website,* is influenced by a variety of elements, as discussed in [7]. The main elements of this approach are a *strategic plane,* which describes the main goals of a website, an overlying *scope plane* that defines basic features and contents, the *structure plane* which describes how these basic features and contents are structured and the *skeleton plane,* that defines single page grids. On top, at the *visual design plane,* the final visual representations are added.

User experience patterns contain proven and applicable design knowledge for the context of use [24]. Patterns follow a strict representation scheme and provide some kind of positive handling advice. In [10] a good categorisation of patterns used in web context can be found. An online textual pattern library is presented in [16]. In [6] and [2] several pattern-oriented design approaches are discussed. Conceptual, implementation-independent patterns are described in [22].

The tool presented in this paper is partially based on the concepts of user experience elements and patterns, described above.

3. THE *INFIGURA* TOOL

3.1 Architecture

The core concept of the *InFigura* tool is the separation of visual, semantic and syntactic representations of web elements. For each element there exists a visual drawing object and a semantic meta data object (Section 3.3). Syntactic representations are generated in the prototyping step using both, semantic data and visual data like element's size and position (Section 4.5).

The architecture of the *InFigura* system is illustrated in Fig. 1. The main actor components of the *InFigura* system are the *Definers* (*SiteDefiner* and *PageDefiner*), which provide functionality for defining the pages, the site structure and individual page elements. The *SiteDefiner* provides functionality for designing the site structure and the users´ tasks, corresponding to the structure plane described in [7] (Section 2). The elements of the individual web pages (the skeleton plane) are defined using the *PageDefiner*. The *Definers* manage the meta data objects stored in *WebsiteMetadata* and keep track of the corresponding drawing objects (e.g., circles and rectangles). The *drawing environment* manages the visual editing of the website model. User events related to website or web page elements, like resizing, moving etc., are processed within the drawing environment. Relevant events like deleting or editing are forwarded to the Page- or SiteDefiner that updates the WebsiteMetadata.

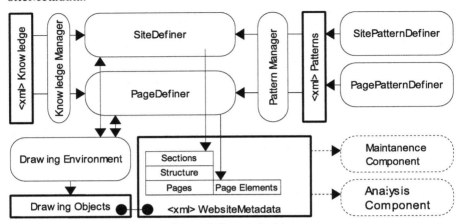

Figure 1. System Architecture.

User experience patterns stored in XML documents are created using the *SitePatternDefiner* and the *PagePatternDefiner*, which are specializations of the Site- and PageDefiner. For applying these patterns the *PatternManager* integrates the patterns´ semantic metadata and visual objects into the website model under development. The website model consists of semantic elements like sections, web pages and navigation elements (links) and is stored in *WebsiteMetadata*, which can later be used by maintenance and analysis components (not described in this paper). The *Usability Knowledge Base* contains guidelines about user experience aspects. The *KnowledgeManager* customizes this stored knowledge to the current development step, e. g. by layering the areas of attention on web pages [1] over the developed page skeleton layout or by checking the site´s structure for maximal link depths [17].

3.2   Actors and Handling

Information architects (IA) are the tool's primary target group. They are responsible for structuring information, for creating the navigation structure and the relevant elements on individual pages. Today many IAs use standard drawing and text editing software for performing the tasks covered by the *InFigura* tool. Other actors are visual and software designers. For each target group, a common user interface ("view") exists, that focuses on the relevant items while still showing their context. The *visual designer* interacts with a view of the visual elements and formatting information. The *software de-*

signer, on the other hand, needs information about the required backend functionality. Finally there is the *customer* of the website agency, who wants to know about the current state of development.

The tool users have different professional backgrounds as described above, so tool handling and visualisation have to be interactive and intuitive. IAs may not be used to work with abstract models and notations like the UML [3]. They often have different ways of thinking and notating things compared to software developers. Most existing interface tools do not support intuitive actions of the tool user. The *InFigura* tool is controlled visually like the drawing applications, the information architects are used to. The notation provided by *InFigura* is similar to *structure trees*, a de-facto-standard for modeling the information architecture of web sites [11]. For designing the individual pages *layout skeletons* [7] are used, consisting of rectangles representing content, function or navigation elements. The user is not bothered by technical details and can focus on website development, not on editing XML files. For example, if the IA moves a web page onto the surface, the PageDefiner creates both a visual representation (e.g., rectangle) of the element in the drawing environment, as well as a web page object in the metadata XML document. The page's visual representation is linked to the meta data object.

3.3   Website Metadata

Triggered by the IA, who defines sections, pages and page elements (see chapter 4), the system builds up a central database of metadata keeping track of each element through all steps of a website's life cycle. This avoids multiple editing and manual translation of data during the design and development process (e.g. from a textual to a visual representation), reducing possible sources of error and the risk of concurrent versions of artefacts. Thus the development life-cycle is shortened and costs are reduced, while development quality is improved. The website's metadata is stored in XML format, which is structured as described in [22]. For every modelled item (section, page, link or page element) conceptual data, technical data and visual data is stored. For example, a function element *delete from list*, has a visual style with two different values (*normal* and *active*), it defines a specific technical functionality *(delete selected item from database)*, and it has a semantic meaning as it realizes a feature claimed in the website's scope.

3.4   User Experience Patterns

The exploitation of user experience patterns speeds up the development life-cycle and helps to achieve better usability of the target system. Patterns used in this tool not only exist as written text, but are directly applicable elements stored in XML containing all relevant items. The patterns can be easily integrated into a website model by transforming their XML elements into website model XML elements (done by the *PatternManager*) and inserting them into the website model XML document (done by the *Site-* or *PageDefiner*). After the insertion, the website model is rearranged, the navigation structure is adjusted and the labelling database is updated.

Compared to the concept of templates, user experience patterns represent a more complex and integrated approach. The patterns used by *InFigura* are compositions of different items, from content and navigation items to sections, some limited to one page, others spanning over several pages. In addition these applicable patterns incorporate tested usability knowledge. *InFigura* classifies them into two main classes according to their range of application: *Structural patterns* describe complex processes, that affect more than one page, like online shopping or user registration.

Structural patterns are composed of linked sequences of pages and elements on every individual page, e.g., information items, functional elements or link elements. Structural navigation patterns include link elements and navigation pages needed for special navigation structures like *index navigation*. Elements implementing knowledge about usability issues, marketing and legal aspects are stored in such patterns, too. For example, see Section 4.3. *Page element patterns* refer to individual web pages. They can be complex content structures, sets of form elements or status information. Page element patterns can also be part of more complex structural patterns which implicitly define specific elements for each page (Section 4.4).

3.5   Usability Engineering

Besides the integration of patterns, the *InFigura* tool supports usability engineering in different ways. A central labelling database helps to provide labelling consistency (e.g., link and page labels). Central style sheet management keeps the visual representation of pages and page elements consistent. Plug-ins add additional usability knowledge.

For example, one plug-in checks the click count to reach a specific goal (the maximum should be three). Attention areas on pages [1] can be layered over the edit canvas, helping the IA and/or visual designer to place page elements on an appropriate position. The automated generation of prototypes (Section 4.5) is another method of usability engineering comprised by *InFigura*.

4. THE *INFIGURA* DEVELOPMENT PROCESS

4.1 Workflow

The *InFigura* workflow can be described as follows (Fig. 2):
1. Definition of page types and their templates
2. Definition of website structure and resources (web pages)
3. Definition of page elements
4. Incremental adjustment and refinement

In the first step, the IA transforms the web site´s features and content items (scope) into a basic structure. Using the tool, he or she defines sections and pages of the website. Structural patterns are applied in this step. Next, primary navigation links are defined. In the following step, the IA edits pages and defines their individual elements. Further, the website model is gradually refined as shown in Fig. 2.

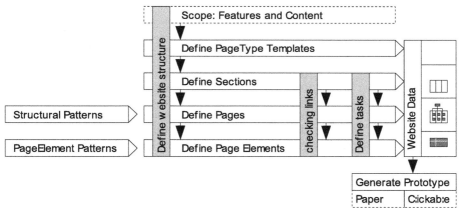

Figure 2. Interaction and Interface Definition Workflow.

InFigura offers a structured workflow, but it still allows for the necessary slack in order to trigger the creativity of the members of the development team. It supports cooperation between IAs, visual designers and software designers (SD), thus enabling an integrated design workflow. The centralized website database prevents team members from doing redundant work and provides consistency over the different development phases. Different views (Section 3.2) of the website model and data focus on elements appropriate for each actor, while still displaying their respective context. For example texters can use a "texter view" to directly write their texts in the correct context of use. An interactive list of the content elements is automatically created from the website metadata. Thus content production and delivery can easily be managed. Additonally *InFigura* supports the documentation of a website, like site-structure and/or style guides. In this chapter we use a shopping website example because it is quite complex and yet a well known example.

4.2   Defining Page Types and Templates

Basic *page types and their templates* are defined first. Table 1 shows examples of page types, based on [22]. In a later step (Section 4.3) pages are assigned to page types in order to provide structural and layout consistency and reduce the modelling effort for individual pages. The visual designer and the information architect define a *universal layout grid* visually, by dividing the page into several semantic canvases and setting a number of attributes, e.g., *fixed-sized* or *dynamic-sized layout* of pages. Based on this, layout grids for all page types are defined, as well as standard page elements. The software designer can check these fundamental decisions with respect to their impact on technical design and implementation.

Table 1. Semantic Page Types

Page Type	Meaning
HomePage	first page of website
FrontPage	first page of a particular section within a website
NavigationPage	page that is mainly used for navigation
ContentPage	page that contains the actual content the user is searching for
RichContentPage	page containing rich media content like videos or sounds
FormPage	page containing a form (as the main element)
FormConfirmation	page confirming the processing of form data
MoodPage	page that stimulates the user's mood and emotions

4.3   Defining Website Structure and Pages

After setting up the project basis with page types, the IA defines the *structure* of the site. This is done by translating the goals, features and content into a navigable structure [5]. The website structure is defined visually by drawing rectangles and circles representing sections and pages on the edit canvas. A page type is assigned to any created page, so the created page contains standard page elements. The IA also sets page attributes that are used for construction, maintenance and analysis of the website (e.g., whether the page is an entry- or exit-page).

Additional attributes are set by the visual designer (colour set) and the software designer (static or dynamic page). All these defined attributes are stored in the central database. Fig. 3 shows a screenshot of the *SiteDefiner*. For an example website the IA defines the following sections: *Shopping* and *Corporate Information*. Afterwards she creates all necessary logical pages (home page, product list, product detail, order form, confirmation, …). For standard processes there are predefined structural patterns that also can be applied by drawing their visual pattern representation on the website edit canvas. Thus all pages, navigation and page elements contained in the pattern are created in a single step. Some structural patterns are listed in Table 2. For example, if the IA creates an online shopping process as described above, she has to consider a multitude of aspects from technical and usability issues to legal regulations.

The *OrderPattern* provides abstract task information together with a sequence of pages containing all necessary link and function elements. As an example, the pattern may contain legal regulations as text blocks displaying some necessary advice and usability issues incorporated in navigation elements with a consistent labelling. Using this pattern reduces modelling time and ensures proven usability for the order process.

Table 2. Structural Patterns

Pattern	Meaning
Login Pattern	login process for registered users
Registration Pattern	process for registration with a website
OrderPattern	process for online shopping (ordering items)
Navigation Pattern	patterns for navigation (grid, index, guided tour, ...)

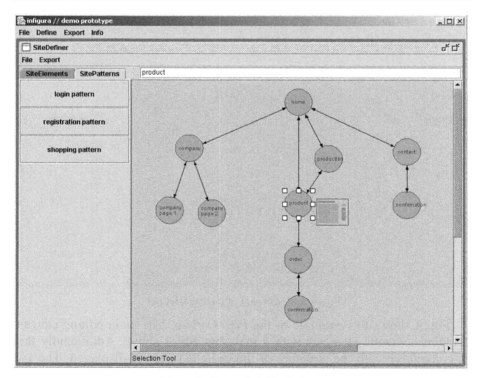

Figure 3. Screenshot SiteDefiner

4.4   Defining Page Elements

After the site's structure has been arranged, the IA defines the layout and the elements of the individual pages (the page's *skeleton*) using the *Page-Definer*. According to its page type, the layout area of each page is already divided into canvases. Standard page elements have already been set automatically on the page or have been added to a list of elements to be set. The IA checks these elements and defines more page elements. Examples can be found in Table 3. In our shopping website the IA would define the following items on the productdetail page (in addition to standard elements, like top navigation elements): content elements (product description, product image), function links (add to cart) and navigation links (related teaser).

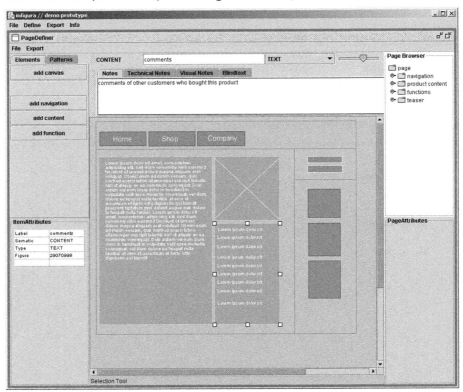

Figure 4. Screenshot of the PageDefiner

Fig. 4 shows this example in the *PageDefiner*. The main editing canvas contains semantic elements with a metadata editor above. Additionally the *PageExplorer* with the structure of the designed page is displayed. The IA can use page element patterns for easy and fast creation of complex components. Table 4 lists examples of page patterns. *InFigura* allows page definition in two ways. An e*xact mode* defines placement and size accurately. This method can be used for rapid development or in projects with a very rigorous style guide. *Bubble mode* gives more flexibility to the visual designer. Here, actual positioning and sizes are not defined at this stage.

Table 3. Examples for semantic page elements

Page Element	Meaning	Syntactic Elements
Content	contains actual content of a web page	text, image, media
Branding	creates branding and image "feeling"	image, text
StatusInformation	information on status of application	text
NavigationLinks	provide main structural navigation	text links, image links
ContentLinks	links in context of the page's content	text links, image links
FunctionLinks	provide functionality	text links, form buttons
InputElements	allow users to enter data	form elements
Notes	notes that help the user use the site	text, image

Table 4. Examples for page element patterns

Page Element Pattern	Meaning
NavigationSelector	user can select one navigation item from a list of items
ItemList	list of linked items with more information available
TeaserElement	linked element that teasers special content
PersonalDataForm	form for input of personal data
Bestof Navigation	list of most visited pages
ShoppingCart	status information and functionality of a shopping cart
PersonalAccount Informat.	status information and functionality of personal account
NavigationGroups	groups of navigational links
ContactElements	elements used for contacting

4.5   Automated Export and Prototyping

After the site's structure and the basic elements have been defined, different types of prototypes can be produced at all steps of the development process. This can be achieved by transforming the XML metadata of the website into different formats like *PDF* for paper prototypes or *HTML* for clickable prototypes. Size and position of each element are gathered from the drawing environment – as well as the page element's hierarchy – and added to the site's model. Its navigation and resource elements are then transformed into PDF or HTML using XSLT (Fig. 2).

The *paper prototype* [17] can be used to test the basic information architecture at early development stages. Also hints for improving the navigation structure can be gathered this way.

The *clickable prototype* allows real-click testing of the information architecture, interaction and navigation design. New ideas can easily be evaluated. This helps information architects to easily prove concepts. Web agencies, dealing with customers, can use the prototypes to illustrate ideas and getting better argumentational support.

Plus, technical system designers can inspect the clickable prototype for required techniques and the needed concrete behaviour of functions. Visual designers can test designs not only on static screen designs or printouts, but in a clickable environment which gives a better impression of the look-and-feel of the created design.

5.   CONCLUSION

The *InFigura* tool presented in this paper focuses on practical aspects of website development. Its intuitive handling concepts and visualization enables non-technical users like information architects to participate in the advantages of an integrated process, while still maintaining the flexibility they need. The tool integrates conceptual, legal, marketing, as well as visual and technical aspects of website development, what makes it a valuable development system for interdisciplinary cooperation. The exploitation of patterns and usability guidelines incorporates important design knowledge into the development life cycle.

Today, where cost optimization is important for all web agencies, the *InFigura* tool increases the efficiency of web development activities and bridges the gap between software developers and creative web designers.

6.   FUTURE WORK

The *InFigura* tool is currently being developed as a joint project between *allevia gbr* and the *usability management project* at the Department of Computer Science at Augsburg University of Applied Sciences. It is now planned to extend the functionality of the existing prototype and to use the tool for the construction of a group of pilot commercial applications. Another goal of our research is the integration of the tool into the AWUSA website usability analysis framework [22], completing the support for the overall website life-cycle. This will lead towards a comprehensive and integrated framework for interactive media development and analysis.

REFERENCES

[1] Bernard, M., Usability News, accessible at: http://psychology.wichita.edu/surl/usabili-tynews/3W/web_object.htm
[2] Borchers, J., *A Pattern Approach to Interaction Design*, John Wiley, New York, 2001.
[3] Conallen, J., *Building Web Applications with UML*, 2nd ed., Addison-Wesley, Boston, 2002.
[4] Costagliola, G., Ferruci, F., and Francese R., *Web Engineering: Models and Methodologies for the Design of Hypermedia Applications*, in S.K. Chang, "Handbook of Software

Engineering & Knowledge Engineering", Emerging Technologies, Vol. 2, World Scientific, 2002, Singapore, pp. 181-199.

[5] Fleming, J., *Web Navigation Designing the User Experience*, O'Reilly & Associates, Sebastopol, 1 September 1998.

[6] Forbrig, P., Limbourg, Q., Urban, B., Vanderdonckt, J. (eds.), *Design, Specification, and Verification of Interactive Systems*, Proceedings of the 9th International Conference on Design, Specification, and Verification of Interactive Systems DSV-IS'2002 (Rostock, June 2002), Lecture Notes in Computer Science, Vol. 2545, Springer, Berlin, 2002.

[7] Garrett, Jesse J., *The Elements of User Experience*, New Riders, Indianapolis, 2002.

[8] Garzotto, F., Paolini, P., and Baresi, L., *Supporting Reusable Web Design with HDM-Edit*, in Proceedings of 34th Hawaii International Conference on System Sciences HICSS'34 (Maui, 3-6 January 2001), IEEE Computer Society Press, Los Alomitos, 2001, accessible at http://csdl.computer.org/comp/proceedings/hicss/2001/0981/07/09817076.pdf

[9] IBM Eclipse, accessible at http://www.eclipse.org/

[10] Gómez, J. and Cachero, C., *Conceptual Modeling of Device-Independent Web Applications*, IEEE Multimedia, Vol. 8, No. 2, April-June 2001, pp. 26-39.

[11] Kahn, P. and Lenk, K., *Websites visualisieren*, Rowohlt, Reinbek, 2001.

[12] Lin, J., Thomsen, M., and Landay, J., *A Visual Language for Sketching Large and Complex Interactive Designs*, in Proceedings of ACM Conference on Human Factors in Computing Systems CHI'2002 (Minneapolis, 20-25 April 2002), ACM Press, New York, 2002, pp. 307-314.

[13] Macromedia Dreamweaver, accessible at http://www.macromedia.com/

[14] Microsoft Frontpage, accessible at http://www.microsoft.com/

[15] Molina, P., Meliá, S., and Pastor, O., *User Interface Conceptual Patterns*, in P. Forbrig, Q. Limbourg, B. Urban, J. Vanderdonckt (eds.), PreProceedings of the 9th International Conference on Design Specification and Verification of Interactive Systems DSV-IS'2002 (Rostock, June 2002), University of Rostock, Univ. catholique de Louvain, 2002, pp. 201-214.

[16] Montreal Online Usability Digital Library, accessible at http://hci.cs.concordia.ca/moudil/

[17] Nielsen, J., *Usability Engineering*, Academic Press, Boston, 1993.

[18] Nielsen, J., *Erfolg des Einfachen*, Markt+Technik Verlag, München, 2000.

[19] Perzel, K. and Kane, D., *Usability Patterns for Applications on the World Wide Web*, in Proceedings of Pattern Languages of Programs PLoP'99 (Urbana, 15-18 August 1999), accessible at http://jerry.cs.uiuc.edu/~plop/plop99/proceedings/Kane/perzel_kane.pdf

[20] Puscher, F. *Das Usability Prinzip*, Dpunkt-Verlag, Heidelberg, 2001.

[21] Rosenfeld, L. and Morville, P., *Information Architecture for the World Wide Web*, O'Reilly, Sebastopol, 1998.

[22] Tiedtke, T., Märtin, C., and Gerth, N., *AWUSA–A Tool for Automated Website Usability Analysis*, in P. Forbrig, Q. Limbourg, B. Urban, J. Vanderdonckt (eds.), PreProceedings of the 9th Design, Specification, and Verification of Interactive Systems DSV-IS'2002 (Rostock, June 2002), University of Rostock, Univ. catholique de Louvain, 2002, pp. 251-266.

[23] van Welie, M., van der Verr, G.C., and Eliens, A., *An Ontology for Task World Models*, in Proceedings of Conference 5th International Eurographics Workshop on Design, Specification and Verification of Interactive Systems DSV-IS'1998 (Abingdon, 3-5 June 1998), Springer-Verlag, Wien, 1998, pp. 57-70.

[24] van Welie, M., van der Verr, G.C., and Eliens, A., *Patterns as Tools for User Interface Design*, in J. Vanderdonckt, Ch. Farenc (eds.), Proceedings of International Workshop

on Tools for Working with Guidelines TFWWG'2000 (Biarritz, 7-8 October 2000), Springer-Verlag, London, 2000, pp. 313-324.

[25] van Welie, M., *Task-based User Interface Design*, Ph.D. Thesis, Amsterdam, 2001, accessible at http://www.cs.vu.nl/~martijn/gta/docs/Welie-PhD-thesis.pdf

[26] Wenzel, O., *Webdesign, Informationssuche und Flow*, Josef Eul Verlag, Köln, 2001.

[27] Wirth, T., *Missing Links*, Hanser Verlag, München, 2002.

[28] Wodtke, C., *Information Architecture Blue Prints for the Web*, New Riders, Indianapolis, 2002.

[29] Wroblewski, L., *Site Seeing: A Visual Approach to Web Usability*, Hungry Minds, New York, 2002.

Chapter 15

INSTRUMENTING BYTECODE FOR THE PRODUCTION OF USAGE DATA

Iain McLeod, Huw Evans, Philip Gray and Rebecca Mancy
Computing Science Department, University of Glasgow,
17 Lilybank Gardens – Glasgow G12 8QQ (Scotland)
E-mail: {mcleodia,huw,pdg,rebecca}@dcs.gla.ac.uk
URL: http://www.dcs.gla.ac.uk/contacts/searchresults.cfm?rowid=362 - (??) -
http://www.dcs.gla.ac.uk/~pdg –http://www.dcs.gla.ac.uk/contacts/searchresults.cfm?rowid=459
Tel: +44 141 330 {4256,(),4933, 0918} – Fax: +44 141 330 4913

Abstract   We have taken the process of software instrumentation, normally used in the creation of profiling and debugging tools, and applied it to the production of usage data for user-computer interaction studies. This paper describes the design and evaluation of a prototype tool called iGuess, that enables an investigator to discover which methods are used within a Java application when particular tasks are carried out, and instrument these to produce usage data. A key feature of the system is that an application can be instrumented without any need for access to the source code. In this paper we describe the system's functionality, briefly explain how it works and present the results of an early informal evaluation.

Keywords: ByteCode instrumentation, Usability testing tools, Usage monitoring, Software visualisation.

1.   INTRODUCTION

In order to study usage data from an application, one must be able to extract it. Various approaches to extraction exist: [1,5,7]. These all require either modification of the source code of the original application or the use of a specially built run-time framework. Consequently, the generation and capture of usage data depends on having the right software in the first place or considerable programming effort. The Grumps project is developing tools to assist in the capture, transport, storage and processing of usage data in a dis-

R. Jacob et al. (eds.), Computer-Aided Design of User Interfaces IV, 185–195.
© 2005 *Kluwer Academic Publishers. Printed in the Netherlands.*

tributed environment. As part of the project, we have addressed the problem of how to make it feasible for investigators to build customised instrumentation of applications, even when they do not have access to the original source code. iGuess, the system described here, is our first attempt at a solution.

2.   INSTRUMENTING AN APPLICATION

Instrumentation is the process of augmenting an application with code which conveys information about the running process. This is achieved through the generation and transmission of events and optionally allows control of the application's execution.

2.1   iGuess Approach to Instrumentation

For each of the tasks that the investigator wishes to study, he or she must identify the methods called within a given application. The iGuess design is based on the notion that an instrumenter can, by interacting with this application, identify those interaction methods they wish to capture. iGuess provides a visualisation and count of the methods being called and allows the investigator to turn instrumentation of every individual class and method on or off (we include constructors in our definition of Method). Initially a fully instrumented version of the application is launched. This generates instrumentation data for every method that is called. Using the feedback from method call counts, the investigator turns off the instrumentation of different methods according to whether they are used during the execution of the task to be studied. By a process of elimination, the investigator determines the methods to be included in the final instrumentation of the application.

Fig. 1 shows this process, demonstrating the instrumentation of an application by iGuess. The application is loaded into iGuess in the form of a Jar file (the box labelled "Original Application"). A fully instrumented Jar file is produced (the box labelled "Instrumented Application") by the process described in Section 2.3.1. There is then an iterative cycle of interaction, visualisation and editing (shown by the processes "Interact with Application", "View set of methods called" and "Refine Instrumentation"). This cycle assists the investigator in discovering the set of methods they wish to instrument. At the end of the iterative process, only a subset of the methods within the application is instrumented. This reduces code bloat and unnecessary event generation. When the investigator is satisfied with the chosen set of methods, the instrumented application can then be deployed amongst the end user population (shown on the diagram by the process labelled "Deploy").

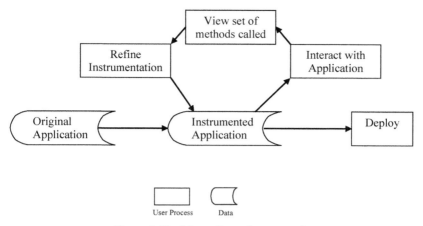

Figure 1. The Macro Recorder approach.

2.2 Instrumenting an Application with iGuess

2.2.1 Classbrowser

iGuess has a classbrowser-style interface (Fig. 2), which displays the application as a tree of packages ( ), classes ( ), methods ( ) and constructors ( ). These are colour coded with their current state of instrumentation so that the user can identify what is currently being instrumented and what is not.

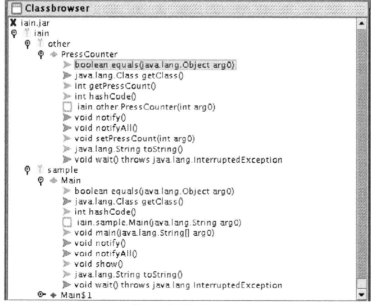

Figure 2. Classbrowser.

2.2.2   Instrumentation Editor

The Instrumentation Content Editor allows fine-grained control over what parts of a method are logged (i.e. its parameters, return types and exceptions) as well as whether a class or method is currently being instrumented. When changes are made, the user is alerted to the fact that any instrumented applications they are currently running must be closed and redeployed to reflect these changes. The Instrumentation Editor for classes and methods are both similar in design, with two tabs:

Standard Controls. *Standard Controls* has a master switch which determines whether the class or method is being instrumented (shown by the checkbox *"Instrumentation on"* in Fig. 3). In the case of the method editor, there is a checkbox for all parameters and exceptions of the method, as well as for the return value if there is one. Note that the names of method parameters, exceptions and return values are not stored in the bytecode of an application and hence are not recoverable.

Figure 3. Standard Controls.

Extra Code. *Extra Code*, shown in Fig. 4 allows the investigator to insert his or her own code into a method or class, over and above the standard instrumentation code. This could be used, for example, to display an incident diary during execution of an instrumented application. Of course, use of this field would require the instrumenter to be a proficient Java programmer.

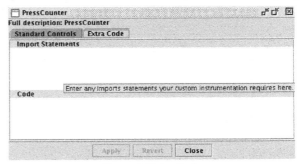

Figure 4. Extra Code.

2.2.3   Viewing an Instrumented Application

There are two ways of viewing the output of an instrument application, within the iGuess system: viewing the output of the application since it was last re-deployed (runtime viewer) and viewing all output from the application since iGuess was last re-started (lifetime viewer). These can be cleared by a *reset* button if desired. The idea behind the runtime viewer and the *reset* button is that a potential strategy for discovery would be to start up a fully instrumented application and wait until construction was finished, then clear the runtime viewer before carrying out an action. Then, the only method calls displayed (assuming no background threads) would be those directly generated by that action. The output can be viewed in two ways: as a tree, via the Call Count Visualiser, and as a list, via the Call Sequence Visualiser.

2.2.4   Call Count Visualiser

The Call Count Visualiser (Fig. 5) is similar to the Classbrowser, showing a tree of packages, classes and methods. This tree (initially empty) is built *on-the-fly* as the events are received from the instrumented application. A count of every method call is stored next to that method entry in the tree. Methods which were called more recently (the cut-off time defining recent is user adjustable via a slider control) are displayed in green, those called less recently are displayed in amber on both the text area and the tree. This is to help the user to distinguish the events generated by the last action they performed from those generated by previous actions.

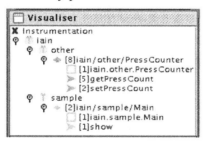

Figure 5. Call Count Visualiser.

2.2.5   Call Sequence Visualiser

The Call Sequence Visualiser (Fig. 6) is a text area showing the instrumentation events received in order of arrival (and hence of generation). Similar to the Call Count Visualiser, these are coloured according to time of arrival. Clicking on a class or method in the Call Count Visualiser highlights the corresponding event in the Call Sequence Visualiser, facilitating the analysis.

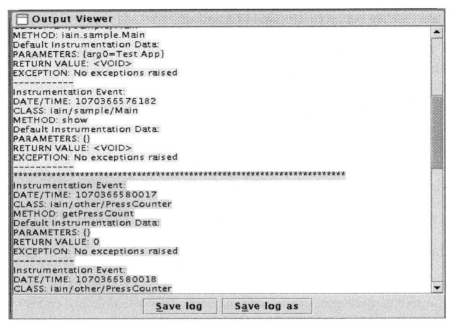

Figure 6. Call Sequence Visualiser.

2.3   The Bytecode instrumentation process

2.3.1   Grumps Bytecode Tool

Grumps Bytecode Tool (GBT) is an API for modifying the bytecode of an application. It uses the Apache Bytecode Engineering Library (BCEL) API [11]. GBT replaces the standard Java bytecode for creating a new object on the heap:

```
SomeObject obj = new SomeObject();
```

with a call to a nominated static method:

```
SomeObject obj = (SomeObject) Util.create ("SomeObject");
```

The static method hands out an instance of a subclass of that object which we generate by inspecting the object using the Java reflection API. Each method we wish to instrument within this subclass will contain the instrumentation code plus a call to the superclass method (which ensures the original application's code is executed). The usage data produced by this code is packaged up into an Instrumentation Event, which is relayed through the Grumps data transport network (GrumpsNet [4]) via a call to a static method in a "Logger" class:

```
Logger.log(InstrumentationEvent evt);
```

2.3.2   Related Work

The technique used by GBT is similar to that of JRat [12], a profiling tool which is also built upon BCEL. JRat and GBT both require pre-processing of the application. JFluid [13] is another profiling tool which can attach to a running process and create instrumentation within a method, as well as before and after the method call (this requires sourcecode). However, it requires a modified Hotspot™ Virtual Machine to run. BIT [8] and JOIE [3] are both bytecode editing tools which provide similar functionality to that of BCEL. Kaldi [1] provides instrumentation by replacing the core Java AWT classes with pre-instrumented ones. This is not instrumentation by bytecode manipulation, instead being instrumentation by replacement of core APIs. However it achieves a similar end result. Chander, Mitchell and Shin [2] discuss the applications of replacing objects with safe subclasses to implement mobile code security.

3.   EVALUATIVE STUDIES

We have carried out a small, informal evaluation of iGuess to test its feasibility and to identify problems in its interaction model and user interface. Six users, with a variety of programming backgrounds, were invited to instrument a computer-based version of the board game Connect4, identifying the occasions when a move was made. We asked them to think aloud during their tasks and we also interviewed them afterwards.

Two trials were carried out with each subject. They were first given a version of iGuess which initially produced a full instrumentation of our sample application, i.e. one in which every method was fully instrumented to produce events. This task was intended to test their ability to cope with large amounts of data being produced by an application and of narrowing down their search by switching off methods within the instrumentation. The method used was thus a process of elimination.

Users were then given a version which started with an empty instrumentation, i.e. one in which none of the methods were initially instrumented. This was designed to evaluate their ability to use the interface to find the method which carried out a given action by looking at the names of packages, classes and methods. This could be described as a process of induction.

The main finding of our evaluation was that unstructured instrumentation (i.e. without any knowledge of the structure of the target application) is not desirable. A large number of events were generated by a fully instrumented application - in the region of 2000 just for the initial construction and display of a small sized application. A number of methods, particularly in user interfaces are low level, and are called many times. Actions such as moving the mouse cursor across the screen of some applications can generate hundreds of method calls as the application repaints. As methods are called in rapid succession, the application slows considerably, so as to be almost unusable in larger applications. See Section 4, Two Way Communication. In contrast, when faced with an empty instrumentation, users did not know where to begin looking within classes and methods to find suitable points of entry for instrumentation. There were a number of other findings, the most important of which are the following:

3.1.1   Problems of Search and Information Management

• Lack of support for key tasks: Displaying full information on a method within the tree of the classbrowser (e.g., "void wait() throws java.lang. InterruptedException") forced the user to scroll and expand the tree horizontally to see all of the information on the method and placed too much burden on users (particularly novice programmers).

• Lack of support for key tasks: The lack of a search facility for finding a given class or method within the Classbrowser or Call Count Visualiser.

3.1.2   Problems of Navigating Code Structure

• Affordance of key tasks: When viewing and instrumenting a class, the methods it declares should be separated from the methods that its super-classes declare. This can easily be identified using the reflection mechanism and the method getDeclaringClass().

3.1.3   Supporting the instrumentation process

• Lack of support for key tasks: The lack of the support for highlighting and annotating a method that the user was interested in looking at.

• Affordance of key tasks: The master switch ("Instrumentation On") for adding or removing a method or class from the currently instrumented set was hidden amongst the controls for fine-tuning the content of the instrumentation (Fig. 3), making it difficult for the user to find.

• Affordance of key tasks: Subjects also found it hard to make the semantic jump from clicking on a method or class in the classbrowser to editing it in the class or method editor. This would have been better implemented via a right click popup menu in the tree.

• Lack of support for key tasks: Another desirable task not supported was to edit the instrumentation of groups of classes or methods simultaneously.

- Integration of key tasks in the instrumentation process: Visualising of instrumentation output and editing of instrumentation should be handled within one part of the user interface, not separated as at present (many users found it hard to distinguish between the Classbrowser and Call Count Visualiser and tried to select methods for editing with the latter instead of the former).

- Lack of support for key tasks: The Call Sequence Visualiser was less useful than the Call Count Visualiser in the process of discovering the methods to instrument. Subjects used it a lot less than expected. Most found it produced overwhelming amounts of information, which was not well structured for digesting. The consensus was that had it provided simply the name of the method, it would have proved to be a more valuable tool.

4. CONCLUSION

iGuess is primarily intended to be a tool for users such as HCI experts and psychologists who may wish to generate data rapidly from specific parts of an application. The major issue uncovered by our study is the level of knowledge required to use the tool. With a classbrowser style interface, iGuess is only realistically usable by someone with training and experience in programming. The challenge, then, is to increase the potential user base of future versions by minimising this specialist knowledge requirement. We believe that this is possible by shifting the focus of iGuess from a package/class/method-centric visualisation to one which more closely resembles what the instrumenter sees when interacting with the application. Specialised applications, such as those described in Section 2.2.2, would still require programming knowledge, although tools such as incident diaries could be pre-instrumented. Suggestions to this end are outlined in the rest of this section, alongside other envisaged improvements to the tool.

- Toolbox of commonly used UI components. The concept of a "Toolbox" of commonly used UI components, such as buttons or menu items could be introduced. These would be pre-instrumented. The user could select a component from the toolbox and apply it to an application during editing of its instrumentation. During the discovery process, the first time an instance of that component is selected by the investigator on the instrumented application; it could initiate a dialogue with the instrumenter to determine instrumentation. In this way, iGuess would shift the necessity for knowledge of the internal structure of the application to knowledge of the structure of its user interface.

- Alternative visualisations of method call sequences. Several complimentary techniques for visualising program execution which could be incorporated are demonstrated by Jerding *et al.* [6] and De Pauw *et al.* [9].
- Creation of instrumentation code. In versions of Java prior to 1.4, there was no support for persistence of an arbitrary object (they had to implement the Serialisable interface). A plug-in architecture was created to allow the content of an instrumentation event to be customisable – with the default implementation simply calling toString(). With the inclusion of the XMLEncoder and XMLDecoder classes in Java 1.4, this is no longer an issue.

- Two way communication. Instrumentation content could be controlled by sending control events to the instrumented application. This would allow the instrumenter to place a limit on the number of times a given method call was logged within an interaction session. This would mean that an instrumenter could be made aware of the fact that a method was being called several times, without this causing the performance degradation described in section 3.

- Machine Learning. The process of discovery could be further automated by using machine learning to analyse the sequence of method calls produced by an instrumented application as the investigator carries out the task he or she wishes to study. This is necessary because these methods may be executed by multiple threads within the instrumented application and events may thus arrive out of order and with spurious events between them.

- Code building. Our current implementation of iGuess does not deal with pathological cases such as anonymous inner classes, final classes and private constructors. These can be dealt with using techniques such as JavaCloak [10].

- Extension to other bytecode-based languages. iGuess is limited to instrumenting Java applications. However, the same approach is applicable to any bytecode-based language, (e.g., C# and other .NET languages). We intend to extend iGuess to handle other languages, as the opportunities allow.

ACKNOWLEDGEMENTS

This work was funded by EPSRC Grant GR/N38114. We wish to thank Hunter Bryce, Steve Draper and Richard Thomas for their valuable contributions to the iGuess design and evaluation.

REFERENCES

[1] Al-Qaimari, G. and McRostie D., *KALDI: A Computer-Aided Usability Engineering Tool for Supporting Testing and Analysis of User Performance*, in A. Blanford, J. Vanderdonckt, Ph. Gray (eds.), Proceedings of the 15th Annual Conference of the British HCI Group IHM-HCI'2001 (Lille, 10-14 September 2001), Springer-Verlag, London, pp. 153-169.

[2] Chander, A., Mitchell J.C., and Shin, I., *Mobile Code Security by Java Bytecode Instrumentation,* in Proceedings of the 2001 DARPA Information Survivability Conference & Exposition DISCEX-II'2002 (Anaheim, 12-14 June 2001), IEEE Computer Society Press, Los Alamitos, 2002, pp. 1027-1040, accessible at http://citeseer.nj.nec.com/chander01mobile.html.

[3] Cohen, G., Chase, J., and Kaminsky, D. *Automatic Program Transformation With JOIE,* In Proceedings USENIX Annual Technical Conference (New Orleans, 15-19 June 1998) USENIX Association, Berkeley, 1998, pp. 167-178.

[4] Evans, H., Atkinson, M., Brown, M., Cargill, J., Crease, M., Draper, S., Gray, P.D., and Thomas, R.C., *The Pervasiveness of Evolution in GRUMPS Software,* Software: Practice and Experience, Vol. 33, No. 2, February 2003.

[5] Hilbert, D.M. and Redmiles D.F., *Extracting Usability Information from User Interface Events,* ACM Computing Surveys, Vol. 32, No. 4, December 2000, pp. 384-421.

[6] Jerding, D.F., Stasko, J.T., and Ball, T., *Visualizing Interactions in Program Executions:* International Conference on Software Engineering ICSE'97 (17-23 May 1997 Boston), ACM Press, New York, 1997, accessible at http://citeseer.nj.nec.com/ jerding97visualizing.html.

[7] Kölling, M., Quig, B., Patterson, A., and Rosenberg, J., *The BlueJ System and its Pedagogy,* The Journal of Computer Science Education, Special Issue on Learning and Teaching Object Technology, Vol. 13, No 4, pp. 249-268, December 2003.

[8] Lee, H.B. and Zorn, B.G., *BIT: A Tool for Instrumenting Java Bytecodes,* In Proceedings USENIX Symposium on Internet Technologies and Systems, 1998.

[9] De Pauw, W., Helm, R., Kimelman, D., and Vlissides, J., Visualizing the Behavior of Object-Oriented Systems, in Proceedings of the Conference on Object-oriented Programming Systems, Languages and Applications OOPSLA '93 (Washington, 26 September-1 October), 1993, accessible at http://citeseer.nj.nec.com/depauw93visualizing.html

[10] Renaud K, Evans H. *JavaCloak: Engineering Java™ Proxy Objects using Reflection.* NET.OBJECTDAYS 2000, Messekongresszentrum Erfurt, Germany, accessible at http://www.netobjectdays.org/pdf/00/papers/jit/evans.pdf.

[11] *BCEL: The Java Bytecode Engineering Library*, accessible at http://bcel.sourceforge.net

[12] *JRat: The Java Runtime Analysis Toolkit*, accessible at http://jrat.sourceforge.net

[13] *JFluid: dynamic bytecode instrumentation*, accessible at   http://research.sun.com/projects/jfluid/

Chapter 16

PATTERNS IN MODEL-BASED ENGINEERING

Daniel Sinnig[1,2], Ashraf Gaffar[2], Daniel Reichart[1], Peter Forbrig[1]
and Ahmed Seffah[2]

[1]*Software Engineering Group, Department of Computer Science,*
University of Rostock, Rostock (Germany)
E-mail: {daniel.reichart, Peter.Forbrig}@informatik.uni-rostock.de
[2]*Human-Computer Software Engineering Group, Department of Computer Science,*
Concordia University, Montreal (Canada)
E-mail: {d_sinnig, gaffar, seffah}@cs.concordia.ca

Abstract   In this paper we demonstrate how patterns can act as a driving force for the development of interactive applications. As knowledge re-use is becoming more and more crucial, patterns can be an effective tool to represent knowledge of the HCI domain. Using a model–based development methodology, it is shown how patterns can act as building blocks for the establishment of these models. Starting from outlining the general process of pattern application, we discuss how and which patterns are suitable for several models. In particular we discuss the application and use of patterns for the task, dialog and presentation models. Furthermore, we suggest an interface for patterns using "generic classes" and give concrete examples to corroborate our approach. This allows for modular patterns reuse and plausible parameter exchange with the underlying system. Tool support is based on XML-representations of patterns using a template engine.

Keywords: Model-based interface design, Patterns, Task modelling, UI engineering.

1.   PATTERNS FOR MODEL-BASED DESIGN

The concept of patterns has been transferred to the software community by [5]. Their book "Design Patterns" contained a collection of patterns for the design of object–oriented software. The book has been widely acknowledged and referenced within the community. Recently, like in the software engineering community, the user interface design community has also been a forum for vigorous discussions on pattern languages for User Interface (UI)

197

R. Jacob et al. (eds.), Computer-Aided Design of User Interfaces IV, 197–210.

design and usability engineering. UI patterns are an effective way to transmit experience about recurrent problems in the HCI domain related to UI design issues. A pattern is a named, reusable solution to a recurrent problem in a particular context of use. Even though patterns serve a number of different purposes (education, discussion ground, re-use, etc.), this paper mainly looks at patterns as vehicles for re-use of existing solution.

Since UI patterns capture the essence of successful solutions to recurring design problems, correctly applying them will help avoid "re-inventing the wheel". They could accelerate the development of initial prototypes and help designers reuse successful, elegant designs without the need to rediscover these designs [5]. In the following, we will introduce our approach of developing a formal notation for patterns within the scope of a model–based design of interactive applications.

1.1   The Impact of Patterns on the Model–Based Framework

In a model based UI design methodology, various models are used to describe the relevant aspects of the user interface. Fig. 1 portrays that many UI facets exist and reflects the relevant models for tasks, business objects (domain), users, dialogue and presentation.

First, design decisions are made to establish the envisioned task model in which the future support of the interactive system is already considered. Additionally, models for capturing user characteristics and business objects are developed. Based on these rather abstract models, a dialog, a presentation and a layout model are derived to reveal some implementation details of the user interface. Due to the lack of tool support and libraries populated with existing solutions and ideas, model based user interface design has not reached the mainstream software developer, yet [14]. We believe that patterns have the potential to overcome this major shortcoming. Therefore, as demonstrated in Fig. 1, in our approach we are aiming to use patterns as building blocks in order to create the various models. In the following we will demonstrate how patterns can impact several models. In particular we will focus on the impact of patterns on the envisioned task model, the dialog model, the presentation model and the layout model.

1.2   The Process of Pattern Application

In the domain of software development, the reuse of ideas and knowledge is becoming more and more crucial as a solution to the stark competition, the demand on more quality and less time-to-market, and the steady increase in complexity [10]. "Reusability" is considered as an important quality factor

[7]. Using patterns can be an effective way to transmit experiences about re-current problems in the software and UI development domain. Therefore a solution should be generic enough to apply to different contexts of use. In other words patterns should be formulated generically enough to withstand variations of context and domain. Before the pattern solution stated in the pattern is really tangible and applicable, it must be adapted to the current context of use.

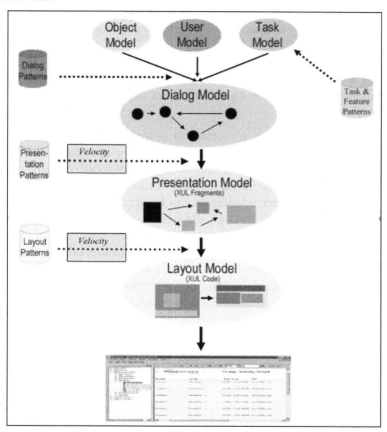

Figure 1. Patterns as building blocks within a model based methodology.

Thus we suggest that patterns contain variables, which can act as place-holders for each particular context of use. In other words, the variables must be bound to concrete values representing the surrounding context. Assuming that patterns are applied to models, the process of pattern applications comprises four sequential steps:

1. **Identification:** A subset M' of the target model M is identified: $M' \subseteq M$. This should reduce the domain size, and help focus the attention on a smaller subset of concern for the next step.

2. **Selection:** An appropriate pattern P is selected to be applied to M'. By focusing on a subset of the domain, the designer can scan M' more effectively to capture potential "spots" that could be improved using some patterns. This is the most important step of all the four. It depends strongly on the experience and the creativity of the designer.
3. **Adaptation:** A pattern is an abstraction that must be instantiated. Therefore in this step the pattern P will be adjusted according to the context of use resulting in the pattern instance S. In a top down process all variable parts will be bound to specific values, resulting in a concrete instance of the pattern.
4. **Integration:** The pattern instance S will be integrated into M' by connecting it to the other elements in the domain. This may require replacing, updating or otherwise modifying other objects to produce a seamless piece of design.

Automatic tool support is important in order to integrate patterns effectively into the development life cycle of interactive applications. Moreover by integrating the idea of patterns into development tools, patterns can be a driving force throughout the entire UI development process. For instance the top-down process of pattern adaptation can be greatly assisted by tools such as Wizards. A Wizard runs through the pattern tree and questions the user each time it encounters a variable that has not been resolved yet. We have developed a prototype of a task pattern wizard (introduced in [11]), which supports all phases of pattern integration for the task model, ranging from pattern selection over pattern adaptation until pattern integration. Which patterns are applicable for the task model is introduced in the next section.

2. PATTERNS FOR THE ENVISIONED TASK MODEL

The envisioned task model describes how activities can be performed to reach the user's goals when interacting with an interactive system [9]. Using task models, designers can develop integrated descriptions of the system from a functional and interactive point of view. Task models typically are hierarchical decompositions of goals, tasks and subtasks into atomic actions [12]. Also the relationships between tasks are described in correlation with the execution order or dependencies between peer tasks. The tasks may contain attributes about the importance, the duration of execution and the frequency of use. In order to speed up the process of establishing the task model and to integrate proven and efficient solution, we suggest using patterns as building blocks. In the following we will explain how patterns for the task model should be written and how they should be applied. In a subtle manner we distinguish between two kinds of patterns that are applicable for the user-task model: Task Patterns and Feature Patterns.

- **Task Patterns** describe the activities the user has to perform while pursuing a certain goal. The goal description acts as an unambiguous identification for the pattern. In order to compose the pattern as generic and flexible as possible, the goal description should entail at least one variable component. As the variable part of the goal description changes, the content solution part of the pattern will adapt and change accordingly. Task Patterns can be composed out of sub-patterns. These sub-patterns can either be task-patterns or feature-patterns.
- **Feature Patterns**, applied to the user-task model describe the activities the user has to perform using a particular feature of the system. For the purpose of this paper we define a feature as an aid or a "tool" the user can use in order to fulfil a task. Examples of these features can be "Keyword Search", "Login" or "Registration". Feature patterns are identified by the feature description, which should also contain a variable part, to which the realization of the feature (stated in the pattern) will adapt. Feature patterns can comprise other sub-feature patterns.

As we mentioned above, the difference between task and feature patterns is subtle, but noticeable. While task patterns concentrate on a specific goal, the same task can be accomplished in different ways using different feature patterns. That is why feature patterns are important as a classification. Similarly, the same feature pattern can be used to accomplish different task patterns. Therefore it is safe to say that there is a many-to-many relationship between the two. To summarise, Task patterns are concerned with the user goals (what we need to do), while feature Patterns are concerned with the system behaviour (how we can do it). A typical task performed in many different applications is to find something. This can range from finding a book at www.amazon.com to finding a used car at www.cars.com, to even finding a computer in a network environment. All these tasks embody the same basic task and can just be distinguished by the particular "Find" object in the goal description. In order to create a generalised *Find* Pattern, we must abstract the particular object we are searching, and replace it with a generic variable.

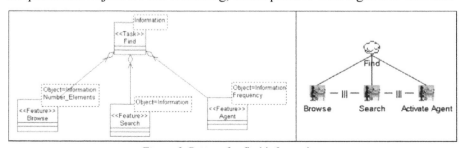

Figure 2. Pattern for find information.

For the sake of simplicity, let us assume that a simplified version of the *Find* pattern suggests that "Find" information can be performed by browsing, searching or using an agent. In the left part of Fig. 2 the *Find* pattern is displayed in an abstract manner. We have used the UML notation for parametric classes is used to portray the pattern. The variable "Information" is utilised as a placeholder for the particular type of information one is trying to find. In the right part of Fig. 2 a possible instance of the pattern is shown. The details of the resulting task tree are illustrated with CTTE notation [9].

Moreover, it is visualised that the *Find* pattern is composed of the feature patterns *Browse*, *Search* and *Agent*. If we place patterns in such an "aggregation" relation we have to pay special attention to the variables. It is shown in Fig. 3 that a variable, defined at the super-pattern level can affect the variables used in the sub patterns. The value of the variable "Information" of the *Find* pattern is used to assign the "Object" variable in all sub patterns. However the variables "Number_Elements", and "Frequency" of the sub-patterns *Browse* and *Agent* remain undefined. During the process of adaptation, the variables of each pattern must be resolved top-down and replaced by concrete values.

In Fig. 3, we have bound the variable "Information" with the value "Book" to create the patterns instance *Find Book*; and with the value "Car" to create the instance *Find Car*. Please note that with the binding of a concrete value to the variable "Information" in the goal description, the body of the pattern has changed accordingly. After the pattern adaptation process, the patterns instance can be integrated in an already existing task model. In Fig. 3, *Find Car* has been integrated into the Car-shop task model. This process of integrations is visualised using the inheritance relationship and can be interpreted as: Car-shop has inherited all methods (tasks) from *Find Car*. Eventually after resolving all variables, the pattern instance will be transformed into a concrete task structure. Practically this integration process is not realised by inheritance. It is supported by a wizard, which is described in [11].

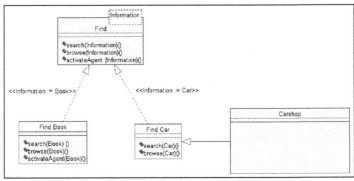

Figure 3. The Find pattern and its instances.

3. PATTERNS IN THE PROCESS OF DERIVING THE UI FROM ABSTRACT DESCRIPTIONS

Until now it was described how patterns can be used as building blocks for establishing task models. Task models as well as user and object models are rather abstract and deal only indirectly with user interface issues. In the following we will explain how an implementation of a user interface can be derived from these abstract descriptions. Moreover it will be shown how patterns can drive and influence this process.

In Fig. 1, we have portrayed four milestones on the way from an abstract description to the implemented user interface. First a dialog model is interactively derived from the task, user and object model. The dialog model associates several tasks to dialog views and defines transitions between these dialog views. At this stage dialog patterns can help grouping the tasks and suggest sequences between dialog views. Next, in order to develop the presentation model the tasks of each dialog view are associated with interaction elements such as buttons, trees and lists. Moreover, some domain objects (tools or artefacts) which are related to the tasks are also mapped to interaction elements. Presentation patterns can be applied in order to map complex tasks (such as advanced search) to a predefined set of interaction elements.

Within our approach presentation patterns are described as Velocity XUL templates [18]. Thus, our presentation model consists of a set of XUL code fragments. Each fragment describes one or a set of interaction objects. After that the interaction objects are positioned following an overall layout or floor plan resulting in the layout model. Additionally, the visual appearance of each interaction element is specified by setting fonts, colours and dimensions. In our framework layout patterns –which are described as XUL templates as well– are used to integrate proven layouts and design solutions. Practically the loose set of XUL fragments of the presentation model is aggregated to XUL code. Finally this XUL code is automatically rendered to a concrete user interface implementation. In the following we will explain in greater detail each phase.

According to our model–based framework the presentation model and layout model are logically separated. We decided to split them into two categories, since we believe that for each model different kinds of patterns apply. The first category contains patterns that describe a set of interaction elements (presentation patterns). The other category contains patterns that describe the layout of the interaction elements (layout patterns).

3.1 Patterns and the Dialog Model

The dialog model specifies the user commands, interaction techniques, interface responses and command sequences that the interface allows during user sessions. It must encompass all static and dynamic information the user needs for the dialog with the machine. This information is grouped into several dialog views. The dialog view contains functionally- and logically related elements of the task model and the business object (domain) model.

In short, the dialog model specifies the navigational structure of the UI and the interaction techniques [15]. It is a more specific model and can be derived in good part from the more abstract task-, user- and business object models.

There are different strategies to design the dialog model. One possibility is the evolution of the task model to a final user interface. Janus [1] uses information mainly from the object model. However, most approaches are based on tasks. TERESA [6] follows an idea of grouping tasks based on preconditions, which allows an automatic generation of dialogue models.

Finding dialog views and transitions is closely connected to the underlying task models. On the one hand, structural information from the task model, which describes the task–subtask hierarchy can be used to group related tasks into task views. On the other hand temporal transitions between sub tasks can be used to constrain and derive possible dialog transitions [9, 15]. Consequently patterns applied to the task model indirectly affect the dialog model and in particular the dialog graph. Let us take the example of the *Multi Value Input Task* Pattern introduced by [2]. For the sake of simplicity let us assume that our *Multi Value Input Task* pattern describes a task structure in which the user edits various values. After all values have been entered the user can submit them.

In the left fraction of Fig. 4 the interface of the dialog pattern *Wizard* is illustrated. It is parameterised with the variable "Number" which stands for the number of dialogs the wizard will run through. Let us assume that we will use the *Wizard* pattern in order to realise the *Multi Value Input Task*. An instantiation for three input tasks of the pattern is depicted in the right fraction of Fig. 4 and visualised as a dialog graph using the notation introduced by [4].

Adopting the semantics of this graph, the user sequentially inputs three values. After entering the third value submit can be performed and the dialog view will be closed. In particular the user runs through a sequence of three single dialogs, starting from dialog one. From each dialog only one of the neighbour dialogs (previous or next) can be reached. After submitting the third dialog the overall dialog view will be closed.

In order to validate, find and apply dialog patterns we have developed a tool called "DialogGraphSimulator" [4]. Using our application the user can interactively "walk through" the dialog graph. The DialogGraphSimulator helps to define multiple dialog structures for one task model. Different attempts can be opposed to each other and the best solution can eventually be extracted. Due to the separation of task and dialog structure, dialog patterns can be brought in independently. As the DialogGraphSimulator processes dialog structures described in XIML [3], our dialog patterns are formalised as XIML fragments as well. Currently we are developing a tool, similar to the TaskPatternWizard, to allow the computer aided adaptation and integration of dialog patterns.

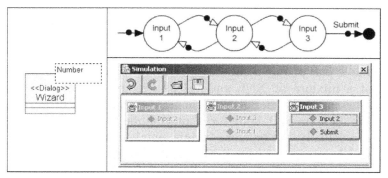

Figure 4. Interface, instance and simulation of the Wizard dialog pattern.

Fig. 4 (lower right corner) contains also a screenshot of the simulation of the *Multi Value Input Task* pattern implemented as a *Wizard*. Each dialog is visualised by a little window. Buttons in each window portray the possible transitions to other dialog views. The third input dialog is currently active. From this dialog it is either possible to go back to the second dialog or to press submit, which would close the dialog view.

3.2   Patterns and the Presentation Model

In the presentation model, a set of abstract UI elements is defined to determine the abstract appearance of the user interface. In particular, the grouped tasks of each dialog view are associated with a set of interaction elements such as buttons, trees and lists. Moreover some domain objects, which will be displayed on the interface, are mapped to interaction elements as well. Please note that all interaction elements should be described in an abstract manner. Style attributes such as size, font, and color remain open and will be defined by the layout model.

We have chosen the generic user interface description language XUL [18] as a medium to describe the presentation model. Thus our presentation model basically consists of a set of XUL fragments. Each fragment represents a single interaction elements or a group of interaction objects.

For the presentation model, presentation patterns embody building interface object blocks. In practice, instantiations of presentation patterns deliver

XUL fragments which -again- describe user interface objects. Therefore each presentation pattern must have a mechanism to generate variants of XUL code depending on the assignment of their variables. We have chosen to employ XUL Velocity templates in order to implement the patterns. Velocity templates can be used to dynamically generate XUL code. If the variable parts of the presentation pattern change, conditions, loops and other control structures are used to adapt the template (pattern) accordingly.

Fig. 5 portrays three different views on a simplified version of the *Input Form* pattern. On the left hand side, the interface of the patterns is displayed showing that only one parameter "Number" is expected. This parameter determines the number of elements to be entered.

The middle part of Fig. 5 shows the formalization of this pattern, which consists of a mixture of XUL and velocity template code. The variable $NUMBER is used to determine the number of iterations of the #foreach loop. Within the loop XUL code for displaying the Input fields and labels is produced. Eventually, the outcome of this template (the instantiation of the pattern), which consists of "pure" XUL code can be rendered to a UI fragment of the target platform. The right part of the illustration shows the screenshot of the result of rendering the *Input Form* pattern instance to Windows XP desktop platform.

Please note that, in practice, the *Input Form* presentation pattern is significantly more complex. Since it must embody information and parameters for the types of data input or the internal alignment of the interaction objects.

Figure 5. Different views on the Input Form presentation pattern.

3.3   Patterns and the Layout Model

In the layout model, the various XUL fragments of the presentation model are merged together resulting in aggregated XUL code. The loosely connected XUL pieces are nested and associated together. The way these fragments are merged together depends on the overall "layout" of the entire application.

Usually a Web site or a GUI consists of several pages or windows. In order to maintain a consistent feeling across them, the same basic layout or floor plan should be kept throughout the entire interface. Depending on the purpose, the complexity, the in-house style and other attributes, a certain basic layout for the UI is chosen. Selecting a basic layout style usually determines the positioning of navigational elements such as search elements and menus or the size and position of information containers. As a result of this merging process, the style attributes of the UI elements -which were not set- are bound to concrete values. Patterns such as *Column Layout, Liquid Layout* or *Card Stack* are used to determine the structure of the layout model.

As Velocity templates can be used to generate XUL fragments (presentation model) they can also be used to aggregate XUL code. Therefore layout patterns are formalised as Velocity XUL templates as well, and the instantiation of these patterns consists of pure XUL code.

Eventually the established layout model (XUL code) is used as input for the automatic generation process in which the concrete interface is generated. Please note that the same layout model can be rendered to different target platforms such as Java Swing and Mozilla /Netscape. XUL has its focus on window-based user interfaces. At the moment XUL specifications cannot be rendered to multiple user interfaces including small devices.

4. RELATED WORK

In [16], van Welie describes how patterns can be used as tools for User Interface Design. He recognised that different kinds of patterns should be formatted in a way, which promotes best its purpose. Within our framework patterns are intended to describe model fragments. Each model is described differently and thus we have introduced different kinds of patterns which have their own formalisation.

According to van Welie's patterns are applicable in different contexts and for each context the adaptation of pattern is necessary. We have adopted this principle and attributed our patterns with variables, which are placeholders for the particular context of use, in which the pattern will be applied.

Van Welie also published a pattern language for interaction design [17]. However all patterns are documented in an informal, narrative way which makes it nearly impossible to implement them in development tools. The overall goal of our approach is the computer aided generation of models, which incorporates patterns as building blocks for re-use. Therefore in this paper we have suggested a possible formalization of patterns.

In [8], Molina also recognised that the mostly-informal description of today's patterns is not suitable for processing them by tools. Within his Just-UI framework, a more precise description of patterns is necessary, which can be interpreted by software tools like validators or code generators. A set of conceptual patterns which realise so-called interaction units is proposed. According to Molina frequent scenarios in user interfaces can be specified with very little effort by combining these interaction units. Molina's patterns are closely connected to the underlying domain object model. They focus on object manipulation and visualization. Compared to our approach Molina's conceptual patterns apply primarily to our presentation model. However, in his work it is also shown how a task description can be extracted and hence the patterns can be applied to underlying task model as well.

Trætteberg [13] recognized that multiple representations should be used in the UI design process and that a uniform modelling language must support the transition between the various presentations. In his work, he suggested RML, TaskMODL and DiaMODL as interlocking fragments of a uniform language for task, domain and dialog modelling. As TaskMODL is quiet similar to our task model DiaMODL is based on the Pisa Interactor and the UML Statecharts notation. Interactors are used to describe the functionality and behaviour of concrete interaction objects, whereas statecharts model the information flow and activation and deactivation of interactors [13].

On the contrary, our dialog model only groups tasks to dialog views and defines transitions between the various dialog views. This allows an earlier generation of a non-functional prototype and thus, earlier user evaluation and earlier iterations. In comparison to Trætteberg's work one could say that within our dialog model the generic interactor is assigned to each task.

Within our framework the definition of interaction objects is described by the presentation model, whereas Trætteberg specifies interactors already during dialog modelling. He uses Statecharts to model the dynamic behaviour including the information flow. At the moment our framework focuses on the generation of non-functional interface prototypes. Thus, the issue of modelling the dynamic behaviour and the information flow between interactors has not been tackled in this work.

In parallel to our approach Trætteberg also suggested to formulate model fragments as patterns in order to facilitate the re-use. In particular he points out the need for patterns in order to describe the mapping between concrete dialog elements to abstract interactors (Presentation and Layout Patterns) and the mapping from tasks to dialogs (Dialog Patterns).

5.   CONCLUSION

In this paper, we demonstrated how patterns could be used in conjunction with models to support the UI development process. The core ideas we introduced were highlighted by some examples.

In our model-based framework the application of patterns has a number of advantages. First, they can reduce the time required for UI engineering since for many of the common problems, some pattern solutions already exists. Moreover, a consequent use of UI patterns help in the comprehension of the system for future maintenance.

In particular we have shown which patterns are suitable for several models. In the case of presentation and layout patterns we have suggested a possible formalisation of patterns using Velocity XUL templates. Even though the validity of our approach can not be formally proven, through the realization of the TaskPatternWizard we have experienced that the concept of patterns is applicable and realizable at least for the task model. Furthermore we are progressing in developing a tool that processes and applies dialog patterns.

For the future we aim to develop an all-embracing tool set that supports the integration of patterns into all steps of our model-based framework. We wish to ground our pattern-driven UI engineering methodology as solidly as possible on empirical data and theoretical principles. Furthermore we will validate and compare design patterns with usability tests, particularly for new and experimental patterns and extend our framework to be able to generate functional UI prototypes. In particular we will try to model the information/data flow between the various UI elements.

REFERENCES

[1] Balzert, H., *From OOA to GUIs: The JANUS System*, Journal of Object-Oriented Programming, Vol. 8, No. 9, February 1996, pp. 43-47.

[2] Breedvelt, I., Paternò F., and Severiins, C., *Reusable Structures in Task Models*, in M.D. Harrison, J.C. Torres (eds.), Proceedings of 4th International Eurographics Workshop on Design, Specification, and Verification of Interactive Systems DSV-IS'97 (Granada, 4-6 June 1997), Springer-Verlag, Vienna, 1997, pp. 251-265.

[3] Eisenstein, J., Vanderdonckt, J., and Puerta, A., *Model-Based User-Interface Development Techniques for Mobile Computing*, in J. Lester (ed.), Proceedings of 5th ACM International Conference on Intelligent User Interfaces IUI'2001 (Santa Fe, 14-17 January 2001), ACM Press, New York, 2001, pp. 69-76.

[4] Forbrig, P., Dittmar, A., Reichart, D., and Sinnig, D., *User-Centred Design and Abstract Prototypes*, in Proceedings of BIR'2003 (Berlin, September 2003), SHAKER, 2003, pp. 132-145, accessible at http://www.dsinnig.de/pdfs/User_Centred_Design.pdf

[5] Gamma, E., Helm, R., Johnson, R., and Vlissides, J., *Design Patterns: Elements of Object-Oriented Software*, Addison-Wesley, Boston, 1995.

[6] Mori, G., Paternò F., and Santoro, C., *Tool Support for Designing Nomadic Applications*, in Proceedings of the 8th ACM International Conference on Intelligent User Interfaces IUI'2003 (Miami, 12-15 January 2003), ACM Press, New York, 1993, pp. 141-148, accessible at http://portal.acm.org/citation.cfm?doid=604045.604069

[7] McCall, J., Richards, P., and Walters, G., *Factors in Software Quality*, Three Volumes, NTIS AD, November 1977.

[8] Molina, P., Belenguer, J., and Pastor, O., *Describing Just-UI Concepts Using a Task Notation*, in J. Falcão e Cunha, N.J. Nunes, J. Jorge (eds.), Proceedings of 10th International Workshop on Design, Specification and Verification of Interactive Systems DSV-IS'03

(Madeira, 4-6 June 2003), Springer-Verlag, Berlin, 2003, pp. 218-230.

[9] Paternò F., *Model-Based Design and Evaluation of Interactive Applications*, Springer-Verlag, Berlin, 2000.

[10] Pressman, R.S., *Software Engineering, A Practitioner Approach*, McGraw-Hill, Berkshire, 2001.

[11] Sinnig, D., Javahery, H., Forbrig, P., and Seffah, A., *The Complicity of Model-Based Approaches and Patterns for UI Engineering*, in Proceedings of BIR'03 (Berlin, September 2003), pp. 120-131, accessible at http://www.dsinnig.de/pdfs/BIR_Pattern_Models.pdf

[12] Souchon, N., Limbourg, Q., and Vanderdonckt, J., *Task Modelling in Multiple Contexts of Use*, in P. Forbrig, Q. Limbourg, B. Urban, J. Vanderdonckt (eds.), Proceedings of 9th International Workshop on Design, Specification and Verification of Interactive Systems DSV-IS 2002 (Rostock, 12-14 June 2002), Lecture Notes in Computer Science, Vol. 2545, Springer-Verlag, Berlin, 2002, pp. 59-73.

[13] Trætteberg, H., *Dialog Modelling With Interactors and UML Statecharts –A Hybrid Approach*, in J. Falcão e Cunha, N.J. Nunes, J. Jorge (eds.), Proceedings of 10th International Workshop on Design, Specification and Verification of Interactive Systems DSV-IS'03 (Madeira, 4-6 June 2003), Springer-Verlag, Berlin, 2003, pp. 346-361.

[14] Trætteberg, H., *Using User Interface Models in Design*, in Ch. Kolski, J. Vanderdonckt (eds.), Proceedings of 4th International Conference on Computer-Aided Design of User Interfaces CADUI'2002 (Valenciennes, 15-17 May 2002), Kluwer Academics Publishers, Dordrecht, 2002, pp. 131-142.

[15] Vanderdonckt, J., Limbourg, Q., and Florins, M., *Deriving the Navigational Structure of a User Interface*, in M. Rauterberg, M. Menozzi, J. Wesson (eds.), Proc. of 9th IFIP TC 13 Int. Conf. on Human-Computer Interaction INTERACT'2003 (Zurich, 1-5 September 2003), IOS Press, Amsterdam, 2003, pp. 455-462.

[16] van Welie, M., van der Veer, G.C., and Eliens, A., *Patterns as Tools for User Interface Design*, in J. Vanderdonckt, Ch. Farenc (eds.), Proceedings of International Workshop on Tools for Working with Guidelines TFWWG'2000 (Biarritz, 7-8 October 2000), Springer-Verlag, London, 2000, pp. 313-324.

[17] van Welie, M., *Patterns in Interaction Design*, 2003, accessible at http://www.welie.com.

[18] XUL, 2003, accessible at http://www.xulplanet.com/

Chapter 17

ANALYSIS AND DESIGN OF MODEL-BASED USER INTERFACES
An Approach to Refining Specifications towards Implementation

Pedro J. Molina[1] and Hallvard Trætteberg[2]
[1]*CARE Technologies S.A., Pda. Madrigueres, 44, 03700 Denia, Alicante (Spain)*
E-mail: pjmolina@care-t.com – URL: http://www.care-t.com
Tel.: +34 96 643 55 55
[2]*Dept. of Computer and Information Sciences Norwegian, University of Science and Technology, Sem Sælands vei 7-9, NO-7034 Trondheim (Norway)*
E-mail: hal@idi.ntnu.no – URL: http://www.idi.ntnu.no/~hal/
Tel.: +47 7359 3443 – Fax: +47 7359 4466

Abstract   This paper proposes a method for user interface development where a model for analysis (Just-UI) and a model for design (DiaMODL) are conveniently combined into an integrated method. Just-UI currently supports automatically refining analysis models, through conceptual patterns to concrete user interface designs. Integrating a dialog modelling language (DiaMODL) into the method, will let the designers take part in the refinement process, hence gaining control and allowing a greater variety of designs. The method encourages the use of code generation for rapid prototyping of the UI. The ultimate objective is to provide a suitable software engineering and user interface design method with coverage to cross through requirements to final implementation of core application code and user interface.

Keywords: Conceptual models, Design models, Model-based user interface development, User interface development

1.   INTRODUCTION

Model-Based User Interface Development (MB-UID) is a field mature enough to be applied into the software industry. However, still now, MB-UID methods have produced little impact into the way User Interface (UI) developers create user interfaces. Such methods are difficult to introduce due

R. Jacob et al. (eds.), Computer-Aided Design of User Interfaces IV, 211–222.

to different problems: learning curve, scalability, expressiveness, lack of adequate tools, code immaturity of generators, etc.

In this context, Novak's rule [9] becomes a painful truth: *people will not use specifications if the spend more time and resources creating the specification and development from such a specification than developing in their classical approach (without formal specification.* In other words, using a model-based approach has to be perceived by developers as an immediate gain (in terms of productivity, quality, resource saving, error reduction, better documentation, ease of maintenance, reduction in time to market, etc.) and not as a useless intermediate step (waste of time, outdated documentation). Therefore, we definitely think that more effort must be put into creating agile methods and tools that are seen as really useful by actual developers and facilitate the adoption of MB-UID in the software industry.

In this work, we try to integrate the advantages of using two proven models for user interface development: one of them for analysis (JUST-UI [7]) and another one for design (DiaMODL [15]), establishing a bridge from the former to the latter. Supported by code generation, the proposed method intends to be interesting not only from the academic point of view, but also useful to develop user interfaces for commercial software, thus increasing the adoption of MB-UID methods and tools in the software industry.

2. RELATED WORK

TRIDENT [16,17] is a reference project in the field of MB-UID tools. A Task Model (Activity Chain Graphs), a simple Domain Model (extended entity-relational model) and Dialog Model are the main artifacts employed to derive user interfaces in a semi-automatic way. Designers can participate in the process choosing design alternatives among presented by an expert system during the process of mapping from Abstract Interaction Objects (AIOs) to Concrete Interaction Objects (CIOs) [16] (SEGUIA [18,19]).

MECANO, MOBI-D and MOBILE [10,13,14] are projects that have had a significant impact in the state of the art of MB-UID tools. In these tools, domain, dialog, task, user and presentation models are used in the process.

Just-UI [7] is the model of OO-Method [11] for the analysis of business user interfaces. It is named "Presentation Model" in OO-Method. This model is based on a conceptual user interface pattern language. It is used to specify UIs from requirements in an abstract way: no design choices or platform considerations are taken. The presentation model complements the domain model resulting from object-oriented analysis of the functionality of the system. OO-Method, including this model, is supported by two commercially available tools: OlivaNova Modeler and Transformation Engines (code generators) to produce implementations for several devices [2]. The model has been used during the last four years in an industrial context and has increased the developer productivity [5].

DiaMODL [15] is a hybrid dialog modelling language based on interconnected abstract interaction objects and UML class/object diagrams and Statecharts. DiaMODL may be used for documenting the function and structure of concrete UIs, abstract specification of UI functionality and for systematic exploration of design alternatives. DiaMODL has also been used for capturing design knowledge in abstract design patterns [20].

PSA (Patterns Supported Approach) [6] is a methodological proposal to use patterns during the whole software life-cycle: from requirements to implementation. The main idea behind the approach is that patterns constitute proven solutions to frequent problems. Patterns are pills of distilled experience and constitute a common *lingua franca* [3] shared by the development team. PSA is not specifically tied with user interface production. On the contrary, it can be applied to general software development.

3. THE PROPOSAL

The method we propose comprises the following steps:

1. Task Analysis and Use Case specification (to organise requirements);
2. User Interface Analysis (using Just-UI);
3. Refine analysis model to abstract design model expressed in DiaMODL;
4. Abstract design to concrete UI specification; and
5. Code Generation and Implementation (producing an executable UI).

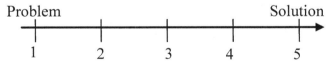

Figure 1. Five steps from design problem to design solution.

The general idea is to gradually move from problem-oriented representations to solution-oriented ones as Fig. 1 suggests. Starting with the problem i.e. the user domain and tasks, the design process breaks down user tasks, moves through abstract descriptions of design to more formal, detailed and concrete descriptions of a solution. By breaking the whole process into smaller steps, we gain several advantages:

- It is easier to apply appropriate design knowledge (whether automatic or manual).
- The process becomes more transparent, since the representation at each step may be examined and manipulated by the designer/analyst.
- Notations and tools may be tailored to each step.
- It is easier to manage changes, as it is easier to trace the relations be-

tween representations at different points from problem to solution.

The steps will be explained in the following subsections accompanied with a small design example to illustrate the concepts.

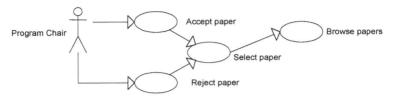

Figure 2. Example of User Task expressed using a Use Case.

3.1 Task Analysis / Use Cases

A task analysis supported by use cases is a good starting point for discovering user goals in a given system. Main objectives and secondary tasks can progressively be discovered and organised in convenient uses cases. These use cases can also be prioritised accordingly to the relevance of the functionality in the system. Care should however be taken when developing the use cases, to avoid a system-centric view. I.e. focus should be put on the user actor's need, rather than on system response. Fig. 2 shows an example of high-level user task described with a use case.

This example will be used to illustrate the following explanations. In the use case, the main task of a Program Chair is to Accept or Reject the papers for a given conference or workshop. As secondary tasks, selecting and browsing papers will be also required to accomplish the first class tasks. In this way, task requirements of the system are depicted: from high-level goals to more concrete user actions that will require interaction with the system through a UI.

3.2 User Interface Analysis with Just-UI

As described in the related work section, Just-UI [7] will be used in the stage of UI analysis. The main objective of this phase is to take requirements into account and focus only on *what* is needed instead of *how* it will be realised. Here, conceptual UI patterns as presented in [8] helps to describe the desired UI. UI patterns represent common configurations of UI elements that support typical user tasks, such as exploration, navigation, search, selection and service invocation.

In Just-UI three levels of UI patterns have been identified, and patterns are structured in a hierarchy to represent how lower-level patterns may be used to build and/or augment higher-level ones. A chart of conceptual user interface patterns used in this approach is shown in Fig. 3.

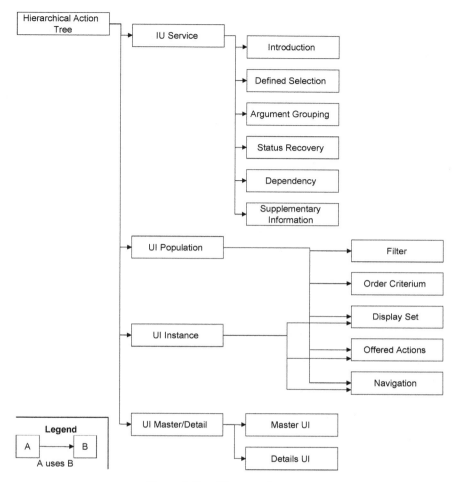

Figure 3. Just-UI pattern language.

One of the central concepts in Just-UI is the Interaction Unit concept (IU). It represents an abstraction of a window, a web page or any other component supporting communication between human and machine. Interaction Units have been categorised as patterns comprising not only presentation aspects, but also behaviour and semantics based on the tasks to be accomplished in each unit. Each pattern shown in Fig. 3 is such an interaction unit.

During the specification, prototypes derived by transformation engines allow to validate requirements with customers in a few and very fast cycles of requirements-gathering, specification and user validation (one-three days per cycle, two-seven iterations). Tool support and code generation for rapid prototyping is crucial to guaranty the agility of approach. Patterns are used as primitives to build a user interface specification. To avoid mixtures of different metaphors, interaction styles and conventions, patterns are tailored for specific domains. In the case of Just-UI, the domain of is user interfaces for business application and information systems. Note however that the approach itself is not particular to a given domain. Only the pattern language used (Just-UI) is oriented towards business applications.

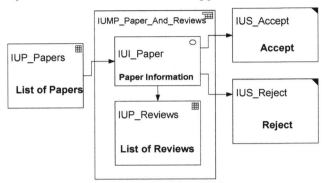

Figure 4. Example of Just-UI diagram.

The pattern language constrains which patterns are meaningful to apply together, in the general case. An actual design for solving a particular use case, is specified by a structure of patterns forming a part-of hierarchy and linked by navigation links, in what is called a Just-UI diagram. Fig. 4 shows an example of specification solving the use case described in Fig. 2. A **population** of papers (`IUP_Papers`) allows browsing among a list of papers. When a paper is selected, information and reviews of that paper appear in a **master/detail** interaction unit (`IUMP_Paper_And_Reviews`). This unit is composed of an **instance** (`IUI_Paper`) as master component and a **population** (`IUP_Reviews`) as a detail. Finally, two services can be launched for the paper: accept and reject, using two **service** interaction units (`IUS_Accept` and `IUS_Reject` respectively).

3.3   Refine Analysis Models to Abstract Design Models

The patterns and Just-UI diagrams are fairly high-level and are similar to Constantine's abstract prototypes [3] in that respect. Nevertheless, it is possible to generate code from Just-UI diagrams, if we let the generator take a lot of design decisions. This is acceptable for the purpose of quickly showing end-users a prototype, but the designer should have the option of taking part in the design process. To give the designer this possibility, the Just-UI diagrams are converted to DiaMODL diagrams, which may be restructured, elaborated, detailed and otherwise manipulated, before later being mapped to a concrete design. The DiaMODL diagrams make it easier to systematically explore alternatives for the design details that are underspecified in the Just-UI diagrams and decisions made by the UI generator.

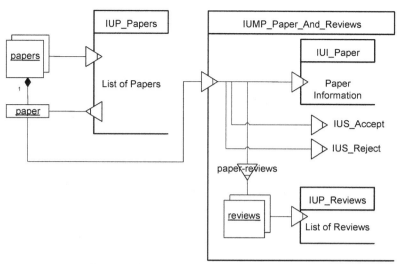

Figure 5. Corresponding DiaMODL diagram.

The example above may be modeled by the DiaMODL diagram shown in Figure. The IUP_Papers interactor presents a set of papers (UML multi-object) to the user and the user may select one of the papers. The selected paper flows into the IUMP_Paper_And_Reviews interactor, where it is presented to the user by the IUI_Paper interactor. In addition, a set of reviews are computed from the paper by the paper-reviews function, and presented to the user by the IUP_Reviews interactor. Finally, the same selected paper is used as input to the IUS_Accept and IUS_Reject functions, which may be triggered by the user (the triggering event is not shown in the diagram).

We see that each basic Interaction Unit in the Just-UI diagram has a corresponding DiaMODL fragment. These fragments are pre-made, i.e. for each of the basic IUs defined by the Just-UI pattern language, we have made corresponding DiaMODL fragments. Just-UI's compositional operators are similarly mapped to DiaMODL's interactor composition and gate interconnection operators, which are used to compose these fragments. This process is mechanical, although currently manual. We are investigating doing the composition automatically, but the result will nevertheless only be a suggestion that the design may want to edit.

3.4   Elaborating DiaMODL Diagrams

A DiaMODL may be more or less explicit about design details, and the designer may want to both add detail and change the existing design. This can happen in at least two ways, as we will illustrate below. First, the decomposition of an interactor may be incomplete (or not present) and the designer may want to add functionality in the decomposition. E.g., the GUI generated for the `IUP_Papers` interactor in the example above, will typically be a listbox with single selection. It may however be relevant to include a search field for limiting the size of the list, in this case the number of papers in the list. Hence, the designer will decompose `IUP_Papers` and add functionality corresponding to a relevant use case. It is for instance, not uncommon that a reviewer is late with his reviews and that the program committee will try to accept/reject papers without the missing reviews. This use case may be supported by letting the user enter the reviewer's name and limit the list of papers accordingly. A possible decomposition of `IUP_Papers` is shown in Fig. 6.

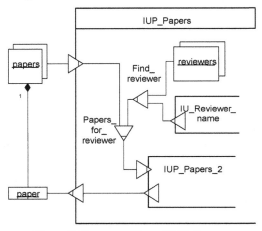

Figure 6. Decomposition of IUP_Papers.

The search field is represented by the `IU_Reviewer_name` interactor. From the entered name and the set of all reviewers (the `reviewers` multiobject) a specific reviewer is computed by the `Find_reviewer` function. A second function (`Papers_for_reviewer`) computes the limited set of papers based on this reviewer, and the result is presented by the `IUP_Papers_2` interactor. Note that this decomposition preserves the outer `IUP_Papers` interactor's gate interface, and that the inner `IUP_Papers_2` corresponds to the original `IUP_Papers` interactor, and hence maps to a single selection list box.

A second way of elaborating the original model, is adding sequencing details. For instance, the diagram in Fig. 5 is not explicit about when the different Interaction Units (or interactors in DiaMODL terminology) are active in the user interface. One possibility is one large window with the `IUP_Papers`, `IUI_Paper` and `IUP_Reviews` are all present simultaneously. This is acceptable for desktop screens and supports locating a paper based on both paper info and reviewers. A medium-sized possibility is adding a transition from `IUP_Papers` and `IUMP_Paper_And_Reviews`, so the latter replaces the former when a paper is selected and a trigger is activated. This is shown left in Fig. 7. It can be argued that the designer should not have to work at this level of detail, and we agree: The pattern and default DiaMODL diagram provides the (most) common default case, while the designer has the freedom to edit the result, e.g., based on user preferences and the target platform.

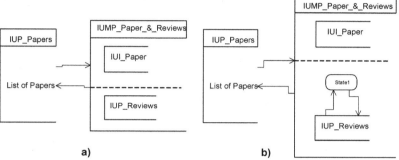

Figure 7. Two variants of interactor activation logic.

3.5 Concrete UI Specification

The DiaMODL diagram elements must be mapped to concrete UI elements, to make the design complete. For each basic IU an appropriate CIO must be found [18], usually selected among several candidate CIOs. In the example, the IUs presenting sets of objects (`IUP_Papers` and `IUP_Reviews`) correspond to list and table interaction objects. The chosen CIO for `IUP_Papers` must support single selection, while IUP_Reviews does not specify a need for selection. The chosen CIO will lead to additional design choices, like which columns to include, fonts and colors to use etc.

The next design step is to select CIOs for triggering action invocations, e.g., whether to use menu items or buttons for invoking the accept-paper and reject-paper object services. Furthermore, rules for triggering transitions between IUs must be specified. If the right variant in Fig. 7 is chosen, triggers for `IUMP_Paper_and_IUP_Reviews` and for `IUP_Reviews` must be specified, e.g., return, double-click and/or a button for the former and a button for the latter.

This mapping process is fairly mechanical, in that the DiaMODL diagram may be used to drive a systematic mapping process. The mapping may be supported by tools, and in many cases diagram elements may be automatically mapped to CIOs. Design patterns may be applied to quickly get a reasonable default design, while the designer is free to edit the result, based on user preferences and target platform constraints and conventions.

3.6   Code Generation / Implementation

Just-UI is supported by a modelling tool and a set of code generators (OlivaNova Model Execution System) to produce user interfaces for different devices (such as desktop and web) directly from an analysis Just-UI specification. This approach has been useful in an industrial environment to produce code for commercial applications.

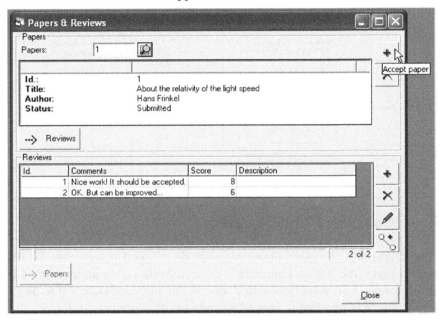

Figure 8. Generated Desktop UI for the example task.

An example of code generated for the case of study directly from a Just-UI model is show in Fig. 8. It contains a UI capable of reviewing papers, revisions and accepting or rejecting the paper. The generated UI is suitable for early validation of user requirements. However, specific design aspects of the user interface code has to be tuned manually due to the lack of a design model capable of expressing different choices, alternatives to the common default values for design choices.

Therefore, the approach presented here, proposes to use DiaMODL just in the point where Just-UI jumps into the implementation using code generators. Refined specifications using DiaMODL can be changed by designers to take in account alternatives designs and selecting platform properties like font, colors, CIO selection and so on [17]. In this way, design models will contain more detail information that the analysis one: enabling a finer tuning of the generation process to suit better the UI needed. DiaMODL is currently integrated with the Just-UI only, and not with the OlivaNova tool. A Java execution engine for the DiaMODL language exists, but it currently cannot generate code and do not support other platforms, as OlivaNova does.

4. CONCLUSION

The method proposed follows a gradual approach focusing on requirements, what (analysis), how (design) and implementation using a continuous and model-based approach. Each step has a clear focus, clear separation of concerns and uses as input the output of the previous steps. A model-based approach for user interfaces has been used, refining a device independent analysis specification to a design specification and progressively reaching a device dependent specification taking in account the capabilities of the target device. This is compliant with modern engineering techniques like Model Driven Approach [10] where Platform Independent Models (PIMs) are refined to specific ones (PSMs) and finally are automatically or semi-automatically converted to source-code. The approach presented enriches engineering methods for producing user interfaces in the way that covers analysis and design of user interfaces. With more design information the generated code will better fit the application and target platform.

REFERENCES

[1] Bodart, F., Hennebert, A.M., Leheureux, J.M., Sacré, I., and Vanderdonckt, J., *Architecture Elements for Highly-Interactive Business-Oriented Applications*, in L. Bass, J. Gornostaev, and C. Unger (eds.), Proceedings of 3rd East-West Conference on Human-Computer Interaction EWHCI'93 (Moscow, July 1993), Lecture Notes in Computer Science, Vol. 153, Springer-Verlag, Berlin, 1993, pp. 83-104.

[2] CARE Technologies, *OlivaNova Model Execution System*, 2003, accessible at http://www.care-t.com.

[3] Constantine, L. and Lockwood, L., *Structure and Style in Use Cases for User Interface Design*, accessible at http://www.foruse.com/Files/Papers/structurestyle2.pdf

[4] Erickson, T., *Patterns Languages as Languages*, in Proceedings of CHI'2000 Workshop Pattern Languages for Interaction Design (The Hague, 1-6 April 2000), 2000, accessible at http://www.pliant.org/personal/Tom_Erickson/PatternLAsLanguage.html

[5] Gartner Inc., OlivaNova Benchmark, 2003, request for examination to care-technologies @care-t.com, http://www.gartner.com.

[6] Granlund, Å. and Lafrenière, D., *A Pattern-Supported Approach to the User Interface*, Design, in Proceedings of 9th International Conference on Human-Computer Interaction HCI'International 2001 (New Orleans, 5-10 August 2001), Lawrence Erlbaum Associates, Mahwah, pp. 282-286, available at http://www.sm.luth.se/csee/csn/publications/ HCIInt2001Final.pdf

[7] Molina, P.J., Meliá, S., and Pastor, O., *Just-UI: A User Interface Specification Model,* in Ch. Kolski and J. Vanderdonckt (Eds.), *Computer-Aided Design of User Interfaces III,* pp. 63-74, Kluwer Academics Publisher, Dordrecht, 2002.

[8]   Molina, P.J., Meliá, S., and Pastor, O., *User Interface Conceptual Patterns*, in P. Forbrig, Q. Limbourg, B. Urban, and J. Vanderdonckt (eds.), *Design, Specification, and Verification of Interactive Systems*, Proceedings of 9th Int. Workshop on Design, Specification, and Verification of Interactive Systems DSV-IS'2002 (Rostock, 12-14 June 2002), Lecture Notes in Computer Science, Vol. 2545, Springer-Verlag, Berlin, 2002, pp. 201-214.

[9]   Novak, G.S., *Novak Rule*, accessible at http://www.cs.utexas.edu/users/novak/index.html.

[10] Object Modeling Group, *Model Driven Architecture*, 2001, accessible at http://www.omg.org/cgi-bin/apps/doc?ormsc/01-07-01.pdf

[11] Pastor, O., Insfrán, I., Pelechano, V., Romero, J., and Merseguer, J., *OO-METHOD: An OO Software Production Environment Combining Conventional and Formal Methods*, in Proc. 9th Int. Conf. on Advanced Information Systems Engineering CAISE'97 (Barcelona, June 1997), Springer-Verlag, London, 1997, pp. 145-159.

[12] Puerta, A.R., *A Model-Based Interface Development Environment*, IEEE Software, Vol. 4, No. 14, July/August 1997, pp. 41-47.

[13] Puerta, A.R. and Maulsby, D., *Management of Interface Design Knowledge With MOBI-D*, in Proceedings of the International Conference on Intelligent User Interfaces IUI'97 (Orlando, 6-9 January 1997), ACM Press, New York, pp. 249-252, accessible at http://camis.stanford.edu/projects/mecano/pubs/iui97.pdf

[14] Puerta, A.R., Cheng, E., Ou, T., and Min, J., *MOBILE: User-Centered Interface Building*, in Proceeding of the ACM Conference on Human Factors in Computing Systems CHI'99 (Pittsburgh, 15-20 May 1999), ACM Press, New York, 1999, pp. 426-433.

[15] Trætteberg, H., *Dialog Modelling With Interactors and UML Statecharts - A Hybrid Approach*, in Proceedings of 10th International Workshop on Design, Specification and Verification of Interactive Systems DSV-IS'2003 (Funchal, June 4-6 2003), Springer-Verlag, Berlin, Lecture Notes in Computer Science, Vol. 2844, pp. 346-361, accessible at http://www.idi.ntnu.no/emner/sif80ap/dsvis-2003.pdf

[16] Vanderdonckt, J. and Bodart, F., *Encapsulating Knowledge for Intelligent Automatic Interaction Objects Selection*, in Proc. of the ACM Conf. on Human Factors in Computing Systems INTERCHI'93 (Amsterdam, 24-29 avril 1993), ACM Press, New York, 1993, pp. 424-429.

[17] Vanderdonckt, J., *Assisting Designers in Developing Interactive Business Oriented Applications*, in H.-J. Bullinger & J. Ziegler (eds.), Proceedings of 8th International Conference on Human-Computer Interaction of HCI International'99 (Munich, 22-26 August 1999), Ergonomics and User Interfaces, Vol. 1, Lawrence Erlbaum Associated Pub., Mahwah, 1999, pp. 1043-1047.

[18] Vanderdonckt, J., *Advice-Giving Systems for Selecting Interaction Objects*, in N.W. Paton & T. Griffiths (eds.), Proceedings of 1st Int. Workshop on User Interfaces to Data Intensive Systems UIDIS'99 (Edinburgh, 5-6 September 1999), IEEE Computer Society Press, Los Alamitos, 1999, pp. 152-157.

[19] Vanderdonckt, J. and Berquin, P., *Towards a Very Large Model-based Approach for User Interface Development*, in N.W. Paton & T. Griffiths (eds.), Proceedings of 1st International Workshop on User Interfaces to Data Intensive Systems UIDIS'99 (Edimburgh, 5-6 September 1999), , IEEE Computer Society Press, Los Alamitos, 1999, pp. 76-85.

[20] van Welie, M., Trætteberg, H., *Interaction Patterns in User Interfaces*, in Proceedings of 7th Pattern Languages of Programs Conference PLOP'2000 (Allerton Park, 13-16 August 2000), accessible at http://www.cs.vu.nl/~martijn/patterns/PLoP2k-Welie.pdf

Chapter 18

INTERACTION TEMPLATES FOR CONSTRUCTING USER INTERFACES FROM TASK MODELS

David Paquette and Kevin Schneider
Department of Computer Science, University of Saskatchewan,
Saskatoon, SK S7N 5A9 (Canada)
E-mail: dnp972@mail.usask.ca, kas@cs.usask.ca

Abstract   Task modelling is well suited to identifying user goals and identifying the ac-
                   tivities a user performs to achieve these goals. Some task model tools provide
                   simulation capabilities and/or aid in the construction of concrete user inter-
                   faces. When it is desirable for the simulated or constructed interface to be real-
                   istic, the task model must be specified in considerable detail. Unfortunately
                   this is usually quite onerous for medium to large size systems, for context-
                   dependent user interfaces, and for highly interactive user interfaces. This paper
                   introduces 'Interaction Templates': pre-defined components that can be
                   plugged into a task model to provide concrete dialogue and presentation. In-
                   teraction Templates define complex, context sensitive interaction that is to be
                   incorporated into the target user interface and can be used when simulating a
                   task model. Interaction Templates are bound to the task model using an ex-
                   plicit data model. We demonstrate the applicability of Interaction Templates
                   with a case study..

Keywords: Methods and languages, Model-based interface design, Task modelling, Tem-
                   plates, User interface design and specification.

1.   INTRODUCTION

Our research applies task modelling approaches to the design of interactive systems. Through a case study we investigated benefits and deficiencies
of using task modelling for the design of an interactive system for the propose of tracking soil samples. In particular we are interested in applying
ConcurTaskTrees [4] and tool support for simulating a user interface. Other

R. Jacob et al. (eds.), Computer-Aided Design of User Interfaces IV, 223–234.
© 2005 *Kluwer Academic Publishers. Printed in the Netherlands.*

task modelling approaches include UAN [2], SUIDT [1] and U-Tel [8].

Our case study shows that task modelling, although useful for modelling an interactive system with a user, becomes tedious when specifying a task model in sufficient detail to benefit from simulation tool support.

We propose the use of Interaction Templates, pre-defined components that can be plugged into a task model to provide concrete dialogue and presentation. Interaction Templates define complex, context sensitive interaction that is to be incorporated into the target user interface and can be used when simulating a task model. Interaction Templates are bound to the task model using an explicit data model.

CTTE [3,4,5] is a tool for building and evaluating ConcurTaskTrees and was used in our case study. It features a visual task model builder and a task model simulator, which is used to validate task models.

The visual task model builder aids in creating models. It is used to create and define tasks as well as define relationships between those tasks. It includes features that help with layout as well as features that help to ensure the mathematical correctness of a model.

The simulator can be useful in validating task models with users, as well as evaluating usability at a very early stage. With CTTE's Task Model Simulator tasks can be selected from a list of available actions. Any one of the actions can be performed by double clicking it. When an action is performed, the list of enabled actions is updated. This allows users to test the system design to ensure that it allows them to reach certain goals and does not allow actions to be performed when they should not be.

A drawback of this simulator is that it does not allow for true simulation of concurrent tasks. It treats concurrent tasks the same as choice tasks.

A tool similar to CTTE provides a simulator that has the ability to simulate concurrent tasks [6]. The simulation is made up of a window that is filled with smaller windows containing play and stop buttons. Each of the smaller windows represents a task from the task model. These tasks can either be active or inactive. A user can activate a task by pressing the play button, or deactivate a task by pressing the stop button. Activating or deactivating a task in the simulator has the same effect as starting or stopping a task in the system. Activities can either be enabled or disabled. This is shown in the simulator by enabling or disabling the play and stop buttons. When a task is activated, all tasks that are enabled or disabled by that task are updated. By playing through different scenarios, it is easy to validate your task model with users. One of the problems of this simulator is that it would get difficult to sort through the many tasks involved in a large system.

In the next section we describe a case study in which we applied task modelling to an existing interactive system.

2. LAB ASSISTANT CASE STUDY

Lab Assistant is an information system for tracking soil samples through a soil–processing lab in Saskatoon, Saskatchewan. The samples are provided to the lab by producers and university researchers. The system is data intensive, interacting with a database containing information about farmers, geographic locations, soil samples and quality control data. The Lab Assistant is used to enter the data, verify the data, and create a variety of reports for the users. The system was built using Borland Delphi 4 and runs on Microsoft Windows operating systems. Fig. 1 is a screen shot of the Lab Assistant soil sample data entry form.

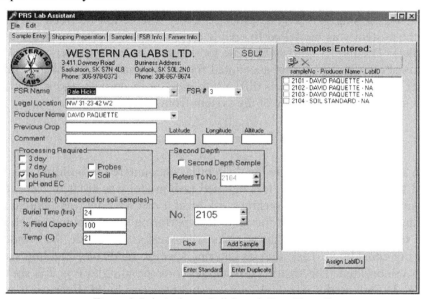

Figure 1. Lab Assistant Soil Sample Data Entry Form.

2.1 Detailed Task Model

The ConcurTaskTree environment (CTTE) was used to model the user interactions with the Lab Assistant. Each window was considered to be an abstract task named after the main task performed in that window. The abstract tasks were modelled in detail to describe the user's interaction. Widgets such as text fields and buttons were modelled as Interaction Tasks. Relationships between tasks showed the effects each widget had on other objects in the system. Fig. 2 shows a small section of the task model that was developed. The model gave a precise definition of the system and allowed for an accurate simulation using CTTE.

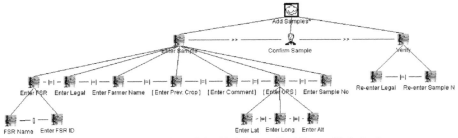

Figure 2. Small section of detailed ConcurTaskTree of Lab Assistant.

Although the task model provided an accurate and precise description of the Lab Assistant, some difficulties were encountered. The process of generating a detailed task model for an information system the size of the Lab Assistant was a long and tedious process. Every interaction between the user and the system was modelled to enable a reasonable simulation of the user interface. The model quickly became too large to be easily understood. The section shown in Fig. 2 only accounted for approximately 10% of the entire model. A model of this size is difficult to view in its entirety and it was difficult to get a good overview of the system from the task model.

2.2   Abstract Task Model

In an attempt to overcome the difficulties encountered in building the detailed task model, a second, less detailed task model was created. Here, the system was modelled at the abstract task level. Each window was again as an abstraction task named after the main task performed in that window. However, the specifics of how those tasks were performed inside the window were not considered. Task such as entering specific fields when adding samples were omitted. The abstract task model corresponding to Fig. 2 is shown in Fig. 3. This model was both quicker and easier to build. Because it was much smaller, it also gave a better overview of the system than the previous model.

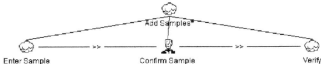

Figure 3. Small section of abstract ConcurTaskTree of Lab Assistant.

Modelling a system at this level of abstraction results in a loss of some of the functionality that CTTE offers. In particular, because some of the detail is missing, CTTE can no longer provide a suitable simulation of the task model. A simulation of entering a sample no longer consists of entering a few required fields and some optional ones. The simulation only consists of entering an abstract sample object, the details of which are unknown. Another problem is that valuable information about the system was lost. It is no longer known what data is verified. In order to fully understand what is occurring in this model, one must already have knowledge of the system.

2.3 User Feedback

In order to get user feedback on the validity of the two task models, the main user involved in the development of the Lab Assistant was introduced to the concept of task models using CTTE. The user is a business computer user with limited technical background, however, she interacts with the Lab Assistant system every day.

First, the user was given an overview of the CTT notation, and taken through an example of modelling a small portion of the Lab Assistant. Together, the task of adding a batch of samples to the database was modelled. The user did not have any difficulties in following the construction of the model, and was able to point out some inaccuracies as the model was built. The user was able to correct a task operator in the model. User feedback allowed for a more accurate model of the Lab Assistant to be built. After analysing the sample task model, the user expressed some concern as to how large the model would be if the entire system were modelled. The small task model built in this example had already covered the entire screen.

Once the small model was built, the user was introduced to the task model simulator. The user was excited by the possibilities of the simulator: the idea of simulating a software system before it was built seemed very useful to her. She commented that if this tool had been available when designing the Lab Assistant, some design flaws would likely have been identified much earlier in the design process. In the current version of the Lab Assistant, the flow of data does not match the flow of samples through the lab. To work around this problem, users must change the way soil is analysed to match the assumptions that were made when the Lab Assistant was built. There are no current plans to fix this problem, as the cost is expected be significant. If this problem could have been identified in a simulation with users at an early stage in design, the cost would have been minimal.

Next the user was shown the detailed task model and the simplified task model that had been previously developed. The user was overwhelmed by the size of the first model. Since the model was too large to view in its entirety, she found it difficult to see the 'big picture' of the Lab Assistant from the model. She was impressed by the functionality available in the simulator as it allowed for a very accurate simulation of the Lab Assistant. The user found the second task model easier to understand. She found that because it lacked detail and was smaller, it gave a better overview of the Lab Assistant.

She did not, however, find the simulation as valuable in this model as it had been in the previous model. Overall the user felt that CTTE would be a useful tool in the analysis and design of Lab Assistant. In particular, she felt that the task model simulator integrated in CTTE would be a very valuable tool in validating proposed designs and catching major problems early in the design process.

2.4   Case Study Summary

CTTE provides a good mechanism for modelling information systems. Task trees provide an excellent overview of a system and offer a powerful simulation capability. Task trees are valuable as a common language for both designers and users. As was seen in the task modelling session with the user, it appears that it is beneficial to actively involve users in the creation of task models using CTTE, and that users are able to understand task models. Once the task models have been built, the simulation capabilities provided in tools such as CTTE can be extremely useful in validating proposed designs with users. A few problems arose when modelling information systems using CTTE. These problems can be summarised as being a problem of scale. Building accurate task models for medium to large systems is a long and tedious process. The models quickly grow to be too large to understand. This can be partially solved by modelling information systems at a more abstract task level, unfortunately with the side effect that simulations become less valuable and validating designs more difficult. The next section tries to address these shortfalls, with a proposal to extend task models with Interaction Templates.

3.   INTERACTION TEMPLATES

Interaction Templates were developed to attempt to find a middle ground between the two models (detailed and abstract) discussed in the Lab Assistant case study. Interaction Templates are intended to help us to build models quickly, and allow for detailed simulation while maintaining a useful system overview.

While building task models for information systems, there are sub trees that repeat throughout the model with only slight variations. These sub trees are associated with common interface interactions found in information systems. Interaction Templates model these common interface interactions. They include a detailed task model, an execution path (i.e., dialog), and a presentation component. Inserting and customising Interaction Templates reduces the need to model the same interaction repeatedly in a system, and thus, greatly reduces the time spent modelling information systems [7]. As well, Interaction Templates can be designed and tested to ensure their usability in accomplishing a task and can be designed to be 'plastic' [9] and thus adapt to different contexts [7].

Two common interface interactions, data table interaction and print dialog interaction, were chosen as examples of Interaction Templates. These examples illustrate how Interaction Templates attempt to solve some of the problems encountered in the Lab Assistant case study. The next two sections describe these Interaction Templates examples. To help illustrate an Interaction Template we provide a snapshot of its presentation for a specific context and its task tree.

3.1   Example 1: Data Table Interaction Template

Information systems typically deal with large amounts of data. This data is often visualised and interacted with by means of a data table component. The data table Interaction Template models the particular data table interaction found in the data tables of the Lab Assistant. With slight modifications, this Interaction Template could be adapted to model different data table components. The screen snap shot of the data table Interaction Template is shown in Fig. 4.

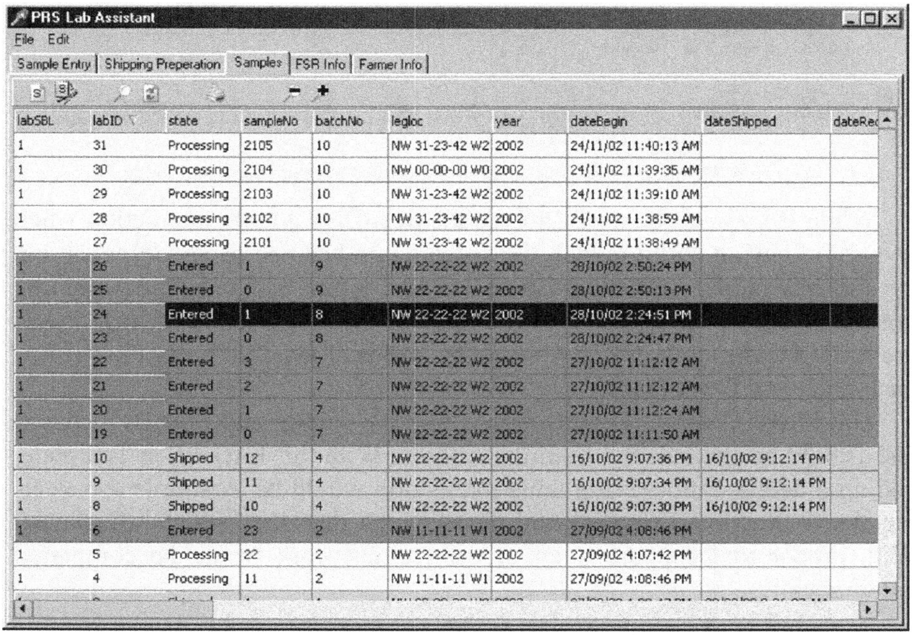

Figure 4. Data Table Interaction Template plugged into the Lab Assistant software.

In the abstract view (Fig. 5), with all sub trees hidden, the data table Interaction Template contains a description of the data the table will be showing. The data is actually expressed with XML but for simplicity we have shown just the key data fields in our figures. Given this abstract view and field information of the data table Interaction Template, the details of the interaction are known without viewing the larger detailed view shown in Fig. 6. Because data tables are common interface interactions in information systems, most users and designers do not need to view the detailed model to understand the interactions that are being described.

This is the feature of the Interaction Template that allows for detailed simulation while maintaining reasonable model size. Hiding the details below the abstraction table interaction task helps to condense the overall size of the model.

Figure 5. Abstract Task Tree of the Interaction Template for a data table.

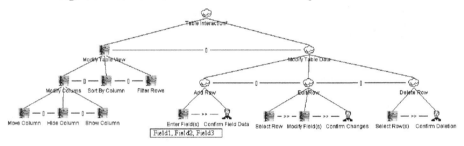

Figure 6. Detailed Task Tree of the Interaction Template for a data table.

While it may not be useful to see the details of a table interaction when trying to view an entire model, these details do become necessary when using the task model simulator. Given the description of the data, it would be possible for a tool to customise the details of the template. With such a tool, the Enter Field(s) task in Fig. 6 would be broken down into Enter Field1, Enter Field2, and Enter Field3.

The Move Column, Hide Column, Show Column, and Sort By Column tasks could be expanded in a similar fashion. With this Interaction Template, adding a detailed model of a table interaction would be as simple as selecting the Interaction Template and defining the data that will be displayed. With proper tool support, a lot of the tedious work would be completed automatically.

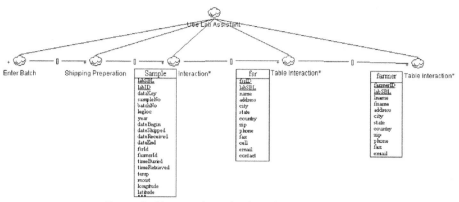

Figure 7. Abstract view of Lab Assistant Task Tree.

The detailed view shows exactly how a user interacts with a data table. The interaction is divided into two subtasks: modify table view and modify table data. When modifying the table view, a user can move, hide and show columns, as well as sort and filter rows. When modifying table data, a user can add, edit and delete rows. With this parameterised Interaction Template, detailed ConcurTaskTrees that are customised for a specific use could be built quickly.

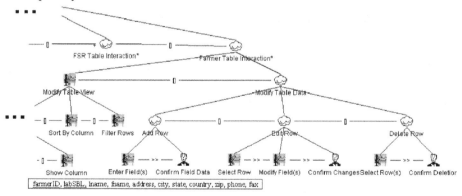

Figure 8. Lab Assistant Task Tree with the Data Table Interaction Template plugged in.

Fig. 7 shows how the data table Interaction Template was used in the Lab Assistant. The abstract view gave a good overview of the system, and helped to keep the model at a manageable size. In Fig. 8, the *fsr* (field service representative) and *farmer* tables fit perfectly with the template. No manual changes to the template were necessary to model these portions of the Lab Assistant. The *sample* table, however, did not match the template exactly. In the *sample* table, it is not possible to add a sample directly to the table. In order to add a sample, the user must go to the abstract task of entering a batch. The *sample* table also does not allow rows to be deleted. Sample deletion is handled in a separate software system called the Lab Manager. The Lab Manager was not modelled in this case study.

Fig. 9 shows how the template was inserted, and easily modified to reflect the differences found in the *sample* table. Under the abstract task *Modify Table Data*, *Add Row* was replaced with the abstract task *Enter Batch*. The abstract task *Delete Row* was simply removed. Although the original template did not match the sample table perfectly, the effort required to manually customise it was minimal.

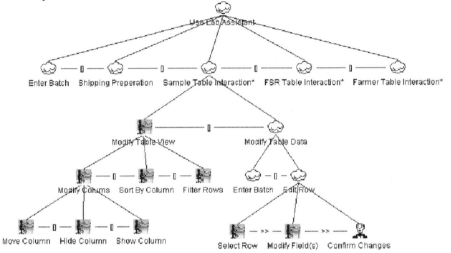

Figure 9. Data Table Interaction modified to fit the sample table.

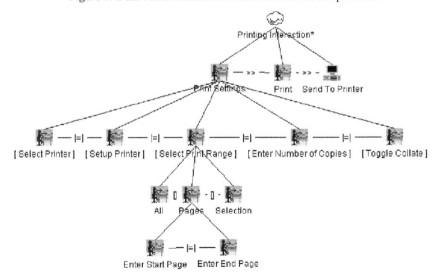

Figure 10. Print Dialog Interaction Template Task Model.

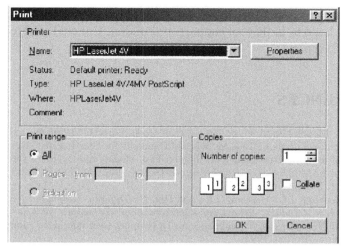

Figure 11. Print Dialog Interaction Template for Windows 9x.

3.2   Example 2: Print Dialog Interaction Template

Another interesting interaction that is commonly found in information systems is the print dialog. Since print dialogs are usually built in to the operating system, they are almost always identical in every place they appear in a software system. This makes them an excellent candidate for Interaction Templates. If they are always the same, an entire print dialog interaction can be added in only one step. The only parameter needed for the Print Dialog Interaction Template is an operating system, because print dialogs differ slightly between operating systems. If an Interaction Template was being built and a printer interaction was needed, the Print Dialog Interaction Template could be selected, and an operating system selected. A model of a print dialog matching the selected OS would then be inserted into the task model. A plastic Interaction Template could be used to provide different behaviour for each operating system. An example of the Print Dialog Interaction Template for Windows 9x is shown in Fig. 10. The Windows 9x print dialog box is shown in Fig. 11.

4.   CONCLUSION

Interaction Templates were developed to solve the problems identified in the Lab Assistant case study. They attempt to solve these problems by taking advantage of common interface interactions found in information systems. The data table interaction and print dialog interaction examples show how

Interaction Templates attempt to solve these problems of scale by condensing the overall model size while maintaining quality of information. In the future we hope to build tool support for building ConcurTaskTrees using Interaction Templates.

REFERENCES

[1]   Baron, M. and Girard, P., *SUIDT: A Task Model Based GUI-Builder*, in C. Pribeanu, J. Vanderdonckt (eds.), "Task Models and Diagrams for User Interface Design", Proceedings of the 1st International Workshop on Task Models and Diagrams for User Interface Design TAMODIA'2002 (Bucharest, 18-19 July 2002), INFOREC Printing House, Bucharest, 2002, pp. 64-71.

[2]   Brandenburg, J.L., Hartson, H.R., and Hix, D., *Different Languages for Different Development Activities: Behavioral Representations Techniques for User Interface Design*, in B. Myers (ed.), "Languages for Developing User Interfaces", Jones and Bartlett Publishers, Boston, 1992.

[3]   Paternò, F., *Model-Based Design and Evaluation of Interactive Applications*, Springer-Verlag, Berlin, 2000.

[4]   Paternò, F., *Task Models in Interactive Software Systems*, in S.K. Chang (ed.), "Handbook of Software Engineering and Knowledge Engineering", Vol. 1, World Scientific Publishing Co., River Edge, 2001, accessible at ftp://cs.pitt.edu/chang/handbook/21.pdf

[5]   Paternò. F., *Tools for task modelling: Where we are, where we are headed*, in C. Pribeanu, J. Vanderdonckt (eds.), "Task Models and Diagrams for User Interface Design", Proceedings of the 1st International Workshop on Task Models and Diagrams for User Interface Design TAMODIA'2002 (Bucharest, 18-19 July 2002), INFOREC Printing House, Bucharest, 2002, pp. 10–17.

[6]   Seffah, A. and Forbrig, P., *Multiple User Interfaces: Towards a Task-Driven and Patterns-Oriented Design Model*, in P. Forbrig, Q. Limbourg, B. Urban, J. Vanderdonckt (eds.), Proceedings of the 9th International Conference on Design, Specification, and Verification of Interactive Systems DSV-IS'2002 (Rostock, 12-14 June 2002), Lecture Notes in Computer Science, Vol. 2545, Springer-Verlag, Berlin, 2002, pp. 118–132.

[7]   Souchon, N., Limbourg, Q., and Vanderdonckt, J., *Task Modelling in Multiple Contexts of Use*, in P. Forbrig, Q. Limbourg, B. Urban, J. Vanderdonckt (eds.), Proceedings of 9th International Workshop on Design, Specification and Verification of Interactive Systems DSV-IS 2002 (Rostock, 12-14 June 2002), Lecture Notes in Computer Science, Vol. 2545, Springer-Verlag, Berlin, 2002, pp. 59-73.

[8]   Tam, R.C.M., Maulsby, D., and Puerta, A.R., *U-TEL: A Tool for Eliciting User Task Models from Domain Experts*, in Proceedings of 3rd ACM International Conference on Intelligent User Interfaces IUI'98 (San Francisco, 6-9 January 1998), ACM Press, New York, 1998, pp. 77-80.

[9]   Thevenin, D. and Coutaz, J., *Plasticity of User Interfaces: Framework and Research Agenda*, in A. Sasse, Ch. Johnson (eds.), Proceedings of 7th IFIP TC.13 Internationa Conference on Human-Computer Interaction Interact'99 (Edinburgh, 30 August- 3 September 1999), IOS Press Publ., Amsterdam, 1999, pp. 110–117.

[10] van Welie, M., van der Veer, G.C., and Eliens, A., *Patterns as Tools for User Interface Design*, in J. Vanderdonckt, Ch. Farenc (eds.), Proceedings of International Workshop on Tools for Working with Guidelines TFWWG'2000 (Biarritz, 7-8 October 2000), Springer-Verlag, London, 2000, pp. 313-324.

Chapter 19

AUTOMATING A DESIGN REUSE FACILITY WITH CRITICAL PARAMETERS
Lessons Learned in Developing the LINK-UP System

C.M. Chewar, Edwin Bachetti, D. Scott McCrickard, and John E. Booker
Center for Human-Computer Interaction and Department of Computer Science,
Virginia Polytechnic Institute and State University, Blacksburg, 24061-0106 VA (USA)
E-mail: {cchewar, mccricks}@cs.vt.edu, {ebachett, jobooker}@vt.edu

Abstract   We propose an interface design process compatible with scenario-based design methods, but specifically intended to facilitate three primary goals: design knowledge reuse, comparison of design products, and long-term research growth within HCI. This effort describes a computer-aided design tool suite, LINK-UP, which supports the design process for specific genre of systems that cross many domains-notification systems. We describe the vision for LINK-UP, contrasting underlying concepts with typical task-based modelling approaches. To achieve its stated goals, the design process is organised and guided by critical parameters, presenting several challenges that we reflect on through the results of a design simulation study. The possibilities envisioned through this approach have important implications for the integration of reusable design knowledge, HCI processes, and design support tools.

Keywords: Claims, Knowledge-based interface design User interface design and specification methods and languages, Notification systems, Task modelling.

1.   INTRODUCTION

Our work probes two themes within human-computer interaction: approaches for reusing and improving design knowledge from project to project, and the design and evaluation of systems used in divided-attention situations (*notification systems*). Central to our goals is a desire to produce automated design support tools that help designers reason and gain inspiration about key questions related to the behaviour of an interface. We envision a system that complements a scenario-based design process [1], in which formative interface development efforts focus on channelling re-

R. Jacob et al. (eds.), Computer-Aided Design of User Interfaces IV, 235–246.
© 2005 *Kluwer Academic Publishers. Printed in the Netherlands.*

quirements and design ideas into narrative scenarios and concise claim statements that evolve through iterative design activities. The majority of the paper discusses the implications of such a system –LINK-UP– developed specifically for our design concern of interest, but extensible to other types of interfaces. However, we first situate this work by providing some background on the prospects of reusing and quantifying design knowledge, as well as our design genre of interest and similar automation efforts.

1.1   Reusing Design Knowledge

As we consider how research growth within Human-Computer Interaction (HCI) can be achieved, supporting design knowledge reuse seems paramount. This goal fits squarely into the movements within the software engineering and HCI communities toward reusable design knowledge. The most dominant approach to software and design knowledge reuse seems to be the patterns movement, coupled with Unified Modelling Language (UML) descriptions. Since patterns include records for design tradeoffs that are observed through actual use, they rely on expression of reasoning about design decisions, which is achieved through claims in scenario-based design methods. *Claims* articulate the positive and negative effects (tradeoffs) of an artefact as feature on a user in accomplishing a task [1]. To achieve design knowledge reuse, Carroll and Sutcliffe argue that research should focus on producing "designer digestible" packets of knowledge in the form of claims, grounded on theory [2,11]. Sutcliffe's Domain Theory provides a structure of abstraction, formal definitions, reuse program evaluation metrics, and generic tasks that can be used to catalog design information [10]. Related work provides approaches for generalising claims for cross-domain reuse [12] and for reuse specifically within the notification systems genre [8].

1.2   Quantifying Design Knowledge

In reflecting on how reuse approaches can include some judgment of design quality, we look to other important arguments with HCI literature. Newman has pointed out the importance of basing design activities on *critical parameters*–figures of merit that are manageable and measurable, transcending specific applications and focusing on the broader purpose of technology [7]. He argues recognising and adopting critical parameters for classes of systems enhances ability to conduct meaningful modelling and recognition of design progress between iterations of a single design and among different designs. To our knowledge, no approach to design reuse or automated design support systems integrates the idea of critical parameters.

1.3   Designing Notification Systems

Our genre of interest, notification systems design, is primarily concerned with interactive or display systems delivering information to users that are primarily engaged in another ongoing task [6]. These interfaces can be found in many implementation forms and on a variety of platforms. Perhaps classic desktop systems are the most readily identifiable–instant messengers, status programs, and stock tickers. However, other familiar examples hint at the range of potential notification systems, such as ubiquitous representations of network traffic, in-vehicle information systems, ambient media, collaboration tools, and multi-monitor or large screen displays. Systems have overarching goals of providing appropriate utility through delivered information in a way that favourably balances demand on user attention. Many examples of claims can be found in [1,2,9,11,12]. For convenience, an example of a simple claim pertinent to notification systems design is:

Use of **tickering text-based animation** to display news headlines in a small desktop window:

+ Preserves user focus on a primary task, while allowing long-term awareness

– BUT is not suitable for rapid recognition of and reaction to urgent information.

Previous work has presented arguments to support the identification of notification system critical parameters [4],[5], which focus design on controlling user *interruption*, *reaction*, and *comprehension*. A claim about a notification system artefact can be quantified with its critical parameters:

Tickering text-based animation ∈ {*low* interruption, *low* reaction, *moderate* comprehension}   (as established in [4])

The example continues in the next section, as a basis for our system vision.

2.   VISION: A SYSTEM FOR DESIGN SUPPORT

In considering how to support design knowledge reuse and growth for notification systems, several arguments from the Computer-Aided Design of User Interfaces (CADUI) community are influential. Since notification systems design is inherently focused on supporting primary and secondary task performance, approaches that seek to understand and model desired task behaviour are key. In particular, the Enhanced Task-Action Grammar (ETAG) provides a proven mechanism to describe interface expectations and connects HCI and software engineering concerns [3]. Wilson and Johnson present considerations for task-based models developing the connection between design phases, identification of optional and compulsory features of the existing task model, and development of the envisioned task model [15]. Building on this foundation, we propose an interface design process compatible with scenario-based design methods, but specifically intended to facilitate three primary goals: design knowledge reuse, comparison of design products, and long-term research growth within HCI.

For example, a designer of a notification system for collaborative work status should be able to benefit from lessons learned in developing previous, similar systems–perhaps a notification system for news headlines or weather information. Claims about appropriate artefacts used in other domains can be accessed for reuse by designers to meet user notification goals. In conceptualizing and developing this system, we have determined that critical parameters provide a meaningful mechanism to specify and describe claims, allowing structured design process transition and reuse.

2.1   LINK-UP, Our Envisioned System

The LINK-UP system (Leveraging Integrated Notification Knowledge through Usability Parameters) operationalises our proposed interface design process. The root concept of the system is to provide notification systems designers with a facility for task-based design advice, consistent with the Wilson and Johnson definition [15], guiding progression throughout an interface design process. This design advice comes in the form of claims, demonstrating an automated approach to claims reuse. In general, claims stem from requirements analysis and provide the basis of the existing and envisioned task model, motivating the design decisions leading to the interface model. Testing of an interface model grounds claims by empirical observation, making them useful and reusable in other design efforts [12]. To continue the example started previously, a designer of a notification system can recognise a need to support notification delivery that results in low user interruption and reaction, but moderate gain of comprehension. In this case, the claim introduced earlier would be returned as a matching technique to meet user requirements.Characterising claims with critical parameters (as illustrated in section 1.3) also allows designers to compare this claim with claims describing other techniques, such as in-place fading and blasting animation. As designers proceed through a design cycle, they continuously question the values of targeted and actual critical parameters for key interface decisions. Claims stored a design knowledge repository are accessed and modified at several points with interactive system tools. Fig. 1 depicts LINK-UP's general architecture, relating it to Norman's conceptual models [8]. Further details about all LINK-UP steps are provided in section 5, but we first focus on Requirements Analysis (1), the initial step where we capture the design model and start to recognise challenges with using critical parameters.

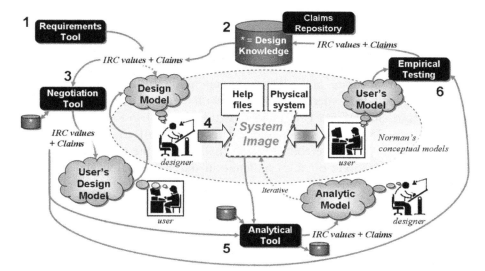

Figure 1. General architecture of LINK-UP. The light grey region in the center depicts Norman's conceptual models [8], which are extended through our work. Numbers refer to steps though the process, and are referenced and explained in sections 2.2 and 5.1.

2.2 Capturing the Design Model

Modelling the usability engineering process, LINK-UP's first step ("1" in Fig. 1) is gathering and analysing user requirements to drive interface design, to include understanding tasks, information characteristics, user background, and other aspects of the situation. In Norman's terms, this forms the *design model* [8], based on dimensions of successful dual-task design recognised in research [14]. Notification systems designers are provided with convenient access to these considerations, as the system ascertains the critical parameter levels of desirable user interruption, reaction, and comprehension (or *IRC values*), expressed simply as triplet of ordinal scale values between 0 and 1.

Using the LINK-UP system, designers search for influential and reusable claims from previous projects and gather them ("2" in Fig. 1) in a manner similar to the Internet shopping cart metaphor used on e-commerce sites. Several indices are used to access this design knowledge within LINK-UP, to include the generic tasks that the system will support (e.g., monitoring or alerting), design choices (e.g., use of colour or animation), and IRC values as the most influential index. Much of this information can be gathered from ETAG specification [3] or direct input by the designer.

In order to use IRC values as indices, they first must be calculated. To facilitate this, a web-based questioning system probes requirements relating to the critical parameters. Using easy to understand questions, LINK-UP guides reasoning about notification tasks and usage factors (such as those summarised in [5]). An algorithm converts designer responses to IRC values (transparent to the designer) accurately and consistently for a wide variety of design models. Section 4 describes the methods used to guide development and validation for accurate and consistent generation of critical parameters, which have included expert walkthroughs with a variety of systems and lab-based design simulation. This process within LINK-UP for characterising the design model to access and judge effectiveness of claims in a design knowledge repository overcomes a key challenge in the use of critical parameters. We elaborate on this challenge in the next section and then describe our related study.

3.   CHALLENGES WITH CRITICAL PARAMETERS

Revisiting the concept of critical parameters, as introduced in [7], experience in developing LINK-UP helped recognise several challenges in using them to guide design knowledge reuse (as we propose in our high-level vision). We introduce each challenge, commenting when appropriate on how it was addressed in the design of the LINK-UP system.

- **Target appraisal.** Designers must be able to transform abstract requirement variables to qualitative critical parameters. Although requirement variables for any class of system (describing the design model) are likely to be quite numerous with wide ranges of possible values, some mechanism must be present that funnels these variables into abstract design goals expressed as critical parameter values. This is the specific focus of step 1 in the LINK-UP system, which we assess in the following section.

- **Iterative assessment.** Designers must be able to estimate critical parameter values throughout the design cycle to gauge the impact of decision-making on design progress. In short, analytical and empirical testing processes must be able to calculate effects necessary to determine whether the critical parameters will be reached. LINK-UP steps that address this challenge are discussed in section 5.

- **Benchmarking.** Through iterative assessment, benchmarks must be established to summarise state-of-the-art effects of actual systems used in real world situations. In this case, design characteristics for specific parameter ranges (e.g., low interruption) would be collected, assisting other designers with understanding implication of various parameter values. This is also a challenge noted by others, which can be used to form reference tasks for research programs [13]. A benefit of an automated system like LINK-UP is acceleration of consensus and collection of benchmarking data.

- **Definition.** A common conception of parameter definitions, as well as acceptable units and methods of measure, must be established so that they can be universally applied–a process worked out through the acceptance of benchmarks. While the researchers may be moving toward common definitions of essential usability metrics, there is still a long way to go. Certainly, related work in the behavioural science fields provides a good starting point that can be bridged to the specific needs of design.

- **Selection.** Researchers must be satisfied that they have exhaustively included the right parameters in consideration of the system class and that all parameters apply to all systems within that class. The LINK-UP system is based on critical parameters of interruption, reaction, and comprehension, argued as essential usability metrics within relevant notification systems literature [4],[5]. As this system and research area matures, acceptance of these parameters will become more widespread.

Our architecture situates the design phases that are important for notification systems. As a vital first step, we consider target appraisal in the study presented in the next section–the first concern a designer would be presented with during requirements analysis in a design process and a topic of interest in the CADUI community.

4. DESIGN SIMULATION STUDY WITH LINK-UP

Without consistency among designers in the determination of critical parameters, effectiveness of the system would be severely limited. If two designers were to specify very different critical parameter values for the same design model, the claims returned in a search result would not fit the needs of this design model. Therefore, our current efforts in implementing and validating LINK-UP probe establishment of a well-defined process for target appraisal. To this end, we have developed a questionnaire and an underlying algorithm in our system, taking designer's abstract requirement variables and transforming them into qualitative critical parameters values. A key validation concern with this tool allows designers to generate accurate and precise results for a full range of notification system design models.

We hypothesize a user test with our tool would validate several system objectives. Our first objective enforces accuracy of critical parameter establishment against expert consensus; we expect agreement within 20%. This value was selected based on the best expert-to-expert parameter assessment agreement rates previously obtained with manual assessment methods. Our second objective ensures that different designers are able to derive similar critical parameter values given an identical design model, for which we also expect agreement within a standard deviation of 20%. These objectives apply throughout the full range of possible parameter values. Of course, we also expect that designers generating critical parameter values with this tool will obtain more accurate and precise results than designers with no tool at all (using manual, heuristic-based estimation). Before beginning formal testing, we tuned the algorithm with a number of system and requirements walkthroughs by different experts, ensuring expert users could achieve agreement between manual and tooled parameter assessment.

4.1   Methodology

The first phase of testing, which probed the accuracy and precision of our tool, consisted of 10 undergraduate computer science students that received credit in an HCI class for their assistance in a design simulation study. These participants were instructed to consider themselves designers of notification systems and were given four design problems, such as the example below:

> *You have been asked to design a desktop notification system that provides sport score updates for several games that users select. You anticipate that users (probably typical college students) will want to glance at this system quite frequently during a course of several hours, as they perform other desktop processing tasks. These primary tasks include word processing, making presentations, chat, and surfing the Internet. Although you feel it will be important for the notification system to be always visible, you don't think it should take up much screen space or be overly distracting. You don't think that users will usually want to click on anything to receive updates–but it is possible they they'll want to use the system to launch to more details about close scores or important games. However, you guess that most users will just want to know scores.*

After reading a given design problem, participants used the tool to answer approximately 16 multiple-choice questions. An example question is *"Which statement describes the general relationship between the importance of the primary task and receiving the notification?"* After answering all questions, the parameter values are calculated via an underlying algorithm and sent to the LINK-UP system. Following the generation of the critical parameter values, participants responded to a post-test survey to determine if the questions addressed all factors they felt impacted interruption, reaction, and comprehension. In addition to testing these novice designers, we obtained benchmark parameter values for each of the four design problems from an impartial expert that assisted in the development of the IRC system. We conducted a second phase of testing to determine if the tool provided designers with more accurate and precise results than designers without the tool. This required 10 additional participants from the same population who solved the same four design problems. Instead of an automated questionnaire, these participants were given a list of general heuristics to guide their reasoning, but then used their best judgment to specify quantitative values for the three critical parameters.

4.2 Results and Conclusion

In interpreting the results, we calculated the absolute difference between each participant's derived parameters and the benchmark results. This yielded an overall difference of 18.0%, which is well within our expected threshold for accuracy. The accuracy per parameter for the IRC values was 16.6%, 17.9%, and 19.5% respectively. While all three individually are also within our threshold, upon further analysis of the comprehension parameter, the majority of the disagreement between expert and novice designers came from two outliers in two of the four design problems. This reveals the only weakness in achieving accuracy across the full range of parameter values.

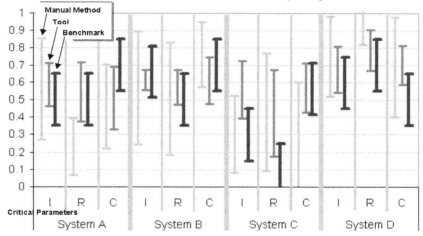

Figure 2. Accuracy and precision results, indicating the superior performance of the tool over the manual critical parameter assessment method, as well as the general match between participant results with the tool and expert derived benchmarks.

Testing for precision was done by taking the raw parameter values and calculating the standard deviation. The results were also favourable, yielding a standard deviation of 14.1%, well within our expected threshold. In looking at the standard deviations by parameter and problem, we note a problem with consistently assessing reaction in one of the design problems, suggesting additional fine-tuning work or perhaps rephrasing the problem.

To ensure that the tool indeed provided better support for calculating critical values, we compared the benchmark differences of results obtained by participants who had used the tool with those that did not. A single factor ANOVA revealed a significant difference ($F(1, 238) = 7.35$, $p<0.01$). Details of results can be seen in Fig. 2. Overall, these results are very favourable for the prospect of integrating critical parameters into a design support system like LINK-UP, since we can at least ensure target appraisal.

5.   GENERAL IMPLICATIONS AND NEXT STEPS

The success in developing and validating the Requirements Analysis module has provided confidence that the other challenges with using critical parameters can be overcome. Just as we were able to develop general questions to characterise essential components of problem situations, we are working on methods to refine details from participatory design processes and analytical and empirical usability test results, making conclusions about actual critical parameter values of notification system artefacts. At this point, we can continue a conceptualisation of the LINK-UP system and comment on broader implications of our general approach.

5.1   LINK-UP, Beyond Requirements Analysis

The claims collected in step 2 assist designers in reasoning about scenario-based design phases [1]. However, to aid participatory design efforts and validate the design model IRC values, the LINK-UP system provides a tool for designers to produce an interactive claims-review session with potential users ("3" in Fig. 1). Designers can present prototypical usage scenarios to the user, who then assesses the claims (and underlying, transparent IRC values). Users accept or reject claims according to their needs, forming the *user's design model (UDM)*—a conception of the system effects gleaned through the IRC values associated with the final claims set. In turn, the agreement of the UDM with the design model helps the designer know when to progress from one stage to the next (in this case, to production of the physical system ("4" in Fig. 1)). This resolves a key concern cited with other task-based design approaches [15]. It is anticipated that designer-user claims negotiation is an iterative process involving multiple users. Once a system image is available, the LINK-UP system supports analytical (expert) evaluation ("5" in Fig. 1), with the hope that most usability problems can be caught early in the development process and without requiring costly user evaluation. Currently to support this stage, we use a heuristic method to analytical evaluation, based on heuristics tailored for notification systems. LINK-UP facilitates execution of the analytic method, recording of results, and estimation of the actual IRC values, or the *analytical model*. In this step, the claims set's corresponding IRC values are assessed in light of the physical product, providing a means for developing practical guidelines and comparing design choices–another limitation noted in other task-based design support techniques [15]. Designers are able to gauge whether targeted critical parameters will be achieved in the design, receiving automated support to pinpoint specific design problems. Similar to the previous step, the next tool within the LINK-UP system facilitates the execution and results analysis for an empirical user testing session ("6" in Fig. 1). Here, the system uses the original set of claims to adapt a general instrument for collecting usage data. Based on users' qualitative feedback and quantitative performance, actual IRC values are determined to characterise the *user's model* (as defined in [8]) and effectiveness of the claims. While the step allows formative and summative testing of the designed interface, it generates new knowledge related to new and existing claims. The key function of the tool assists the designer in comparing actual with intended efforts, informing the next design iteration.

5.2 Implications: Integrated Design Knowledge Reuse

The conclusions drawn from our studies suggest several implications for integrated design knowledge reuse. The LINK-UP system provides continuous and integrated access to the design knowledge repository, facilitating knowledge reuse. Through access to the claims database, designers are able to build from and test previous design claim tradeoffs, contributing to a growing body of knowledge. To enable these features in a manner that preserves content quality and user trust, the system includes meta-analysis and maintenance features for expert administrators, such as full claims editing, association of claims with related theories, example systems, and design artefacts. The concept of this system extends the existing notion of claims analysis [1] to one of *claims engineering*–design efforts will continuously improve the quality of reusable claims.

As we continue to develop the system, validation efforts will be structured around lab-based simulation studies, and content creation will result mainly from student design efforts and conversion of existing related literature. However, as soon as possible, we would like to start testing the system's support for actual long-term development efforts. We welcome opportunities to challenge LINK-UP's utility (and that of its critical parameters) through collaborative design efforts within the notification systems field, seeking to broaden its functionality by integrating and extending CADUI research.

To summarise, the LINK-UP system provides a web-based interface to guide the usability engineering process for a notification system. Designers interact with five major design support tools, saving and building on progressive session results throughout the process. These tools include support for requirements analysis and negotiation, analytical and empirical testing, and design knowledge access. Design progress within a single design and through a meta-analysis of several systems is guided by a set of claims (serving as design hypotheses) and associated critical parameters (acting as engineering targets and results). The design knowledge repository will grow and improve through use, becoming a living record of notification systems research made possible by thinking about design through critical parameters.

We have begun formalising the way we develop and evaluate notifications systems. To generalise this effort, we have recognised potential for a similar process of design knowledge reuse to be applied in the areas of information visualisation and community networks. Based on initial success, we feel that the general process, integrated with critical parameters, can be valuable to other genres in the user interface community.

REFERENCES

[1] Carroll, J.M., *Scenario-based Design: Envisioning Work and Technology in System Development*, John Wiley and Sons, New York, 1995.

[2] Carroll, J.M., Singley, M.K., and Rosson, M.B., *Integrating Theory Development With Design Evaluation*, Behavior and Information Technology, Vol. 11, pp. 247-255, 1992.

[3] de Haan, G., *ETAG-based Design: User Interface Design as Mental Model Specification*, in "Critical Issues in User Interface Systems Engineering", Springer-Verlag, pp. 81-92.

[4] McCrickard, D.S., Catrambone, R., Chewar., C.M., and Stasko, J.T., *Establishing Tradeoffs that Leverage Attention for Utility: Empirically Evaluating Information Display in Notification Systems*, International Journal of Human-Computer Studies, Vol. 8, No. 5, May 2003, pp. 547-582.

[5] McCrickard, D.S., Chewar, C.M., Somervell, J.P, and Ndiwalana, A., *A Model for Notification Systems Evaluation–Toward Assessing Usability for Multitasking Activity*, ACM Trans. on Computer-Human Interaction, Vol. 10, No. 4, December 2003, pp. 312-338.

[6] McCrickard, D.S., Czerwinski, M., and Bartram, L., *Introduction: Design and Evaluation of Notification User Interfaces*, International Journal of Human-Computer Studies Vol. 8, No. 5, May 2003, pp. 509-514.

[7] Newman, W.M., *Better or Just Different? On the Benefits of Designing Interactive Systems in terms of Critical Parameters*, in Proceedings of the ACM 2nd Symposium on Designing Interactive Systems DIS'97 (Amsterdam, 18-20 August 1997), ACM Press, New York, 1997, pp. 239-245.

[8] Norman, D.A., *Cognitive Engineering*, in D.A., Norman, S.W., Draper (eds.), "User Centered Systems Design: New Perspectives on Human-Computer Interaction", Lawrence Erlbaum Associates, New Jersey, 1986, pp. 31-61.

[9] Payne, C., Allgood, C.F., Chewar, C.M. Holbrook, C., and McCrickard, D.S., *Generalizing Interface Design Knowledge: Lessons Learned from Developing a Claims Library*, in Proceedings of 2003 IEEE International Conference on Information Reuse and Integration IRI'03 (Las Vegas, 27-29 October 2003), Los Alamitos, 2003, pp. 362-369.

[10] Sutcliffe, A., *The Domain Theory: Patterns for Knowledge and Software Reuse*, Lawrence Erlbaum Associates, New Jersey, 2002.

[11] Sutcliffe, A., *On the Effective Use and Reuse of HCI Knowledge*, ACM Transactions on Computer-Human Interaction, Vol. 7, No. 2, June 2000, pp. 197-221.

[12] Sutcliffe, A.G. and Carroll, J.M., *Designing Claims For Reuse In Interactive Systems Design*, Int. J. of Human-Computer Studies, Vol. 50, No. 3, March 1999, pp. 213-241.

[13] Whittaker, S., Terveen, L., and Nardi, B.A., *Let's Stop Pushing the Envelope and Start Addressing It: A Reference Task Agenda for HCI*, Human-Computer Interaction, Vol. 15, No 2-3, 2000, pp. 75-106.

[14] Wickens, C.D. and Hollands, J.G., *Engineering Psychology and Human Performance,* 3rd ed., Prentice Hall, New Jersey, 2000.

[15] Wilson, S. and Johnson, P., *Bridging the Generation Gap: From Work Tasks to User Interface Design*, in J. Vanderdonckt (ed.), "Computer-Aided Design of User Interfaces", Proceedings of the 2nd Workshop on Computer-Aided Design of user Interfaces CADUI'96 (Namur, June 1996), Presses Universitaires de Namur, Namur, 1996, pp. 77-94.

Chapter 20

XICL – AN EXTENSIBLE MARK-UP LANGUAGE FOR DEVELOPING USER INTERFACE AND COMPONENTS

Lirisnei Gomes de Sousa and Jair C. Leite
Department of Informatics and Applied Mathematics, Federal Univ. of Rio Grande do Norte,
Av Sen. Salgado Filho, 3000 - Lagoa Nova - Campus Universitario, Natal (Brazil)
Tel.: +55 84 215 3814 - Fax: +55 84 215 3813
E-mail: lirisnei@lcc.ufrn.br, jair@dimap.ufrn.br
URL: http://www.lcc.ufrn.br/~lirisnei, http://www.dimap.ufrn.br/~jair/

Abstract   The development of browser-based User Interface (UI) components is important to enhance Web Systems Usability. There are several solutions to the development of UI components. Some of them are proprietary and requires specific high-cost development tools and run-time plug-in. DHTML – the W3C client-side recommended technologies – provides resources to the development of new UI components. However, the development of new UI components using DHTML is a very hard work because of the lack of standardised models and application programming interfaces. Reusability and Extensibility is also very difficult to achieve. This work presents the XICL, a mark-up language to describe user interfaces and UI components. This language defines a description format and a semantic model that standardises UI components development. XICL is based on DHTML and follows the component-based software development paradigm to promote reuse, extension and portability. We also present the XICL Studio, a development environment composed of an editor, a library of components and a compiler.

Keywords: DHTML, Mark-up languages, User interface components, User interface specification methods and languages, Web-based interfaces.

1.   INTRODUCTION

As the World Wide Web increases, many browser-based applications are available to a great number of users with very different profiles. Usability is a very important issue in this scenario. However, browser-based user inter-

R. Jacob et al. (eds.), Computer-Aided Design of User Interfaces IV, 247–258.

face (UI) development technologies have important limitations to allow usability with portability, extensibility and reusability. DHTML, the WWW
Consortium recommended technologies [12], has only a limited set of UI
components and only allows the implementation of few interaction techniques [7]. It is possible to develop legacy UI components such as pop-up
menus, dialog boxes, toolbars, toolboxes and others using DHTML. However, there are no models and standardised Application Programming Interfaces (APIs) to drive UI component development and to component-based
UI software development. Others UI development technologies also have
some limitations that are discussed in Section 2.

This work presents the XICL, an extensible XML-based mark-up language to UI and UI components development to Web systems and Browser-
based software application. UI components are developed in XICL using
HTML elements and others XICL UI components. The language also describes additional information to allow XICL to be used in UI builders. The
goals of XICL are to provide a standardised way to UI component-based development and to promote reusability, extensibility and portability. The
XICL Studio is an associated tool to the development of UI and UI components. It has an editor, a library of components, and an interpreter to generate
DHTML code from XICL descriptions.

2.   USER INTERFACE COMPONENT-BASED DE-
VELOPMENT TECHNOLOGIES

In this section we analyse the reusability, extensibility and portability
features of some UI component-based development technologies. The main
software industry solutions are the Microsoft IE WebControls [9], the Macromedia Flash MX 2004 and the Sun Java Applets. The Internet Explorer
WebControls are a collection of ASP.NET server controls that generate
HTML 3.2 content that renders in all commonly used browsers [9]. A *Tree-
View, ToolBar, MultiPage,* and *TabControl* user interface are included in the
Internet Explorer WebControls. There are others solution from Microsoft but
they are also based on the .NET (COM/ActiveX) technologies that are spe-
cific for Windows platform.

The Macromedia Flash MX 2004 is a proprietary and closed technology
to the development of Web UI Components [1]. It provides a Component
Architecture that uses the ActionScript 2 language to define Classes and Interfaces for Web components. However, the development of the components
and their execution in the resulting user interface requires a proprietary plug-
in that is not available to all operating platforms.

The Java-based technologies for UI components should be developed in the Java language using some specific development framework and API (e.g., *Java Swing*). The running time UI components are *Java Applets* and they require the Java Virtual Machine to be executed in a browser. Applets are a powerful and flexible solution but they are limited to the Java development and operating platforms.

There are others solutions to developing UI and UI components that are based in XML. We analyse some of this language-based approach to UI development.

AUIML (Abstract User Interface Mark-up Language) is "an XML vocabulary which has been designed to allow the intent of an interaction with a user to be defined." This clearly contrasts with the conventional approach to user interface design, which focuses on appearance. With an intent based approach, designers are able to "concentrate on the semantics of the interactions without having to concern themselves with which particular device type(s) need to be supported." Being an XML vocabulary, AUIML allows device independent encoding of information. All the interaction information can be encoded once and subsequently rendered using 'device dependent rendering' so that users can actually interact with the system. AUIML is therefore intended to be independent of the client platform on which the user interface is rendered, the implementation language and the user interface implementation technology [2]

XIML (*eXtensible Interface Mark-up Language*) is an XML-based "interface representation language for universal support of functionality across the entire lifecycle of a user interface: design, development, operation, management, organisation, and evaluation" [6,11]. The main concern of the XIML approach is model-based development. It provides a standard mechanism to data interchange among tools and application from design to operation. XIML allows design models to be transformed in multi-device implementation solution [11]. This language has an interested purpose but it does not offers reusability and extensibility of components.

The UIML (*User Interface Mark-up Language*) aim is to allow platform independent UI development – hardware devices, operating systems and programming languages [10]. It was designed conforming to XML and has HTML-like syntax. From a unique specification in UIML it is possible to generate User Interfaces to several platforms in different programming languages. The main purpose of UIML is similar to that of XICL. However, it is not possible the development, reuse and extension of UI components.

XUL is a multi-platform language to describe application UI. The most of GUI components could be create using XUL – buttons, text-boxes, check-boxes, menus, dialog boxes, trees and others [3]. It is similar to the Java approach but it uses the Mozilla engine instead of the Java Virtual Machine. It chine. It is the ideal solution to Web system when it is not possible to install a standard browser. It is also possible to design on-line and off-line application. The main disadvantage is the low portability because it cannot be used in every browser.

Xforms is a W3C initiative and it is an XML-based language to the creation of UI form elements to provide portability in different platforms [5]. However it is not possible to create menu, windows, dialog boxes, toolbar and other UI component.

There is another project that is similar with the purpose of our work and it also uses a mark-up language. The SEESCOA (*Software Engineering for Embedded Systems using a Component-Oriented Approach*) project goal [8] is to adapt the CBD (Component Based Development) technology that was developed for mainstream software to the needs of embedded systems.

3.   THE XICL LANGUAGE

XICL is a mark-up language to UI and UI component development for browser-based software. Its syntax is based on XML, HTML and ECMAScript and also follows the Document Object Model [11]. Our intention is to provide a familiar syntax to Web system developer. The main goals are (1) the development of UI component to browser-based software and (2) the development of UI using HTML elements and XICL components.

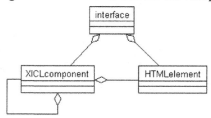

Figure 1. The XICL components and HTML elements relationships.

New UI components are described in XICL using HTML elements and XICL components by reuse and extension mechanisms. A XICL component could be composed of reusable components stored in a library (XICL Lib) or it can extend an existing component modifying specific propertied. The relationship among HTML elements and XICL elements are illustrated using UML in Fig. 1.

3.1   Developing User Interfaces in XICL

The development process using XICL is described as follows and Fig. 2 illustrates it. The developer of the UI specifies it in the XICL code using a text editor. He/she could reuse a XICL component from the library (XICL Lib). The interpreter analyzes the XICL code and generates the resulting UI in DHTML code. The resulting DHTML code could run in all browsers that follow W3C recommendations.

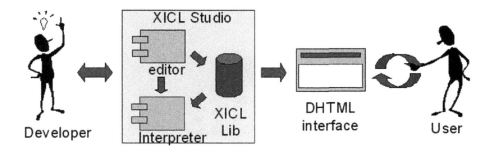

Figure 2. The development process.

The following sub-sections describe how a UI and its components are developed using XICL.

3.2   Specifying the UI in XICL

To illustrate the features and the expressive power of XICL we present a short example of the basic structure and the associated behaviour of a user interface composed of HTML elements and XICL components.

The Fig. 3 shows a screenshot of the Presenta, a browser-based tool to the development of slide presentations [4]. To open an existing presentation in Presenta the user should open a file. This is done by entering a file name in a dialog box window as shown in Fig. 3. The user interface of the Presenta application was developed using XICL. The dialog box could be implemented with DHTML but this requires several lines of Javascript and HTML programming code. The development is easier and faster using XICL than using DHTML technologies.

Fig. 4 shows a small part of the specification of the Presenta user interface structure and behaviour. The XICL specification is a XML document. Its syntax follows the mark-up style that is familiar to the most of web developers. The <XICL> is the root element of the specification. All others elements must be inside its scope.

A XICL specification can contain zero or more component descriptions and one or zero interface descriptions. It also can make reference to components that were defined in another XICL documents. To use these outside components it is necessary to import the specification documents using the

IMPORT element. Fig. 4 (line 2) illustrates a use of the IMPORT element.

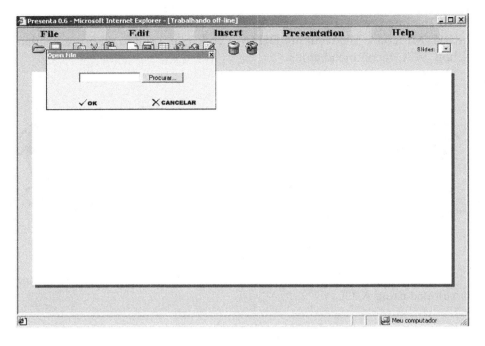

Figure 3. A UI developed using XICL.

The INTERFACE element is used to describe the user interface structure and behavior specification. The HTML components and its associated events are specified using the XHTML syntax (remember that a XICL document is a XML document). In our example, the paragraph <P> element and the table (<TABLE>, <TR> and <TD>) are used in the specification. The DHTML *onclick* event is also used in line 5.

The XICL components are described in a similar way as HTML elements. The *menuOption* element (line 5) is a part of the menu component specification that is not described here. The WINDOW component creates the *Open File Dialog Box*.

It is identified by the *"OpenFile"* name. The structure of this window is defined using the <TABLE> element. It contains an input file element (line 14) and two buttons. *BtnOk* is a button used to confirm the operation and to close the window. *BtnCancel* is used to cancel the operation and also to close the window.

The behaviour of the *OpenFile* window is defined by the methods *show()* and *close()*. Each function should be associated to others UI components. The *show()* function displays the *OpenFile* window to the user when the user click on the corresponding menu option. This is specified in XICL by associating the *onclick* event of the *menuOption* element (line 5) to the function *OpenFile.show()*. The two buttons of the *OpenFile* window associate the user click to the corresponding functions. The *BtnOk* button triggers the *confirm()* and *close()* functions whereas the *BtnCancel* triggers only the *close()* function.

```
1.  <XICL>
2.  <IMPORT src= "lib1.xml">
3.  <INTERFACE>
4.  ...
5.    <menuOption onclick="OpenFile.show()">Open File </menuOption>
6.  ...
7.
8.    <Window title="Open File" id="OpenFile" width="250" top="200" left="200" height="200">
9.       <table width="100%" border="0" >
10.         <tr>
11.            <p align="center"> Enter with the file (path) </p>
12.         </tr>
13.         <tr>
14.            <p align="center"><input type="file" onBlur="eval(file=this.value)"/></p>
15.         </tr>
16.         <tr>
17.            <td align="right"><BtnOk  onclick="confirm(); OpenFile.close()" /> </td>
18.            <td align="left"><BtnCancel value="Cancelar" onclick=" OpenFile.close()" />   </td>
19.         </tr>
20.       </table>
21.    </Window>
22. </INTERFACE>
23. </XICL>
```

Figure 4. The XICL specification.

3.3   Developing XICL Components

Using the XICL language the developer can specify the user interface and also new UI components. The component-based software development paradigm recommends the definition of a conceptual model to drive the developers in defining and reusing a component.

XICL defines its own component conceptual model that is composed by its *structure, properties, events, methods* and *interaction model*. Fig. 5 shows the relationship between them.

In the Presenta example describe in last section, a WINDOW component is reused to create the *OpenFile dialog box*. This component offers a structure to developers to create different kinds of windows in an easy way but it is must to be created before reuse.

This section describes the development of the WINDOW component by specifying it in XICL.

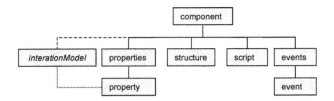

Figure 5. The component conceptual model.

The specification begins with the <COMPONENT name=...> tag informing the component name (see Figure 6 and ends with the </COMPONENT> tag. The *name* attribute is used to reserve a *namespace* to the component so the component can be used on the interface description only putting its name between tag marks (*<compName>*). Components can be defined extending others components. In order to do it we use the *extends* attribute.

The structure of the WINDOW component is defined using HTML elements and XICL components. The WINDOW is a box with top and left positions. The interface described on the Fig. 3 use XICL component (TEXT) and HTML elements (DIV, TABLE and others). A component instance can appear and disappear when its methods *show()* and *close()* is activated by an event.

A component can have another component as a *child*. The CHILDREN element is used to specify the position of the child in the component structure so the compiler knows how to compose the components when necessary. It is an important mechanism to reusability. Fig. 6 (line 17) shows that the component WINDOW can have children in the table cell.

The PROPERTY element is used to describe the component properties. This element has the attributes *name* and *dataType*. Although the type of the data is not necessary in DHTML, it is necessary in XICL to explicitly declare the type of the data. A set of component properties should be specified inside of the PROPERTIES element.

```
1.   ...
2.   <COMPONENT name="Window" >
3.     <STRUCTURE>
4.       <div id="$id">,
5.         <div style="position:absolute; top:$top; left:$left; ">
6.           <table border="1" style=" width:$width; height:$height; ">
7.             <tr height="12">
8.               <td align="left" border="0">
9.                 <TEXT style="color:blue; font-size:12 ">  $title  </TEXT>
10.              </td>
11.              <td width="2" align="right" border="0">
12.                <a  onclick="$id.close()" name="fig1">
13.                   <img src="close.gif"/>
14.                </a>
```

```
15.                    </td>
16.                  </tr>
17.                  <tr ><td colspan="2">        <CHILDREN/>        </td> </tr>
18.               </table>
19.            </div>
20.         </div>
21.
22.     </STRUCTURE>
23.     <METHODS>
24.        <METHOD name="close" function="closeWindow" />
25.        <METHOD name="show" function="showWindow" />
26.     </METHODS>
27.
28.     <EVENTS>
29.        <EVENT name="onClose" objEvent=" fig1.click " when="during" />
30.        <EVENT name="afterClose" functionExec=" closeWindow " when="after" />
31.     </EVENTS>
32.     </COMPONENT>
33.     <SCRIPT><!— ... —> </SCRIPT>
```

Figure 6. Component definition in XICL.

DOM allows the mapping of events into script function in a HTML user interface element. The DOM events are *primary events* and the associated functions are *primary functions* in XICL. It is not necessary to define primary events. The *onclick* is an example of a primary event. New events can be defined to new components in XICL. The new events are *secondary events* and they should be defined in XICL in the scope of a component definition specification using the EVENT element. This element has the attributes *name, objEvent, functionExe* and *when*. A new event can be based in a primary event that are associated to an element – an *element-event pair* – that belongs to the component structure. All the EVENT elements of a component should be specified inside the EVENTS element.

The WINDOW component has two secondary events. The *onClose* event is associated with the event-element *fig1.click* and it triggers the *close* primary function. The function is activated only during the event occurrence. The *afterClose* event specifies that it occurs only after the *closeWindow()* function has been executed. The afterClose event is applied in the WINDOW reuse described in the last section.

The METHODS element encloses the definition of the components methods. Each method is a script function that determines the behavior of the component. Actually, the METHOD element maps a method name into a scripting function.

The SCRIPT element is used to delimit the code of the scripting functions that are methods of the component. The scripting function could be coded in Javascript or ECMAScript.

4.   XICL STUDIO – A DEVELOPMENT ENVIRON-MENT

The UI development process using XICL requires a basic environment composed of an editor, a library of components (XICL Lib) and an interpreter. The current version of XICL Studio environment consists of a very basic editor where the developer edits the XICL code. Using the editor is possible to edit the specification of user interfaces or components. When editing components the developer should store its source XICL code in the XICL lib to be reused in future user interfaces.

To develop a complete UI, it is necessary to write the specification in XICL code using the editor and then call the interpreter to generate the DHTML final code. This code can be executed in any common browse.

The reuse of XICL components can be done by importing a component from XICL Lib. The developer specifies the component by using the *import* statement. The interpreter joins the source code of the component to that of user interface and translates them into a DHTML code.

The XICL Studio environment is a browser-based software that integrates the basic editor, the XICL Lib and the interpreter in the same application. The developer executes it in a browser and it provides commands to store a component in the XICL Lib, to call the interpreter and to view the final DHTML code.

The XICL Lib has some pre-defined components that can be reused by the developers. The *Window* component described in a previous section of this paper is a pre-defined component that is available to reuse. The Window is composed of a title bar, a button to close the window and an empty area where others component could be put. The *MessageBox* component extends the Window and could be reused to error messages and warnings. The *Dialog Box* is also an extension of the Window and it contains a text box, a OK button and a Cancel button.

The *ToolBar* and *MenuBar* are components that present options to the user to activate specific commands. The *ToolBar* presents a set of images representing the corresponding functions. The *MenuBar* presents a set of words representing the functions and opens a set of *Pulldown MenuOptions*. The user interface of the Presenta reuses both of these components.

5.   CONCLUSION

Developers need always to construct new UI components to achieve more system usability. The W3C recommends the client-side user interface DHTML technologies to increase application portability. However, DHTML only provides a few basic UI components such as *button, drop-down menu, text fields, check-box, radio-button*, etc. and developing in DHTML is a very hard work. Also, there are no models and standards to the development of DHTML UI components.

XICL is a language to User Interface development by specifying its structure and behaviour in an abstract level than using only DHTML. It also promotes reuse and extensibility of user interface components. The developer can create new and more abstract UI components.

XICL is based on the XML syntax and it follows a basic component model to provide a well-structure code. The XICL code smoothly integrates with DHTML technologies promoting also interoperabilty.

UI development in XICL can be done using the XICL Studio environment. This basic environment provides a simple editor, a library of components and an interpreter that translate XICL code into DHTML code. The final user interface is implemented using DHTML technologies and can run in common Web browsers.

ACKNOWLEDGEMENTS

The authors would like to thanks to CNPq (Brazilian Council for Scientific and Technological Development), PRH22 - ANP/MCT and to the Federal University of Rio Grande do Norte for their financial support.

REFERENCES

[1] Anbar, W., *Exploring Version 2 of the Macromedia Flash MX 2004 Component Architecture*, 2004, accessible at http://www.macromedia.com/devnet/mx/flash/articles/

[2] Azevedo, P., Merrick, R., and Roberts D., *OVID to AUIML - User-Oriented Interface Modelling*, in N.J. Nunes (ed.), Proceedings of the UML200 Workshop "Towards a UML Profile for Interactive Systems Development" TUPIS'2000 (York, 2-3 October 2000), accessible at http://www.math.uma.pt/tupis00/submissions/azevedoroberts/azeve doroberts.html.

[3] Boswell, D., King, B., Oeschger, I., Collins, P., and Murphy E., *Introduction to XUL*, in "Creating Applications with Mozilla", O'Reilly, Sebastopol, September 2002.

[4] De Sousa, L.G, Oliveira, E.S., and Leite, J.C., *Implementação de técnicas de interação no Presenta – uma ferramenta para edição de apresentações na Web*, in E. Furtado, J.C. Leite (eds.), Proc. of 5th Symposium on Human Factors in Computer Systems IHC'2002 (Fortaleza, 7-10 October 2002), Fortaleza, 2002, pp. 141-152.

[5] Dubinko, M., Klotz L., Merrick, R., and Raman, T.V., *XForms 1.0 W3C Working Draft*, accessible at http://www.w3.org/TR/xforms/.

[6] Eisenstein, J., Vanderdonckt, J., Puerta, A., *Model-Based User-Interface Development Techniques for Mobile Computing*, Proc. of 5th ACM Int. Conf. on Intelligent User Inter-

faces IUI'2001 (Santa Fe, 14-17 January 2001), ACM Press, New York, 2001, pp. 69-76.

[7]   Goodman, D., *Dynamic HTML – The Definitive Reference*, O'Reilly, Sebastopol, 1998.

[8]   Luyten, K., Van Laerhoven, T., Coninx, K., and Van Reeth, F., *Runtime Transformations for Modal Independent User Interface Migration*, Interacting with Computers, Vol. 15, No. 3, 2003, pp. 329-347.

[9]   Microsoft Corporation, *Internet Explorer WebControls Reference*, The MSDN Library, accessible at http://msdn.microsoft.com/library/

[10] Phanouriou, C., *UIML: A Device-Independent User Interface Markup Language*, Ph.D. Thesis, Virginia Polytechnic Institute, Blackburg, 26 September 2000.

[11] Puerta, A. and Eisenstein, J., *XIML: A Universal Language for User Interfaces*, in Proc. of 7th ACM Conference on Intelligent User Interfaces IUI'2002 (San Francisco, 13-16 January 2002), accessible at http://www.iuiconf.org/02pdf/2002-002-0043.pdf

[12] W3C, accessible at http://www.w3c.org, 2003.

Chapter 21

UIML.NET: AN OPEN UIML RENDERER FOR THE .NET FRAMEWORK

Kris Luyten and Karin Coninx
Limburgs Universitair Centrum, Expertise Centre for Digital Media
Universitaire Campus, B-3590 Diepenbeek (Belgium)
Tel.: +32 11 26 84 11 – Fax: +32 11 26 84 00
E-mail: {kris.luyten,karin.coninx}@luc.ac.be – URL: http://www.edm.luc.ac.be

Abstract   As the diversity of available computing devices increases it becomes more difficult to adapt User Interface development to support the full range of available
devices. One of the difficulties are the different GUI libraries: to use an alternative library or device one is forced to redevelop the interface completely for the
alternative GUI library. To overcome these problems the User Interface Mark-up
Language (UIML) specification has been proposed, as a way of glueing the interface design to different GUI libraries in different environments without further efforts. In contrast with other approaches UIML has matured and has some
implementations proving its usefulness. We introduce the first UIML renderer
for the .Net framework, a framework that can be accessed by different kinds of
programming languages and can use different kinds of widget sets. We show
that its properties, among them its reflection mechanism, are suitable for the development of a reusable and portable UIML renderer. The suitability for multi-
device rendering is discussed in comparison with our own multi-device UI
framework Dygimes. The focus is on how layout management can be generalised in the specification to allow the GUI to adapt to different screen sizes.

Keywords: Automatic User Interface Generation, Multi- and multiple-device User Interfaces, User-interface design and specification methods and languages, UIML.

1.   INTRODUCTION

It is a known fact that all computing environments become more heterogeneous every day. Instead of emerging to a common set of hardware and
software platforms, computing gains at diversity. Nevertheless, a lot of attention is given to open standards supporting interoperability between different
devices and software platforms. The diversity raises the opportunity for new

R. Jacob et al. (eds.), Computer-Aided Design of User Interfaces IV, 259–270.

methodologies and techniques to support multi- (and multiple-) device User Interfaces (UIs). Several initiatives exist in the academic world as well as in the industry. Managing the reuse of interactive software components over several different kinds of devices is one of the problems tackled in this paper. One of the noticeable methodologies is the use of Model-Based User Interface Development (MBUID). Another one is the use of User Interface Descriptions Languages (UIDL), nowadays mostly based on the XML syntax. This work concentrates on the latter: the goal is to develop an adaptive, flexible UIDL renderer so it can be deployed easily in MBUID for multiple devices. In the existing literature there are several publications describing the usage of the UIDL within MBUID to support the design of multi-device UIs. XIML [6,17], XWeb [14], XForms [20], XUL [7] and TERESA XML [12,15] are especially worth mentioning here. They provide solutions for multi-device UI design and creation on different levels of abstraction. Another initiative is the Dygimes framework [5]: it combines several techniques like task modelling, UIDL, web services and constraint-based layout management to generate UIs for mobile and embedded systems at runtime.

Unfortunately, once the design reaches the presentation level it remains difficult to specify this in a device-independent manner. Very few UIDLs succeed in being generic enough to be really independent of the widget set (e.g., some can only be used with Java widgets, or are only suitable with web browser support). The User Interface Mark-up Language (UIML) [2,16] is a specification that is independent of a widget set and claims to be device-independent as well. Because the specification has matured over the years and efforts are emerging to submit it as a World Wide Web Consortium (W3C) specification, it is beneficial to develop renderers for the specification. Some of the current research efforts include creating better support for multi-platform UIs [3,16]. Targeting multi-device environments implies the UIML renderer has to be very flexible: on different devices there could be different widget sets, or the widget set API can be slightly different due to the different device profiles. This work also aims at creating a UIML renderer managing and supporting evolution in widget set APIs and differences in widget set vocabularies without the need for changing the renderer itself.

The remainder of this paper is structured as follows: Section 2 gives a short introduction into the UIML language. It provides the necessary details of the specification to understand the following sections. In Section 3 some related work and underlying technologies are discussed evaluating the use of UIML to illustrate the context of the work. This is followed by a description of the implemented renderer in Section 4. Several aspects will be highlighted with the emphasis on the flexibility of the renderer. Section 5 identifies the layout management problem and proposes a solution for future UIDL renderers. Section 6 concludes the paper with an example.

2. UIML OVERVIEW

The UIML specification is currently under revision for submission as a W3C standard. Consequently this means some changes in the specification can be expected and current renderer software design should support easy refactoring to adopt these changes. An UIML document exists of several parts [1] that are shown in Fig. 1. Together they form the Meta-Interface Model (MIM):

1. **Interface** describes four parts of the UI:
   - **Structure**: describes the "widget hierarchy" of the UI. It defines the different parts that are contained in the UI, and the abstract widget name of each part.
   - **Style**: describes properties of the parts defined in the structure. This allows to change properties of the widgets like color, font, text,...The layout is also defined as a style of the parts in structure. Unfortunately the current way of defining a layout is not suitable for multi-device UIs, Section 5 will elaborate further on this.
   - **Content**: separates the content of the interface (e.g., the list that has to appear in a list presentation) of the other parts.
   - **Behavior**: defines rules with actions that are triggered when some condition is met. Some kind of event mechanism is offered to the UI designer this way.
2. **Vocabularies** are referred to as *peers* in the UIML specification: this contains the mapping with the concrete UI toolkit. To allow the use of different devices and different GUI libraries, one can define several peers for the same UIML document while choosing the appropriate peer at runtime. The renderer described in this paper is limited to 2D widget sets.
3. **Logic** defines how to bind the UI with the application logic. More precise it describes the mappings with the software interface to communicate with the application logic.

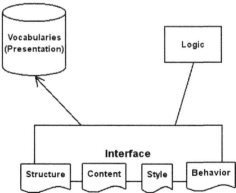

Figure 1. The UIML Meta-Interface Model.

3.   RELATED WORK

Until now, we are not aware of any previous work describing the actual implementation of an UIML renderer and releasing the source code. There were some initiatives in the past, but most of these projects only implemented parts of an obsolete specification version or are no longer supported. [4] describes how UIML can be converted into program code. Harmonia [3] offers a Java-based UIML renderer that implements most of the specification. Several other implementations are gathered on `http://www.uiml.org`, but most of them are deprecated and/or no source code has been released.

It is clear that UIML was designed with Object-Oriented programming languages in mind. Most mappings on the UI toolkit and the relations with the application logic rely on the existence of "classes" in the OO sense. The most mature implementation of the UIML renderer is the one provided by Harmonia, and is implemented in Java. However, the .Net framework offers some new possibilities to develop a UIML renderer. For example it supports on-the-fly executable code generation and better integration with web services. This is the first attempt to write a UIML renderer for the .Net Framework.

The widget set that is used to generate the UI is the GTK# (`http://gtk-sharp.sourceforge.net`) widget set. Although it is still in a development stage, and only few applications are implemented using this widget set, it is mature enough to use as a basis. The most well-known widget set is the Windows Forms library. This one is not chosen for two reasons: the first one is that it is more complex to use than most other .Net widget sets, the second reason is to keep the renderer independent of the Microsoft implementation. Portability to different platforms and availability are important issues, so the renderer was not implemented in the Microsoft .Net Framework, but in the Mono (`http://www.go-mono.com`) implementation of .Net. Both .Net Frameworks implement the same ECMA standard, so the implementation should be reusable as is.

4.   THE RENDERER

4.1   Overall Design

A UIDL can be processed in two different ways: either it can be *compiled* or *rendered*. The former transforms the specification into program code, the latter provides a rendering engine that can interpret the UIML document. When the UIML document is transformed into source code ("compiled"), on its turn the resulting source code needs to be compiled. Transforming the UIML document into program code is advantageous when the code still needs to be manually changed afterwards.

The rendering approach is more complex to implement, but is more flexible: it allows fast prototyping because an UIML document can be tested directly, it can offer dynamic changes in the UI and a transparent mechanism for connecting the rendered UI with the application logic. Several parts of the renderer can be distinguished:

- **Vocabulary Generator.** One of the most cumbersome and tedious tasks is to create a vocabulary for a particular widget set. When the vocabularies are manually edited this often results in different incompatible vocabularies and incomplete mappings. When the widget set API gets updated, often the vocabulary has to be updated manually if one wants to support the latest version of the widget set. This process can be automated when the implementation language supports reflection, e.g., Java and C# have reflection support. Reflection allows software to inspect implementation code and APIs at runtime.

- **Interface reader.** In the initial stage the UIML document has to be processed. The Interface reader processes the document and stores it in an appropriate data structure. Notice that it is recommended to keep this data structure in memory during the lifespan of the UI: dynamic changes in the style and the UI structure can be supported better this way.

- **Style repository.** The style properties included in a UIML document are implemented in a repository-like manner. On the one hand the part that is specified beforehand is queried using XPath expressions. On the other hand there is support for properties that are added at runtime by an internal data structure.

- **Rendering Backends.** The specification allows different peers to co-exist for the same interface specification. A peer defines the language bindings for the interface, thus which widget set is being used and how it can interact with the application logic.

- **System Glue.** The system glue connects the concrete interface with the application logic. There are different ways to do this; by means of direct method invocation, remote method invocation or through web services. All three ways are supported by the .Net framework making it a powerful choice for implementing the renderer.

Fig. 2 gives an overview of the architecture of the renderer. Fig. 3 illustrates the rendering process of the uiml.net renderer.

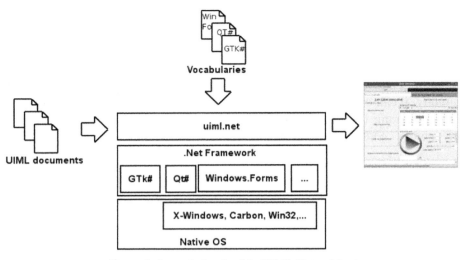

Figure 2. A rough sketch of the UIML.Net architecture.

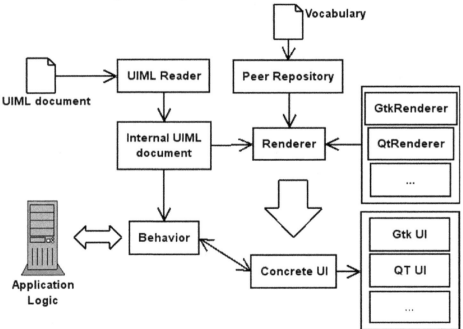

Figure 3. Processing an UIML file with UIML.net.

4.2   Dynamic Core

Roughly spoken, there are two ways of implementing a renderer for a UI mark-up language:

- **Static renderer.** The implementation relies on specific knowledge of the widget set. The types offered by the target GUI library are loaded and used at compile-time.

- **Dynamic renderer.** The implementation does not rely on specific knowledge of the widget set. The types offered by the target GUI library are loaded and used at runtime.

The former is more robust but less flexible and requires more program code. The latter takes full advantage of the information offered by the peer descriptions (vocabularies); it requires a detailed mapping description in the vocabulary.

Reflection is a very powerful tool to use when mapping the Abstract Interface Objects (AIO) to Concrete Interface Objects [18]. AIOs are abstract representation of widgets, and CIOs are the concrete representation; e.g., a "range indicator" is an AIO and can be mapped to a slider widget (CIO). The rendering engine itself has no notion of concrete widgets, but will be guided by the vocabulary to search for the appropriate mapping. Even when the concrete widgets are found (including its class name and properties), the renderer will avoid using the explicit class names. Instead it queries the available libraries containing possible widget sets with the information retrieved from the vocabulary. The reflection mechanism allows to construct new objects using solely this information. This has several advantages:

- The rendering engine is **reusable** for other widget sets, since it does not explicitly creates the concrete widgets directly.
- The vocabulary can be extended **independently** of the renderer. When the widget set is updated, only the vocabulary has to be updated. New entries in the vocabulary can be used without further adaption of the program code.
- The renderer is more **portable** across devices, e.g., it can be ported to platforms that only offer a limited version of the same widget set.

5. THE LAYOUT PROBLEM

One of the pitfalls making UIML less suitable for multi-device interfaces is the lack of support for uniform layout management. We propose to use spatial hierarchical layout constraints to overcome this problem. [13] rightfully argues that constraint-based systems have not caught on for UIs, nevertheless *simple* constraints can be succesfull for specifying the layout of a system. Since the very beginning of GUI creation constraints are investigated to obtain better layout management. [10] gives an overview of different techniques using constraints for the layout of graphical interfaces. Thinglab used constraints for graphical simulation [8]. In [19] some techniques are discussed that a renderer could implement to obtain a visually pleasing result. Typically the layout of the UI is influenced by the interface and style parts of the UIML document. Our approach differs with traditional approaches in the sense that we also use the hierarchy as described by UIML in the structure element instead of directly referring to the individual parts. Most available vocabularies have the layout specified as parts of the properties that can be defined in the style section of a UIML document.

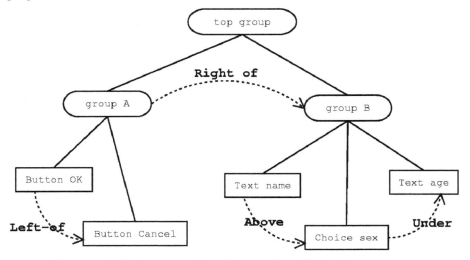

Figure 4. A visual representation of the contraint definition for a structure tree.

In the way we implemented the renderer, the interface part determines how the concrete UI will be nested and the style part specifies the more widget-set related possibilities using layout managers. Using spatial layout constraints this separation can be preserved, while adding adaptability when rendering the UI. Constraints are only defined between siblings in the structure tree. A visual representation of this related to the example in section 6 is shown in Fig. 4.

The hierarchy divides the interface in groups. These groups can be subdivided in other groups and so on. All widgets that are part of the same group, have a logical relation with respect to each other. Some rules can be applied here:

- A group describes a set of **logically related** abstract interactors or groups of abstract interactors. The designer should decide which widgets are gathered in a group.
- A group can be specified **splittable** (as a UIML property). This specifier allows the layout manager to show the abstract interactors or groups of abstract interactors in separate spaces.
- The group specifier **non-splittable** (as a UIML property) forces the layout manager to show the children of the group as a whole to make

sense to the user. Note that "non-splittable" is only valid for the direct children of the group, and does not affect the further offspring.

For now, we have not implemented this into the UIML.Net renderer because it would break the current specification. The layout management should be generic and not related to any widget set and modalities. By consequence this requires adding new elements into the UIML specification, e.g., tags to define constraints. The spatial constraints are implemented in the Dygimes framework [5,11] for testing purposes and has proven to be a feasible solution for UIs containing a limited amount of widgets. Results obtained in this experiment to combine UIDL with spatial constraints can be seen in Fig. 5. The figure shows how a hotel registration form described in a UIDL can be rendered to different devices.

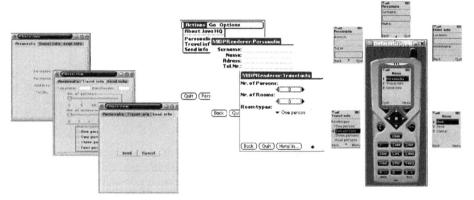

Figure 5. Hotel registration form on an IPaq 3970 (a), a Palm IIIc (b), and a cell phone (c).

6.   A MULTI(PLE)-DEVICE PICTURE BROWSER

To provide the reader with a clear understanding we introduce a simple example here: the *multi(ple)*-device picture browser. We will show how to create a simple picture browser that can be rendered on multiple different devices, distributing the interface over several devices. Imagine the following scenario: nowadays most people have a digital camera. It would be nice to design one application for browsing your pictures that works on most devices. Sometimes it is even usefull to distribute several parts of the UI over several devices. For example suppose you want to give a presentation showing your pictures on a large screen. The controls for browsing the pictures (e.g., the "previous" and "next" button) can be shown on a PDA, while the pictures can use the full screen space of the available monitor. An extract of the UIML document can be seen in Fig. 7.

When the UIML document shown in Fig. 7 is rendered for the desktop, the UI depicted in Fig. 6(a) is the result. Suppose we are only interested in a part of the UI being rendered for our PDA, more specific the controls section (thumbnails and buttons) of the picture browser. This results in only a selection of the structure tree being rendered as shown in Fig. 6(b). The interesting feature is that the pruning can be done at runtime, without manual intervention (apart from the user interaction to initiate this action).

Figure 6. The Multi(ple) device Picture Browser on a desktop (a)
and controls rendered separately (b) .

```
<uiml>
 <interface>
  <structure>
   <part class="Frame" id="picbrowser">
    <part class="Frame" id="theimg">
     <part class="Image" id="image"/>
    </part>
    <part class="Frame" id="remote">
     <part class="Frame" id="thumbnails">
     <part class="Image" id="prev2"/>
      ...
      <
 </structure> part class="Button" id="previous"/>
     </part>
    </part>
   </part>
    ...
```

Figure 7. Part of the UIML document.

7. CONCLUSION

We discussed the implementation of a User Interface Markup Language (UIML) renderer and a possible extension: better adaptability for multiple/ multi-device environments throughout the usage of spatial constraints. Our goals are to compare the UIML specification with the UIDLs supported by the Dygimes framework and to contribute to the development of UIML; the leading specification for multi-device UI development. We explored how the .Net framework allows to create a renderer that is bound to a widget set at runtime (through reflection) instead of at compile-time. This results in an easy extensible rendering engine that supports evolution of widget set vocabularies. The source code of uiml.net is accessible at `http://www.edm.luc.ac.be/software/uiml.net/`.

ACKNOWLEDGEMENTS

The authors would like to thank Bert Creemers for his help implementing the spatial layout constraints in Dygimes. The research at the Expertise Centre for Digital Media (EDM/LUC) is partly funded by the Flemish government and EFRO (European Fund for Regional Development).

REFERENCES

[1] Abrams, M. and Helms J., *User Interface Markup Language (UIML) Specification Version 3.0.*, Technical report, Harmonia, 2002.

[2] Abrams, M., Phanouriou, C., Batongbacal, A.L., Williams, S.M., and Shuster, J.E., *UIML: An Appliance-Independent XML User Interface Language*, Computer Networks, Vol. 31, No. 11-16, 1999, pp. 1695-1708.

[3] Ali, M.F., Perez-Quiñones, M.A., Abrams, M., and Shel, E., *Building Multi-Platform User Interfaces With UIML*, in [9], pp. 255-266.

[4] Binnig, C. and Schmidt, A., *Development of a UIML Renderer for Di erent Target Languages: Experiences and Design Decisions*, in [9], pp. 267-274.

[5] Coninx, K., Luyten, K., Vandervelpen, C., Van den Bergh, J., and Creemers, B., *Dygimes: Dynamically Generating Interfaces for Mobile Computing Devices and Embedded Systems*, in L. Chittaro (ed.), Proc. of 5th International Symposium Human-Computer Interaction with Mobile Devices and Services Mobile HCI'2003 (Udine, 8-11 September 2003), Lecture Notes in Computer Science, Vol. 2745, Springer-Verlag, Berlin, 2003, pp. 256-270.

[6] Eisenstein, J., Vanderdonckt, J., and Puerta, A., *Model-Based User-Interface Development Techniques for Mobile Computing*, in Proc. of 5th ACM International Conference on Intelligent User Interfaces IUI'2001 (Santa Fe, 14-17 January 2001), ACM Press, New York, 2001, pp. 69-76.

[7] Hyatt, D., Goodger, B., Hickson, I., and Waterson, C., *XML User Interface Language (XUL) Specification 1.0. World WideWeb*, 2001, accessible at http://www.mozilla.org/projects/xul/

[8] Maloney, J., Boming, A., and Freeman-Benson, B.N., *Constraint Technology for User Interface Construction in ThingLab II*, in Proceedings of ACM Conference on Object-Oriented Programming: Systems, Languages, and Applications OOPSLA'1989 (New Orleans, 1-6 October 1989), ACM Press, New York, 1989, pp. 381-388.

[9] Kolski, C. and Vanderdonckt, J. (eds.), *Computer-Aided Design of User Interfaces III*, Proceedings of 4th Int. Conf. on Computer-Aided Design of User Interfaces CADUI' 2002 (Valenciennes, 15-17 May 2002), Kluwer Academic Publishers, Dordrecht, 2002.

[10] Lok, S. and Feiner, S., *A Survey of Automated Layout Techniques for Information Presentations*, in Proceedings of SmartGraphics 2001 SG'2001 (Hawthorne, March 2001), pp. 61-68.

[11] Luyten, K., Creemers, B., and Coninx, K., *Multi-device Layout Management for Mobile Computing Devices*, Technical Report, TR-LUC-EDM-0301, Limburgs Univeristair Centrum, Expertise Centre for Digital Media, September 2003, accessible at http://lumumba.luc.ac.be/kris/research.

[12] Mori, G., Paterno, F., and Santoro, C., *Tool Support for Designing Nomadic Applications*, in Proceedings of 7th ACM International Conference on Intelligent User Interfaces IUI'2003 (Miami, 12-15 January 2003), ACM Press, New York, 2003, pp. 141-148.

[13] Myers, B., Hudson, S.E., and Pausch, R., *Past, present, and future of user interface software tools*, ACM Transactions on Computer-Human Interaction, Vol. 7, No. 1, 2000, pp. 3-28.

[14] Olsen, D.R., Jefferies, S., Nielsen,T., Moyes, W., and Fredrickson, P., *Cross-modal interaction using XWeb*, in Proc. of the 13th Annual Symposium on User Interface Software and Technology UIST'00 (San Diego, 5-8 November 2000), ACM Press, New York, pp. 191-200.

[15] Paterno, F. and Santoro, C., *One Model, Many Interfaces*, in [9], pp. 143-154.

[16] Phanouriou, C., *UIML: A Device-Independent User Interface Markup Language*, Ph.D. Thesis, Virginia Polytechnic Institute, Blackburg, 26 September 2000.

[17] Puerta, A. and Eisenstein, J., *XiML: A Common Representation for Interaction Data*, in Proceedings of 6th ACM International Conference on Intelligent User Interfaces (San Francisco, 13-16 January 2002), ACM Press, New York, 2002, pp. 214-215, 2002.

[18] Vanderdonckt, J. and Bodart, F., *Encapsulating Knowledge for Intelligent Automatic Interaction Objects Selection*, in Proc. of the ACM Conf. on Human Factors in Computing Systems INTERCHI'93 (Amsterdam, 24-29 April 1993), ACM Press, New York, 1993, pp. 424-429.

[19] Vanderdonckt, J. and Gillo, X., *Visual Techniques for Traditional and Multimedia Layouts*, in Catarci, T., Costabile, M.F., Levialdi, S., Santucci, G. (eds.), Proceedings of 2nd ACM Workshop on Advanced Visual Interfaces AVI'94 (Bari, 1-4 June 1994), ACM Press, New York, 1994, pp. 95-104.

[20] World Wide Web consortium, *XForms*, World Wide Web, 2001, accessible at http://www.w3.org/TR/xforms/

Chapter 22

THE UBIQUITOUS INTERACTOR – DEVICE INDEPENDENT ACCESS TO MOBILE SERVICES

Stina Nylander, Markus Bylund, and Annika Waern
Swedish Institute of Computer Science
Box 1263, 16429 Kista (Sweden)
Tel.: +46 70 {3530369, 6615460, 3363916} – Fax: +46 8 751 7230
E-mail: {stina.nylander, markus.bylund, annika.waern}@sics.se – URL: www.sics.se

Abstract   The Ubiquitous Interactor (UBI) addresses the problems of design and development arising around services that need to be accessed from many different devices. In UBI, the same service can present different user interfaces on different devices by separating user-service interaction from presentation. The interaction is kept the same for all devices, and different presentation information is provided for different devices. This way, tailored user interfaces for many different devices can be created without multiplying development and maintenance work. In this paper we describe the system design of UBI, the system implementation, and two services implemented for the system: a calendar service and a stockbroker service.

Keywords: Device independence, Interaction acts, Mobile services, Multiple user interfaces.

1.   INTRODUCTION

The Ubiquitous Interactor (UBI) is a system addressing the problems with design and development that arise when service providers face the vast range of computing devices available on the consumer market. Today, users have a wide range of devices at their disposal for accomplishing different tasks: desktop and laptop computers, wall-sized screens, PDAs and cellular phones. The range of services is equally wide: information services, shopping and entertainment. This creates a need for service use from different devices in different situations. Users could for example access their shopping

R. Jacob et al. (eds.), Computer-Aided Design of User Interfaces IV, 271–282.
© 2005 *Kluwer Academic Publishers. Printed in the Netherlands.*

services from a desktop computer at home and from a cellular phone on the bus. Unfortunately, this is often not possible since devices and services cannot be freely combined. Devices have different capabilities for user interaction and presentation, and most services cannot adapt their user interfaces to these differences. This means that users often have to use different versions of a service from different providers to access the same functionality, which causes problems of synchronisation and compatibility.

The main approach to making services accessible from multiple devices today is versioning. However, with many different versions of services, development and maintenance work get very cumbersome, and it is difficult to keep consistency between different versions. Another popular method is to use Web user interfaces since most devices run a Web browser. However, adaptations are still needed, for example translation between mark-up languages and layout changes for small screens. It is also difficult to take advantage of device specific features and to control how user interfaces will be presented to end-users. Thus, we need new and robust methods for developing services that can adapt to different devices [6]. It is not reasonable to force users to use different services for different devices to get the same content [11]. UBI offers a possibility to develop a single device independent version of a service, and then create device specific user interfaces for it. To accomplish this, UBI uses *interaction acts* [8] (Section 4.1) to describe the user-service interaction in a device independent way. This description is used by all devices to generate an appropriate user interface. The presentation of user interfaces can be controlled through *customisation forms* [8] (Section 4.2), which contain service and device specific information of how user interfaces should be presented. This makes it possible to develop services once and for all, and tailor their user interfaces to different devices.

2.   BACKGROUND

Our interest and need for device independent services are results from previous work with the next generation electronic services [1,2]. However, the need for device independent applications is not new. During the seventies and eighties, developers faced large differences in hardware. That time the problem disappeared when personal computers emerged. The hardware got standardized to mouse, keyboard and desktop screen, and direct manipulation user interfaces worked similarly in different operating systems [6].

The situation that we face today is different. We are currently experiencing a paradigm shift from application-based personal computing to service-based ubiquitous computing. In a sense, both applications and services can be seen as sets of functions and abilities that are packaged as separate units

[4]. However, while applications are closely tied to individual devices, typically by a local installation procedure, services are only manifested locally on devices and made available when needed. The advance of Web based services during the nineties can be seen as the first step in this development. Instead of accessing functionality locally on single personal computers, users got used to access functionality remotely from any Internet connected PC. This will change though. With the development of the multitude of different devices that we see today (e.g., cellular phones, PDAs, and wearable computers) combined with growing requirements on mobility and ubiquity, the Web based approach is no longer enough.

The multitude of device types we see today is not due to competition between vendors as before, but rather motivated by requirements of specialisation. Different devices are designed for different purposes and thus their diverse appearance. As a result, the solution this time needs to support simple implementation and maintenance of services without losing the uniqueness of each type of device. This is what we set out to solve with UBI.

3.   RELATED WORK

Much of the inspiration for the Ubiquitous Interactor (UBI) comes from early attempts to achieve device independence or in other ways simplify development work by working on a higher level than device details.

Mike [10] and ITS [13] were among the first systems that made it possible to specify presentation information separately from the application, and thus change the presentation without changes in the application. However, they only handled graphical user interfaces, and they had other important limitations. Mike could not handle application specific data. In ITS, presentation information was considered as application independent and stored in style files that could be moved between applications, something that was not very useful [13]. In UBI, we instead consider presentation as application specific and tailor it to different devices.

Personal Universal Controllers (PUC) [7] encode the data sent between application and client in a device independent format using a set of state variables combined with dependency information, and leaves the generation of user interfaces to the client. Unlike UBI, PUC does not provide any means for service providers to control the presentation of the user interfaces. It is completely up to the client how a service will be presented to end-users.

Unified User Interfaces (UUI) [12] is a design and engineering framework that aims to provide user interfaces tailored to different user groups and situations of use in terms of users' physical capabilities, preferences and usage context. Since UUI is a project with very large scope, making all user interfaces accessible to all users, they take into account a large number of factors (e.g., contextual and environmental) that make the system more complex than we believe is necessary to solve the problems UBI is addressing.

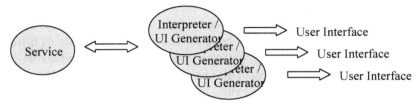

Figure 1. Services offer their interaction expressed in interaction acts, and an interpreter generates a UI based on the interpretation. Different interpreters generate different UIs.

4.   DESIGN

In the Ubiquitous Interactor (UBI), we have chosen the interaction between users and services as our level of abstraction in order to obtain units of description that are independent of device type, service type, and user interface type. Interaction is defined as *actions that services present to users, as well as performed user actions, described in a modality independent way.* Some examples of interaction according to this definition would be: making a choice from a set of alternatives, presenting information to the user, or modify existing information. Pressing a button, or speaking a command would *not* be examples of interaction, since they are modality specific actions. By describing the user-service interaction this way, the interaction can be kept the same regardless of device used to access a service. It is also possible to create services for an open set of devices.

The interaction is expressed in interaction acts that are exchanged between services and devices. User interfaces are generated based on interaction acts and additional presentation information (Fig. 1). In the standard case, interaction acts are interpreted and user interfaces generated on the device side, but for thin clients the interpretation and generation can be made on a server. Although we are aiming for general solutions, which cover interaction with many sorts of applications via a large range of interface types, we realise that it might be difficult and in some cases not even desirable to develop services using interaction acts. Some services might be too complex, while others might be too device dependent (like a high-end multi-player game) to benefit from this approach. For the time being, we are therefore limiting our vision to a few interface types, (mainly windows-based GUIs, command-line interfaces, and speech interfaces), and more simple services (e.g., information services). However, these types of services and UIs cover most of what is available today and will be available in the near future.

4.1   Interaction Acts

Interaction acts are abstract units of user-service interaction that contain no information about modality or presentation. This means that they are independent of devices, services and interaction modality. Throughout this work, we assume that most kinds of interaction can be expressed using a fairly limited set of interaction acts. User-service interaction for a wide range of services can be described by combining single interaction acts and groups of interaction acts.

The set of interaction acts have been established through analysis of existing services and applications [8]. We examined functionality and user-service interaction in services on the Web, such as ticket reservation services for trains and movie theatres, telephone services such as bank services and train time tables, a desktop home care planning tool, and computer games. Live face-to-face instructions were also studied informally. The current set have eight members supported in UBI: `input`, `output`, `select`, `modify`, `create`, `destroy`, `start` and `stop`. `Input` and `output` are defined from the systems point of view. `Select` operates on a predefined set of alternatives. `Create`, `destroy` and `modify` handles the life cycle of service specific data, while `start` and `stop` handles the interaction session. All interaction acts except `output` returns user actions to services. `Output` only presents information that users cannot act upon.

During user-service interaction, the system needs more information about the interaction acts than its type. Interaction acts are uniquely identifiable, so that user actions can be associated with them and interpreted by services. It is also possible to define for how long a user interface component based on an interaction act should be present in the user interface before being removed. Otherwise only static user interfaces can be created. It is possible to create modal user interface components based on interaction acts, e.g. components that lock the user-service interaction until certain user actions are performed. This way, user actions can be sequenced when needed. All interaction acts also have a way to hold information, as a default base for the rendering of interaction acts. Finally, meta-data can be attached to interaction acts. Metadata can for example contain domain information, or restrictions on user input that are important to the service.

In more complex user-service interaction, there is a need to group several interaction acts together, because of their related function, or the fact that they need to be presented together. An example could be the play, rewind, forward and stop functions of a CD player. The structure obtained by the grouping can be used as input when generating the user interfaces. These groups allow nesting.

4.2   Controlling the Presentation

To give service providers a way to specify how their services will be presented to end-users, services must be able to provide detailed presentation information. Control of presentation has proven to be an important feature of methods for developing services [3,6], since it is used for e.g., branding.

In UBI, presentation information is specified separately from user-service interaction. This allows for changes and updates in the presentation information without changing the service. The main forms of presentation information are *directives* and *resources*. Directives link interaction acts to for example widgets or templates of user interface components. Resources could be pictures or sounds that are used in the rendering of an interaction act.

It is optional to provide presentation information in UBI. If no presentation information or only partial information is provided, user interfaces are generated with default settings. However, by providing detailed information service providers can fully control how their services will be presented.

5.   IMPLEMENTATION

The Ubiquitous Interactor (UBI) has three main parts: the Interaction Specification Language (ISL), customisation forms, and interaction engines. ISL is used to encode the interaction acts sent between services and user interfaces, customisation forms contain presentation information, and interaction engines generate user interfaces based on interaction acts and information from customisation forms. The different parts are defined at different levels of specificity, where interaction acts are device and service independent, interaction engines are device dependent, and customisation forms are service and device dependent.

5.1   Interaction Specification Language

Interaction acts are encoded using the Interaction Specification Language (ISL), which is XML compliant. Each interaction act has a unique id that is used to map performed user interactions to it. It also has a life cycle value that specifies when components based on it are available in the user interface. The life cycle can be *temporary, confirmed*, or *persistent*. Interface components based on temporary interaction acts are available in the user interface for a specified time and then removed by UBI, confirmed components are available until the user has performed a given action, and persistent components are available in the user interface during the whole user-service interaction. The default value is persistent. All interaction acts can be given a symbolic name, and belong to a named presentation group in a customisation form. This will be discussed further in Section 5.2.

Interaction acts also have a modality value that specifies if components based on them will lock other components in the user interface. The value of the modality can be true or false. If the modality value is true, the component is locking other components in the user interface until the user performs a given action. The default value is false. All interaction acts contain a string value used to hold default information. It is also possible to attach meta data to all interaction acts. Listing 1 shows the ISL of a select interaction act.

```
<select>
  <id>235690</id>
  <life>persistent</life>
  <modal>false</modal>
  <string>browseList</string>
  <alternative>
    <id>5463</id>
    <name>alt</name>
    <string>Previous</string>
    <retVal>0</retVal>
  </alternative>
  <alternative>
    <id>5893</id>
    <name>alt</name>
    <string>Next</string>
    <retVal>1</retVal>
  </alternative>
</select>
```

Listing 1: ISL encoding of a select interaction act with id, life cycle, modality, and default content information.

Interaction acts can be grouped using a designated tag `isl`, and groups can be nested to provide more complex expressions of interaction. These groups contain the same type of information assigned to single interaction acts. The ISL code sent from services to interaction engines contains all information about the interaction acts: id, name, group, life cycle, modality, default information and metadata. A large part of this information is only useful for the interaction engine during generation of user interfaces. Thus, when users perform actions, only the relevant parts of interaction acts are sent back to the service. Two different DTDs have been created for this, one for encoding interaction acts sent from services to interaction engines, and one for encoding interaction acts sent from interaction engines to services. The DTDs are available at http://www.sics.se/~stny/UIB/DTDs/dtd.html.

5.2   Customisation Forms

Customisation forms contain device and service specific information about how the user interface of a given service should be presented. Information can be specified on three different levels: group level, type level or name level. Information on group level affects all interaction acts of a group, information at type level provides information for all interaction acts of the given type; and information on name level provides information about all interaction acts with the given symbolic name. The levels can also be combined, for example creating specifications for interaction acts in a given group of a given type, or in a given group with a given name.

The Interaction Specification Language contains attributes for creating the different mappings. Each interaction act or group of interaction acts can be given an optional symbolic name that is used in mappings where the name level is involved. This means that each interaction act with a certain name is presented using the information mapped to the name. Interaction acts or groups of interaction acts can also belong to a named group in a customisation form. All interaction acts that belong to a group are presented using the information associated with the group (and possibly with additional information associated with their name or type).

```
<output>
  <id>235690</id>
  <name>sicsLogo</name>
  <group>calendar</group>
  <life>persistent</life>
  <modal>false</modal>
  <string>SICS AB</string>
</output >
```

Listing 2: ISL encoding of an output interaction act with a symbolic name, and that belongs to a customisation form group called calendar.

Listing 2 shows an encoding of the output interaction act from listing 1 with a symbolic name, and as a member of a customisation form group.

Customisation forms are structured and can be arranged in hierarchies which allows for inheriting and overriding information between forms. A basic form can be used to provide a look and feel for a family of services, with different service specific forms adding or overriding parts of the basic specifications to create service specific user interfaces. A customisation form does not need to be complete. Interaction acts that do not map to any presentation information specified in the form are rendered with defaults.

Customisation forms are encoded in XML and a DTD can be found at http://www.sics.se/~stny/UBI/DTDs/dtd.html. An entry in a customisation form can be either a directive or a resource. Directives are used for mappings to widgets or other user interface components and resources are used to associate media resources to interface components. Both directive mapping and resource association can be made on all three levels, group, type and name. Listing 3 shows an example of a directive mapping based on the type of the interaction act, in this case output.

```
<element name"output">
  <directive>
```

```
<data>
  se.sics.ubi.swing.OutputLabel
</data>
</directive>
</element>
```

Listing 3: A mapping on type level for an `output` interaction act that maps a named interaction act to a Java class that is used to render it.

5.3   Interaction Engines

Interaction engines interpret interaction acts and generate suitable user interfaces of a given type for services on a given device or family of devices. They also encode performed user actions as interaction acts and send them back to services. During user-service interaction, interaction engines parse interaction acts sent by services, and generate user interfaces by creating presentations of each interaction act. If specific presentations, or media resources, are specified for an interaction act in the customisation form of a service, that presentation takes precedence. Otherwise, defaults are used. For example, an output could be rendered as a label, or speech generated from its default information, while an input could be rendered as a text field or a standard speech prompt. We have implemented interaction engines for Java Swing, Java Awt, HTML, and Tcl/Tk user interfaces. All four interaction engines can generate user interfaces for desktop computers, but the Tcl/Tk and the Java Awt engine are designed for PDA and cellular phone respectively. The HTML interaction engine generates HTML code and sends it to a browser via HTTP. The Tcl/Tk interaction engine is designed to generate Tcl/Tk code and send it to a PDA that will interpret the code and render the user interface. In these cases, the interpretation and generation is not executed on the PDA to save computational resources. Both the Java Swing and the Java Awt interaction engines interpret interaction acts and generate user interfaces on the target device.

6.   SERVICES

We will present two different services to illustrate how the Ubiquitous Interactor (UBI) works, a calendar service and a stockbroker service.

6.1   Calendar Service

The calendar provides an example of a service that it is useful to access from different devices. Calendar data may often be entered from a desktop computer at work or at home, but mobile access is needed to consult the information on the way to a meeting or in the car on the way home. Sometimes appointments are set up out of office (in meeting rooms or restaurants) and it is practical to be able to enter that information immediately.

The calendar service supports basic calendar operations as entering, edit and delete information, navigate the information, and display different views of it. The service is accessible from three types of user interfaces: Java Swing and HTML user interfaces for desktop computers, and Tcl/Tk user interfaces for handheld computer. Two different customisation forms have been created for Java Swing, and one each for Tcl/Tk and HTML. These four forms generate different user interfaces from the same interaction acts. See Fig. 2 for pictures of three of the generated user interfaces.

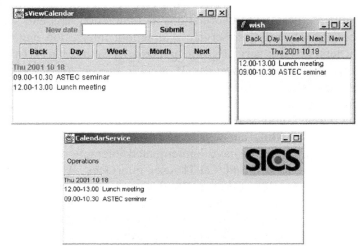

Figure 2. User interfaces for the calendar service. The two to the left are generated by the Java Swing interaction engine using two different customisation forms. The one to the right is generated by the Tcl/Tk interaction engine.

6.2   Stockbroker Service

The stockbroker service TapBroker [9] has been developed as a part of a project at SICS that works with autonomous agents that trade stocks on the behalf of users [5]. Each agent is trading according to a built in strategy, and users can have one or more agents trading for them. TapBroker provides feedback on how their agents are performing so that users know when to change agent, or shut them down.

The TapBroker service provides agent owners with feedback on the agent's actions: order handling, and performed transactions. It also provides information on the account state (the amount of money it can invest), status (running or paused), activity level (number of transactions per hour), portfolio content, and the current value of the portfolio. However, it does not provide any means to configure or control the agent. Agents work autono-mously and cannot be manipulated from outside for security reasons. We have implemented customisation forms for Java Swing, HTML and Java Awt (Fig. 3).

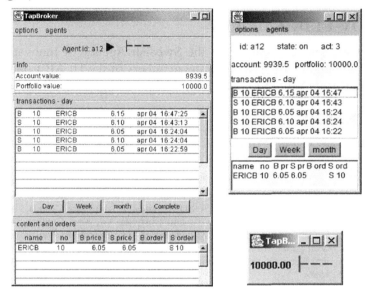

Figure 3. Three user interfaces to the TapBroker: a Java Swing UI for desktop computers (a), a Java AWT UI for mobile phone (b), and a UI for a very small device (c).

7. FUTURE WORK

We will investigate how to handle dynamic resources in UBI. Services that use dynamic media resources extensively, e.g., a service for browsing a video database, might need an extension of our customisation form approach to work efficiently for different modalities. One solution could be to handle the choice of media type outside the customisation form.

8. CONCLUSION

We have presented the Ubiquitous Interactor (UBI), a system for devel-opment of device independent mobile services. In UBI, user-service interac-tion is described in a modality and device independent way using interaction acts. The description is combined with device and service specific presenta-tion information in customisation forms to generate tailored user interfaces. This allows service providers to develop services once and for all, and still provide tailored user interfaces to different services by creating different customisation forms. Development and maintenance work is simplified since only one version of each service need to be developed. New customisation forms can be created at any point, thus services can be developed for an open set of devices.

ACKNOWLEDGEMENTS

This work has been funded by the Swedish Agency of Innovation Systems (www.vinnova.se). Thanks to the members of the HUMLE laboratory, in particular Anna Sandin for help with the HTML interaction engine.

REFERENCES

[1]   Bylund, M., *Personal Service Environments - Openness and User Control in User-Service Interaction*, Licentiate thesis, Department of Information Technology, Uppsala University, 2001.

[2]   Bylund, M. and Espinoza, F., *sView - Personal Service Interaction*, in Proceedings of 5th International Conference on The Practical Applications of Intelligent Agents and Multi-Agent Technology PA EXPO'2000 (Manchester, 10-14 April 2000), 2000.

[3]   Esler, M., Hightower, J., Anderson, T., and Borriello, G., *Next Century Challenges: Data-Centric Networking for Invisible Computing. The Portolano Project at the University of Washington*, in Proceedings of 5th ACM International Conference on Mobile Computing and Networking MobiCom'1999 (Seattle, 15-20 August 1999), ACM Press, New York, 1999.

[4]   Espinoza, F., *Individual Service Provisioning*, Ph.D. thesis, Department of Computer and Systems Science, Stockholm University/Royal Institute of Technology, 2003.

[5]   Lybäck, D. and Boman, M., *Agent Trade Servers in Financial Exchange Systems*, accessible at http://arxiv.org/abs/cs.CE/0203023.

[6]   Myers, B.A., Hudson, S.E., and Pausch, R., *Past, Present and Future of User Interface Software Tools*, ACM Transactions on Computer-Human Interaction, Vol. 7, No. 1, 2000, pp. 3-28.

[7]   Nichols, J., Myers, B.A., Higgings, M., Hughes, J., Harris, T.K., Rosenfeld, R., and Pignol, M., *Generating Remote Control Interfaces for Complex Appliances*, in Proceedings of 15th Annual ACM Symposium on User Interface Software and Technology UIST'2002 (Paris, 27-30 October 2002), ACM Press, New York, 2002, pp. 161-170.

[8]   Nylander, S., *The Ubiquitous Interactor - Mobile Services with Multiple User Interfaces*, Licentiate Thesis, Department of Information Technology, Uppsala University, 2003.

[9]   Nylander, S., Bylund, M. and Boman, M., *Mobile Access to Real-Time Information - The case of Autonomous Stock Brokering*, Journal of Personal and Ubiquitous Computing, Vol. 8, No. 1, 2003, pp. 42-46.

[10]   Olsen, D.J., *MIKE: The Menu Interaction Kontrol Environment*, ACM Transactions on Graphics, Vol. 5, No. 4, 1987, pp. 318-344.

[11]   Shneiderman, B., *Leonardo's Laptop*, The MIT Press, Cambridge, 2002.

[12]   Stephanidis, C., *The Concept of Unified User Interfaces*, in C. Stephanidis (ed.), "User Interfaces for All - Concepts, Methods, and Tools" Lawrence Erlbaum Associates, Mahwah, 2001, pp. 371-388.

[13]   Wiecha, C., Bennett, W., Boies, S., Gould, J., and Greene, S., *ITS: a Tool for Rapidly Developing Interactive Applications*, ACM Transactions on Information Systems, Vol. 8, No. 3, 1990, pp. 204-236.

Chapter 23

GENERATING CONTEXT-SENSITIVE MULTIPLE DEVICE INTERFACES FROM DESIGN

Tim Clerckx, Kris Luyten, and Karin Coninx
Limburgs Universitair Centrum
Expertise Centre for Digital Media, Universitaire Campus, B-3590 Diepenbeek (Belgium)
E-mail: {tim.clerckx,kris.luyten,karin.coninx}@luc.ac.be – URL: http://www.edm.luc.ac.be
Tel.: +32 11 26 84 11 – Fax: +32 11 26 84 00

Abstract   This paper shows a technique that allows adaptive user interfaces, spanning multiple devices, to be rendered from the task specification at runtime taking into account the context of use. The designer can specify a task model using the ConcurTaskTrees Notation and its context-dependent parts, and deploy the user interface immediately from the specification. By defining a set of context-rules in the design stage, the appropriate context-dependent parts of the task specification will be selected before the concrete interfaces will be rendered. The context will be resolved by the runtime environment and does not require any manual intervention. This way the same task specification can be deployed for several different contexts of use. Traditionally, a context-sensitive task specification only took into account a variable single deployment device. This paper extends this approach as it takes into account task specifications that can be executed by multiple co-operating devices.

Keywords: ConcurTaskTrees Notation, Context Sensitive, Model-Based User Interface Design, Multiple Devices, Task Modelling.

1.   INTRODUCTION

Recent advances in mobile computing devices and mobile communication support more complex interaction between different devices. This allows users to migrate from their single "computer on the desk" setup to a heterogeneous environment where he/she uses several devices to accomplish his/her tasks. Although the provided hardware and software becomes more powerful, it makes designing the interface more complex. Different contexts (device constraints, environment of the mobile user,…) have to be taken into

R. Jacob et al. (eds.), Computer-Aided Design of User Interfaces IV, 283–296.
© 2005 *Kluwer Academic Publishers. Printed in the Netherlands.*

account. The nomadic nature of future applications also demands a way to design interaction using multiple devices.

Combining our previous work [6,8] with context-sensitive task specifications [14,15] we realise a supporting framework for the design and creation of context-sensitive multiple- and multi-device interaction. By multiple-device interaction we mean the user interface (UI) is distributed over different devices. The implementation has been tested as a component of the Dygimes framework [6].

The remainder of this paper is structured as follows: Section 2 discusses the related work, introducing the state of the art in context-sensitive task modelling. To illustrate the context and test bed of this work, our framework Dygimes is introduced in Section 3. This is followed by an overview of the design process needed to create a context-sensitive UI in Section 4. Three stages are described: the creation of the task model, the extraction of the dialog model and the generated presentation model. This is followed by a case study to show how things work in practice. Finally, the obtained results and their applicability are discussed in the conclusion.

2.   RELATED WORK

Pribeanu *et al.* [14] proposed several possible approaches to adapt the ConcurTaskTrees notation [12] for context-sensitive task modelling. As pointed out in [14] and [15], the context of use of the application influences which parts of the task model are executed. A context-sensitive (or dependent) and a context-insensitive (or independent) part of the task model can be identified and processed accordingly. The context-sensitive part can be related to the context-insensitive part in multiple ways [14]:

- Both parts are specified in one task model: the *monolithic approach.*
- The context-insensitive parts are connected to the context-sensitive parts with general arcs: *graph-oriented approach.*
- The context-insensitive parts are connected to the context-sensitive parts with special arcs that can constitute a decision tree: *separation approach.*

The last approach in particular is interesting: although it allows different parts for different contexts of use to be integrated in one model, there is a *decision tree* that provides a nice separation. We choose to insert *decision nodes* in the task specification instead of decision trees. Of course, decision nodes can have other decision nodes as descendants. The children of a decision node are possible sub trees where one of them will be chosen in a pre-processing step. Section 4 explains in detail how a concrete task specification can be obtained by pre-processing the decision nodes.

Paternò and Santoro [13] present a method to generate multiple interfaces for different contexts of use starting from one task model. The TERESA tool for supporting this approach is discussed in [13]. In contrast with their approach, we do not focus on the design aspect as much as they do, but emphasize the runtime framework necessary for accomplishing this. To our knowledge, the TERESA tool supports the creation of one task model for multiple devices, but currently does not take into account multiple devices interacting at once or the interface migrating from one device to another.

Calvary *et al.* [3,4] describe a process where a *Platform* and *Environmental Model* are used to represent context information. The process allows creating UIs for two running systems in different contexts. Although at several stages in the UI design process (Task Specification, Abstract UI, Concrete UI, Runtime Environment) a translation can take place between the two systems, the designer will have to change the task specification manually in the process if the context has an influence on the tasks that can be performed.

Nichols *et al.* [11] defined a specification language and communication protocol to automatically generate UIs for remotely controlled appliances. The language describes the functionalities of the target appliance and contains enough information to render the UI. In this case, the context is secured by the target appliance represented by its definition.

Ali and Pérez-Quiñones [2] also use a task model, together with UIML [1], to generate UIs for multiple platforms. The task model has to increase the abstraction level of the UIML specification, which is necessary to guide the UI onto different devices.

3. DYGIMES

Most of the presented work is integrated in our framework Dygimes [6]. Besides supporting the ConcurTaskTree task specification, it uses high level user interface Descriptions (specified in XML) to define the set of abstract interactors necessary for completing the tasks specified in the task specification. One of the aims of this framework is to support design through selected models from Model-Based User Interface Design, and add support for transforming the design into multi/multiple-device UIs at runtime.

The Dygimes framework supports roughly the following steps for creating UIs (a more detailed description can be found in [6]):
1. Create a context-sensitive task specification with the ConcurTaskTrees notation.
2. Create UI building blocks for the separate tasks.
3. Relate the UI building blocks with the tasks in the task specification.
4. Define the layout using constraints.
5. Define custom properties for the UI appearance (e.g., preferred colours,

concrete interactors,…).

6. Generate a prototype and evaluate it (the dialog model and presentation model are calculated automatically).

7. Change the task specification and customisations until satisfied.

On the one hand it supports a clear separation between the creation of the UIs and the implementation of the application logic that underlies the UI. On the other hand there is built-in support to connect the UIs with the application logic without manual intervention [18]. The next section will describe how the design process for the context-sensitive UI and the generation of the UI works.

4.   DESIGN PROCESS

The proposed approach extends the process for automatically generating prototype UIs from annotated task models introduced in [8]. Fig. 1 shows the extended process where a context-sensitive task model is considered to generate UIs depending on the context at the time the UI is rendered.

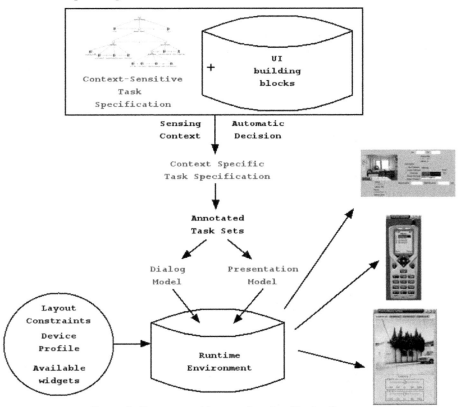

Figure 1. Context-sensitive user interface Design Process.

First, a context-sensitive task model is constructed and high-level UI building blocks are attached to the leaves as described in the previous section. Next, the context is captured and the proper context-specific Concur-TaskTree will be generated automatically. Subsequently the Enabled Task Sets (ETSs) are calculated. These are sets of tasks that can be enabled at the same time [12] and therefore contain the proper information to be rendered together in the resulting UI.

After this step, the appropriate dialog model is extracted automatically from the task model using the temporal operators [8]. Each dialog still is related to the set of tasks it presents, thus also to the appropriate UI building blocks it can use to present itself. The context-sensitive information in the task specification is taken care of in a "pre-processing" step, which we will explain now into further detail.

4.1   The Context-Sensitive Task Model

As pointed out in section 2, there are three proposed approaches to model context-sensitive task models. Instead of collecting decision trees, we propose another way where the context-insensitive part points directly to context-sensitive sub-trees through *decision nodes*. These nodes are marked by the **D** in the example of Fig. 4. Although this resembles the graph-oriented approach, the context-sensitive sub-trees are the direct children of the decision node. When the context-sensitive parts are resolved, the decision node will be removed and replaced by the root of the selected sub-trees of that decision node.

The decision nodes are executed in the first stage of the UI generation process. This results in a normal ConcurTaskTree specification, but also one that is suitable according to the rules defined in the decision nodes. The normal ConcurTaskTree specification enables the provided algorithm to extract the dialog model automatically adapted to the current context.

In order to link the context detection and the task model, some information about which sub-tree has to be performed in which case is added to the decision node. Fig. 1 shows a simple scheme (as a Document Type Definition) defining how rules can be specified for selecting a particular subtree according to a given context. Conditions can be defined recursively and numerical and logical operators are provided ($=$, $<$, $>$, $\vee$, $\wedge$) to cope with several context parameters. In Fig. 2, an example is presented where the current context will be decided on the basis of comparing X and Y coordinates provided by a GPS module. The XML specification provides a way to exchange context information. Tool support is required encapsulate the use of XML from the designer.

Note the approaches described in [14,15] focus on the design of the interface at the task level. This work shows how the task model is used at runtime to generate context-dependent UIs. This will be done by providing a framework (Dygimes, Section 3) that can interpret a task specification and generate a presentation for the given task specification. The framework resolves the context dependencies beforehand, resulting in a presentation that is adapted to the context of use. The next section explains how we proceed from the task specification to the presentation of the UI by using a dialog model.

```
<?xml version="1.0"?>
<!ELEMENT decision ((cond,true,false) |(value,case+))>
<!ELEMENT cond (value,value)>
<!ATTLIST cond type CDATA IMPLIED>
<!ELEMENT value ( cond | PCDATA )>
<!ATTLIST value type CDATA IMPLIED>
<!ELEMENT true (PCDATA)>
<!ATTLIST true platform IMPLIED>
<!ELEMENT false (PCDATA)>
<!ATTLIST false platform CDATA IMPLIED>
<!ELEMENT case (value|cond)> <!ATTLIST case platform CDATA IMPLIED>
```

Figure 2. Decision DTD.

```
<decision>
  <cond type="and">
    <value type="cond">
      <cond type="lt">
        <value type="context"> GPS:Xcoord </value> <value type="int"> 1 </value>
      </cond>
    </value>
    <value type="gt">
      <cond type="equals">
        <value type="context"> GPS:Ycoord </value> <value type="int"> 54 </value>
      </cond>
    </value>
  </cond>
  <true platform="context">left</true> <false platform="context">right</false>
</decision>
```

Figure 3. Decision XML example

4.2   The Dialog Model

Before applying further processing of the task model, it has to be transformed into a concrete one (resolve all the decision nodes) in order to extract a dialog model. The *context-specific* task model is a normal ConcurTask-Tree, suited for the current context of use and can be processed as any other ConcurTaskTree. The transformation can be done by replacing the decision node with the appropriate subtree representing a subtask suitable for the current context of use.

In [8] we proved it is possible to generate simple UIs directly from the task specification. This was done through the automatic generation of a dialog specification from the task specification. In our approach, the dialog model is expressed as a State Transition Network (STN) and each state in the STN equals an ETS. In the UI, the information about the tasks in an ETS have to appear together in the resulting UI. The transitions between dialogs are represented in the STN by transitions between states, marked with the tasks that can *trigger* the change. The transitions between the different ETSs ("dialogs") are identified by the different temporal operators connecting selected tasks located in the different ETSs. An extensive description of the algorithm can be found in [8]. An open source tool is provided that implements this algorithm and calculates a dialog model from the task specification at: http://www.edm.luc.ac.be/software/TaskLib/.

4.3   The Presentation Model

The last step has to render the dialog model on the available output devices. This is the presentation of (the different parts of) the concrete UI. The nodes in the dialog model are ETSs. One such node represents all UI building blocks that have to be presented to complete the current ETS (Section 3 showed that UI building blocks were attached to individual tasks). The tasks in an ETS are also marked with their target device, so two different situations are possible:

1. All tasks in an ETS are targeted to the same device
2. Not all tasks in an ETS are targeted to the same device

Situation (1) allows the UI to be rendered completely on one device. (2) demands that the UI to be *distributed* over different devices. For this purpose the device-independence of the abstract UI description has to be extended towards the use of multiple devices. On the level of the presentation model, the Abstract UI descriptions of a dialog are rendered as concrete dialogs, this can be accomplished by using two important techniques:

*   Customised mappings from Abstract Interaction Objects (AIOs) to Concrete Interaction Objects (CIOs) [17]. The rendering engine for each device can choose for itself the concrete widget selected to present an AIO. This can be customised afterwards by the designer [16].
*   Positioning of the widgets is done through constraints which are defined in a language-independent manner. The renderer can use the information about the hierarchical widget containment to split up the UI in different parts. Details of this approach can be found in [9].

Customised mapping rules and device-independent layout management are two important techniques for realising device-independent distributed UIs. It is possible several concurrent tasks located in the same ETS have to be rendered on different devices. Since the presentation building blocks are attached to the tasks as XML documents, the presentation for an individual device can be calculated for each device separately. Notice when concurrent tasks are rendered on separate devices, some kind of middleware will be necessary to support data-exchange between both tasks in a heterogeneous environment. In contrast with e.g. WebSplitter [7], the focus is not on distribution of content, but distributed support of task execution.

5.   A CASE STUDY: MANAGE STOCK

Fig. 4 shows the *manage stock* example. The following situation occurs: the storekeeper of a warehouse keeps track of the stock using two devices. First a desktop PC is used to manage the purchase and sales of articles. Second an employee checks and updates the stock amounts using his PDA to note the changes immediately. When the amount of a certain article is updated by the desktop PC, for example when new goods are purchased, the employee receives a message on his PDA. When he/she stands in the vicinity of a printer supporting Radio Frequency Identifier (RFID) tags, this can be detected and the information of the product can be viewed and printed.

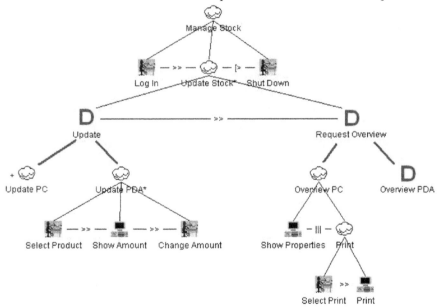

Figure 4. Context-Sensitive Task Model of the *Manage Stock* example.

As a result, the example contains two types of context denoted by the decision tasks: platform (*Update* and *Request Overview*) and location (*Overview PDA*). To link the context handler to the appropriate decision node, decision rules need to be attached to these nodes. Fig. 6 shows an example for the *Overview PDA task*. In this case there will be a call for the *canPrint* function in the RFID Reader.

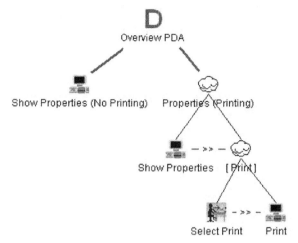

Figure 5. Overview PDA sub-tree.

```
<decision>
 <cond type="equals">
  <value type="context"> RFID:Reader:canPrint </value>
  <value type="boolean"> true </value>
 </cond>
 <true platform="context"> Show Properties (No Printing)</true>
 <false platform="context"> Properties (Printing)</false>
</decision>
```

Figure 6. Decision rules for the *Overview PDA* task.

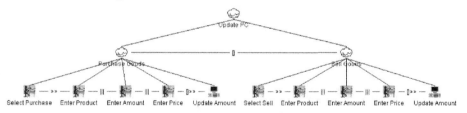

Figure 7. Update PC sub-tree.

The first step to automatically generate the UI is to convert the context-sensitive task model into a context-specific task model. This is why the condition in the decision XML has to be evaluated for each decision node and the decision node is replaced by its sub-tree which matches the current context. In the *Overview PDA* task example, there will be an evaluation of the *canPrint* function. If the return value equals *true* the *Properties (Printing)* subtree will replace the decision node, else the *Show Properties (No Printing)* will. Fig. 8 shows the context-specific task model in case of using the PC to change the stock amounts and the PDA to notify the employee within the reach of an RFID supporting printer.

The *next* step uses a custom algorithm (described in [5]) to calculate the *enabled task sets* (ETSs):

ETS_1 = $\{LogIn\} \Rightarrow P_{all}$

ETS_2 = $\{SelectPurchase(P_{pc}), SelectSell(P_{pc}), ShutDown\} \Rightarrow P_{pc}$

ETS_3 = $\{EnterProduct(P_{pc}), EnterAmount(P_{pc}), EnterPrice(P_{pc}),$
$ShutDown\} \Rightarrow P_{pc}$

ETS_4 = $\{EnterProduct(P_{pc}), EnterAmount(P_{pc}), EnterPrice(P_{pc}),$
$ShutDown\} \Rightarrow P_{pc}$

ETS_5 = $\{UpdateAmount(P_{pc}), ShutDown) \Rightarrow P_{pc}$

ETS_6 = $\{UpdateAmount(P_{pc}), ShutDown) \Rightarrow P_{pc}$

ETS_7 = $\{ShowProperties(P_{pda}), ShutDown) \Rightarrow P_{pda}$

ETS_8 = $\{SelectPrint(P_{pda}), ShutDown) \Rightarrow P_{pda}$

ETS_9 = $\{Print(P_{pda}), ShutDown) \Rightarrow P_{pda}$

P_x indicates on which platform the tasks can be executed. $x = all$ means the platform does not matter, and the task can be executed both on a PC or on a PDA. This example only contains tasks restricted to either a PC or a PDA because no ETS contains tasks marked P_{pc} and P_{pda}. Remark that the only difference between ETS_3 and ETS_4, and ETS_5 and ETS_6 is they are children from another task. Afterwards, the dialog model (Fig. 9) is automatically extracted. Finally the actual UI is rendered by the runtime environment. Fig. 10 shows the dialog model with the rendered UIs.

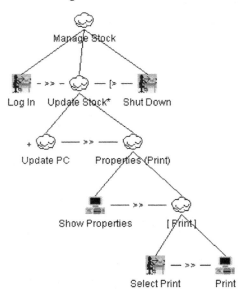

Figure 8. Context-specific Task Model.

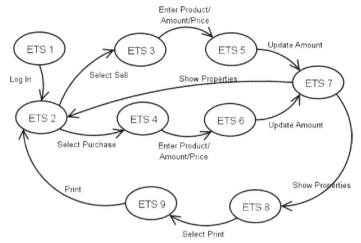

Figure 9. Dialog Model.
(The accepts state caused by the *Shut Down* task is omitted to avoid cluttering the picture).

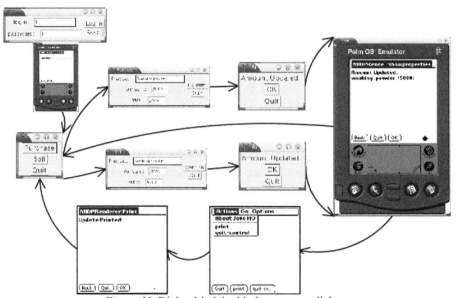

Figure 10. Dialog Model with the concrete dialogs.

6. CONCLUSION AND FUTURE WORK

This paper shows how context information can be integrated in interface design to generate multi- and multiple-device user interfaces at runtime. The ConcurTaskTrees formalism is combined with decision nodes and rules to allow the user interface to adapt to the context while still being consistent w.r.t. the design. An important case is where the context can indicate the change in interaction device while executing a task. Our model allows this change by providing an appropriate dialog model including the transitions between dialogs on the same device *and* transitions between dialogs on different devices. The presentation model also supports dialogs that are distributed over several devices. The precondition to make this work is the context must be frozen from the start until the end of the main task.

Future work involves finding a way to switch the context-concrete task model on a context change in order to recalculate the dialog and presentation model. This approach however comes with a lot of complications. First of all, the new dialog model may not be compatible to the old one and disrupts the continuity of the user interface. This is because the current state might not occur in the new dialog model. Also it is dangerous to adjust the user interface every time the context changes. In some cases the user can become confused about a sudden changed user interface.

Finally we believe the presented process is a first practical step towards involving context in design.

ACKNOWLEDGMENTS

Our research is partly funded by the Flemish government and European Fund for Regional Development. The SEESCOA (Software Engineering for Embedded Systems using a Component-Oriented Approach) project IWT 980374 and CoDAMoS (Context-Driven Adaptation of Mobile Services) project IWT 030320 are directly funded by the IWT (Flemish subsidy organisation). The authors would like to thank Bert Creemers for his contribution.

REFERENCES

[1]   Abrams, M., Phanouriou, C., Batongbacal, A.L., Williams, S.M., and Shuster, J.E., *UIML: An Appliance-Independent XML User Interface Language*, in Proceedings of 8th World-Wide Web Conference WWW'8 (Toronto, 11-14 May 1999), Computer Networks, Vol. 31, No. 11-16, 1999, pp. 1695–1708, accessible at http://www8.org/w8-papers/5b-hypertext-media/uiml/uiml.html

[2]   Ali, M.F. and Pérez-Quiñones, M.A., *Using Task Models to Generate Multi-Platform User Interfaces while Ensuring Usability*, in Proceedings of ACM Conf. on Human Aspects in Computing Systems CHI'2002 (Minneapolis, 20-25 April 2002), Extended Abstracts, ACM Press, New York, 2002, pp. 670-671.

[3]   Calvary, G., Coutaz, J., and Thevenin, D., *Embedding Plasticity in the Development Process of Interactive Systems*, in P.L. Emiliani, C. Stephanidis (eds.), Proceedings of the 6th ERCIM Workshop "User Interfaces for All" UI4ALL'00 (Florence, 25-26 October 2000), CNR-IROE, Florence, 2000, accessible at http://ui4all.ics.forth.gr/UI4ALL-

2000/files/Short_papers/Calva ry.pdf

[4]   Calvary, G., Coutaz, J., and Thevenin, D., *Supporting Context Changes for Plastic User Interfaces: A Process and a Mechanism*, in A. Blanford, J. Vanderdonckt, Ph. Gray (eds.), Proceedings of Joint AFIHM-BCS HCI Conference on Human-Computer Interaction IHM-HCI'2001 (Lille, 10-14 September 2001), Springer-Verlag, London, 2001, pp. 349-363.

[5]   Clerckx, T. and Coninx, K., Integrating Task Models in Automatic User Interface Design. Technical Report TR-LUC-EDM-0302, EDM/LUC, 2003.

[6]   Coninx, K., Luyten, K., Vandervelpen, C., Van den Bergh, J., and Creemers, B., *Dygimes: Dynamically Generating Interfaces for Mobile Computing Devices and Embedded Systems*, in L. Chittaro (ed.), Proc. of 5th International Symposium Human-Computer Interaction with Mobile Devices and Services Mobile HCI'2003 (Udine, 8-11 September 2003), Lecture Notes in Computer Science, Vol. 2745, Springer-Verlag, Berlin, 2003, pp. 256-270.

[7]   Han, R., Perret, V., and Naghshineh, M., *WebSplitter: a Unified XML Framework for Multi-device Collaborative Web Browsing*, in Proceedings of the 8th ACM Conference on Computer Supported Cooperative Work CSCW'2000 (Philadelphia, 2-6 December 2000), ACM Press, New York, 2000, pp. 221–230.

[8]   Luyten, K., Clerckx, T., Coninx, K., Vanderdonckt, J., *Derivation of a Dialog Model from a Task Model by Activity Chain Extraction*, Jorge, J., Nunes, N.J., Falcão e Cunha, J. (eds.), Proc. of 10th International Conference on Design, Specification, and Verification of Interactive Systems DSV-IS'2003 (Madeira, 4-6 June 2003), Lecture Notes in Computer Science, Vol. 2844, Springer-Verlag, Berlin, 2003, pp. 203-217.

[9]   Luyten, K., Creemers, B., and Coninx, K., *Multi-Device Layout Management for Mobile Computing Devices*, Technical Report TR-LUC-EDM-0301, EDM/LUC, 2003.

[10]   Mori, G., Paternò, F., and Santoro, C., *Tool Support for Designing Nomadic Applications*, in Proceedings of the 8th ACM International Conference on Intelligent User Interfaces IUI'2003 (Miami, 12-15 January 2003), ACM Press, New York, 2003, pp. 141–148.

[11]   Nichols, J., Myers, B.A., Higgins, M., Hughes, J., Harris, T.K., Rosenfeld, R., and Pignol, M., *Generating Remote Control Interfaces for Complex Appliances*, in Proceedings of the 15th annual ACM Symposium on User Interface Software and Technology UIST'2002 (Paris, 27-30 October 2002), ACM Press, New York, 2002, pp. 161–170.

[12]   Paternò, F., *Model-Based Design and Evaluation of Interactive Applications*, Springer-Verlag, Berlin, 1999.

[13]   Paternò, F. and Santoro, C., *One Model, Many Interfaces*, in Ch. Kolski, J. Vanderdonckt (eds.), Proceedings of the 4th International Conference on Computer-Aided Design of User Interfaces CADUI'2002 (Valenciennes, 15-17 May 2002), Kluwer Academics Publishers, Dordrecht, 2002, pp. 143–154.

[14]   Pribeanu, C., Limbourg, Q., and Vanderdonckt, J., *Task Modelling for Context-Sensitive User Interfaces*, in Ch. Johnson (ed.), Proceedings of 8th International Workshop on Design, Specification, and Verification of Interactive Systems DSV-IS'2001 (Glasgow, 13-15 June 2001), Lecture Notes in Computer Science, Vol. 2220, Springer-Verlag, Berlin, 2001, pp. 60–76.

[15]   Souchon, N., Limbourg, Q., Vanderdonckt, J., *Task Modelling in Multiple Contexts of Use*, in P. Forbrig, Q. Limbourg, B. Urban, J. Vanderdonckt (eds.), Proc. of 9th Int. Workshop on Design, Specification, and Verification of Interactive Systems DSV-IS'2002 (Rostock, 12-14 June 2002), Lecture Notes in Computer Science, Vol. 2545, Springer-Verlag, Berlin, 2002, pp. 59-73.

[16]   Van den Bergh, J., Luyten, K., and Coninx, K., *A Run-time System for Context-Aware Multi-Device User Interfaces*, in Proceedings of 10th International Conference on Human-Computer Interaction HCI International'2003 (Heraklion, 22-27 June 2003), Volume 2, Lawrence Erlbaum Associates, Mahwah, 2003, pp. 308-312.

[17] Vanderdonckt, J. and Bodart, F., *Encapsulating Knowledge for Intelligent Automatic Interaction Objects Selection*, in Proc. of the ACM Conf. on Human Factors in Computing Systems INTERCHI'93 (Amsterdam, 24-29 April 1993), ACM Press, New York, 1993, pp. 424-429.

[18] Vandervelpen, Ch., Luyten, K., and Coninx, K., *Location Transparent User Interaction for Heterogeneous Environments*, in Proceedings of 10th International Conference on Human-Computer Interaction HCI International'2003 (Heraklion, 22-27 June 2003), Volume 2, Lawrence Erlbaum Associates, Mahwah, 2003, pp. 313–317.

Chapter 24

A LIGHTWEIGHT EXPERIMENT MANAGE-MENT SYSTEM FOR HANDHELD COMPUTERS

Phil Gray[1], Joy Goodman[1] and James Macleod[2]
[1]*Computing Science Department, University of Glasgow,*
17 Lilybank Gardens – Glasgow G12 8QQ (Scotland)
E-mail: {pdg, joy-www}@dcs.gla.ac.uk
URL: http://www.dcs.gla.ac.uk/~{pdg, joy}
Tel: +44 141 330 {4933, 3541} – Fax: +44 141 330 4913
[2]*Division of Immunology, Infection & Inflammation, University of Glasgow,*
Western Infirmary – Glasgow G11 6NT (Scotland)
E-mail: d.i.stott@clinmed.gla.ac.uk
URL: http://www.gla.ac.uk/immunology/people/stott.htm
Tel.: +44 141 211 2442 – Fax: +44 141 337 3217

Abstract   This paper describes a system that helps HCI practitioners and researchers manage and conduct experiments involving context-sensitive handheld applications, particularly related to navigation assistance. The system provides a software framework in which application, user interface and interaction monitoring components can be plugged, offering a simple interconnection protocol and minimising the programming overheads of implementation. We have focused our attention on dealing with the challenges presented by the limited memory and processing of handheld devices and the variety of data sources for mobile context-sensitive applications. In this paper we give an overview of the system's functionality and architecture, discuss key challenges of supporting field-based experiments on handhelds and consider further developments of the system.

Keywords: Evaluation of user interfaces and tools, Mobile applications, Usage monitoring

1.   INTRODUCTION

The use of mobile technologies has been growing rapidly, primarily of mobile telephones but also of other handheld devices. Together with the exploitation of new technologies such as GPS and 3G and improvements in

R. Jacob et al. (eds.), Computer-Aided Design of User Interfaces IV, 297–308.
© 2005 *Kluwer Academic Publishers. Printed in the Netherlands.*

wireless capabilities, this has inspired the development of a wider and more ambitious range of mobile applications. Additional challenges and opportunities are posed by context-awareness, which can be used to provide information related to the user's current location, e.g., to aid navigation.

However, less is known about how to make the resulting applications and devices usable. If this is to be achieved, usability experiments on handheld devices are of key importance, both to test and improve the usability of existing and developed devices, and to gain information on how such devices can be designed in general, for example, by comparing alternative interfaces. Such experiments are important for groups that can particularly benefit from these devices but are most likely to be excluded by them -disabled people and older age groups. The design of handhelds for the older population is especially poorly understood and more work needs to be done in this area. Experiments with older users themselves on different handhelds and user interfaces are important to improving this understanding. It is within this context that the work described in this paper takes place [3,4].

Sadly, the management of such experiments can often be a time-consuming and complicated task, as indicated in Table 1, meaning that evaluations are often limited. However, this process can be improved using software tools. Such tools have been shown to be of use in designing and testing desktop applications in the past, and similar tools could prove useful in mobile situations.

Table 1. Issues in managing experiments.

Category	Example	Examples of management issues	Examples of particular issues with handhelds
Participants	16 participants aged 18-40 who don't know the area, gender-balanced	Obtaining and keeping track of participants, assigning them to conditions, coping with them dropping out	Changes may have to be made to the list of participants in the field
Conditions	Interface A is tested in condition C1 and interface B in condition C2	The right interface should be brought up at the right point in the experiment	Limited screen space and memory, rendering storage and selection of interfaces less easy
Tasks	1. Find your way from the library to the butchers 2. Find your way from the supermarket to the school	The right tasks must be matched with the right conditions for each participant to prevent order and other effects	Familiarity with the area in the 1st task should affect the 2nd as little as possible. Tasks may need to be changed due to external conditions, e.g., roadworks
Equipment	A handheld computer with the application, a GPS receiver, consent form, questionnaires, notebook and pen	Ensuring that the right equipment for each participant and set of conditions is available	Equipment must be carried. This may include equipment for several participants if the experimenter cannot return to base between trials

Category	Example	Examples of management issues	Examples of particular issues with handhelds
Data Collection	Start and end times for each condition, notes of when the participant got lost and which interface elements were used and how often	The data must be collected, collated and stored	Limited storage space on the device. Difficulties taking notes while on the move and trying to manage several pieces of paper at once.

There are many issues that such tools can support. Our eventual aim is to create a tool that would support the entire experiment process, including all the issues described in Table 1, as well as support for activities before and after the actual experiments. This paper, however, describes a prototype of an experiment management tool for mobile devices, incorporating support for managing the user interfaces and collecting usage data. In Section 2 we describe and discuss other experiment management tools and how this work relates to them. In Section 3 we then describe in more detail what our system does and how it works. We map out and discuss key challenges of supporting field-based experiments on handhelds and consider further developments of the system in Section 4, before concluding in Section 5.

2.   RELATED WORK

Several experiment management tools exist for desktop applications and, while they are not generally suitable for mobile devices, some of the techniques used within them can be adapted to this setting. These tools have usually focused on either support for generating the User Interface (UI) or on capturing data from the participants.

The system described in this paper does not provide support for generating interfaces *per se*, such as in the work on automatic interface generation. Rather it supports the process of generating different interfaces for the same data and then swapping between them so that they can be easily compared in an experiment. The emphasis is on aiding the running of experiments, rather than on generating good interfaces for a finished product. Worth mentioning here is the TAE Plus system [12] which, while not aimed at supporting experiments, separates the user interface and the program code making it easier to swap between interfaces.

Previous work on capturing experimental usage data has followed two main avenues – video and screen capture and event logging.

Video capture (e.g., [9]) involves videoing the participant and/or the screen during the experiment. This method is not easily transferred to the mobile domain without specialist equipment and/or wireless communication [10]. Screen capture (e.g., [1]) may be more feasible as it stores the images appearing on the computer screen at regular intervals and therefore does not require additional equipment. However, the resulting files are large and are likely to take up too much memory for a mobile device. In addition, it does not capture the context of use. Taken together with the simpler UIs on mobile devices, this renders it not much more useful than event logging if the latter is done at an appropriate level of detail.

Event logging systems [8] are potentially more useful for mobile studies, but existing logging systems place heavy demands on processing, storage, and communications. However, our understanding of interaction with mobile devices is rather poor and many opportunities remain for carrying out useful studies on or with relatively simple handheld user interfaces. Given the limitations of handhelds, these opportunities depend on keeping processing, memory and communication demands to a minimum. In addition, although some current systems do allow the experimenter to choose the user actions to be logged (e.g., [1]), this is complicated, and a simpler system is needed and indeed possible for a mobile device.

In addition, mobile devices have a greater need for an integrated experiment tool providing support for easily generating and swapping between experimental conditions as well as easy data capture and analysis. The limited memory and processing power of these devices and the difficulties associated with moving the program and data around means it is best to have a single program managing the experiment as a whole.

Although data capture and analysis have been integrated (e.g., [1,7]), less work has been done on combining support for the interface with support for data capture. One example is UsAGE [13], which added event logging to the UI development system, TAE Plus [12], although not as a single unified program, and not for mobile devices.

3.   SYSTEM FEATURES

3.1   An Example

The motivating example for the system described in this paper is the navigation aid, a typical mobile application that provides directions to the user to enable him or her to find a location. Such directions can be provided in a wide variety of formats, including maps, photographs and arrows, as well as using different modalities, but little work has been carried out comparing these different approaches [2].

Let us imagine that we want to evaluate and compare three such interfaces, shown in Fig. 1. One way of doing this would be to write three applications, one with each interface, and create data sets for each for the test and pilot routes. We would then have to run the experiment, ensuring that the right interface with the right route was brought up at the right time. Code would have to be included in each application to monitor any usage data we wanted collected, such as timings and button clicks or alternatively these could be noted by hand by the experimenter. Although this process is possible, it is rather complicated, and our system aims to simplify and support it.

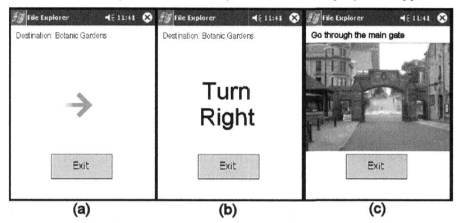

Figure 1. Three possible navigation aid interfaces.

3.2   Supporting Adaptation

Our system supports the adaptation of a context-aware handheld application to different experimental conditions, by separating application data and operations, such as geographical information about the location or context (the Model) from the user interface components used to present this information to the user (the View). For example, in Fig. 1, the same Model is used (information is presented about the same route) but using different Views (different interface methods).

It is possible to create very general models that contain enough information for a variety of different views. In addition, the framework supports more limited models, if less extensive surveying of the environment is desired. However, these models may only be suitable for some views. For example, the view shown in Fig. 1(c) requires a model with images or pointers to images of locations, while those shown in Fig. 1(a) and (b) only need to contain the directions to turn at particular coordinates. The same reduced model could therefore be used for (a) and (b) but not for (c).

Our system matches model and view as well as possible, leaving spaces in the resulting interface rather than crashing if they do not match completely, so that reasonable interfaces can still be produced if the model and view do not match but are not far apart. This separation of model and view makes it easier to:

- Create all of the experimental conditions. In context-aware applications such as navigation aids, the conditions typically consist of all possible combinations of the different test locations with the different interfaces being tested. Using the method above, models can be shared between views rather than having to create a separate application for each combination.
- Select the experimental condition to be tested. Rather than having to keep track of which application corresponds to which combination of conditions, the model and view can be chosen separately but at the same time. Currently this is done through XML configuration files, as shown in the example in Fig. 2, which chooses a model called ArrowModel and a view called ArrowView, generating the interface shown in Fig. 1(a).
- Move the experiment to different locations, which may be necessary due to constraints outside the experimenter's control, such as roadworks. In this case, only the models need to be changed.
- Test new interfaces by creating a new view for an existing model.

This process is further supported by the use of templates and C# interfaces for the models and views, reducing the amount of coding necessary to create new sets of location data and new interfaces. Since we are working with complex and potentially unusual navigation and map-based user interfaces, we chose to represent our design options in term of parameterisable components.

In particular, components can be linked by identifying data values in models to be listened to (and potentially updated by) view components. An alternative approach would be to employ a user interface specification language, like UIML [14], from which the actual user interface components could be generated by a "renderer". While this would increase genericity, there would be too high a cost in terms of the complexity and usability of the specification and specification language, especially given the potentially complex and non-standard character of interaction in our target applications.

```
<configuration>
    <Model>ArrowModel</Model>
    <View>ArrowView</View>
    <Data>
       <Item>ArrowChange</Item>
       <Item>LocationChange</Item>
       <Item>DirectionChange</Item>
    </Data>
 </configuration>
```

Figure 2. XML configuration for the data and view shown in Fig. 1(a).

3.3   Supporting Observation

The system supports experimental observation by collecting usage run-time information. This may include, for example, information on which buttons or other interface elements were selected, when they were selected, when other important events occurred and the length of time taken for the whole experiment. We log information at this level of complexity, rather than lower-level actions and events, because we consider it to be the most useful level for analysing the results of the experiment and because lower-level events are of little use due to the reduced number of UI elements in a handheld interface and the simplicity of the standard input methods.

Each item of loggable information is given a label in the code for the model or the view. The experimenter can then use these labels to indicate which information is to be logged, thus customising the experiment and only collecting information of interest to that experiment. This reduces the sizes of the logs and simplifies their later analysis.

The selection of items to be logged is given in the experiment's XML configuration file, as shown in the example in Fig. 2. This example generates the interface shown in Fig. 1(a) and logs three events in addition to the application's starting and closing time. It logs when changes occur in the displayed arrow, the sensed GPS location and the direction. This particular interface does not contain any interactive UI components. If it did, their use could also be logged by generating suitable logging events in the code for the view, labelling them and including their labels in the configuration file.

3.4   System Architecture

We have created an implementation of our system written in C#, using Microsoft's .Net Compact Framework, which runs on PocketPC devices.

A runnable application consists of a single model object (the model object can also accommodate additional components, such as a GPS proxy object), a single view object, and an optional data collection object connected together and managed by an overall manager component (Fig. 3). The interconnection of the model, view and data collector is carried out with the aid of event generation interfaces made available via class methods: get-DataItems() and getSchema(), which both return a set of identifiers from the model and view. getDataItems() returns a set of identifiers of active values that can be logged - "loggables" - and getSchema() returns a set of identifiers of active values that form the model-view link (i.e., values that the model reveals to the view and values that the view is capable of presenting to a user for interaction) - "linkables". The manager creates a working application by:

- Connecting the model and view by finding name matches in the value sets returned by the model and view via getSchema() and using the results to instantiate the actual user interface.
- Determining what will be logged by finding name matches between the value sets returned by the model and view via getDataItems() on the one hand and the names of desired data to be logged located in the configuration file on the other hand.

On startup the framework reads in an experiment configuration file, such as that shown in Fig. 2. The model and view classes specified in this file are then loaded and instantiated, and a data collection object is also instantiated. Using the name matching algorithms described above, event listeners are created for each matched loggable and linkable, with a predefined logging callback (Fig. 3).

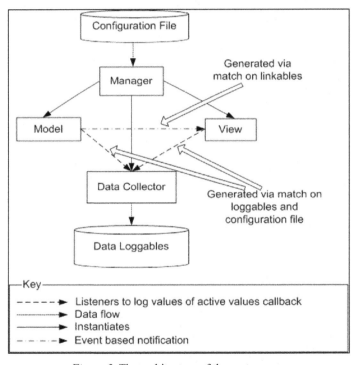

Figure 3. The architecture of the system.

The ability to construct running, loggable applications from simple configuration files removes the need to pre-construct the several application variants necessary for a comparative study. The cost to the developer lies in the need to add into the source code the information used by the framework manager to connect the components together, viz., the names of data items that notify changes to their state. Such data items can be used to update views or can be logged by a data collector component. Furthermore, model and view operations that can change the state of these data items must include in the relevant method a call to a method to fire an appropriate event.

Automatic linking of data items between model and view also demands that the system can determine a unique and sensible mapping between model and view. In the simple applications we currently envisage testing, such a mapping is possible and not costly to embed in the source code. However, this limits the generality of our automatic generation system and future versions may have to explore semi-automated approaches [5,6,11].

4. KEY CHALLENGES AND SUGGESTIONS FOR FURTHER DEVELOPMENT

The system as described above has been implemented in prototype form. We have constructed several alternative models and views and used these with configuration files to construct and run the simple navigation applications described in section 3. We have yet to use it "in anger", however, as part of a usability study. This trial will be taking place in the near future. Our study will investigate the relative effectiveness of several different methods of providing navigation information to older users, such as maps, sequenced landmarks and step-by-step directions. Consequently there will be a number of combinations of models and views that must be trialled, and it will also be necessary to change the configuration in the field with each individual participant.

There are many ways in which our current relatively primitive system might be enhanced, including making it easier to specify an experiment and adding tool support for other aspects of the process of conducting an experiment.

XML is a useful data interchange language, but not very easy to generate or read. A tool is needed to support the initial specification of an experimental platform that will hide the XML and that can present to an experimenter lists of model and view components that can be combined and the type of events that can be logged from each. Given that this information is available from the components via reflection, it would be possible to build a running example of the experimental application at design test. This example could be used to test the configuration before using the application in the experiment itself.

There are several additional aspects of the conduct of an experiment that it would be useful to add to our system. Currently, the system only handles a single trial. Typically data will be collected during a number of trials, with different user participants and different conditions (e.g., counterbalanced combinations of user, location and user interface version). We intend to add to the framework an Experiment Manager component that holds this information, read from an augmented experiment configuration file, so that trials can be set up and run either automatically, in sequence, or via experimenter selection. The Experiment Manager is distinct from the current Manager component in the framework that can only handle a single trial.

As the amount of logged data increases, e.g., via multiple trials, one might run into storage difficulties due to the limited memory of a handheld device and the space occupied by other application data, such as a geographic database. Our system will have to take appropriate action in such cases, including compressing the logfiles during creation, transferring to other devices if possible or alerting the experimenter to a possible loss of data prior to data loss. In the latter case, this should occur between trials based on an analysis of the amount of data logged in previous trials and the current space available. This would give the experimenter adequate warning to take action to make more memory available.

More ambitiously, we would like to add the ability to combine the logged data with data collected concurrently by one or more observers. For example, an observer might use a separate hand-held, entering time-stamped notes or experimental protocols, or taking photos or videos or audio recordings. These could be combined with the logged data later, if the timed data can be suitably synchronised.

Indeed, if the experimenter is using a separate device in the field, such as another handheld or a laptop, additional experimental support is possible. For example, using a peer-to-peer wireless connection between the participant's handheld and the experimenter's device, the experimenter may be able to monitor the handheld application (see real-time logged data, view a copy of the participant's screen) or modify the application if necessary. Also, it may be possible to shift data to the experimenter's device as a backup or to free memory on the participant's handheld.

It would also be desirable to integrate additional tools for data archiving, preparation and analysis in to the overall system. However, these operations are unlikely to be performed on the handheld device and thus are not a particular issue for the support of mobile-oriented experiments.

5.   CONCLUSION

Interaction with mobile devices, such as handhelds, and the user interfaces that support such interaction, remain less well understood than with desktop applications. Ironically, it is more difficult to collect logged data from handheld applications than from workstations. In addition, although several experiment management tools exist for desktops, little has been done in this area for the evaluation of handheld devices, with its different characteristics and challenges. Experiments in the mobile domain have a greater need for an integrated experiment environment and for methods for managing multiple data sources and for coping with limited memory and resources.

Our approach, as reported in this paper, has been to provide a relatively simple tool that makes it easy for evaluators to construct experimental prototypes and to log data from them. Although this system is in its early stages, it provides a useful framework for managing experiments on handhelds and a useful basis on which to build other features and tackle the other challenges of this area.

ACKNOWLEDGEMENTS

This work was funded by SHEFC through the UTOPIA project (grant number: HR01002), which is investigating the design and development of usable technology for older people. We would also like to thank Kartik Khammampad who built and evaluated a navigation system for us using an interface similar to that shown in Fig. 1(c) and Professor Steve Brewster for his useful comments on an earlier draft.

REFERENCES

[1] Al-Qaimari, G. and McRostie, D., *KALDI: A Computer-Aided Usability Engineering Tool for Supporting Testing and Analysis of User Performance*, in Blanford, A., Gray, P. and Vanderdonckt, J., (eds.), Proc. of the Joint AFIHM-BCS Conf. on Human-Computer Interaction IHM-HCI'2001 (Lille, 10-14 September 2001), People and Computers XV, Springer-Verlag, London, 2001, pp. 153-169.

[2] Bradley, N.A. and Dunlop, M.D., *Understanding Contextual Interactions to Design Navigational Context-Aware Applications,* in Paternò, F., (ed.), Proceedings of 3rd Workshop on Mobile Computing and HCI Mobile'2002 (Pisa, 18-20 September 2002), Lecture Notes in Computer Science, Vol. 2411, Springer-Verlag, Berlin, 2002, pp. 349-353.

[3] Eisma, R., Dickinson, A., Goodman, J., Syme, A., Tiwari, L., and Newell, A.F., *Early User Involvement in the Development of Information Technology-Related Products for Older People,* Universal Access in the Information Society, Vol. 3, No. 2, April 2004.

[4] Goodman, J., Gray, P.D., *A Design Space for Location-Sensitive Aids for Older Users,* in Schmidt-Belz, B. and Cheverst, K., (eds.), in Proceedings of 17th BCS-HCI Annual Human-Computer Interaction Conference HCI'2003 (Bath, 8-12 September 2003), Springer-Verlag, London, 2003, pp. 12-16.

[5] Gray, P.D. and Draper, S.W.D., *A Unified Concept of Style and its Place in User Interface Design*, in Sasse, M.A., Cunningham, J., and Winder, R.L., (eds.), Proceedings of BCS-HCI Annual Human-Computer Interaction Conference HCI'96 (London, 20-23 August 1996), People and Computers XI, Springer-Verlag, London, 1996, pp. 49-62.

[6] Griffiths,T., Barclay, P.J., Paton, N.W., McKirdy, J., Kennedy, J., Gray, P.D., Cooper, R., Goble, C.A., and Pinheiro da Silva, P., *Teallach: A Model-Based User Interface De-*

velopment Environment for Object Databases, Interacting With Computers, Vol. 14, No. 1, 2001, pp. 31-68.

[7] Hammontree, M., Hendrikson, J., and Hensley, B., *Integrated Data Capture and Analysis Tools for Research and Testing on Graphical User Interfaces,* in Bauersfeld, P., Bennett, J., and Lynch, G., (eds.), Proceedings of ACM Conference on Human Factors in Computing Systems CHI'92 (Monterey, 3-7 May 1992), ACM Press, New York, 1992, pp. 431-432.

[8] Hilbert, D.M. and Redmiles, D.F., *Extracting Usability Information from User Interface Events,* ACM Computing Surveys, Vol. 32, No. 4, December 2000, pp. 384-421.

[9] Macleod, M., Bowren, R., Bevan, N., and Curson, I., *The MUSiC Performance Measurement Method*, Behaviour and Information Technology, Vol. 16, No. 4-5, 1997, pp. 279-293.

[10] Noldus Information Technology, accessible at http://www.noldus.com

[11] Pribeanu, C. and Vanderdonckt, J., *Exploring Design Heuristics for User Interface Derivation from Task and Domain Models,* in C. Kolski, J. Vanderdonckt (eds.), Proceedings of 4th Int. Conf. on Computer-Aided Design of User Interfaces CADUI'2002 (Valenciennes, 15-17 May 2002), Kluwer Academics Pub., Dordrecht, 2002, pp. 103-110.

[12] Szczur, M. and Sheppard, S., *TAE Plus: Transportable Applications Environment Plus: A User Interface Development Environment*, ACM Transactions on Information Systems, Vol. 11, No. 1, January 1993, pp. 76-101.

[13] Uehling, D. and Wolf, K., *User Action Graphing Effort (UsAGE)*, in Katz, I., Mack, R. and Marks, L., (eds.), Proceedings of ACM Conference on Human Factors in Computing Systems CHI'95 (Denver, 7-11 May 1995), Companion volume 2, ACM Press, New York, 1995, pp. 290-291.

[14] UIML website, accessible at http://www.uiml.org

Chapter 25

GENERIC INTERACTION TECHNIQUES FOR MOBILE COLLABORATIVE MIXED SYSTEMS

Philippe Renevier[1], Laurence Nigay[1], J. Bouchet[1], and L. Pasqualetti[2]

[1]*CLIPS-IMAG Laboratory, IIHM Team, University of Grenoble*
BP 53, 38041 Grenoble Cedex 9 (France)
E-mail: {Philippe.Renevier, Laurence.Nigay, Jullien.Bouchet} @imag.fr
URL: http://iihm.imag.fr/renevier
[2]*FT R&D-DIH/UCE 38-40 rue G. Leclerc 92794 Issy-lesMoulineaux (France)*
E-mail: laurence.pasqualetti@francetelecom.fr

Abstract   The main characteristic of a mobile collaborative mixed system is that augmentation of the physical environment of one user occurs through available knowledge of where the user is and what the other users are doing. Links between the physical and digital worlds are no longer static but dynamically defined by users to create a collaborative augmented environment. In this article we present generic interaction techniques for smoothly combining the physical and digital worlds of a mobile user in the context of a collaborative situation. We illustrate the generic nature of the techniques with two systems that we developed: MAGIC for archaeological fieldwork and TROC a mobile collaborative game.

Keywords: Computer-Supported Collaborative Work, Interaction Techniques, Mixed Reality.

1.   INTRODUCTION

Mixed systems seek to smoothly link the physical and data processing environments. This is also the objective of other innovative interaction paradigms such as Ubiquitous Computing, Tangible Bits, Pervasive Computing and Traversable Interfaces. These examples of interaction paradigms are all based on the manipulation of objects of the physical environment [5]. Typically, objects are functionally limited but contextually relevant [8]. The challenge thus lies in the design and realisation of the fusion of the physical and

R. Jacob et al. (eds.), Computer-Aided Design of User Interfaces IV, 309–322.

data processing environments (hereafter called physical and digital worlds). The object of our study is to address this issue in the context of a collaborative mobility situation. Context detection and mixed reality are then combined in order to create a personalised augmented environment.

The structure of the paper is as follows: first, we define the context of our study by defining what mobile collaborative systems, mobile mixed systems and finally collaborative mixed systems are. We present related work and characterize existing systems highlighting the power and versatility of such systems. We then clarify the notion of mobile collaborative mixed systems. Having defined the goal and challenge of mobile collaborative mixed systems, we then present generic interaction techniques for smoothly combining the physical and digital worlds of a mobile user in the context of a collaborative situation. We illustrate the generic nature of the techniques with two systems that we developed: MAGIC for archaeological fieldwork and TROC a mobile collaborative game.

2.   RELATED WORK

The objective of our study is to address the fusion of the physical and data processing environments in the context of a collaborative mobility situation. We therefore identify three intertwined ingredients: mobile systems, collaborative systems and mixed systems. In this section, we respectively study mobile collaborative, mobile mixed, and collaborative mixed systems.

2.1   Mobile Collaborative Systems

As computers become more and more prevalent, the need for systems that support coordination, communication and shared production between and within groups increases markedly. Such multi-user systems also called groupware have been made possible thanks to the advances of network technologies. A groupware may support synchronous interaction between users, such as a chat and/or asynchronous interaction between users such as email. In our study, we focus on mobile groupware. Mobile groupware are rapidly finding widespread use due to the recent progress in networking technologies. For example, a new protocol of continuous real time transport between a wireless network and a fixed network such as Ethernet is presented in [9]. This protocol is compatible with the quality of service of the current wireless networks. Moreover the studies carried out by the UMTS® consortium foresee, in the short run, flows of data of about 2Mbit/s. An example of existing collaborative systems is RAMSES [1], in the archaeology domain. Each archaeologist in the field takes notes on a Palmtop connected to a radio frequency (2 Mb a second) network so that notes can be shared by the group of archaeologists working in the same field. Amongst mobile CSCW, the objective of our study is to understand the use of mobile supports and services required in a collaborative situation for a user's task in the real world. The aim is to create a seamless collaborative operational field between the physical and digital worlds, thanks to a so-called mixed system.

2.2   Mobile Mixed Systems

As we defined in [3], a mixed system is an interactive system combining physical and digital entities. Two classes of mixed systems are identified:

- *Augmented Virtuality systems*: Systems that make use of real objects to enhance the interaction between a user and a computer.
- *Augmented Reality systems*: Systems that enhance interaction between the user and her/his real environment by providing additional capabilities and/or information.

On the one hand, the Tangible User Interface paradigm [5] belongs to Augmented Virtuality: physical objects such as bricks are used to interact with a computer. On the other hand, the NaviCam system [10] and our Computer Assisted Surgery system CASPER [3] are two examples of Augmented Reality systems: the two systems display situation-sensitive information by superimposing messages and pictures on a video see-through screen (HMD, Head Mounted Display). The common design challenge of mixed systems (Augmented Virtuality as well as Augmented Reality systems) lies in the fluid and harmonious fusion of the physical and digital worlds.

In our study we focus on Augmented Reality systems, one class of mixed systems. The first Augmented Reality systems were designed for a specific use in a fixed environment. Progress made in wireless networks in terms of quality of services make it possible to build mobile Augmented Reality systems [6]. We believe that mobile Augmented Reality systems have a crucial role to play for mobile workers, bringing computer capabilities into the reality of the different workplaces. Systems already exist such as the Touring machine system of the project MARS (Mobile Augmented Reality Systems) [4] or the NaviCam system [10]. The user, while walking in a building such as a museum, in the streets or in a campus, obtains contextual information about the surrounding objects or about a predefined path to follow.

A mobile Augmented Reality system is one in which augmentation occurs through available knowledge of where the user is (the user's location and therefore the surrounding environment). Even though the user's location has an impact on the augmentation provided by the system, the latter does not necessarily maintain this location. Indeed, as explained in [6], on the one hand, the user's location and orientation are generally known by outdoor systems such as the Touring machine system, the position being tracked by a GPS. On the other hand, for indoor Augmented Reality systems, such as the NaviCam system, objects and places identify themselves to the system (RF, IR or video based tags): hence the system does not maintain the user's location. To sum up, amongst mobile mixed systems, we focus on mobile Augmented Reality systems that enhance the interaction between the mobile user and her/his current real environment by providing additional capabilities and/or information.

2.3   Collaborative Mixed Systems

Several collaborative mixed systems have been developed. As for mobile mixed systems, we focus on one class of mixed systems, the Augmented Reality systems. As defined above, in Augmented Reality, interaction with the real world is augmented by the computer in order to assist a user in performing a task in the real world (i.e., modifying the real world). As a consequence, systems such as the StudierStube [13] that allows multiple collaborating users to simultaneously study three-dimensional scientific visualizations in a dedicated room is not part of our study because the task of studying a virtual object, is not in the real world. The shared real environment of the group of users is augmented by the computer but the task remains in the digital world.

An Augmented Reality system may provide support for shared production, communication and/or coordination amongst users. We call such systems Augmented Reality and Collaborative systems. We make a distinction between such Augmented Reality and Collaborative systems and the ones that we call Collaborative Augmented Reality systems that depict systems in which the physical environment of a group of users is collaboratively augmented. A Collaborative Augmented Reality system is one in which augmentation of the physical environment of one user occurs through the actions of other users. The main characteristic of a Collaborative Augmented Reality system is that augmentation of the physical environment of one user no longer relies on information pre-stored by the computer. Links between the physical and digital worlds are therefore dynamic, based on the users' actions and not defined in advance as for example in an augmented museum (the NaviCam system) [10]. Several Collaborative Augmented Reality systems exist and take on a variety of forms: In [11] we introduce a taxonomy of Collaborative Augmented Reality systems based on the classical distinction in groupware, that is the distance between users, as well as the distance between one or several users and the object of the task that belongs to the real world.

Amongst collaborative mixed systems, we focus on Collaborative Augmented Reality systems in which the physical environment of a group of users is collaboratively augmented.

3.   MOBILE COLLABORATIVE MIXED SYSTEMS

Having introduced the context of our research, we now define what a mobile collaborative mixed system is. Such a system combines the characteristics of a mobile mixed system and of a collaborative mixed system. First a mobile mixed system, as defined above, is one in which augmentation occurs through available knowledge of where the user is (the user's location and therefore the surrounding environment). Second a collaborative mixed system is one in which augmentation of the physical environment of one user occurs through the actions of other users and no longer relies on information pre-stored by the computer. Links between the physical and digital worlds are therefore dynamic, based on the users' actions. Combining the characteristics of a mobile mixed system and of a collaborative mixed system, a mobile and collaborative mixed system is one in which augmentation occurs through available knowledge of where the user is and what the other users are doing.

Although mobile collaborative systems are now possible and systems already exist as explained in the previous section, and while some existing mixed systems are mobile and some are collaborative, few mixed systems combine the mobile and collaborative aspects. The main application domain of such systems is game and one of our developed system, TROC, is a game. Indeed, instead of recreating a virtual world, the existing games are based in the real world, the system only adding the magical possibilities related to the game rules. WARPING [12] is one example, but one of the users is not mobile, since s/he is in front of an augmented desktop. ARQuake [14] and Human-Pacman [2] are two additional examples of games. The users are mobile and they must kill digital enemies (ARQuake) or collect digital cookies (Human-Pacman). In these two examples, we can nevertheless notice that the links between the physical and digital worlds are predefined (positions of enemies or cookies) and the users can only destroy them, they cannot create new "links" such as putting a new cookie in the game field.

Beyond the HCI classical design approach, mobile collaborative mixed systems make it compulsory to use a multidisciplinary design approach that embeds complementary methods and techniques for the design and evaluation phases. In [7] we present a scenario-based design approach for mobile collaborative mixed systems. In particular scenarios enable the description of how the system would affect the way mobile users carry out their individual and collective activities. Based on the functions integrated in the so-called "projected scenarios", different interaction techniques can be designed. The interaction techniques, described in the following section, are generic and are those supported by our two mobile collaborative mixed systems: MAGIC dedicated to archaeological fieldwork and TROC, a mobile collaborative game.

3.1 Generic Interaction Techniques

In order to explain the generic interaction techniques, we first describe the underlying hardware platform. This is an assembly of commercial pieces of hardware. The platform includes a Fujitsu Stylistic pen computer. This pen computer runs under the Windows operating system, with a Pentium III (450 MHz) and 196 Mb of RAM. The resolution of the tactile screen is 1024x768 pixels. In order to establish remote mobile connections, a Wave-Lan network by Lucent (11 Mb/s) was added. Connections from the pen computer are possible at about 200 feet around the network base. The hardware platform also contains a Head-Mounted Display (HMD), a SONY LDI D100 BE: its semi-transparency enables the fusion of computer data (opaque pixels) with the real environment (visible via transparent pixels). Secondly, a (D-)GPS is used to locate the users. Finally, capture of the real environment by the computer is achieved by the coupling of a camera and an orientation sensor. We first used an absolute orientation sensor, the magnetometer HMR3000 by Honeywell. We now use an intertrax 2 that is more accurate. The camera orientation is therefore known by the system. Indeed the orientation sensor and the camera are fixed on the HMD, in between the eyes of the user. The system is then able to know the position (GPS) and orientation (magnetometer or intertrax) of both the user and the camera.

Figure 1. A user wearing and holding the hardware platform

Fig. 1 shows a user, fully equipped: the equipment is quite invasive and suffers from a lack of power autonomy. Our goal is to demonstrate the feasibility of our interaction techniques by assembling existing commercial pieces of hardware and not by designing specific hardware out of the context of our expertise. For a real and long use of the platform in a "real" site, a dedicated hardware platform must clearly be designed.

The mobile users manipulate objects that are either digital or physical. Interaction techniques must be designed in order to let them manipulate the two types of objects: physical and digital. For flexibility and fluidity of interaction, such manipulation is either in the physical world or in the digital world. We therefore obtain four cases, by combining the two types of objects and the two worlds: the physical world (i.e., the archaeological field or the game ground) and the digital world (i.e., the screen of the pen computer):

1. Interaction with a physical object in the digital world: Mixed interaction.
2. Interaction with a digital object in the physical world: Mixed interaction.
3. Interaction with a physical object in the physical world: Interaction purely in the real world.
4. Interaction with a digital object in the digital world: Interaction in the digital world (graphical user interface).

In [7] we fully describe the four types of interaction. We focus here on the interaction techniques corresponding to the types (1) and (2). For both cases, passive and active interaction techniques are designed. Passive interaction techniques are based on tracking mechanisms (such as localisation and orientation of the mobile user). With passive techniques, the user does not explicitly issue a command to the system as opposed to active interaction techniques that correspond to the case where the user issues a command to the system, for example a drag and drop of an object.

The two types of mixed interaction ((1) and (2)) respectively imply (i) that physical objects must be manageable in the digital world (ii) that digital objects must be manageable in the physical world. To do so we designed a generic interaction technique, **a gateway** that plays the role of a door between the physical and digital worlds. As a door belongs to two rooms, the gateway exists in both worlds:

• The gateway is an area of the physical world, delimited by a rectangle displayed in a semi-transparency Head-Mounted Display (HMD) as shown in Fig. 2b,

• The gateway is a rectangular area in the digital world, on the pen computer screen as shown in Fig. 2a (window entitled "Head Mounted Display").

Concretely the gateway is simply a window both displayed on the HMD (Java JFrame) on top of the physical world and on the pen computer screen (Java JInternalFrame). As opposed to the Touring Machine system [4] in which the pen computer is used to display information about the surrounding physical environment of the user that is not displayed in the HMD, objects in the gateway are visible on the HMD (i.e., in the physical world) as well as on the pen computer screen (i.e., in the digital world), as shown in Fig. 2. Based on the gateway, we designed two interaction techniques, namely the "clickable reality" and the "augmented field".

- **The "Clickable reality" technique: from the physical world to the digital world.** If the object is physical (1), the object is transferred to the digital world thanks to the camera (fixed on the HMD, between the two eyes of the user). The real environment captured by the camera is displayed in the gateway window on the pen computer screen as a background. We allow the user to select or click on physical objects: we therefore call this technique "the clickable reality". Before taking a picture, the camera must be calibrated according to the user's visual field. Using the stylus on screen, the user then specifies a rectangular zone thanks to a magic lens (a type of camera lens). The cursor displayed on the pen computer screen is also displayed on top of the physical world. The corresponding specified zone (magic lens), displayed in the gateway window on screen and on the HMD, corresponds to the physical object to be captured. The picture can then be stored in the shared database along with the location of the object. Note that although the user is manipulating a magic lens using the stylus on screen, s/he perceives the results of her/his actions in the physical world.

- **The "Augmented field" technique: from the digital world to the physical world.** If the object is digital (2) dragging it inside the gateway makes it visible in the real world. For example the user can drag a drawing or a picture stored in a database to the gateway window. The picture will automatically be displayed on the HMD on top of the physical world as shown in Fig. 2b. Moving the picture using the stylus on the screen will move the picture on top of the physical world. This action is for example used if a user wants to compare an object from a database with a physical object in the field. Putting them next to each other in the real world will help their comparison. The motion of a digital object (ex: drag and drop on the pen computer) can be viewed by the user without looking at the pen computer screen. This is because in using the HMD the user can simultaneously view digital objects and the real world. Although the user is manipulating a digital object, s/he perceives the results of her/his actions in the physical world.

First, transfer of digital objects to the physical world can be explicitly managed by the user by drag and drop (active interaction technique) as explained above or can be automatic (passive interaction technique). Automatic transfer is performed by the system based on the current location of the user.

Second, transfer of digital objects to the physical world can be transient or persistent. Indeed, on the one hand, transfer of digital objects to the physical world can be transient as for comparing a digital object from a database with a physical found object. On the other hand, transfer of digital objects to the physical world performed by one user can be persistent so that later on other users can discover such digital objects that augment the physical environment. Such a technique is called "augmented field". When a user walks in the site, s/he can see discovered objects specified by colleagues. The "augmented field" is an example of asynchronous collaboration. It is therefore a generic technique for mobile collaborative Augmented Reality system.

These generic interaction techniques (i.e., the "gateway" technique on which the "clickable reality" as well as the "augmented field" techniques rely) are supported by two mobile collaborative mixed systems that we developed: MAGIC dedicated to archaeological fieldwork and TROC a mobile collaborative game.

4. SYSTEMS: MAGIC AND TROC

4.1 MAGIC for Archaeological Fieldwork

The design of the MAGIC system is based on a study of the tasks of archaeological fieldwork, interviews and observations in Alexandria (Egypt) [7]. The archaeological fieldwork in Alexandria is time-constrained because the archaeological site must be explored in less than three months (rescue archaeology). Tools that can make such fieldwork more efficient are therefore important. This is a suitable application domain for mobile collaborative mixed systems because archaeologists work in groups, moving in a delimited site and requiring collections of data. Fig. 2a presents the graphical user interface of MAGIC on the pen computer. Coordination between users relies on the map of the archaeological site, displayed within a dedicated window (at the bottom left corner of Fig. 2a). For each found object, archaeologists fill a form describing the object, draw some sketches or very precise drawings and take pictures using the "clickable reality" technique. Analysis of objects relies on comparisons with known objects ("Augmented field" technique) from other archaeologists or reference manuals (database) and on discussions with other archaeologists in the site or with a distant expert. Fig. 2b, a reconstituted picture, presents such comparison. After validation, the object is then added to the shared database and is visible on the map of each user. Because a picture is stored along with the location of the object, we can restore the picture in its original real context (2D representation). When an archaeologist walks in the site, s/he can see discovered objects removed from the site and specified in the database by colleagues ("Augmented field" technique). S/he can then see the object as it was before being removed from the site. The "augmented field" technique is particularly useful to see objects belonging to a stratum higher than the current one, because by definition the objects have all been removed. The MAGIC system along with its software architecture is fully described in [11]. Although the design is based on task and activity analysis performed in Alexandria, we were not able to experimentally test MAGIC on a site there. In order to show the generic aspect of our techniques and also to be able to perform experimental tests we developed a second application, TROC, a collaborative game.

4.2   TROC: a Mobile Collaborative Game

TROC (barter in French) is a mobile collaborative game. Each player has to collect a list of digital objects that are positioned in the game field at the beginning of the game. As shown in part B of Fig. 3, the digital objects to be collected are animals (cat, gull, etc.). Thanks to the "augmented field" technique, the player while moving discovers the objects. TROC also includes 3D sounds that help the player to find the objects. In addition the player can use "magical tools" to locate the objects as well as the other players on the map displayed on the pen computer (part D of Fig. 3, the round circle specifying the zone of observation). The player can also specify filters (part A of Fig. 3) so that s/he will only see one kind of digital object, in the physical world (the game field) as well as on the map. Digital objects collected by a user are stored in four physical cubes carried by the player. The content of the four cubes is displayed on the pen computer (part C of Fig. 3) as well as on top of the physical cube recognized by a vision algorithm thanks to the camera fixed on the HMD.

To collect a digital object, the player has two possibilities: first s/he can use the "clickable reality" technique or s/he can present a physical cube to the camera fixed on the HMD while issuing the voice command "take". The player can also empty a cube and put back on the game field a previously collected digital object ("augmented field" technique). This is an example of asynchronous collaboration between players. In order to win and collect her/his assigned list of objects, the players must collaborate and exchange collected objects. The game is based on the barter technique. During exchanges, a player can lie saying that s/he has a given object and can also give a trapped object to another player.

We performed a first set of experimental tests of TROC. Two functions were simulated (wizard of oz technique): the voice recognition and the location of a player. We had one wizard per player. In addition, during this first set of tests, the players did not have to manipulate the physical cubes.

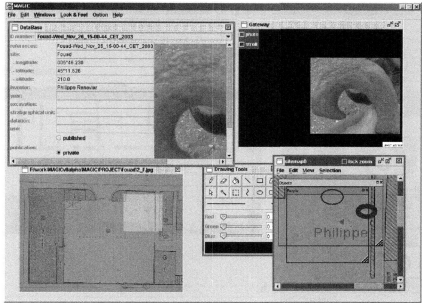

a)

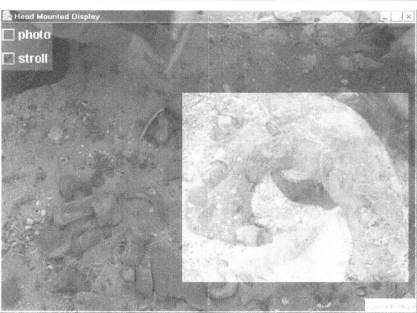

b)

Figure 2. MAGIC system (a) User interface on the pen computer (b) View displayed on the HMD

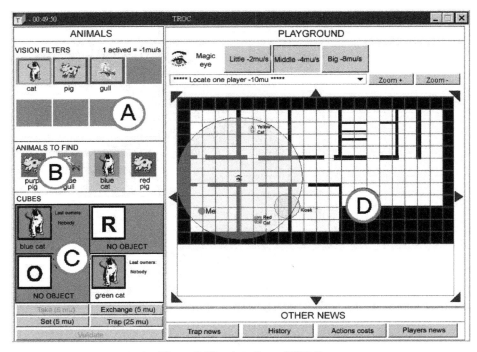

Figure 3. User interface of TROC

Eight volunteers all familiar with computers participated in the experiment. A first phase enables the players to get familiar with the rules of the game and the techniques. Then four experimental settings were studied. (1) without 3D sound (2) with 3D sound (3) in a game field without physical landmark, (a big empty room) (4) in a game field with physical landmarks, (with rooms and a corridor). Four players played the game twice in the two following experimental settings: first, without 3D sound and then with 3D sound in a field without physical landmark. The four other players also played the game twice in the two following experimental settings: first with 3D sound and then without 3D sound in a game field with physical landmarks. So each player played four games. For each game, the test was finished when a player collected all the objects assigned to her/him. After each game, interviews were conducted with the players.

The primary analysis of the collected data shows that 3D sounds facilitate the location of digital objects, sound being available before the object is visible. In addition, the players underlined the fact that the sound reinforces the link between the physical and digital worlds, by making digital objects more real. In addition, it has been observed that digital objects, the focus of the players, had a strong presence to the point that players forgot the physical obstacles. Players underlined the inconsistency of seeing an object through a through a wall and having to go inside the room to be able to pick it up. Although such a possibility was presented as a magical tool which allows one to see through the walls, it confirms the fact that consistency must be maintained while combining the physical and digital worlds. The participants also wanted to pick up objects by hand. In particular such behaviour has been observed when the objects were very close to the players and therefore very big. Moreover players had more difficulties to locate objects in a game field without physical landmarks. Indeed, they adopted an approach of blind searching, while with physical landmarks they first located the objects on the map and then went to pick them up.

5.   FUTURE WORK

The generic techniques, "gateway", "clickable reality" and "augmented field", define a reusable hardware and software platform. As ongoing work, we are pursuing two avenues.

First, we are currently reusing and extending the platform for new applications: we are developing a system that allows users to annotate physical locations with digital notes, which are then read/remove by other mobile users. The presented interaction techniques therefore constitute the first bricks of a toolkit for developing mobile collaborative mixed systems. Reusability of the code and independence of part of it with the hardware are guaranteed by the software architecture model that we applied for developing the platform [11].

Our second research avenue is experimental. Further experimental tests will be performed with the TROC game and the new applications developed with the platform. Our objective is to gain understanding of how the users perceive and interact within the combined physical/digital world. For example, we plan to study when the player selects interaction techniques in the physical world as opposed to interaction techniques in the digital world. To do so, functionally equivalent interaction techniques such as manipulation of physical cubes and direct manipulation on the pen computer are provided.

ACKNOWLEDGEMENTS

This work is supported by France Telecom R&D, under contract Houria N° AJC067CH. Special thanks to G. Serghiou for reviewing the paper.

REFERENCES

[1]   Ancona, M., Dodero, G., and Gianuzzi, V., *RAMSES: A Mobile Computing System for Field Archaeology*, in Proc. of 1st International Symposium on Handheld and Ubiquitious Computing HUC'99 (Karlsruhe, 27-29 September 1999), Lecture Notes in Computer

Science, Vol. 1707, Springer-Verlag, Berlin, 1999, pp. 222-233.

[2] Cheok, A., Fong, S., Goh, K., Yang, X., Liu, W., Farbiz, F., and Li, Y., *Human Pacman: A Mobile Entertainment System with Ubiquitous Computing and Tangible Interaction over a Wide Outdoor Area*, in Proc. of 5th International Symposium on Human-Computer Interaction with Mobile Devices and Services Mobile HCI'2003 (Udine, 8-11 September 2003), Lecture Notes in Computer Science, Vol. 2795, Springer-Verlag, Berlin, 2003, pp. 209-223

[3] Dubois, E., Nigay, L., Troccaz, J., Chavanon, O., and Carrat, L., *Classification Space for Augmented Surgery, an Augmented Reality Case Study*, in M. Rauterberg, M. Menozzi, J. Wesson (eds.), Proceedings of 9th IFIP TC 13 International Conference on Human-Computer Interaction INTERACT'2003 (Zurich, 1-5 September 2003), IOS Press, Amsterdam, 2003, pp. 353-359.

[4] Feiner, S., MacIntyre, B., Höllerer, T., Webster, A., *A Touring Machine: Prototyping 3D Mobile Augmented Reality Systems for Exploring the Urban Environment*, in Proc. of 1st International Symposium on Wearable Computers ISCW'97 (Cambridge, 13-14 October 1997), IEEE Computer Society Press, Los Alamitos, 1997, pp. 439-449, accessible at http://computer.org/conferen/proceed/8192/pdf/81920074.pdf

[5] Ishii, H. and Ullmer, B., *Tangible Bits: Towards Seamless Interfaces between People, Bits and Atoms*, in Proceedings of ACM Conference on Human Factors in Computing Systems CHI'97 (Atlanta, 22-27 March 1997), ACM Press, New York, 1997, pp. 234-241.

[6] Kangas, K. and Röning, J., *Using Code Mobility to Create Ubiquitous and Active Augmented Reality in Mobile Computing*, in Proceedings of International Conference on Mobile Computing and Networking Mobicom'99 (Seattle, 15-20 August 1999), ACM Press, New York, 1999, pp. 48-58.

[7] Nigay, L., Salembier, P., Marchand, T., Renevier, P., Pasqualetti, L., *Mobile and Collaborative Augmented Reality: A Scenario Based Design Approach*, in Paternò, F., (ed.), Proceedings of 3rd Workshop on Mobile Computing and HCI Mobile'2002 (Pisa, 18-20 September 2002), Lecture Notes in Computer Science, Vol. 2411, Springer-Verlag, Berlin, 2002, pp. 241-255.

[8] Norman, D., *The design of everyday things*, Basic Books, September 2002.

[9] Pyssyalo, T., Repo, T., Turunen, T., Lankila, T., and Röning, J., *CyPhone – Bringing Augmented Reality to Next Generation Mobile Phones*, in Proceedings of Designing Augmented Reality Environments DARE'2000 (Elsinore, 12-14 April 2000), ACM Press, New York, 2000, pp. 11-21.

[10] Rekimoto, J., *Navicam: A Magnifying Glass Approach to Augmented Reality*, Presence: Teleoperators and Virtual Environments, Vol. 6, No. 4, 1997, pp. 399-412.

[11] Renevier, P. and Nigay, L., *Mobile Collaborative Augmented Reality: the Augmented Stroll*, in Proceedings of 8th IFIP Working Conference on Engineering for Human Computer Interaction EHCI'01 (Toronto, 11-13 May 2001), Lecture Notes in Computer Science, Vol. 2411, Springer-Verlag, Berlin, 2001, pp. 315-334.

[12] Starner, T., Leibe, B., Singletary, B., and Pair, J., *MIND-WARPING: Towards Creating a Compelling Collaborative Augmented Reality Game*, in Proceedings of 5th ACM International Conference on Intelligent User Interfaces IUI'2000 (New Orleans, 9-12 January 2000), ACM Press, New York, 2000, pp. 256-259.

[13] Szalavári, Z., Schmalstieg, D., Fuhrmann, A., and Gervautz, M., *Studierstube An Environment for Collaboration in Augmented Reality*, Journal of the Virtual Reality Society "Virtual Reality: Research, Development and Application", Virtual Press Ltd., 1997.

[14] Thomas, B., Close, B., Donoghue, J., Squires, J., De Bondi, P., and Piekarski, W., *First Person Indoor/Outdoor Augmented Reality Application: ARQuake*, Personal and Ubiquitous Computing, Vol. 6, No. 1, 2002, pp. 75-86.

Chapter 26

THE CONTINUITY PROPERTY IN MIXED REALITY AND MULTIPLATFORM SYSTEMS: A COMPARATIVE STUDY

Murielle Florins[1], Daniela G. Trevisan[1,2], and Jean Vanderdonckt[1]

[1]*Université catholique de Louvain, Institut d'Administration et de Gestion,*
Place des Doyens, 1 - B-1348 Louvain-la-Neuve (Belgium)
E-mail: {florins, trevisan, vanderdonckt}@isys.ucl.ac.be
URL: http://www.isys.ucl.ac.be/bchi/members/{mfl, dtr, jva}
Tel.: +32 10 47 {83 91, 85.55, 85 25} – Fax: +32 10 47 83 24
[2]*Université catholique de Louvain, Faculté de sciences appliquées, Laboratoire TELE*
Place du Levant, 2 - B-1348 Louvain-la-Neuve (Belgium)
E-mail: trevisan@tele.ucl.ac.be

Abstract   Continuity as usability property has been used in mixed reality systems and in multiplatform systems. This paper compares the definitions that have been given to the concept in both fields. Continuity is then given in a consolidated definition.

Keywords: Augmented reality, Continuity, Mixed reality, Multiplatform systems.

1.   CONTINUITY IN THE LITERATURE

The concern about continuity as a usability property has appeared in two fields: Mixed Reality systems and Multiplatform systems.

Mixed Reality (MR) systems are systems that combine real and computer-based information. Milgram [12,13] defines the Reality-Virtuality continuum shown in Fig. 1. MR is the region between the real world and totally virtual environments. Augmented reality lies near the real world end of the continuum. In AR systems, the perception that predominates is the real world augmented by additional capabilities or information provided by the computer system. Vallino [18] gives a list of 7 application domains where the use of AR reality systems has been investigated: medical domain, entertainment, military training, engineering design, robotics/telerobotics, manufacturing & maintenance, and consumer design. Augmented virtuality is a

323

R. Jacob et al. (eds.), Computer-Aided Design of User Interfaces IV, 323–334.
© 2005 *Kluwer Academic Publishers. Printed in the Netherlands.*

term created by Milgram to identify systems which are mostly synthetic with some added real world sources such as texture mapping video onto virtual objects. Vallino [18] expects that this distinction will fade as the technology improves and the virtual elements in the scene become less distinguishable from the real ones. Therefore we can say that AR and AV are parts of the Mixed Reality systems and MR systems are any possible combination of real and virtual information. We use the terms "digital" and "virtual" indiscriminately to refer to a world that is not physical or real. We also consider that "real" and "physical" share the same meaning of "not digital or virtual".

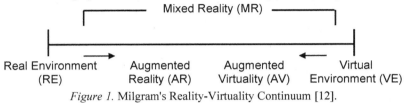

Figure 1. Milgram's Reality-Virtuality Continuum [12].

An example of Mixed Reality is the Transfiction system [10] (more details about this technology can be found in http://www.alterface.com) where extracted video images are analysed, in order to capture the users' movements. Afterwards, the video images are integrated into a virtual graphical scene, which reacts in an interactive manner to the behaviour of the filmed subject(s) (Fig.2).

Figure 2. Transfiction system, example of a Mixed Reality system [10].

Multiplatform systems, as an extension of the notion of multidevice systems proposed by [4], are systems whose versions are available from a range of platforms, where the platform is a specific combination of a hardware (the device) and a software (the operating system, the browser and the available graphical toolkits). Some application fields such as personal information management (e-mails, diary, address book, etc.), travel planning, real time information management (weather, stock exchange, news, etc.) or e-banking are particularly suitable for this kind of use [4].

In the last years continuous interaction has been the interest of works such as those related in [6,9,11,16,17,18]. As results of those studies we can see continuity as being particularly concerned with activity over a period of time. At a low level, this can involve real-time aspects of technologies such as gesture recognition. At a higher level, providing for continuity during a user's interaction with an application can be quite a challenge, as the context of use, environmental conditions and device platform may all change repeatedly. In this work we propose to investigate the definition of the continuity properties in the field of mixed reality and multiplatform systems. Are these definitions compatible or are we speaking of different concepts under the same term?

2.   CONTINUITY IN MIXED REALITY SYSTEMS

The interaction in MR systems is no longer based only on the exchange of discrete messages that could be considered as atomic actions. Instead, the input provided by the user and/or the outputs provided by the computing system are a continuous process of exchange of information at a relatively high resolution. As almost all tools used to interact with virtual world are separated from those used to interact with the real world it forces the user to switch between operation modes resulting in a discontinuous interaction. Another potential discontinuity can be found for different or not similar representations of the real data in the virtual world. In this way we define the continuity as a capability of the system to promote a smooth interaction scheme with the user during task accomplishment considering perceptual, cognitive and functional properties [17]. These properties will be presented in the next sections.

2.1   Augmentation in Mixed Reality Systems

The main goal of the MR system is to augment the user's cognition, perception and/or interaction. User's cognition can be augmented by providing additional virtual information into real world or by providing additional real information into virtual world.

User's perception can be augmented by providing all needed information for the user to perform his/her task in an adequate place or device. User's interaction can be augmented by providing similar mode of operation or interaction (e.g., use of tangible interfaces). These elements are responsible to guarantee the continuous interaction in the MR systems.

2.2 Continuity Properties in Mixed Reality Systems

Cognitive continuity is defined as an ability of the system to ensure that the user will correctly interpret perceived information and that the perceived information is correct with regards to the internal state of the system. In other words the system may provide similar virtual representation of the real data. Perceptual continuity is defined as an ability of the system to make all data involved in the user's task available in one perceptual environment in order to avoid changes in the user's focus.

According to the principle of interaction robustness mentioned in Gram [7] we have introduced the functional property to provide a complete analysis of continuous interaction. Functional continuity is defined as an adaptability level of the user to change or learn new modes of operation. It is related to the similarity level between real and virtual interaction modes. In Dubois [6] two ergonomic properties of augmented reality systems are discussed: continuity and compatibility.

At the perceptual level, the perceptual compatibility extends the observability property [7] to the case where N concepts have to be observed at the same time. The factors influencing perceptual compatibility are the geographical dispersion of concepts within the environment and the human senses necessary to perceive those concepts. At the cognitive level, the cognitive compatibility extends the honesty property [7] to the case where N concepts have to be observed at the same time. Cognitive compatibility is achieved when the user is able to interpret correctly the N concepts. Table 1 summarises these ergonomic properties when applied for an Augmented Reality system.

Table 1. Ergonomic properties of observability, honesty, compatibility and continuity in Augmented Reality systems [6].

Perceptual Level	Observability	Perceptual Compatibility	Perceptual Continuity
Cognitive Level	Honesty	Cognitive Compatibility	Cognitive Continuity
	1 concept 1 representation	N concepts, 1 representation each	1 concept, N representations

3.   NORMAN'S THEORY AND CONTINUOUS IN-TERACTION

Designing for continuous interaction requires designers to consider the way in which human users can perceive and evaluate an artefact's observable behaviour, in order to make inferences about its state and plan and execute their own continuous behaviour [9]. By exploring the Theory of Action [14], it is possible to identify two main levels in the execution cycle of a task: *execution* and *evaluation* flows (Fig. 3). The execution level consists of how the user will accomplish the task corresponding to the functional continuity property. The evaluation level consists of three phases: *user's perception*, *interpretation* and *evaluation*. The perception corresponds to how the user perceives the environment state. The interpretation level consists of how much cognitive effort the user needs to understand the system state corresponding to the cognitive continuity property. The last phase corresponds to the evaluation of the system state by the user with respect to the goals.

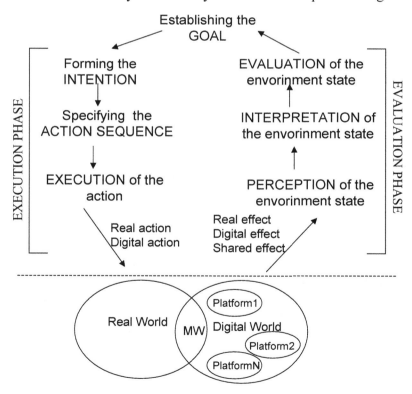

Figure 3. The Norman's action theory applied for Mixed Reality and Multiplatform systems.

During the execution phase the user can interact with a physical object (Real Action) or with a digital object (Digital Action). As results of these actions during the evaluation phase we can have (Fig.3):
- A real effect if the action (real or digital) has affected the real world
- A digital effect if the action (real or digital) has affected the digital world
- A shared effect if the action (real or digital) has affected both worlds.

The shared effect is rarer to produce and an example of that can be found in systems such as remote environment visualization and manipulation for monitoring and exploration in distant or hazardous locations. For instance in [1] they have developed an augmented virtual world that contains real world images as object textures that are created in an automatic way, these are called *Reality Portals*. Using Reality Portals with the robotic system, a human supervisor can control a remote robot assistant by issuing commands using the virtual environment as a medium. The action-effect tuples can be applied for both paradigms (e.g., Mixed Reality and Multiplatform).

4.   THE CONTINUITY PROPERTY IN MULTIPLATFORM SYSTEMS

Denis and Karsenty [4] consider continuity of multiplatform systems at two levels: knowledge continuity and task continuity:
1. Knowledge continuity is based on "the retrieval and adaptation of knowledge constructed from the use of other devices"
2. Task continuity is based on "the memory of the last operations performed with the service, independently from the device used, and the belief that this memory is shared by the system". Task continuity requires that the user recover the state of data and the context of the activity.

Task continuity goes far beyond our study field and beyond the notion of functional continuity as defined by the authors in [17]. For this reason, we will now focus on the other dimension: *knowledge continuity*.

In [4], one identifies three requirements for knowledge continuity:
1. Access to the same functions available on each device
2. Access to the same data available on each device
3. Same presentation of the service on each device

Generally, due to constraints on the different platforms, the whole set of tasks and concepts are not available in each system version. Starting from that consideration, [4] identifies three kinds of relationships between system versions: redundant, when all the versions give access to the same tasks and concepts, exclusive, when each version gives access to different tasks and concepts and complementary, when the versions have a zone of shared tasks and concepts, but at least one version gives access to tasks or concepts unavailable in the other versions. Problems identified at that level obviously belong to the execution phase in the Norman's model and this form of continuity is thus closely related to the functional continuity. Beside the problems of task availability on the different versions, Denis and Karsenty [4] also mention procedural discontinuity: i.e. discontinuity when the same high-level task is present on each system version, but the function is not accomplished in the same way (different subtasks or actions required on the different platforms). At the presentation level they report two kinds of usability problems:

1. Problems caused by graphical differences:
- Differences in spatial organization of information can cause users to fail to locate an object quickly
- Differences in the shape of an interface object can cause users to fail to associate the object with its function
2. Problems caused by terminological differences: when a graphical object is labeled inconsistently between two versions of the system, the user must follow a reasoning process to establish whether the object has the same function in both versions.

Continuity issues identified at the presentation level belong respectively to the perception stage (perceptive screen display) and to the interpretation stage (interpretation of the terminological and graphical differences). In summary, there are also three forms of continuity in multiplatform systems: perceptual continuity, cognitive continuity, and functional continuity.

Perceptual continuity is an extension of the observability property to the case where an *interaction space* has to be observed in different system versions. An Interaction Space (IS) is assumed to be the complete presentation environment required for carrying out a particular interactive task. A given IS could not be observable in the same way in different system versions. It entails also the concepts of *perceptive surfaces* discussed in [8]: the adequacy of a surface for action and/or observation depends on its attributes (such as size, weight and material) and properties (e.g., fluidity, flexibility, opacity, transparency, etc.). For instance the quantity of observable elements directly in an interaction space can be reduced or augmented in function of screen size constraints. Fig.4 illustrates this on the prototype of a health-care information system where the PDA version only display a limited view of the desktop version IS.

Cognitive continuity is an extension of the honesty property to the case where N representations of the same concept have to be observed in different system versions. Fig. 4 shows how the same concept (the patient's personal effects) can be represented by a textual label (on the desktop version) or by an icon (on the PDA version).

Functional continuity depends on the differences between the functionalities available on each system version and between the low-level user's actions required in order to achieve those functionalities.

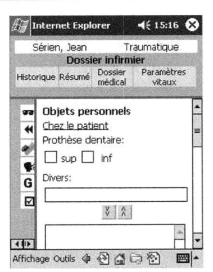

Figure 4. Example of an interaction space to be rendered into other surfaces of interactions.

5. THE CONTINUITY PROPERTY: COMPARISON

The concepts of continuity and potential sources of discontinuities are quite different in mixed reality systems and in multiplatform systems. These aspects are summarised in Table 2.

Table 2. Comparative table between continuity concepts in Mixed Reality systems and Multiplatform systems.

	Mixed Reality Systems	Multiplatform Systems
Continuity	Based on interaction modes and similar representations of real and digital information	Similar functionalities, similar operation procedures, similar data representation and same data set
Source of potential discontinuities	Different interfaces to interact with different worlds (real and digital)	Variations of interfaces caused by platform constraints

On the other hand both share the same three levels distribution following the Norman's action theory:

- Perceptual continuity (perception phase in Norman's theory).
- Cognitive continuity (interpretation phase in Norman's theory).
- Functional continuity (execution phase in Norman's theory).

The definitions of perceptual continuity and cognitive continuity are similar in both paradigms:

- Cognitive continuity corresponds to the honesty of multiple representations of a single concept.
- Perceptual continuity corresponds to the observability of a determined interaction space.

However, the relation between concept and concept representation is quite different in mixed reality systems and multiplatform systems.

In an AR system, "1 concept, N representations" means: there are 2 or more objects (typically: one real object and one software object) that represent the same concept and that have both to be perceived at the same time (during the same interactive task) by the user during a given interactive use of the system. An example in the CASPER system [5] is the needle concept, materialised at the same time by a real object (the surgical needle) and a software object (two crosses on a screen that represent the needle axis and the position of its extremity). This should not be confused with the case where one single concept has multiple representations within the same system version but that the different representations do not have to be perceived at the same time (because they do not participate in the same interactive task). It this case, we will rather use the term coherence, defined by Bastien and Scapin [2,3] as "the way interface design choices (codes, naming, formats, procedures, etc.) are maintained in similar contexts".

On the other side, in a multiplatform system, the phrase "1 concept, N representations" will mean: there are 2 or more objects (always software objects) that have to be recognised by the user as representing the same concept during different interactive uses of different system versions. This leads us to consider that the perceptual continuity and cognitive continuity properties in the multiplatform field are different from those properties defined in MR field.

Do we have to establish the same kind of distinction at the functional level? In MR systems, functional continuity is achieved when "operation modes between workspaces are similar", i.e. when the user who was trained in a task is able to reuse this knowledge in the mixed reality system. Thus, task continuity refers to the comparison between the operation mode in the real world and in the mixed reality. In multiplatform systems, there are two criteria influencing the functional continuity:

- The availability of the function on different system versions.
- The operation procedures (how the function is realised in terms of tasks and sub-tasks sequences). Those distinctions are summarised in Table 3.

Table 3. Interpretation of continuity properties for Mixed Reality and Multiplatform systems.

Continuity properties	Mixed Reality Systems	Multiplatform Systems
Cognitive	Similar digital representation (behavioural and graphical) of the real information	Similar data set and similar data representation (graphical, terminological, spatial)
Perceptual	Observable objects in the same perceptive environment	Same distribution of objects/functions between inter-action spaces
Functional	Similar interaction modes	Similar functionality and similar sequence of operations

6.   CONCLUSION

In conclusion, continuity is a notion that:

- Has to be considered at different levels in the Norman's action theory, namely the functional, perceptual and cognitive levels
- Has to be assessed between two ore more comparison elements that can be of different nature (tasks or concepts and their representation)
- The compared elements can be inserted in different entities. Possible entities are the real world, an information system or a given version of an information system.

Continuity can be described at the same three abstraction levels in mixed reality systems and multiplatform systems. On the other side, the comparison elements are quite distinct and they belong to distinct entities. The major difference between continuity for mixed reality system and for multiplat-form UIs is that the former works on digital and real worlds with only one interactive system, while the last works only on the digital world, but with N variations of the interactive system or N interactive systems.

ACKNOWLEDGMENTS

We gratefully acknowledge the support of the Salamandre Project, funded by the "Initiatives III" research program of the Ministry of Walloon Region, DGTRE (http://www.isys.ucl.ac.be/bchi/research/salamandre.htm).

REFERENCES

[1] Akesson, K.P. and Simsarian, K., *Reality Portals,* in Proceedings of the ACM Sympo-sium on Virtual Reality Software and Technology VRST'99 (London, 20-22 December 1999), ACM Press, New York, 1999, pp. 11-18.

[2] Bastien, C., *Validation de Critères Ergonomiques pour l'évaluation d'interface Utilisa-teurs*, Research report No. 1427, INRIA, Rocquencourt, May 1991.

[3] Bastien, C. and Scapin, D., *Evaluating a User Interface With Ergonomic Criteria*, Re-search report No. 2326, INRIA, Rocquencourt, 1994.

[4] Denis, C. and Karsenty, L., *Inter-usability of Multi-device Systems: A Conceptual Framework*, in A. Seffah and H. Javahery (eds.), Multiple User Interfaces: Engineering and Application Framework, John Wiley and Sons, New Jersey, 2003.

[5] Dubois, E., *Chirurgie Augmentée: un Cas de Réalité Augmentée, Conception et Réalisa-tion Centrée sur l'Utilisateur*, Ph.D. thesis, University Joseph Fourier, Grenoble, July 2001.

[6] Dubois, E., Nigay, L., and Troccaz, J., *Assessing Continuity and Compatibility in Aug-mented Reality Systems*, International Journal on Universal Access in the Information Society, Special issue on Continuous Interaction in Future Computing Systems, Vol. 1, No. 4, 2002, pp.263-273.

[7] Gram, C. and Cockton, G. (eds.), *Design Principles for Interactive Software*, Chapman & Hall, London, 1996.

[8] Lachenal, C. and Coutaz, J., *A Reference Framework for Multi-Surface Interaction*, in Proceedings of 10th International Conference on Human-Computer Interaction HCI In-ternational'2003 (Crete, 22-27 June 2003), Lawrence Erlbaum Associates, Mahwah, 2003.

[9] May, J., Buehner, M.J., and Duke, D., *Continuity in Cognition*, International Journal of Universal Access in the Information Society, Vol. 1, No. 4, 2002, pp. 252-262.

[10] Marichal, X., Macq, B., Douxchamps, D., Umeda, T., and Art.live consortium, *Real-Time Segmentation of Video Objects for Mixed-Reality Interactive Applications*, in Pro-ceedings of International Conference on Visual Communication and Image Processing VCIP'2003 (Lugano, July 2003).

[11] Massink, M. and Faconti, G., *A Reference Framework for Continuous Interaction*, Inter-national Journal of Universal Access in the Information Society, Vol. 1, No. 4, 2002, pp. 237-251.

[12] Milgram, P. and Kishino, F., *A Taxonomy of Mixed Reality Visual Displays*, IEICE Transactions on Information Systems E77-D, Vol. 12, 1994, pp. 1321-1329.

[13] Milgram, P., Takemura, H., Utsumi, A., and Kishino, F., *Augmented Reality: A Class of Displays on the Reality-Virtuality Continuum*, in H. Das (ed.), SPIE Proceedings on Telemanipulator and Telepresence Technologies, SPIE Vol. 2351, 1994, pp. 282-292, accessible at http://vered.rose.utoronto.ca/people/paul_dir/SPIE94/SPIE94.full.html

[14] Norman, D.A. and Draper, S.W. (eds.), *User Centered System Design: New Perspectives on Human-Computer Interaction*, Lawrence Erlbaum Associates, Hillsdale, 1986.

[15] Rogers, Y., Scaife, M., Gabrielli, S., Smith, H., and Harris, E., *A conceptual framework for mixed reality environments: Designing novel learning activities for young children*, Presence, Vol. 11, No. 6, 2002, pp. 677-686.

[16] TACIT project, accessible at http://kazan.cnuce.cnr.it/TACIT/

[17] Trevisan, D., Vanderdonckt, J., and Macq, B., *Continuity as a Usability Property*, in Jacko, J., Stephanidis, C. (eds.), Proc. of 10th Int. Conf. on Human-Computer Interaction HCI International'2003 (Heraklion, 22-27 June 2003), Vol. 1, Lawrence Erlbaum Associates, Mahwah, 2003, pp. 1268-1272.

[18] Trevisan, D., Vanderdonckt, J., and Macq, B., *Analyzing Interaction in Augmented Reality Systems*, in G. Pingali, R. Jain (eds.), Proceedings of ACM Multimedia'2002 International Workshop on Immersive Telepresence ITP'2002 (Juan Les Pins, 6 December 2002), ACM Press, New York, 2002, pp. 56-59.

[19] Vallino J., *Augmented Reality Page*, Rochester Institute of Technology, Department of Software Engineering, accessible at http://www.se.rit.edu/~jrv/research/ar /index.html

Chapter 27

BUILDING RICH USER INTERFACES FOR DIGITAL TALKING BOOKS

Luís Carriço, Carlos Duarte, Rui Lopes, Miguel Rodrigues, and Nuno Guimarães
Human-Computer Interaction and Multimedia Group, LaSIGE, Department of Informatics, C5, Piso 1, Faculty of Sciences, University of Lisbon, Campo Grande, 1749-016 Lisbon (Portugal)
E-mail: {lmc,cd,rlopes,mrod,nmg}@di.fc.ul.pt
Tel.: +351-21-{7500247 ext. 26329, 7500124} – Fax: +351-21-7500084

Abstract   This paper presents a framework for the automatic production of Digital Talking Books (DTB). The production process converts existing audio tapes and OCR-based digitalisation of text books into full-featured, multi- synchronised, multimodal digital books. The framework deals with the standardisation processes, media enrichment and User Interface definition. The latter is based on abstract, yet DTB specific, pattern-based UI specifications. This allows the definition of various forms of interaction and presentation, required by the diversity and constraints of targets users (e.g. visually impaired persons) and situations of use (e.g., learning). Balancing the focus of production between personalised, situation-based UI and adaptive ones is also considered. The article also summarises some usability tests on generated DTBs that contributed to the refinement of the framework.

Keywords: Accessibility, Model-based tools, User diversity, UI generation.

1.   INTRODUCTION

Audiotapes have served as an important medium, and sometimes the only alternative, for print-disabled reader's access to books. In several public libraries, in particular in the Portuguese National Library, a long time effort was made in speech recording of a large amount of printed material. However, the limitations of this analogue approach, even when compared with

R. Jacob et al. (eds.), Computer-Aided Design of User Interfaces IV, 335–348.

their printed counterparts are noteworthy (e.g., difficulties in indexing, annotation and cross-referencing). Moreover, for particular disabilities and situations of use the visual complement is also required.

Digital Talking Books (DTBs) are a logical answer. Involving several groups related with visually impaired people, DTB work identifies requirements, directions and recently a standard based on emerging Web technology [2,9]. Nevertheless, the standard, wisely, does not intentionally propose specific solutions for interaction. In fact, the required combination of synchronisation, structural navigation and annotations management, using visual, audio, speech and standard interaction devices, poses ambiguity and cognitive problems that must be dealt with at the UI design level [5,12,27]. These issues are further stressed by the diversity of targeted users, their particular disabilities and perspectives. It is essential to explore and evaluate distinct UIs for the same book, with different multimodal combinations, eventually enriched with new media contents not present in the original book. Balancing DTBs modes and media, for example, can be explored to overcome the cognitive limitations of human perception and attention [17].

This paper describes DiTaBBu (Digital Talking Books Builder), a framework for the production of DTBs based on media indexing, speech alignment and multimodal interaction elements. The work has been carried out in the context of the IPSOM project, joining the Portuguese National Library (owner and publisher of analogue talking books), speech processing technology experts (providing tools for speech recognition and speech alignment) and multimedia interaction designers and engineers. The framework balances its requirements between: (1) the existence of large amounts of recorded material; (2) the flexibility and simplicity needed for the generation of UIs; (3) the DTB recommendations and standards; and (4) the ability to integrate, explore and adjust multimedia units in the production process. At its current status, the framework already builds on a set of results from usability evaluation studies over produced DTDs, which consolidated and refined several decisions on the execution platform and particularly on the UI specification.

In the following section this article presents the requirements imposed on the production framework by: the particular project needs; the related standards and recommendations; and the results of evaluation tests. Design decisions are also referred. Next, the architecture of the DTBs generated by DiTaBBu framework is presented. The following section describes the frameworks itself, covering the book's content organisation and the modular UI generation. Afterwards, some related work is discussed. The paper ends drawing conclusions and delineating future work.

2. REQUIREMENTS AND DESIGN OPTIONS

The construction of the DiTaBBu framework is the result of a set of requirements and design decisions that evolved throughout the project.

2.1 Project Needs

The Portuguese National Library (BN) provides services for visually impaired persons. It possesses a large amount of analogue spoken books, recorded by volunteers and stored in analogue audio tapes. At the same time the BN is also committed to build a digital version of books – actually scanned books within a XML/HTML envelope. Although both results are available, a need for its integration, along with the introduction of DTB general functionalities, was clearly felt, particularly by the visually impaired community. Two basic problems were raised at this level:

- The huge amount of existing books, audio tapes and digital copies – requiring an automated form to produce the integrated multimodal books.
- The poor quality of the audio tapes – making it very difficult to automatically generate computable digital audio versions.

The first issue should, of course, consider mechanisms for easy and reusable specifications of books' UIs. Those should adapt to different book contents and cope with various types of users and use settings.

The latter problem was solved by recording a clean audio version of some books, or using existing digital forms. The initial pilot corpus was the "O Senhor Ventura" (a novel by Miguel Torga), read by a professional reader in a sound proof booth. Other digital versions were later used [35]. For the moment, then, the automation process departs from a digital (and computable) version of the audio and from the existing scanned text. Refinement of the speech alignment component is currently under work, in order to depart from the original analogue tapes.

2.2 DTB Recommendations and Standards

The work around DTBs has recently resulted in a standard specification [2]. Throughout the process a list of features and functions was identified [28]:

- Support basic navigation (advancing one character, word, line, sentence, paragraph or page at a time, and jumping to specific segments).
- Fast forward and reverse, reading at variable speeds.
- Navigation through tables or control files (allowing the user to obtain an overview of the material in the book).
- Reading notes, cross-reference access, index navigation, bookmarks,

highlighting, taking excerpts, searching, and other capabilities.

All these requirements are fully considered in the generated DTBs, except for the variable speed reading and the thinner (character and sometimes word based) basic navigation support. For the first one, a complete speech model must be available in order to maintain low voice distortion. An alternative, currently under evaluation, is the reduction or extension of sentence separation (silence, or breathing times), combined with small speed changes. The implementation of the second feature strongly depends on the ability to isolate character and word sounds from the continuous speech recording. An alternative is the introduction of speech synthesis. Here, cognition issues are raised [18], which should still be a focus of further evaluation studies. Currently the production framework allows the definition of DTBs minimum synchronisation unit, from word up, that determines the basic navigation and playback granularity.

Another result from the DTBs specification process is a categorisation of DTBs [9], according to the functionalities that could be made available to the user under different scenarios:

- Full audio with title element only – allows sequential playback and is particularly useful for small devices and mobile settings.
- Full audio with navigation control – adds direct access through structural items (e.g., table of contents).
- Full audio with navigation control and partial text – adds textual search on specific components.
- Full audio and full text – all features available and usually requires fix desktop settings with sophisticated resources.
- Full text and some audio – allows listening to some textual components (e.g., pronunciation aids).
- Text and no audio – structured text, allowing Braille production.

On this multifaceted perspective of a DTB, the same book "edition", and to some extent the same book (structure and content), could be presented and interacted in different ways, using different devices [29] and different media and mode combinations. As a direct consequence, the DTB production mechanism or the DTB execution platform or both should build on an architecture that promotes a clear separation between the books' contents, including the logical and semantic structure (e.g., media correspondence) and the books' user interface (UI). This will reinforce coherence between the several usage settings of the same book, facilitating the maintenance and the specification of UI and navigation.

The DiTaBBu framework enforces this architectural separation and allows the generation of all these categories including the most complex DTB format – full audio and full text.

Finally, the proposed standard [2] defines a model of DTBs around a set

XML-based Document Type Definitions. A basic architecture is also proposed identifying the modules (files) that should be present (Navigation files, Media files, Synchronisation files). Presentation specifics are handled with style sheets (CSS or XSL) and for synchronisation purposes, SMIL 2.0 is recommended. The proposed DTB architecture enables different presentation and interaction designs, and the choice of web-based technology ensures the required wide dissemination.

However, in the final representation, content and presentation are dispersed and intermixed in several modules. For example, for the book's content, the media correspondence is defined in the Synchronisation file, where the presentation sequence and timings are also established. On the other hand, for navigation elements, the media correspondence (e.g., table of contents text and speech) is specified in the Navigation file, whereas the time-related presentation is in the Synchronisation module. This DTB proposed architecture, although coping with several configurations for the same book (a DTB for each configuration), hardly embraces the intrinsic correspondence among them. It can (as a standard) be used as a final format for DTBs, but a clearer separation of content and UI is required, either on DTB production frameworks or on DTBs architectures that provide an enhanced run-time flexibility or even adaptability [13]. Furthermore, other final DTB formats should also be made available, that, for example run on off-the-shelf browsers and common devices. The DITaBBu framework can produce different arrangements and different formats for final DTBs.

2.3 Impact of DTB's Evaluation Results

A set of usability studies on several UIs variants were done. The variants, generated by the first versions of the DiTaBBu framework, departed from the same book ("O Senhor Ventura"). Different synchronisation units and different visual and audio marks for the synchronisation of navigation anchors, playback and annotation were used, as well as different forms of interaction (pure voice-based, mouse, keyboard and combined). Wizard of Oz tests were conducted to solve the language related problems of speech recognition software.

In terms of the DiTABBu framework the impact of the usability tests was essentially felt in the identification and characterisation of the UI specification language that enables DiTaBBu to generate UI variants for the DTDs. In accordance with the results, the components controlling the interface generation were classified into several main classes, each with a different focus, covering presentation and interaction aspects, for the main book content, as well as for annotations, navigation structures, enriching media, etc. Particular relevant results where obtained for the synchronisation facet. For example, on DTBs with multiple media presentations, users require contextual information (such as containing sentence, paragraph or section) when navigation or continuous presentation occurs. Furthermore, evaluation results point to the need for different temporal and spatial based contextual units (e.g., the further the navigation "jump" the bigger the required context). The detailed test results can be seen elsewhere [5,12].

3.   DTB ARCHITECTURE AND PLATFORM

In view of the above-mentioned recommendations, the generated DTBs must cope with a diversity of devices and modality combinations, which address the specific characteristics of the books' content, the situation of use and the users. Thus a DTB architecture design that handles a flexible execution is a major prerequisite. Additionally, an easy form of dissemination and integration, with emerging digital publication technologies, is not only a requirement imposed by the source material provider (BN), but for the main target users in general.

A Web-based technology approach was adopted, based on DTB and XML related recommendations, but several final DTB formats and organisations are possible. The general architecture for a generated DTB includes:

- An XML-based content specification, embracing text and other media (in specific formats), media anchoring points, media correspondence (to text or between media) and structure. No UI presentation or synchronisation issues are considered at this level.
- A set of XSLT-based specifications enabling the creation of UIs for the content.
- The UI, including presentation and specific interaction objects when required. Presentation could follow several formats and organisations, from plain SMIL (plus CSS), to versions compliant with the DTB standard architecture.

The introduction of the XSLT level permits to build the several UIs, using alternative DTB formats and still maintaining the coherence with the books' content. On the other hand, it also allows balancing the generation of the UI, between the production framework and the execution platform itself (Fig. 1 shows an example with a DTB using an HTML+TIME format). If the execution platform is able to process XSLT, a book following the above three-layer organisation could be directly used. If performance is an issue or the execution platform does not support it, the DiTaBBu framework could generate the final DTB configurations (e.g., a DTB fully compliant with the standard or a simpler SMIL version, in any DTB category).

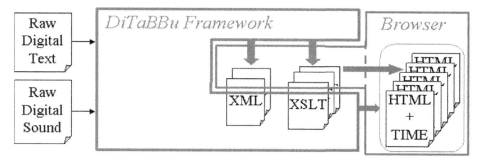

Figure 1. Balancing performance and run-time flexibility.

As a basic, yet powerful, execution platform, Internet Explorer 6, was adopted. This choice enabled the use of HTML+TIME (and CSS), as a representative of a SMIL 2.0 profile, and Microsoft's variant of VoiceML, for voice interaction. Both architectural organisations are supported, since the browser processes XSLT. In the simplest form, the digital book is a (set of) HTML+TIME, CSS and media specific files. An initial version of the generated DTBs used HTIMEL [7], instead of HTML+TIME. Both languages are still available as a result of the DTB production process. However, only HTML+TIME is currently maintained. For voice interaction, off-the-shelf products, recognizing Portuguese language, were initially used with very bad performance results. The Microsoft's implementation of VoiceML, provided better results, but using English as interaction language. Currently, Portuguese speech recognition software, developed within the IPSOM project's teams, is being integrated.

4.   THE FRAMEWORK

The DiTaBBu framework generates DTBs through an automatic production process, configured by a set of specification files that allow the required flexibility. Fig. 1 presents the framework's inputs and outputs. Internally the framework can be decomposed into two main phases: content organisation and UI-generation.

4.1   The Content Organisation Phase

The content organisation phase is represented in Fig. 2. The first step is to determine the time of the written words on the recorded speech (alignment). The book's original text is initially expanded (e.g., abbreviations and numerals are replaced by their complete textual representation) and stripped from punctuation signs. This is feed in the alignment module that generates a table with the audio stream timings for each of the spoken words. Besides the words, this process also identifies the silences (reader's pauses) present in the narration - details on the alignment process can be found elsewhere [34]. From the alignment table, the expanded text (text as spoken) and taking again the digital copies of the source text (raw digital text), two XML tagged descriptions are generated. In the first one, derived from the source text, an ID is assigned to every word and the correlation between written and "as spoken text" is maintained whenever is needed (e.g. <word id="10" sounds="one">I</word>). The second file contains the words' timing (e.g. <anchor id="10" unit="word" begin="13"/>) and silences and represents the anchors into the media file (e.g. an "mp3" file with the book's narration).

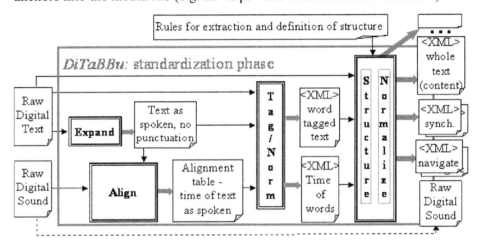

Figure 2. DiTaBBu: the content organisation phase

The final step on the content organisation phase is actually twofold: the book structure is included in the XML-based content file and the remainder DTBs standard files are generated. In the first process a set of rules in terms of regular expressions are used to extract the structure (e.g., paragraphs, sections) from the digital source text. Alternatively and additionally specific structure definitions can be introduced. The second process provides the main DTB file, the navigation files (extracting table of contents, etc.) and the connection between different media (referred as synchronisation). Synchronisation units for syntactic constructs and for spoken divisions (breathing and pauses) are added, enabling an easier (tagged based) production of multi unit DTBs [12].

This phase result is mostly compliant with the ANSI/NISO recommendations. Exceptions are the inexistence of UI elements, including the SMIL-based synchronisation specification defined on the standard. Instead, the synchronisation file generated in this phase of DiTaBBu describes simple media correspondence (through common id tags or meta-information).

4.2   The UI Generation Phase

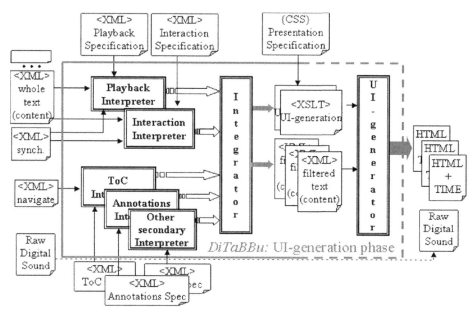

Figure 3. DiTaBBu: UI generation phase.

The UI-generation phase is represented in Fig 3. In the initial steps of this phase the framework presents a set of interpreter modules. Each module receives as input: a set of XML-based files with content; and a specification file, describing the patterns and rules to be applied to that content. Those specification files follow XML-based dialects dependent on the module. Internally the module also uses XSLT code and XSLT templates that are selected and adjusted according to the specification, in order to generate the module's output (XML + XSLT files). Cocoon [23] is used in the transformation process. Two groups of interpreters can be identified relating to primary and secondary material. The primary material modules are the playback and interaction interpreters. Basically they deal with the main book content, not considering footnotes, margin notes and navigation auxiliaries (i.e., indexes, tables of content). The respective dialects handle the visual and audio logical markup and their synchronisation. For example:

- <showsync delay="2s" sunit="silence"/> means that playback will show visual synchronisation marks (the visual effect is specified later in the CSS) delayed by 2 seconds and using the words between reading silences as a unit - the whole unit is marked (e.g., underlined) as narration evolves.
- <onsearch sunit="word, paragraph" basedon="paragraph, section" />

means that in result of a search, the narration (sound) should start on the word found or on the beginning of the paragraph containing that word depending on how distant (paragraph of section) from the current reading position the searched text is (see impact of evaluation results).

The secondary modules handle auxiliary navigation structures, user annotations, side margin notes, etc. Apart from the specificity of their dialects (e.g., <show summary> on annotations), the synchronisation rules with the primary content are also specifiable. The remainder steps of the UI generation phase provide the integration and filtering of the results of the interpretation modules and the (optional) generation of the final presentation. The former generates a set of XSLT and XML content files that can be also interpreted by the execution platform.

5.   RELATED WORK

Multimodal systems have a high degree of complexity. Even if considering only the integration of speech into a point and click interface, there are a great number of problems to be considered [30]. Nevertheless, research has indicates that speech input is advantageous in several circumstances [30], and identified the task characteristics that better suit speech input [8,37]. Those tasks are the ones where the user has to issue brief commands using a small vocabulary, which are approximate to the interaction characteristics of a DTB. However, research on the effectiveness of speech as an input mode has not been conclusive [26,39]. As such, there is still need to experiment systems with different configurations of voice and other mode commands. DiTaBBu platform offers the advantage of flexibility in the creation of DTBs with different presentation and interaction characteristics. That will allow us to try out different ways to convey document structure and assist navigation, such as the use of 3D audio [19], auditory icons [3,16], multiple speakers and sound effects [21], etc.

Referring to DTB formats and architectures, the use of the DTB standard has recently gained momentum. Several software [11,20,41] and hardware [40] players were made available. However, other web-based solutions should be envisaged, if a wider dissemination and ease of evolution is pursued. For example, formats fully compatible with common Web browsers, like the one proposed in this work, potentially executable in general purpose mobile devices and adopting the mentioned flexible architecture should definitely be available.

Our platform of DTBs and its UI generation shares some of the characteristics of model-based UI development environments, namely, the infrastructures needed for the automation of tasks related with the design and implementation of UI processes [36], and the higher level of abstraction in the description of the interface [33,38,43]. For example, model-based approaches were adopted to handle flexible generation of UIs for different users and devices [31]. There are several model-based projects addressing the issue of creating UIs for multiple devices [1,14,24] or to adapt to different devices [4]. This, in fact, is a field where the transition to the commercial software world has not yet occurred, in part because of the abstraction level used in the specification of the models, which contradicts adopted user interface design techniques. However, in the case of DTB production, with the particularities of the domain, there is not such a great emphasis on abstraction. The generation process can, thus, be more easily adopted. Besides, the common notion of "book collection" can definitely compel to reuse, a characteristic reinforced by the automation process.

Still related to model-based UI development is the use of several specifications that are conceptually similar to the models employed in those environments: application model, task model, dialogue model and presentation model. Future developments, which target the construction of an intelligent interface for the DTBs, will see the inclusion of new specifications to allow an adaptation to the reader and the reading environment. This is similar to the introduction of user and environment models presented by some model-based frameworks [15,25,32,38].

6. CONCLUSION AND FUTURE WORK

This paper presented DiTaBBu, a framework for the production of DTBs. We have described the requirements and design options taken in view of those requirements and of the usability tests already performed on generated DTBs. Currently, the produced DTBs provide most of the functionalities intended in the standards literature, including audio and text synchronisation, annotations, navigation through mouse and keyboard interaction and through voice commands.

The platform itself was described. Its architecture based on modules that derived from DTB specific concepts, enables the required flexibility for the creation of multiple UI for DTBs, maintaining the automatic generation premise. The fact that those modules are rule based and template-supported stresses that flexibility.

As ongoing work, we are integrating tools for an higher level of specification for the modules specification files. In line of hypermedia related works [6,22] its being defined an UML description of those specification dialects, that in turn will generate the XML specifications. Some work has also started in the integration of images as secondary book material, including speech based description of such images. The enrichment book process already present in the framework will handle explicit and semi-automatic inclusion of other multimedia related contents in the produced DTBs.

REFERENCES

[1] Ali, M.F. and Pérez-Quiñones, M.A., *Using Task Models to Generate Multi-Platform User Interfaces While Ensuring Usability*, in Proceedings of ACM International Conference on Human Factors in Computing Systems CHI'2002 (Minneapolis, 20-25 April 2002), Extended Abstracts, ACM Press, New York, 2002, pp. 670-671.

[2] ANSI/NISO, *Specifications for the Digital Talking Book*, ANSI/NISO Z39.86-2002, Use and Maintenance, 2002, accessible at http://www.loc.gov/nls/z3986/v100/index.html.

[3] Blattner, M.M., Sumikawa, D.A., and Greenberg, R.M., *Earcons and Icons: Their Structure and Common Design Principles*, Human-Computer Interaction, Vol. 4, 1989, pp. 11-44.

[4] Calvary, G., Coutaz, J., and Thevenin, D., *A Unifying Reference Framework for the Development of Plastic User Interfaces*, in Proceedings of 8th IFIP Working Conference on Engineering for Human Computer Interaction EHCI'01 (Toronto, 11-13 May 2001), Lecture Notes in Computer Science, Vol. 2411, Springer-Verlag, Berlin, 2001, pp. 173-192.

[5] Carriço, L., Guimarães N., Duarte, C., Chambel, T. and Simões, H., *Spoken Books: Multimodal Interaction and Information Repurposing*, in Jacko, J., Stephanidis, C. (eds.), Proc. of 10th Int. Conf. on Human-Computer Interaction HCI International'2003 (Heraklion, 22-27 June 2003), Vol. 1, Lawrence Erlbaum Associates, Mahwah, 2003.

[6] Carriço, L., Lopes, R., Rodrigues, M., Dias, A., and Antunes, P., *Making XML from Hypermedia Models*, in Proceedings of the IADIS International WWW/Internet Conference, ICWI'03 (Algarve, November 2003), accessible at http://www.di.fc.ul.pt/~paa/papers/icwi-03.pdf

[7] Chambel, T., Correia, N., Guimarães, N., *Hypervideo on the Web: Models and Techniques for Video Integration*, International Journal of Computers & Applications, Vol. 23, No. 2, 2001, pp. 90-98.

[8] Christian, K., Kules, B., Shneiderman, B., and Youssef, A., *A Comparison of Voice Controlled and Mouse Controlled Web Browsing*, in Proceedings of 4th ACM Conference on Assistive Technologies ASSETS'00 (Arlington, 13-15 November 2000), ACM Press, New York, 2000, pp. 72-79.

[9] DAISY, *Daisy Structure Guidelines*, 2002, accessible at http://www.daisy.org/publications/guidelines/sg-daisy3/structguide.htm.

[10] DAISY, *Statement of Principles for the Creation and Production of Accessible Books and Materials*, 1999, accessible at http://www.daisy.org/dtbook/guidelines/draft/principles.htm.

[11] Dolphin Audio Publishing, *EaseReader - the next generation DAISY audio eBook software player*, 2003, accessible at http://www.dolphinse.com/products/easereader.htm.

[12] Duarte, C., Chambel, T. Carriço, L., Guimarães N., and Simões, H., *A Multimodal Interface for Digital Talking Books*, in Proceedings of the IADIS International WWW/Internet Conference ICWI'03 (Algarve, November 2003).

[13] Duarte, C. and Carriço, L., *Identifying Adaptation Dimensions in Digital Talking Books*, in Proceedings of 9th ACM Conference on Intelligent User Interfaces IUI'2004 (Funchal, 13-16 January 2004), ACM Press, New York, 2004, pp. 241-243.

[14] Eisenstein, J., Vanderdonckt, J., and Puerta, A.R., *Applying Model-based Techniques to the Development of UIs for Mobile Computers*, in Proceedings of 6th ACM International Conference on Intelligent User Interfaces IUI'2001 (Santa Fe, 14-17 January 2001), ACM Press, New York, 2001, pp. 69-76.

[15] Elwert, T. and Schlungbaum, E., *Modelling and Generation of Graphical User Interfaces in the TADEUS Approach*, in Ph. Palanque, R. Bastide (eds.), Proceedings of 2nd Eurographics Workshop on Design, Specification, Verification of Interactive Systems DSV-IS'95 (Toulouse, 7-9 June 1995), Springer-Verlag, Vienna, 1995, pp. 193-208.

[16] Gaver, W., *Synthesizing Auditory Icons*, in Proc. of the ACM Conf. on Human Factors in Computing Systems INTERCHI'93 (Amsterdam, 24-29 April 1993), ACM Press, New York, 1993, pp. 228-235.

[17] Gazzaniga, M.S., Ivry, R.B., and Mangun, G.R., *Cognitive Neuroscience - the Biology of the Mind*, W.W. Norton & Company, 1998.

[18] Gong, L. and Lai, J., *Shall we Mix Synthetic Speech and Human Speech? Impact on user's Performance, Perception, and Attitude*, in Proceedings of the ACM Conference on Human Factors in Computing Systems CHI'2001 (Seattle, 31 March-5 April 2001), ACM Press, New York, 2001, pp. 158-165.

[19] Goose, S. and Moller, C., *A 3D Audio Only Interactive Web Browser: Using Spatialisation to Convey Hypermedia Document Structure*, in Proceedings of the 7th ACM Conference on Multimedia Multimedia'99 (Orlando, 30 October-5 November 1999), ACM Press, New York, 1999, accessible at http://www.kom.e-technik.tu-darmstadt.de/acm mm99/ep/goose/.

[20] Innovative Rehabilitation Technology Inc., *eClipseReader*, 2003, accessible at http://www.eclipsereader.com/.

[21] James, F., *Presenting HTML Structure in Audio: User Satisfaction with Audio Hypertext*, Proceedings of International Conference on Auditory Display ICAD'96 (Palo Alto, 4-6 November 1996), ICAD, 1996, accessible at http://www.icad.org/websiteV2.0/Conferences/ICAD96/proc96/james.htm

[22] Kraus, A. and Koch, N., *Generation of Web Applications from UML Models using an XML Publishing Framework*, in Proceedings of 6th World Conference on Integrated Design and Process Technology IDPT'2002 (Pasadena, 23-28 June 2002), Society for Design and Process Science, 2002, accessible at http://www.pst.informatik.uni-muenchen.de/~krausa/publications/UWEXML-Kraus-Koch-pn1.pdf

[23] Langham, M. and Ziegler, C., *Cocoon: Building XML Applications*, SAMS, New Riders, 2002.

[24] Lin, J. and Landay, L., *Damask: A Tool for Early Stage Design and Prototyping of Multi-Device User Interfaces*, in Proceedings of the International Workshop on Visual Computing during the 8th International Conference on Distributed Multimedia Systems VC'2000 (San Francisco, 26-28 September 2002), San Francisco, 2002, accessible at http://guir.berkeley.edu/projects/damask/pubs/damask-vc2002.pdf

[25] Markopoulos, P., Pycock, J., Wilson, S., and Johnson, P., *ADEPT - A Task Based Design Environment*, in Proceedings of the 25th Hawaii International Conference on Systems Sciences HICSS'92 (Koloa, 9 January 1992), Vol. 2, IEEE Computer Society Press, Los Alamitos, 1992, pp. 587-596, accessible at http://www.idemployee.id.tue.nl/p.markopoulos/downloadablePapers/Markopoulos-P-1992.HICSS25.pdf

[26] Martin, G., *The Utility of Speech Input in User-Computer Interfaces*, International Journal of Man-Machine Studies, Vol. 30, No. 4, 1989, pp. 355-375.

[27] Morley, S., *Digital Talking Books on a PC: A Usability Evaluation of the Prototype DAISY Playback Software*, in Proceedings of the 3rd ACM Conference on Assistive Technologies ASSETS'98 (Marina del Rey, 15-17 April 1998), ACM Press, New York, 1998, pp. 157-164.

[28] NISO, *Document Navigation Features List*, 1999, accessible at http://www.loc.gov/nls/z3986/background/navigation.htm.

[29] NISO, *Playback Device Guideline*, 1999, accessible at http://www.loc.gov/nls/z3986/background/features.htm.

[30] Oviatt, S., Cohen, P., Wu, L., Vergo, J., Duncan, L., Suhm, B., Bers, J., Holzman, T., Winograd, T., Landay, J., Larson, J., and Ferro, D., *Designing the User Interface for*

Multimodal Speech and Gesture Applications: State-Of-The-Art Systems and Research Directions, Human-Computer Interaction, Vol. 15, No. 4, 2000, pp. 421-456.

[31] Paternò, F., *Model-Based Design and Evaluation of Interactive Applications*, Springer-Verlag, Berlin, 2000.

[32] Puerta, A.R., *The Mecano Project: Comprehensive and Integrated Support for Model-Based Interface Development*, in J. Vanderdonckt (ed.), Proceedings of the 2nd Workshop on Computer-Aided Design of User Interfaces CADUI'96 (Namur, 5-7 June 1996), Presses Universitaires de Namur, Namur, 1996, pp. 19-25.

[33] Puerta, A. and Maulsby, D., *Management of Interface Design Knowledge with MODI-D*, in Proceedings of 2nd ACM Conference on Intelligent User Interfaces IUI'97 (Orlando, 6-9 January 1997), ACM Press, New York, 1997, pp. 249-252.

[34] Serralheiro, A., Caseiro, D., Meinedo, H., Trancoso, I., and Neto, J., *Spoken Book Alignment Using WFSTS*, in M. Marcus (ed.), Proceedings of 2nd Conference on Human Language Technology Conference HLT'02 (San Diego, 24-27 March 2002), Association for Computational Linguistics, Morgan Kauffman, 2002, accessible at http://www.l2f.inesc-id.pt/documents/papers/Serralheiro02.pdf

[35] Serralheiro, A., Trancoso, Caseiro, D., Chambel, T. Carriço, L. & Guimarães, N., *Towards a repository of Digital Talking Books*, in Proceedings of 8th European Conference on Speech Communication and Technology Eurospeech'2003 (Geneva, 1-4 September 2003), International Speech Communication Association, Geneva, 2003, pp. 1605-1608.

[36] Szekely, P., Sukaviriya, P., Castells, P., Muthukumarasamy, J. and Salcher, E. (1996). *Declarative Interface Models for User Interface Construction Tools: the MASTERMIND Approach*, in L. Bass, C. Unger (eds.), Proceedings of the 6th IFIP TC 2/WG 2.7 Working Conference on Engineering for Human-Computer Interaction EHCI'95 (Grand Targhee Resort, 14-18 August 1995), Chapman & Hall, Londres, 1995 pp. 120-150.

[37] Van Buskirk, R. and LaLomia, M., *A Comparison of Speech and Mouse/Keyboard GUI Navigation*, in Proceedings of ACM Conference on Human Aspects in Computing Systems CHI'95 (Denver, 7-11 May 1995), ACM Press, New York, 1995, pp. 96-97.

[38] Vanderdonckt, J. and Berquin, P., *Towards a Very Large Model-based Approach for User Interface Development*, in N.W. Paton, T. Griffiths (eds.), Proc. of 1st Int. Workshop on User Interfaces to Data Intensive Systems UIDIS'99 (Edimburgh, 5-6 September 1999), IEEE Computer Society Press, Los Alamitos, 1999, pp. 76-85.

[39] Visick, D., Johnson, P., and Long, J., *The Use of Simple Speech Recognizers in Industrial Applications*, in B. Shackel (ed.), Proceedings of 1st IFIP International Conference on Human-Computer Interaction Interact'84 (London, 4-7 September 1984), North-Holland, Amsterdam, 1984.

[40] VisuAide, *Victor Reader Classic*, 2003, accessible at http://www.visuaide.com/victor-classic.html.

[41] VisuAide, *Victor reader soft*, accessible at http://www.visuaide.com/victorsoft.html.

[42] W3C, Synchronized Multimedia Integration Language SMIL 2.0, 2001, accessible at http://www.w3.org/TR/smil20/.

[43] Wiecha, C. and Boies, S., *Generating User Interfaces: Principles and Use of its Style Rules*, in S.E. Hudson (ed.), Proceedings of 3rd Annual Symposium on User Interface Software and Technology UIST'90 (Snowbird, 3-5 October 1990), ACM Press, New York, 1990, pp. 21-30.

Chapter 28

A FRAMEWORK FOR DEVELOPING CONVER-SATIONAL USER INTERFACES

James Glass[1], Eugene Weinstein[1], Scott Cyphers[1], Joseph Polifroni[1], Grace Chung[2], and Mikio Nakano[3]

[1]MIT Computer Science and Artificial Intelligence Laboratory,
Cambridge, MA 02139 Cambridge (USA)
E-mail:{glass, ecoder, cyphers, joe}@csail.mit.edu
[2]Corporation for National Research Initiatives, Reston, VA (USA)
E-mail: gchung@cnri.reston.va.us
[3]NTT Corporation, Atsugi (Japan)
E-mail: nakano@atom.brl.ntt.co.jp

Abstract   In this work we report our efforts to facilitate the creation of mixed-initiative conversational interfaces for novice and experienced developers of human language technology. Our focus has been on a framework that allows developers to easily specify the basic concepts of their applications, and rapidly prototype conversational interfaces for a variety of configurations. In this paper we describe the current knowledge representation, the compilation processes for speech understanding, generation, and dialogue turn management, as well as the user interfaces created for novice users and more experienced developers. Finally, we report our experiences with several user groups in which developers used this framework to prototype a variety of conversational interfaces.

Keywords: Conversational interaction, Spoken dialogue systems.

1.   INTRODUCTION

In recent years, many sophisticated conversational interfaces have been developed that enable fluent, spoken communication between humans and machines. Such systems are developed by speech and language experts, and require significant effort over a sustained period to achieve good perform-ance. For this reason, non-experts must overcome a significant hurdle to use human language technologies (HLTs) for their own applications. To address this issue, we have been developing a utility (called SPEECHBUILDER),

R. Jacob et al. (eds.), Computer-Aided Design of User Interfaces IV, 349–360.
© 2005 *Kluwer Academic Publishers. Printed in the Netherlands.*

which enables rapid prototyping of spoken dialogue systems by both novice and expert developers. In this paper we motivate the need for this research, describe our approach and progress, and describe several experiments we have performed with novice users creating their own speech-based interfaces. In the following section, we briefly provide additional background on the current state of directed and mixed-initiative dialogue interaction, and motivate the need for mechanisms to facilitate the development of mixed-initiative conversational interface prototypes. We then describe the approach that we have taken for our research in this area, and give an overview of the user interface we have created. We then describe the speech understanding, generation, and dialogue framework used, and describe several experiments we have conducted with different groups of users. Finally we compare our research to related work, and describe our ongoing research in this area.

1.1   Background

Although all spoken dialogue systems can be considered conversational to some degree, they may be differentiated by the degree with which the system maintains control of the conversation, and the inherent amount of flexibility provided to the user to ask for a) what they want, b) in the way they want to ask for it, and c) when they want to ask it. In the most conservative approach, the computer takes complete control of the interaction. These *directed-dialogue* applications typically require that the user answer a set of prescribed questions, much like the touch-tone implementation of interactive voice response systems. Since the user's options are restricted, completion of such transactions is easier to attain, and it is therefore not surprising that such systems have been the first to be successfully deployed on a wide scale [3,5,16]. An alternative approach to human-computer interaction is based on the idea of *mixed-initiative* dialogue between the user and the machine. This approach employs a more flexible dialogue strategy that allows both the user and the machine to participate actively to solve a problem interactively using a conversational paradigm. Systems which are built with the mixed-initiative paradigm must typically process more complex queries than their directed-dialogue counterparts [33], and are inherently more difficult to design and deploy. For this reason, the majority of these kinds of systems remain under development in research laboratories [1,7,20,21,27], although some are beginning to be deployed publicly as well [12].

1.2   Motivation

Although mixed-initiative conversational interfaces are a natural and efficient means of communication, there are two fundamental technical barriers which limit their widespread use. First, it is difficult to configure the HLT required to create a prototype system, and second, performance optimisation is typically an iterative process that is application specific, and not fully automated. Creating a robust, mixed-initiative conversational interface for a new application area currently requires a tremendous amount of effort from speech and language experts. The development of speech recognition and language understanding technologies is mostly domain and language specific, requiring a large amount of annotated training data. Dialogue management is typically also fine-tuned for the application, often with domain-dependent functionality. System development proceeds iteratively, with prototypes being used to collect data that can then be used for system development, training, and evaluation. This iterative process is crucial to achieve good performance. For example, the initial prototype of a mixed-initiative weather information system trained from several thousand utterances collected from a simulated "wizard-of-oz" scenario saw its error rates more than triple when it was first deployed over the telephone to a wide user population [34]. As utterances were continuously collected, the performance slowly improved to the point where it ultimately exceeded the original laboratory performance. However, this level of performance was only achieved through continuous data collection and system refinement over a period of time.

For conversational interfaces to become as ubiquitous as the telephone, researchers must make it easier for developers to create systems that learn and improve their performance automatically. However, there are many hurdles to even allowing developers to create an initial prototype. For example, we must address the problems of producing a conversational system in a new domain and language given at most a small amount of domain-specific training data. To achieve this goal, we must strive to cleanly separate the algorithmic aspects of the system from the application-specific aspects. We must also develop automatic or semi-automatic methods for acquiring the acoustic models, language models, grammars, and semantic structures for language understanding, and dialogue models required by a new application. The issue of portability spans across different acoustic environments, databases, knowledge domains, and languages. The following section describes the approach we have taken to begin to address some of these challenging issues.

2. APPROACH

The approach we have adopted is to leverage the basic technology which has been successfully deployed in more sophisticated conversational systems (e.g., [23]). There are many reasons for this. First, we have devoted considerable effort over the last decade to developing HLT to support conversational interaction. By employing these HLT components we minimise duplication of effort and maximise our ability to adopt any technical advances which are made in any of these areas. Second, by using our most advanced HLT components we widen the pool of potential users to include both novice and expert developers, since the latter can use the web-interface to rapidly prototype a new domain and subsequently modify it manually. Third, since we are not limiting any of the HLT capabilities in any way, we allow for the potential for prototype systems to eventually scale up to the same level of sophistication as our most capable systems. Lastly, by focusing attention on portability, we can identify weaknesses in existing HLT, which can lead to better solutions which can benefit all of our conversational systems.

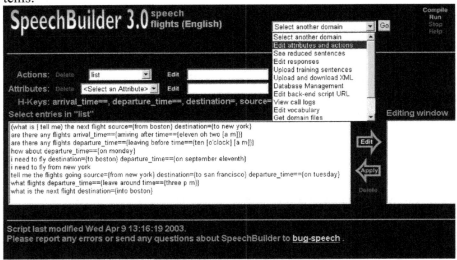

Figure 1. The SPEECHBUILDER user interface used to prototype conversational interfaces.

We have also attempted to use as simple a user interface as possible, while providing mechanisms to incorporate any needed complexities. To accomplish this, we have developed a web-based interface, illustrated in Fig. 1, that is used by developers to specify information about the nature of the interactions that will take place between a human and a spoken dialogue system. More experienced developers wishing to bypass the web-interface, but still desiring to leverage SPEECHBUILDER to configure HLT components may use a voice configuration syntax (VCFG) illustrated in Fig. 2. To configure understanding, the developer defines semantic concepts, known as *attributes*, and general functions, known as *actions*, that may be invoked by a user in the domain. The developer can also configure system responses and dialogue functionality for their application. This information can be automatically generated from uploaded database tables, or via third-party programs, or entered manually by the developer. All information is stored as a human-readable description (XML) that is compiled to configure the appropriate HLT components.

```
<actions>
 <request_name> = I would like a restaurant | can you (show|give) me a Chinese restaurant in Arlington;
 </actions>
<attributes>  <cuisine> = Chinese|Taiwanese; <city> = Washington | Boston | Arlington; </attributes>
<discourse> name masks(city cuisine neighborhood); </discourse>
<constraints> <request_name> (city|neighbourhood) {prompt_for_city}; </constraints>
```

Figure 2. Partial VCFG file for a restaurant query domain.

Once a developer has configured their application domain, they use the web-interface to *compile* it. This process uses the specified information, along with example sentences provided by the developer to configure all necessary HLT components. This process is usually quite rapid (i.e., one or two minutes), although it depends on the domain complexity. Once the domain has been compiled, the developer can examine the resulting grammar, *deploy* the system, talk to it, and subsequently iteratively refine aspects of the understanding, generation, dialogue, etc. Using this interface, a spoken language interface to query database content can thus be created without requiring any programming on the part of a developer. Applications requiring connections to external functionality (e.g., controlling the lights in a house) require the developer to provide code to invoke the external functions.

3.   HUMAN LANGUAGE TECHNOLOGIES

When a user speaks, audio data is sent through a speech recogniser to a natural language understanding component that produces a plausible context-independent semantic representation of what the user spoke. Then context resolution is used to incorporate dialogue history context to resolve unknown references in the sentence. For example, if the user asked, "Is there a cheaper one?" and hotels were being talked about, "hotel" might replace "one" in the semantic representation. Next, the dialogue manager determines how to respond, either by taking an action or asking for additional information. In either case, it generates a semantic representation for a response which a natural language generator converts into the words for the response to the user. All HLT components use the open source GALAXY architecture [24]. The recogniser, natural language, context resolution, dialogue management, and generation components are all configurable. The SPEECH-BUILDER compiler generates the appropriate configuration files for each of these components. SPEECHBUILDER also allows the dialogue management component to invoke arbitrary user code. The following sections describe the configuration of some of these components in greater detail.

3.1 Understanding

The speech recogniser [11] uses generic telephone-based acoustic models, phonetic descriptions of the words in the vocabulary, and an n-gram grammar, which provides likelihoods for sequences of n words, to describe the ways words occur in sentences. The recogniser finds sequences of words that maximise the combined likelihood of the word sequence based on its component n-grams and the likelihood of each individual word given the waveform. The n-gram grammar is derived from the language understanding grammar rules and example sentences provided by the developer, while likelihoods for individual words are based on pronunciations. Baseform word pronunciations can come from large on-line dictionaries, be generated by rule [6], or be provided by the domain developer. We have incorporated an out-of-vocabulary model to handle spoken words which are not in the vocabulary [4]. The recogniser produces a ranked list, called an N-best list, of most likely word sequences. Because an n-gram grammar is used, each word sequence is only locally grammatical, i.e. each sub-sequence of n words is likely, but the entire sequence may not be. The natural language component, TINA [25], uses a probabilistic context-free grammar to combine the word sequences in the N-best list into the semantic representation of the most likely parse tree. Developers do not actually specify a parsing grammar for their application. Instead, a grammar is inferred using example-based specification [10] from *attributes*, which are semantic concepts specified by phrases, and *actions* which are sentences that use attribute phrases. When one phrase of an attribute appears in an action sentence, the generated grammar will permit any other phrase for the same attribute. For example, in Fig. 2, the "cuisine" attribute can be "Chinese" or "Taiwanese." In the "request_name" action, only "Chinese" is listed, but the user could ask about any other cuisine. The actual phrase used in a spoken sentence will be associated with "cuisine" in the semantic representation. The generated grammar provides a complete parse where possible, and backs off to concept spotting when a complete parse is not found. Although this mechanism works fairly well, the generated parsing grammar is very simple compared to those that are written by experts, and does not allow domains to reuse sub-grammars for concepts such as times, dates and prices. We have begun to address this issue by allowing developers to incorporate sub-grammars catering to common semantic concepts such as dates and times. We have also developed a new process that converts these concepts into a standard semantic representation. Fig. 2 also shows an example of configuring the context resolution component [9]. The "discourse" section states that if a name is specified, then the city, cuisine, and neighbourhood should not be inherited from the dialogue history context into the semantic representation of the sentence.

3.2   Dialogue Management

Developers must be able to configure complete mixed-initiative conversational interfaces. Our initial interface constrained developers with no programming experience to database query applications. Those with programming experience could perform more sophisticated dialogue functions via a remote CGI script. However, these two alternatives clearly limited the ability of inexperienced developers to create the kinds of conversational interfaces that can be created by experts.

To provide for more flexible dialogues, we have been developing a more generic dialogue manager [17]. As part of this work, we have begun to abstract a suite of easily configurable dialogue flow functions from our mixed-initiative dialogue systems using a text-based domain specification format. As illustrated in Figure 2, in the "constraints" section, if the user seems to be invoking the "request_name" action and a city or neighborhood has not already been specified, then the dialogue manager should invoke the "prompt_for_city" routine to ask for the city. The generic dialogue manager and functions supporting common semantic concepts have been applied to several new domains.

3.3   Language Generation

The natural language generation process converts semantic representations to text [2]. The most obvious role for generation is to produce a response for the user via a speech synthesizer. These responses can be configured by the developer via the web-interface, by modifying default generation templates generated by the initial compilation process. The language generation process is also used to generate other internal representations. For CGI-based applications, a generated URL-encoded version of the semantic representation is passed to the remote application via an HTTP GET request. For database query applications, the generation process also formulates an SQL query from a semantic representation of a request. Finally, when the generic dialogue manager is used, the generator is used to create an internal "E-form" representation used by the context resolution and dialogue components. E-forms are a simple semantic representation of the meaning of the query, and can be augmented by the discourse and dialogue components based on the query's context.

3.4   HLT Infrastructure

Over the last few years, we have developed several ways to deploy domains to fit particular needs. Originally, users accessed their domains by a shared telephone line with dialogue processing running on a remote server. We now also offer support for developers who want to run domains on local hardware, and, as part of our research on pervasive computing, there is support for handheld devices [29]. We have made it easier for speech-interfaces to communicate with external applications. This was initially accomplished via HTTP requests which provided an encoded version of the semantic frame to an application running on a web server. To eliminate the need for a web server, and to allow applications to incorporate state information when desired, we provide ways to extend a system with Perl, Python, or Java.

All systems generate log files showing the details of user interactions and individual component input and output. We provide tools to allow domain developers to view the logs as hypertext and listen to recordings of the dialogue. To further ease discourse and dialogue testing and debugging, a system can also be run in *batchmode*. In this mode, previously recorded waveforms, *N*-best lists, or text input can be sent through the system and the output examined. These capabilities are helpful for developers trying to improve the performance of their initial prototype.

4.   DEPLOYMENT

Over the last few years, we have had numerous experiences with developers using the SPEECHBUILDER utility to create a wide variety of speech-based applications. To familiarise new developers with the SPEECHBUILDER system, we have developed an introductory laboratory exercise. Our first experiences were with users interacting with database applications with limited dialogue functionality, or controlling applications via the CGI interface. As the dialogue management component was made available, we extended the laboratory to explore this component in more depth within the context of a hotel information domain. In the current laboratory, students develop a restaurant query system, starting from a database table containing simple attribute-value pairs (i.e., names, addresses, cuisines, etc., plus associated values). An initial recogniser and natural language component are created automatically using the values in the table. Discourse and dialogue components are then configured and modified within the VCFG file; system responses are also modified. The students use both batchmode and a telephone to communicate with their systems.

The laboratories we have developed have been used both locally and remotely. In a recent remote workshop on pervasive computing [14], a class of over 30 researchers created a speech interface to an instant messenger client. The web-based utility has also been used as a laboratory for Computational Linguistics students at Georgetown University, and as part of summer school classes at Johns Hopkins University. Courses have varied from one to three sessions where students with little prior background have learned to build simple restaurant and hotel query applications using the web-based interface.

Finally, as part of collaboration with speech researchers at NTT, we have been developing a Japanese version of this technology. As part of this work, researchers have built several prototype applications including a bus timetable information system and a weather information system.

5.   RELATED WORK

Other research groups have also been attempting to make it easier for non-experts to create new domains. Systems which modularise their dialogue manager try to take advantage of the fact that a dialogue can often be broken down into a set of smaller sub-dialogues (e.g., dates, addresses), in order to make it easier to construct dialogue for a new domain (e.g., [3]). For example, researchers at OGI have developed a rapid development kit for creating spoken dialogue systems, which is freely available, and which has been used by students to create speech-based systems [30]. Starkie *et al.* describe a spoken dialogue system creation toolkit that is able to infer complex natural language grammars from examples specified by the developer [28]. On the commercial side, there has been a significant effort to develop the Voice eXtensible Markup Language (VoiceXML) as a standard to enable internet content and information access via voice and phone [32]. To date these approaches have been applied only to directed-dialogue strategies. In addition, example-based specification of user interfaces has also been addressed in the literature (e.g., [8]), but this work has focused on visual interfaces, and has not been significantly explored in the area of spoken dialogue.

Additionally, several attempts have been made at simplifying the process of creating dialogue systems to query databases. Toth *et al.* [31] have created a toolkit to allow a developer to efficiently configure human language technology components around relational database tables. However, the user must first learn keywords to converse with the system. Microsoft English Query is a commercial product that allows a developer to configure a typed natural language interface to database content [13]. The system provides a great deal of flexibility in specifying mappings from linguistic content to database constructs; however, no speech interface is provided, and there is no support for dialogue or discourse. [19] describes a tool similar to English Query in purpose, which achieved better NL-to-SQL translation performance on a corpus of queries from several popular domains.

6. CONCLUSION

This paper has summarised our progress in developing a utility to enable rapid prototyping of spoken dialogue systems. However, as was pointed out initially, and as any experienced developer knows, a prototype is only the initial step in the creation of a conversational interface. Creating a high-performance system requires sustained data collection, continuous development, evaluation, and refinement. To help developers achieve this goal will require additional work on unsupervised learning. In our lab, we have begun to improve system performance by processing untranscribed utterances [15], but there is clearly much more research necessary.

The current compilation process configures the speech recogniser and language understanding grammar in parallel, based on the domain description. Recently, we have added the ability to configure our recogniser based on information in the natural language parsing grammar [26]. We plan to integrate this new method into the compiler, to provide increased flexibility to developers in the future. In other areas of research, we have been developing a dynamic vocabulary capability within our speech recogniser and language understanding components [22]. This will give the developer increased flexibility to modify system capabilities during run-time. This work will also allow us to take advantage of more flexible response planning techniques we are developing [18].

Finally, as part of our recent efforts on multimodal interfaces, we have augmented attribute values with timing information to indicate when a concept was spoken. We have used this information to modify a SPEECH-BUILDER-created application, so that it can incorporate pen-based input. Future versions of the SPEECHBUILDER utility will probably include a connection to our new multimodal component to enable more flexible interactions.

ACKNOWLEDGEMENTS

This research was supported in part by DARPA under contract N66001-99-8904 monitored through Naval Command, Control and Ocean Surveillance, and contract N66001-00-2-8922, monitored through SPAWAR Systems Center, San Diego, under an industrial consortium supporting the MIT Oxygen Alliance, and by NTT.

REFERENCES

[1] Allen, J., Schubert, L., Ferguson, G., Heeman, P., Hwang, C.H., Kato, T., Light, M., Martin, N., Miller, B., Poesio, M., and Traum, D., *The TRAINS Project: A Case Study in Defining a Conversational Planning Agent*, Journal of Experimental and Theoretical

Artificial Intelligence, Vol. 7, 1995, pp. 7-48.

[2] Baptist, L. and S. Seneff, GENESIS-II: *A Versatile System for Language Generation in Conversational System Applications*, Proceedings of International Conference on Spoken Language Processing 2000 ICSLP'2000 (Beijing, 16-20 October 2000), Vol. 3, ISCA Archive, 2000, pp. 271-274.

[3] Barnard, E., Halberstadt, A., Kotelly, C., and Phillips, M., *A Consistent Approach to Designing Spoken-Dialog Systems*, in Proceedings of Workshop ASRU'99 (Keystone, 13-15 December 1999), accessible at http://asru99.research.att.com/abstracts/6_4490_invited.html

[4] Bazzi, I. and Glass, J., *Modeling Out-Of-Vocabulary Words for Robust Speech Recognition*, in Proceedings of International Conference on Spoken Language Processing 2000 ICSLP'2000 (Beijing, 16-20 October 2000), ISCA Archive, 2000, pp. 401-404.

[5] Billi, R., Canavesio, F., and Rullent, C., *Automation of Telecom Italia Directory Assistance Service: Field Trial Results*, in Proceedings of 4th IEEE Workshop on Interactive Voice Technology for Telecommunications Applications IVTTA'98 (Turin, 29-30 September 1998), IEEE Computer Society Press, Los Alamitos, 1998, pp. 11-16.

[6] Black, A., Lenzo, K., and Pagel, V., *Issues in Building General Letter to Sound Rules*, in Proceedings of 3rd ESCA/COSCOSDA International Workshop on Speech Synthesis (Jenolan Caves, 26-29 November 1998), 1998.

[7] Blomberg, M., Carlson, R., Elenius, K., Granström, B., Gustafson, J., Hunnicutt, S., Lindell, R., Neovius, L., and Nord, L., *An Experimental Dialogue System: Waxholm*, in Proceedings of European Conference on Speech Communication and Technology Eurospeech'93 (Berlin, September 1993), ISCA Archive, 1993, pp. 1867-1870.

[8] Derthick, M. ans Roth, S., *Example-Based Generation of Custom Data Analysis Applications*, in Proceedings of 6th ACM Conference on Intelligent User Interfaces IUI'2001 (Santa Fe, 14-17 January 2001), ACM Press, New York, 2001, pp. 57-64.

[9] Filisko, E. and Seneff, S., *A Context Resolution Server For The* GALAXY *Conversational Systems*, in Proceedings of 8th European Conf. on Speech Communication and Technology Eurospeech'2003 (Geneva, 1-4 Sept. 2003), ISCA Archive, 2003, pp. 197-200.

[10] Glass, J. and Weinstein, E., SPEECHBUILDER: *Facilitating Spoken Dialogue Systems Development*, in Proceedings of 7th European Conference on Speech Communication and Technology Eurospeech'2001 (Aalborg, 3-7 September 2001), ISCA Archive, 2001, pp. 1335-1338, accessible at http://www.sls.lcs.mit.edu/sls/publications/2001/Speech Builder.pdf

[11] Glass, J., *A Probabilistic Framework for Segment-Based Speech Recognition*, Computer, Speech, and Language, Vol. 17, 2003, pp. 137-152.

[12] Gorin, A., Riccardi, G., and Wright, J., *How may I help you?*, Speech Communication, Vol. 23, 1997, pp. 113-127.

[13] Microsoft SQL Server: English Query, October 2000, accessible at http://www.microsoft.com/sql/evaluation/features/english.asp

[14] MIT Project Oxygen web site, accessible at http://oxygen.lcs.mit.edu

[15] Nakano, M. and Hazen, T., *Using Untranscribed User Utterances for Improving Language Models Based On Confidence Scoring*, in Proceedings of 8th European Conference on Speech Communication and Technology Eurospeech'2003 (Geneva, 1-4 September 2003), ISCA Archive, 2003, pp. 417-420.

[16] Nuance Communications, http://www.nuance.com

[17] Polifroni, J. and Chung, G., *Promoting Portability in Dialogue Management*, in Proceedings of 7th International Conference on Spoken Language Processsing ICSLP'2002 (Denver, 16-20 September 2002), ISCA Archive, 2002, pp. 2721-2724.

[18] Polifroni, J., Chung, G., and Seneff, S., *Towards the Automatic Generation of Mixed-Initiative Dialogue Systems From Web Content*, in Proceedings of 8th European Conference on Speech Communication and Technology Eurospeech'2003 (Geneva, 1-4 September 2003), ISCA Archive, 2003, pp. 193-196.

[19] Popescu, A.M., Etzioni, O., and Kautz, H., *Towards a Theory of Natural Language Interfaces to Databases*, in Proceedings of ACM Int. Conference on Intelligent User Interfaces (Miami, 12-15 January 2003), ACM Press, New York, 2003, pp. 149-157.

[20] Rosset, S., Bennacef, S., and Lamel, L., *Design Strategies for Spoken Language Dialog Systems*, in Proc. of 6th European Conf. on Speech Communication and Technology Eurospeech'99 (Budapest, 5-9 September 1999), ISCA Archive, 1999, pp. 1535-1538.

[21] Rudnicky, A.I., Thayer, E., Constantinides, P., Tchou, C., Shern, R., Lenzo, K., Xu W., and Oh, A., *Creating natural dialogs in the Carnegie Mellon Communicator system*, in Proc. of 6th European Conference on Speech Communication and Technology Eurospeech'99 (Budapest, 5-9 September 1999), ISCA Archive, 1999, pp. 1531-1534, accessible at http://www.speech.cs.cmu.edu/Communicator/papers/NaturalDialogs2.pdf

[22] Schalkwyk, J., Hetherington, L., and Story, E., *Speech Recognition With Dynamic Grammars Using Finite-State Transducers*, in Proceedings of 8th European Conference on Speech Communication and Technology Eurospeech'2003 (Geneva, 1-4 September 2003), ISCA Archive, 2003, pp. 1969-1972.

[23] Seneff, S. and Polifroni, J., *Dialogue Management in the MERCURY Flight Reservation System*, in Proceedings of ANLP-NAACL Satellite Workshop on Conversational Systems (Seattle, 4 May 2000).

[24] Seneff, S., Hurley, E., Lau, R., Pao, C., Schmid, P., and Zue, V., *GALAXY-II: A Reference Architecture for Conversational System Development*, in R.H. Mannell, J. Robert-Ribes (eds.), Proceedings of 5th International Conference on Spoken Language Processsing ICSLP'98 (Sydney, 30 November-4 December 1998), Vol. 3, Australian Speech Science and Technology Association, Incorporated (ASSTA), Canberra, 1998, pp. 931-934, accessible at http://www.sls.csail.mit.edu/sls/publications/1998/icslp98-galaxy.pdf

[25] Seneff, S., *TINA: A Natural Language System for Spoken Language Applications*, Computational Linguistics, Vol. 18, No. 1, 1992, pp. 61-86.

[26] Seneff, S., Wang, Ch., Hazen, T.J., *Automatic Induction of N-Gram Language Models from a Natural Language Grammar*, in Proceedings of 8th European Conference on Speech Communication and Technology Eurospeech'2003 (Geneva, 1-4 September 2003), ISCA Archive, 2003, pp. 641-644.

[27] Souvignier, V., Kellner, A., Rueber, B., Schramm, H., and Seide, F., *The Thoughtful Elephant: Strategies for Spoken Dialogue Systems*, IEEE Transactions on Speech and Audio Processing, Vol. 8, No. 1, 2000, pp. 51-62.

[28] Starkie, B., Findlow, G., Ho, K., Hui, A., Law, L., Lightwood, L., Michnowicz, S., and Walder, Ch., *Lyrebird: Developing Spoken Dialog Systems Using Examples*, in Proceedings of 6th International Colloquium on Grammatical Inference ICGI'02 (Amsterdam, 23-25 September 2002), Amsterdam, 2002, pp. 309-311.

[29] Steele, K., Waterman, J., and Weinstein, E., *The Oxygen H21 Handheld*, MIT Lab. for Computer Science Research Summary, March 2003.

[30] Sutton, S., *Universal Speech Tools: The CSLU Toolkit*, in R.H. Mannell, J. Robert-Ribes (eds.), Proceedings of 5th Int. Conf. on Spoken Language Processsing ICSLP'98 (Sydney, 30 November-4 December 1998), Vol. 3, Australian Speech Science and Technology Association, Incorporated (ASSTA), Canberra, 1998, pp. 3221-3224.

[31] Toth, A., *Towards Every-Citizen's Speech Interface: An Application Generator for Speech Interfaces to Databases*, in Proceedings of 7th International Conference on Spoken Language Processsing ICSLP'2002 (Denver, 16-20 September 2002), ISCA Archive, 2002, pp. 1497-1500.

[32] VoiceXML, accessible at http://www.w3.org/TR/voicexml/

[33] Zue, V. and Glass, J., *Conversational interfaces: Advances and challenges*, Proceedings of the IEEE, Vol. 88, No. 8, 2000, pp. 1166-1180.

[34] Zue, V., Seneff, S., Glass, J., Polifroni, J., Pao, C., Hazen, T., and Hetherington, L., *JUPITER: A Telephone-Based Conversational Interface for Weather Information*, IEEE Transactions on Speech and Audio Processing, Vol. 8, No. 1, January 2000, pp. 85-96.

Chapter 29

A SYSTEM FOR MANIPULATING AUDIO INTERFACES USING TIMBRE SPACES

Craig Nicol, Stephen Brewster, and Philip Gray
Computing Science Department, University of Glasgow,
17 Lilybank Gardens – Glasgow G12 8QQ (Scotland)
E-mail: {can,stephen,pdg}@dcs.gla.ac.uk - URL: http://www.dcs.gla.ac.uk/~{can,stephen,pdg }
Tel.: +44 (0)141 330 {4256, 4966, 4933} – Fax: +44 141 330 4913

Abstract   The creation of audio interfaces is currently hampered by the difficulty of designing sounds for them. This paper presents a novel system for generating and manipulating non-speech sounds. The system is designed to generate Auditory Icons and Earcons through a common interface. It has been developed to make the design of audio interfaces easier. Using a Timbre Space representation of the sound, it generates output via an FM synthesiser. The Timbre Space has been compiled in both Fourier and Constant Q Transform versions using Principal Components Analysis (PCA). The design of the system and initial evaluations of these two versions are discussed, showing that the Fourier analysis appears to be better, contrary to initial expectations.

Keywords: Auditory Icons, Earcons, Multimedia interfaces, Timbre Spaces, User interface design and specification methods and languages.

1.   INTRODUCTION

Many authors, for example Gaver [6,7] and Mynatt [13], declare a lack of clear design tools for sounds or auditory interfaces. This paper presents ongoing work on a system to address this need. The system we are developing will use a more natural interface than the current tools and allow sounds to be described not in terms of their wave properties, but in terms of the sources that produce those sounds, with an advanced level to edit sounds via auditory properties. It is hoped that this system will help sound designers find useful sounds for their interfaces, and from this, a complete set of design guidelines for sonic interactions can be realised.

R. Jacob et al. (eds.), Computer-Aided Design of User Interfaces IV, 361–374.

The interface will be designed around the timbre space concept typified by work by Hourdin *et al.* [9,10], who based their work on perceptual models developed in human experiments [8]. Sounds will be analysed and loaded into this timbre space where they can be manipulated before being output via a suitable synthesiser. After a short discussion on why this is an important topic, Section 3 discusses the current level of research in sound and in sonic interfaces, and contains brief discussions of human perception and other auditory interfaces. Section 4 overviews the technology and design behind the current implementation of the system that has been designed, in the context of the work that has been completed. Section 5 provides a quick summary of work to be completed on the project and possible future directions.

2.   OVERVIEW

As computer displays get smaller on devices such as mobile phones and PDAs, audio interfaces will become even more important for providing information to users. Audio has also been used to enrich a user's information awareness by presenting information non-intrusively [5]. With these new challenges, new methods of designing and prototyping audio interfaces need to be developed that can be understood not just by experts in music and acoustics, but also by designers with a background in HCI and psychology.

Sound has always been an important part of interacting with the physical world. Sound tells us when someone is coming up behind us, when we have drilled though the wall and when we need to change our spark plugs. Against our rich sonic environment, the computer interface is a poor cousin. Most sounds from our computers are static sounds that do not change to reflect changes in the environment and often have little to do with the events that trigger them. Gaver noticed this [6] and developed a system of Auditory Icons whose sound was related to the action to which they were connected, and whose properties could be adjusted to reflect changes in the underlying environment.

Since then, many people have developed sonic interfaces to various virtual environments and data sets, but each one is distinct, and despite numerous guidelines defining how each type of interface should be designed, and how people will interpret these, there is no common tool for developing or evaluating these sonic interactions. In the design of Audio Aura [14] for example, the following guidelines were followed to prevent an "alarm response" in the users:

"[Background sounds are designed to avoid] sharp attacks, high volume levels, and substantial frequency content in the same range as the human voice (200-2,000 Hz)."

The quote is then followed by a note that current audio design often induces this alarm response, intentionally or otherwise. The computer music community on the other hand has defined many methods for creating and manipulating sounds through a small number of common interfaces, each method having its own strengths and weaknesses.

The most basic musical interface is the MIDI standard, which defines a series of commands that specify musical notes and operations on these such as sustain, pan and instrument used. Short musical segments generated from these commands are known as Earcons [1,3]. The biggest problem with MIDI is that the output sound is not guaranteed. Although there has been some recent standardisation, the basic MIDI specification does not guarantee any particular sound is available on the playback device or that the device will reasonably interpret all the commands. In the most extreme cases, MIDI devices will ignore commands and only play one note at a time, ignoring any other notes requested at the same time.

Another popular field within computer music concerns the transformations made available by the various Analysis-Synthesis techniques, a review of which was done by Masri *et al.* [12]. Analysis-Synthesis allows composers to manipulate sounds directly rather than via the sources that produce them. It allows sounds to be sliced, stretched, reversed and slowly changed into other sounds. It achieves this by presenting the sound in a different format to that used for recording and storage. Since the aims of the MIDI and Analysis-Synthesis techniques has been musical production, little thought has been given to their perceptual relevance or their use as a design tool for non-musical sounds.

The aim of this project is to go a long way to combining the work in these two areas, allowing interface designers access to complex acoustic and musical methods for developing sound through an interface defined in terms of human perception and design methodologies.

3. HEARING, ANALYSING AND PRODUCING SOUND

This section discusses current research in the fields of audio perception and sound analysis. The focus here is on tools or the results of experiments that have been or could be applied to the production of a generic sonic design tool.

3.1 Perception of Sound

There are four components to the way we hear a single sound: the pitch, the loudness, the duration and the timbre. Where sounds are combined, the relative values of these are important as is the temporal pattern of the sounds. This section concentrates on the issues of single sounds and leaves the sound combination components to the discussion of Earcons in Section 3.3. The timbre of the sound is what differentiates two sounds whose pitch, loudness and duration are equal. Unlike these other measures, the timbre is a result of complex interactions of frequencies in the sound.

The objective measurement of timbre has been a long-running problem in acoustics. Although Helmholtz did a lot of experiments in the 1870's [16], it has only been with recent advances in signal analysis techniques that timbre has been seriously investigated in papers such as [8] and [9].

3.2   Playing Sounds

Once the sound has been designed, an appropriate and efficient output algorithm is needed to play it to the user. In this section, the most common synthesis techniques used on the desktop are discussed.

Sampled Sounds. A sound sample is simply a pre-recorded sound that can be played back at will. Most modern GUIs have support for sound samples that can be triggered in response to a user action such as closing an application. Sound samples are almost identical across a wide range of computers and generally have low performance requirements. One of the major drawbacks of using sound samples in an audio interface is the size of the files. Even compressed samples are several orders of magnitude larger than the parameter definitions for synthesis algorithms such as FM synthesis or additive synthesis described below. Sampling also requires recording a different sample for every type of interaction we want to simulate. Not only does this require a large amount of storage space, but is also labour-intensive in the sound capture stage and may be impossible if you do not know all possible interactions beforehand.

Wave Synthesis. For sounds generated algorithmically by the machine, the simplest forms of synthesis are based on the manipulation of simple waves. The algorithm will start with one or more simple input waves and modifies them through various filters to create a complex output wave. The input wave is usually a simple sine wave, although others such as sawtooth and square waves are also common. Waves can be shaped by an *envelope*, which defines the shape of one of the attributes of the wave such as the amplitute. At each point on the wave, the attribute is multiplied by the value of the envelope. We say that the wave attribute has been *convolved* with the envelope. In Fig. 1, the amplitude of a sine wave has been convolved with the envelope shown.

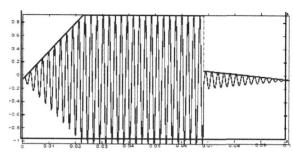

Figure 1. A sine wave shaped by an amplitude envelope. The thin line is the wave, the thick line is the envelope.

Additive Synthesis. Additive synthesis is the basis of Gaver's Auditory Icons [7]. An additive synthesiser generates several waves, giving each wave has its own frequency, phase and amplitude envelopes. The output is the weighted sum of these input waves. Gaver used these to generate contact sounds. The phase and amplitude envelopes are parameterised in order to produce realistic timbre for a variety of real-world contacts. Additive synthesis, though simple and powerful, is often a slow process as it can require many individual waves to reproduce a complex sound. Synthesis with 10 or more waves is not uncommon. This means that additive synthesis cannot be used in real-time without sacrificing sound quality.

FM synthesis. In the 1970's, Yamaha released a series of keyboards that used Frequency Modulation (FM) synthesis to generate their sounds, as developed by Chowning [4]. Since then, the technique has found its way into many soundcards available on modern machines, although in a more limited form. For modern computers without a built-in FM synthesiser, the process is fast enough to be computed in real time on the main processor during an interactive session. A simple sine wave known as the carrier has its frequency perturbed by a modulating wave. The effect is to induce a range of tones around the original frequency, creating a complex sound from a small number of input waves. As a consequence, the output of an FM synthesiser is difficult to predict from its inputs, and it is non-trivial to achieve a desired output sound. The characteristic FM sound is fairly metallic so the sound is then filtered in order to produce a more natural sound. The most useful filter for this purpose is the envelope, which is used to soften the onset and termination of the sound by modifying the amplitude.

3.3   Interfaces and Design

Our system is to be developed for a desktop environment, for situations where the expressiveness and flexibility of the sound development is far more important than accurately recreating a sound from the real world. An example given by Gaver is his Auditory Icon illustrating a file being copied

[7]. In this icon, the expressiveness of the pouring sound he uses is more important than using a less expressive realistic photocopying sound. The idea behind an auditory interface is that the sounds produced will reflect the current state of the system. In some cases, as in Gaver, this is used to provide feedback and information on user actions. Others, such as Conversy [5], use the sounds as a non-intrusive way of providing status information on background tasks. A short review of current audio interface concepts on the desktop follows.

Auditory Icons. Auditory Icons were devised by Gaver [7]. They are auditory representations motivated by real-world sounds. In his paper, Gaver discusses a variety of sounds designed to resemble tapping, scraping, pouring and other real-world actions. The tapping sounds are used to represent the act of clicking on an icon, the scraping to represent dragging an icon over the desktop and the pouring is used as a progress indicator. The sounds are parameterised such that different file types are associated with sounds of taps on different materials and the size of the material being tapped represents the file size. The major problem with Auditory Icons is that the parameterisation is a hard problem. Even where the mapping between a perceptual description of a sound and the system state it represents is obvious, it is rarely easy to modify the sound signal in the correct way as standard sound editors operate at the signal rather than the perceptual level. All the icons Gaver presents have been developed after studying the processes that create the sound, which is a slow process.

Earcons. In contrast to Auditory Icons, Earcons [1] do not attempt to describe an event with a real-world sound. Earcons are short musical segments that are abstract representations of a computer process. Earcons are constructed as patterns of musical notes, where the instrument, duration, pitch, volume and other attributes are modified according to the state of the process. As Earcons are made of many notes, the rhythm and tempo of those notes and their relative volume and pitch are also important attributes that are used in Earcon design. Unlike Auditory Icons, the connection between state and the sound is arbitrary. Hierarchical Earcons, as used in the experiments by Brewster *et al.* on the effectiveness of Earcons [2], attempt to assign some structure to Earcons by mapping different attributes to different levels of description of the interface. For example, menus are described by the timbre of the sound, and menu items are described by the rhythm of the sound, providing a consistency across the interface. Earcons allow a much richer space of sound than Auditory Icons since Auditory Icons are independent of each other and can only be parameterised with respect to simple object interactions, such as a scrape. Earcons can be parameterised with a wide range of musical features as listed above, allowing a single Earcon to present much more information than an Auditory Icon.

Combined approach. A single Earcon is a complex unit formed of many notes. Earcons treat timbre as a single dimension, which is categorical rather than numerical. Earcons use musical concepts such as pitch, rhythm, duration and tempo as further dimensions, which modify the notes within them and the relative positions of those to reflect changes in the underlying process. Auditory Icons, however, treat timbre as the combination of many dimensions, and rarely use other dimensions, such as pitch and tempo.

A rare example being Gaver's bouncing objects where the temporal proximity of events is an indication of the original height and the springiness of the dropped object. By combining the complex timbral manipulation of Auditory Icons with the complex combination and musical manipulation of Earcons, we can see that a system that allows control over both timbre and musical dimensions will have a much richer design space than either idea on its own. Whether this richer space will provide a more flexible and useful design space is a matter for investigation.

3.4   Timbre Spaces

To effectively control sound, we need a representation that is flexible enough to allow designers a variety of ways to adapt it. A timbre space is one such representation, and has been chosen for our work because the studies detailed below suggest a link between human perception and a timbre space representation. This implies that designers should find it easier to create a desired sound with a timbre space representation than via traditional synthesis algorithms, where the parameters do not necessarily adapt the sound in the way the designer wishes.

Timbre Spaces. In 1977 Grey published a paper describing an experiment he had done on perception of timbre [8]. In this, he played a series of sounds to volunteers and asked them to rate how similar the sounds were. Grey then constructed a 3-dimensional space to represent the sounds, such that each axis represented a property of the sound, for example, he related the first axis to the spectral distribution of energy. In 1997, Hourdin *et al.* [9] first demonstrated an automated way to generate this space, although their space has ten dimensions to Grey's three.

They compared their space with that of Grey, showing a correlation between the axes of the two. They then used this space to drive a synthesis system [10]. In their automated analysis, a set of input sounds is analysed to produce a sonogram representation where the sound is described by how its frequencies change over time.

Taking each frequency as a separate dimension, and the sound as a path through this multi-dimensional space, the sound can be projected into a lower dimensional space known as the timbre space, where each dimension represents some higher-level description of the sound based on its frequency components. There are many possible timbre spaces and each one has its own strengths and weaknesses for different tasks. Each combination of analysis method and dimensionality reduction produces a different space, and other spaces have been used for different tasks, such as for instrument recognition [11].

Signal Analysis. Signal analysis is the first stage in producing a timbre space. It is the process by which an input signal is broken into its constituent frequencies. There are many different methods for doing this, and good explanations for many of these techniques can be found in Roads [15] and in [12]. In the analysis, the frequency axis is separated into a number of frequency bins, each of which covers a range of frequencies. This range is known as the bandwidth of the bin.

In general, a smaller bandwidth gives a more accurate frequency representation and a less accurate time representation. The time axis is also split into a number of shorter fragments which may have a window envelope applied, such as a Gaussian bell curve, to smooth the signal over the time segment. Unlike the frequency axis, the time segments can overlap, and this is used to retain any information lost by applying a window envelope.

The two main analysis methods used for this project are the Short-Time FourierTransform (STFT) and the ConstantQTransform(CQT), both described in Roads (1996). In the STFT, the frequency scale is linear. In the CQT, the frequency scale is logarithmic. In general, the CQT will produce a smaller output but the STFT will compute faster and will have greater resolution across the frequency range. Fig. 2 shows how the Flute sound from our dataset is represented in the CQTand STFT forms. As you can see, due to the higher frequency resolution in the CQT presented here, the frequency data is spread across far more frequency bins than in the STFT.

Dimensionality Reduction. The dimensionality reduction techniques presented here take a set of data in n dimensions and create a mapping to convert the data into m dimensions where m is less than n. The output m dimensions are chosen to represent the directions of most importance in the data and are ordered such that the first dimension is the most important. Principal Components Analysis (PCA) is the simplest of the dimensionality reduction techniques and the most susceptible to any noise in the input data. It is the technique used by Kaminskyj [11] in his timbre space paper. In PCA, the data is rotated such that the direction where the data has the most variance is aligned with the primary axis and the other axes are aligned similarly with the remaining variance in the data.

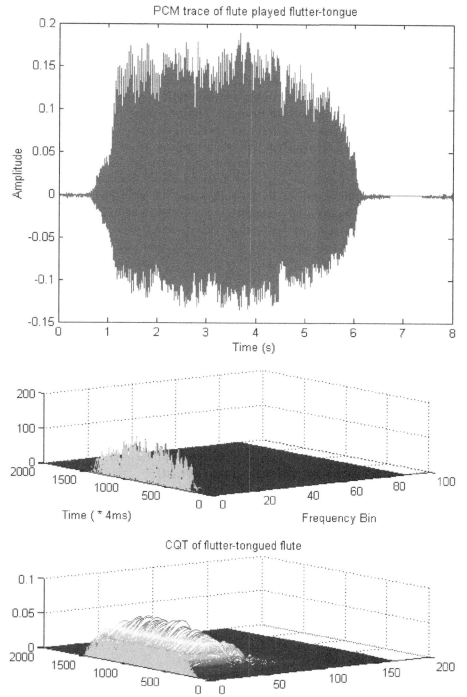

Figure 2. One of the 27 sounds used in our Timbre Space as PCM data and as analysed by two different techniques.

4.   SYSTEM DETAILS

The complete system we are developing comprises an analysis engine based on the Timbre Space work described above. New sounds presented to the system are converted into paths in this space. The system allows manipulation of these sounds via their path representation. When an output is required, the system maps the path from the Timbre Space onto an FM synthesiser which then outputs the sound to a specified device. The sound manipulation component of the system allows morphing between sounds in the space. To generate completely new sounds, the paths can be warped into any shape in the space. Certain warps will describe easily heard transformations of the sound and these can easily be coded into the interface, added by the designer by hand or added by comparing two different sounds for the change required to convert one into the other. This section will now discuss the work and evaluations completed so far on the system and will give preliminary analysis of the results given.

4.1   System Overview

Fig. 3 shows how data is processed by the system that has been developed. There are 4 data stages and 3 translation stages that map one data type to another. The intermediate data is stored on disk and can be passed between separate devices if required. The seven stages of the process are:

1. Get sounds (Wave Data).
2. Create timbre space representation of the sound.
3. Manipulate path in timbre space (Point List).
4. Create control parameters for the output synthesiser.
5. Send parameters to synthesiser (Event List).
6. Run synthesiser over parameter list.
7. Output sound to disk or speakers (Wave Data).

Of these, Step 1 and Steps 5-7 are complete. Current experiments are being run to determine the best timbre space to use for Step 2. Preliminary results for these are defined below. Since Step 4 depends on the type of timbre space created, this will be completed after the experiments.

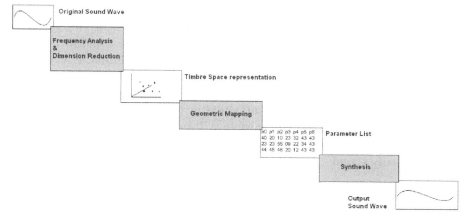

Figure 3. Data flow model of the system.

4.2   Analysis of Timbre Spaces

Analysis has been performed on a range of musical and synthetic signals including output from an FM synthesiser and across a selection of sounds selected to match those in Hourdin et al.'s experiments. Out of their 40 sounds, 27 have been chosen based on those available to us. Versions of the STFT and CQT algorithms have been tested with various configurations. The CQT has proved to be quicker than the STFT and produces less output data for the same input, suggesting a greater likelihood of a fixed number of dimensions being able to capture the input signal. Both methods take several minutes to complete the analysis once the input signal is much longer than 400,000 samples (or 9 seconds at a 44.1kHz sampling rate).

A set of functions has been developed to automatically generate a set of timbre spaces that will be compared on their compilation speed, timbre space size and accuracy of sound reproduction. These experiments are ongoing since each timbre space takes as long as 5 days to compile using all 27 input sounds.

Once the space is compiled however, it takes under 5 minutes to process each new sound through to its path representation. The test suite covers CQT and STFT based Timbre spaces with 8 different window conditions, including some where the input is not smoothed by a window before analysis. These are tested against 3 different time resolutions. In the case of the CQT, all these are tested against 3 separate frequency resolutions. When passed through a Timbre Space, the CQT appears to lose a lot more information that the STFT, producing a lower quality sound. This is contrary to expectations as the CQT produces a smaller output and so has less information to lose. The STFT is much more memory intensive however and will not compile at its highest resolution setting as the resultant output is too large for the PCA algorithm under Matlab with 512Mb system memory and 2Gb virtual memory. When the STFT is compiled without a window, the consequent PCA compilation takes exponentially longer with the time resolution. Every other case appears to grow linearly against time resolution. This suggests that there is much less structure to the STFT output when no window is applied, which makes the PCA much less effective in this circumstance. Once this testing is complete, the complete system will be tested for accuracy against previous Timbre Space work and FM synthesis analysis to ensure the results are perceptually sound.

4.3   Design of Interface

The completed tool will be implemented within a MIDI environment in order to take advantage of existing work on Earcon design. It will accept MIDI signals to control pitch and amplitude and will add an interface to allow real-time editing of timbre. This editing can be performed interactively by a human operator or by another machine process. The interface will allow selection of any of the pre-selected 27 timbres included in the timbre space as well as any others the user has added to the system. For each of these preset timbres, a selection of transforms will be made available. These transforms will include morphing between two or more presets, looping the sound within a preset, scaling the pitch of the preset or any other user-defined transformation within the timbre space. The strength of each transform, or the relative strengths of the timbres affected by the transform, can be controlled by any MIDI controller. This allows the transform to be adjusted over time by any external input and allows the change in the timbre to be recorded in the same place as the change in the melody.

In addition to the preset timbres, the timbre space will also include a series of timbral effects. This will include, for example, 'Alarm sounds' as defined by Mynatt [14]. These effects will be defined as a region of timbre space where the effect is greater the closer the path is to the region. When these effects are used in a transformation, a timbre can be modified to be more like the effect or less like the effect as required. These effects can also be user defined and are expected to be based on psychoacoustic experiments performed by practitioners in that field.

5.   FUTURE PLANS

With this system complete, a range of experiments will be possible. In particular, sounds can be developed according to both Auditory Icon and Earcon principles such that in any given interaction, the most important information will be mapped to parameters relating to the Auditory Icon portion of the sound (i.e., the note) and subsidiary information will be mapped to the Earcon properties of the sound (i.e. the pattern of notes). We could perform experiments to see how much of our perceptual space each synthesiser covers in order to decide upon the best synthesiser or configuration to use for any particular sound. If any synthesiser is found to cover a particularly wide or narrow area of this space, this will be a major consideration in its ongoing usage.

6.   CONCLUSION

We have set out to enable designers more flexibility when developing sounds. The project has so far completed the design stage and is currently evaluating the best way to represent the sounds to maximise this flexibility. The Timbre Space has been chosen for this representation due to the perceptual basis afforded to it by the work of Grey. Preliminary results show that the Timbre Space is heavily reliant on the quality of the audio analysis stage. STFT looks to produce the best quality output at this moment, but experiments on other techniques are ongoing.

REFERENCES

[1]   Blattner, M.M., Sumikawa, D.A., and Greenberg, R.M., *Earcons and Icons: Their Structure and Common Design Principles*, Human Computer Interaction, Vol. 4, No. 1, 1989, pp. 11-44.

[2]   Brewster, S., Wright, P., and Edwards, A., *A Detailed Investigation into the Effectiveness of Earcons*, in G. Kramer (ed.), Proceedings of the 1st International Conference on Auditory Display ICAD'92 (Santa Fe, 28-30 October 1992), "Auditory Display, Sonification, Audification and Auditory Interfaces", Addison-Wesley, New York, 1992, pp. 471-498.

[3]   Brewster, S., Wright, P., and Edwards, A., *An evaluation of Earcons for Use in Auditory Human-Computer Interfaces*, in Proc. of the ACM Conf. on Human Factors in Computing Systems INTERCHI'93 (Amsterdam, 24-29 April 1993), ACM Press, New York, 1993, pp. 222-227.

[4]   Chowning, J., *The Synthesis of Complex Audio Spectra by Means of Frequency Modulation*, Journal of the Audio Engineering Society (JAES), Vol. 21, No. 7, 1973, pp. 526-534.

[5]   Conversy, S., *Ad-Hoc Synthesis of Auditory Icons*, in S.A. Brewster, A.D.N. Edwards (eds.), Proceedings of 5th International Conference on Auditory Display ICAD'98 (Glasgow, 1-4 November 1998), British Computer Society Press, eWiC series, 1998, accessible at http://www.icad.org/websiteV2.0/Conferences/ICAD98/papers/CONVERSY.PDF

[6]   Gaver, W.W., *How do we Hear in the World? Explorations in Ecological Acoustics*. Ecological Psychology, Vol. 5, No. 4, 1993, pp. 285-313.

[7]   Gaver, W.W., *Synthesizing Auditory Icons*, in Proc. of the ACM Conf. on Human Factors in Computing Systems INTERCHI'93 (Amsterdam, 24-29 April 1993), ACM Press, New York, 1993, pp. 222-235.

[8] Grey, J., *Timbre Discrimination in Musical Patterns*, Journal of the Acoustical Society of America, Vol. 64, 1977, pp. 467-472.

[9] Hourdin, C., Charbonneau, G., and Moussa, T., *A Multidimensional Scaling Analysis of musical Instruments' Time-Varying Spectra*, Computer Music Journal, Vol. 21, No. 2, 1997, pp. 40-55.

[10] Hourdin, C., Charbonneau, G., and Moussa, T., *A Sound-Synthesis Technique Based On Multidimensional Scaling of Spectra*, Computer Music Journal, Vol. 21, No. 2, 1997, pp. 56-68.

[11] Kaminskyj, I., *Multidimensional Scaling Analysis of Musical Instrument Sounds' Spectra*, in Proceedings of the Australasian Computer Music Conference ACMC'99 (Wellignton, 1999), pp. 36-39.

[12] Masri, P., Bateman, A., and Canagarajah, C.N., *A Review of Time Frequency Representations, With Application to Sound/Music Analysis-Resynthesis*, Organised Sound, Vol. 2, No. 3, 1997, pp. 193-205.

[13] Mynatt, E.D., *Designing with Auditory Icons: How Well do we Identify Auditory Cues?*, in Proceedings of ACM Conference on Human Factors in Computing Systems CHI'94 (Boston, 24-28 April 1994), ACM Press, New York, 1994, pp. 269-270.

[14] Mynatt, E.D., Back, M., Want, R., Baer, M., and Ellis, J.B., *Designing Audio Aura*, in Proceedings of ACM Conference on Human Factors in Computing Systems CHI'98 (Los Angeles, 18-23 April 1994), ACM Press, New York, 1994, pp. 566-573.

[15] Roads, C., *The Computer Music Tutorial*, Massachusetts Institute of Technology, Cambridge, 1996.

[16] von Helmholtz, H.L.F., *On the Sensations of Tone as a Physiological Basis for the Theory of Music*, Dover, 1954.